A PERILOUS PATH

THE MISGUIDED FOREIGN POLICY OF
BARACK OBAMA, HILLARY CLINTON, & JOHN KERRY

ANNE R. PIERCE, Ph.D.

A POST HILL PRESS BOOK

A PERILOUS PATH
The Misguided Foreign Policy of Barack Obama, Hillary Clinton, and John Kerry
© 2016 by Anne R. Pierce
All Rights Reserved

ISBN: 978-1-68261-058-9
ISBN (eBook): 978-1-68261-059-6

Cover Design by Quincy Alivio
Interior Design and Composition by Greg Johnson/Textbook Perfect

PRESS

Post Hill Press
275 Madison Avenue, 14th Floor
New York, NY 10016
posthillpress.com

Printed in the United States of America
10 9 8 7 6 5 4 3 2 1

CONTENTS

*To people everywhere
longing to express their freedom
and secure their rights—
this book is for you.*

ACKNOWLEDGMENTS

To my sweet, smart, and steady husband who puts up with my intensity, reads the chunks of manuscript I throw at him with a keen and patient eye, and makes me laugh.

To my Chicago dissertation advisers, who taught me so much and gave me so much encouragement, and remain an inspiration.

To my guys.

To my parents and grandparents.

To my friends.

Thank you to editor Jon Ford for his impressive skill and talent, calmness and kindness. He allowed me to be, in my words, "proprietary about my writing," and gently guided me toward changes that made this a better book.

Thank you to publisher Anthony Ziccardi for believing in this book from the beginning. He has no idea how much that meant to me.

Thank you to research assistant Melanie Heinichen Barloh, who dropped everything to provide information and moral support whenever I needed it, and repeatedly undertook the daunting task of getting me organized.

PREFACE

At about the time of President Barack Obama's first inauguration, I began to compile material for a book on the foreign policy speeches of presidents from George Washington to George W. Bush. I felt no urgency. But as the foreign policy approach of President Obama and his secretary of state Hillary Clinton was articulated and put into place, I felt, first, a sense of dread, then, a sense of urgent purpose. Why would they disregard our best foreign policy principles, traditions, and strategies? And why was there so little discussion of the drastic change their approach entailed? Further, why did those analysts who did question President Obama's foreign policy give Secretary Clinton a "pass"? I began to do intense in-time research, looking at every action, every word that affected America's stance toward the world, and position in the world. Once I dug in, I knew I would write this book.

A *Perilous Path* records and assesses the Obama administration's foreign policy ideas and decisions, and reveals how we got into the mess we're in now—with the Arab Spring in shambles; Syria a cataclysm; Iraq, Yemen, Lebanon, Libya, and Ukraine in crisis; the Middle East beset by terrorism; Iran and North Korea ever closer to becoming serious nuclear powers; the Russian "reset" an obvious failure; the Iranian, Russian, and Syrian regimes increasingly aligned and aggressive; China flexing its geopolitical muscle; Islamic extremism, anti-Semitism, persecution of Christians, and targeting of religious minorities on the rise; human rights violations, violence, and global instability much worse than in 2008; and democratic allies and pro-democracy groups disillusioned with the United States.

American foreign policy at its best combines moral and practical concerns. It emphasizes the security of the free world (necessary in a world where global threats lie just beneath the surface) and the principles of freedom (essential to expanding the realm of human dignity). Some American presidents and secretaries of state have emphasized either the exigencies of power or democratic ideals, but none have emphasized neither—until now. Too often, Obama, Clinton, second-term secretary of state John Kerry, and their foreign policy teams stood idle as terrible events unfolded, as if the United States were the least influential country in the world. The result of de-emphasizing American power and American ideals is a more hostile, more oppressive world.

Nowhere do concerns of the heart and of the mind so converge and recoil as in response to today's foreign policy—a policy that ignores human rights, caters to dictators, "deconstructs" national security strategy, and degrades democratic principles. I wrote A Perilous Path because I believe we are on the wrong path, a dangerous and immoral one. We are paying too little attention to America's geopolitical position in the world and too little attention to the world's suffering and oppressed. We are inadequately focused on growing threats from hostile regimes and extremists, and on the growing number of people who are traumatized, hardened, or radicalized through repression, indoctrination, and displacement.

This book is a lament for the brave young Iranians (now missing, dead, or facing routine torture) who marched to the future chanting, "Obama are you with us?" It is a heartfelt American apology to the Syrian people, whose movement for freedom was at first a genuine democracy movement (and for many Syrians still is) who long ago gave up asking, "Don't you see what Assad is doing to us?" It is for the poor souls in the ghastly camps of North Korea, a country where the human rights situation is so dire that the country itself can be said to be a concentration camp. It is for the United States I used to know that valued freedom above all else and for an American foreign policy tradition rooted in democratic ideals. It is, finally, a tribute to the post–World War II presidents and secretaries of state who did so much to protect the free world, to project principles of political freedom and human worth, and to ensure that a world war would never happen again.

American foreign policy today rejects the idea of "peace through strength" and denies the power of truth when it is raised up against propaganda. It revolves around "talking" with tyrants, being careful not to offend them, and offering them concessions in exchange for keeping their ruthlessness confined within their own borders. As it was when Nazi Germany and the Empire of Japan ascended, truth is being sacrificed on the altar of hope and fear: hope that radical regimes will be reasonable if presented with the right diplomatic openings, and fear that if we "insult" hostile powers we'll provoke them. We've sold others short, and we've sold ourselves short as well.

AUTHOR'S NOTE

I wrote this book in a continuous stream as events unfolded. It is based upon in-time research and analysis, and includes documents, speeches, congressional testimony, political commentary, and historical works that were available at the time. I benefited from Capitol Hill briefings, and from participating in or attending forums and panels at the James Madison Program in American Ideals and Institutions, the United States Institute of Peace, the Liberty Fund, the Foreign Policy Initiative, the Heritage Foundation, the Institute of Current World Affairs, the American Political Science Association, and the Fund for American Studies. I resisted the temptation to rely upon memoirs by those who served in the administration or to read other authors' books on President Obama's foreign policy. I did not want to jeopardize what is hopefully a freshness and independence of thought in this book by relying on latter-day criticism or latter-day flattery. I wanted to show how little attention was paid to escalating hostilities and atrocities early on. Before Syria devolved into chaos, Russia invaded Ukraine, China engaged in frenzied island building in the South China Sea, and Iran secured an advantageous nuclear deal, there was need for focus on the amoral, anti-strategic trajectory of American foreign policy. I hope this will serve as a cautionary tale about the perils of complacency.

CHAPTER 1

THE STAGE IS SET

Forgotten History and Lessons of World War II and the Cold War

After Adolf Hitler and the Axis powers put the world through living hell, there were lessons to be learned. The "total war" wrought by Nazi Germany and the Empire of Japan was an apocalypse. Sixty million casualties, the Holocaust, mass executions of civilians, death marches, routine torture of POWs, and the desecration of everything held sacred to religions and civilizations were among the markers of this extraordinary period.

If anything good were to come from all this loss, it would be our new understanding of what allows totalitarians to come to power, to consolidate power, and to make war. From now on, we would see the signs. We would do things differently. With these lessons of history absorbed, recorded, and analyzed, we would avoid another Hitler, wouldn't we? We would prevent genocide, stop expansionist aggression in its tracks, and counter fascist ideologies with ideas of political freedom and human worth. We would keep both the ideals and the armies of totalitarians at bay. We finally, collectively, knew that if we did not take the lead in influencing and helping others, they would take the lead in diminishing and harming us. We finally, collectively, saw the folly of isolationism and of unilateral disarmament. In a world where global threats and fanaticism lay just beneath the surface, America had to enhance its defenses and project its principles.

Although the Allied powers emerged victorious from World War II, the United States was the only country with a tradition of political

1

liberty that *also* had the moral stature and the economic and military power to lead the free world's postwar efforts. Thus, the twentieth century became the "American Century," a phrase first coined by magazine publisher Henry Luce in a 1941 editorial. This was a period in which fascists and communists often met their match in the ideals, the power, and the resolve of the American people.

It must be stipulated that America's greatest successes came when its influence *was* used, but was not *misused, overused,* or *unwisely* used. However, it must also be emphasized: None of our successes came from downplaying atrocities, from denying or ignoring the aggression of hostile powers, from appeasing tyrants, from buying security and comfort at the expense of those living in camps and political prisons, from standing up for no one or standing for nothing. Each time the free world outdid the world of repression and horror, it did so with an emphasis on the differences between the two and a willingness to make sacrifices to keep the one world safe from the other. When the Cold War ended with communist dictatorships collapsing one after another, this was a victory not just for our military and material power, but also for the human rights and individual rights that the free world, at its best, embodies.

Everyone who witnessed the Soviet empire unravel and combust knew this instinctively, if not enthusiastically. Mesmerized, the world watched as Berliners "tore down" their wall, as joyful, hope-filled East Germans streamed across to the West, as the Solidarity movement triumphantly soared to success in Poland, and as, all across the Eastern Bloc, Soviet-sponsored dictatorships succumbed to the human spirit. Inspired by American freedom and success and eager to form their own democratic republics, country after country looked to the US Constitution and Declaration of Independence for inspiration and guidance.

After all of this, who would believe that presidential candidates would deem foreign policy of relative unimportance and base their campaigns entirely on the economy?[1] Who would then believe, in a post-9/11 world, when what French intellectual Jean-François Revel called "the totalitarian temptation" was a clear and present danger—not only in the form of terrorism in service to extremist ideologies, but also in the form of terror-sponsoring states that sought nuclear weapons and kept dissenters in prisons and torture chambers—that we would have a president, Barack Obama and secretary of state, Hillary Clinton, who treated the problems of people living under totalitarian rule as matters of indifference to American foreign policy? They were *such* matters of indifference that speaking out for the people living within the dark night of totalitarianism and dictatorship was deemed "arrogant" and "counterproductive," while speaking *with* the brutal heads of these regimes, even when they declared our destruction as their goal and broke treaties before our eyes, was deemed the progressive and sensible approach. And, who would believe our new approach to the world would go even further than that—that it would call for the partial but unilateral dismantling of our defense structure, and the diminution of our democratic ideals?

Engagement, outreach, and indulgent negotiations—with tyrants—have, remarkably, become a defining feature of American foreign policy. It has become the policy of the United States to downplay the differences between democracies and nondemocratic states, to discount the role ideology plays in those differences, and to provide hostile adversaries with enabling compromises and friendly gestures.

Since President Obama and Secretary Clinton refashioned US policy, the United States has expended more effort in creating good relations with dictatorships and dictators than in strengthening alliances with democracies young and old, and in encouraging and disseminating ideas of freedom. In a manner befitting Greek tragedy, we have given potential enemies just the words, the support, and the time they need to succeed, while we have left potential friends to fend for themselves, thus forcing them back into the orbit and control of nondemocratic powers all too eager to "help" them.

All of this could have been avoided if we had paid even casual attention to the lessons of World War II. Remember the refrain "Never again"? It was born out of reaction to Hitler's concentration camps. It stated the importance of focusing on the suffering and repression of others, not just ourselves. It warned of complacency, for how many at first thought that what was happening in Germany, Austria, Poland, and Czechoslovakia was not our problem? It implied that, had not so many individuals and nations looked the other way, Hitler's plan for world domination would not have come so close to fruition.

Hitler's ascendancy taught us not only of the danger of complacency but also of the danger of ideas, for the Nazi movement, which

Hitler defined as a "struggle," was not primarily geopolitical, but rather ideological. Nazism was a toxic brew of nihilism, socialism, racism, determinism, nationalism, atheism, economic expansionism, and territorial imperialism. Indeed, the story of the twentieth century is the story of unchecked "central planners," lusting for power and fueled by ideologies that deny the existence of human rights and the innate worth of individuals.

The "will to power" actuated in the terrible cruelties of the twentieth century bore little resemblance to the American understanding of will, as in free will, but it spoke volumes about the obstacles with which the American tradition was faced. Let us pause, then, to look at, and learn from, Hitler's rise to power and his near success in achieving his goal of a radically new world order.

■ ■ ■

Shell-shocked from World War I, holding onto the hope that *that* war, in all its obvious horror, had been "the war to end all wars"—finding it impossible to believe that the world would ever subject itself to such horror again—the Western powers signed disarmament treaties and focused on the economic side of relations between states. Many believed that the connected and global nature of modern economic activity would lead to more peaceful political ties. Although some feared the rise of communist and fascist ideologies in Russia and Germany, the socialist and statist aspects of these ideologies appealed to those who were tired of the "messy" business of checks and powers and parliamentary procedure and longed for a more efficient path to what we now call social justice. Even among those who saw how hostile German and Russian ideas were to democracy, there were many who convinced themselves that accepting our differences was requisite for peace; we might not agree with Nazism or Bolshevism, but we could "live and let live" for the sake of avoiding war. If hostility ever actually manifested itself, negotiation was to be the first line of defense. Negotiation was rightly considered an underused tool in a world that, until then, had allowed small shifts in the balance of power to lead to seismic conflagrations.

The attempt to use negotiation to solve the problem of Hitler's military mobilization and acts of war is often acknowledged as the crucial lesson: While England and France negotiated, Hitler continued on with his plans, violated every agreement, and played England and France for fools. Seen through the lens of history, the attempt to conciliate Germany, even when it meant allowing others to absorb Hitler's aggression, is a lesson in the dangerous futility of appeasement and the moral vacuity of self-absorption. As the most widely acknowledged case in point, Czechoslovakia, the only new democracy surviving the post–World War I settlement, was, in the words of British historian Ian Kershaw, "deserted by its friends and devoured by its enemies."[2] The case of Czechoslovakia remains instructive.

Czechoslovakia's "Sudeten Crisis" was fanned by Nazi propaganda that claimed Sudeten Germans were a brutally oppressed Czechoslovakian minority and by Sudeten Nazis under the leadership of Konrad Henlein who intentionally provoked turmoil and violence. The Nazi propaganda machine operated according to Hitler's assertions that "if you tell a big enough lie and tell it frequently enough, it will be believed" and that "the victor will never be asked if he told the truth."

Although the French at first reminded Germany of their mutual aid pact with the Czechs, with Britain and Russia following suit, the closer Germany came to war, the more other powers retracted, desiring above all else to avoid war themselves. Through the mission of Lord Walter Runciman and other diplomatic efforts, the British pressured the Czechs to comply with German demands. Czech president Eduard Benes eventually bowed to the pressure, but the Germans added more demands, with Hitler ramping up his tirades. Prime Minister Neville Chamberlain decided he needed to meet with Hitler personally, and came away from the meeting convinced that "self-determination" for the Sudetens would satisfy German claims. Again, the British pressured the Czechs to compromise, this time by giving up territory in exchange for guarantees against unprovoked aggression. Without options or allies, the Czechs yielded again, and their concessions were formalized when Chamberlain, Hitler, Italian dictator Benito Mussolini, and French prime minister Edouard Daladier met at Munich, where they signed a pact turning the Sudetenland over to Germany.

The rest is history, so to speak. Hitler was, of course, not satisfied with the Sudetenland. One Nazi conquest would follow another. After the rape of Czechoslovakia (which was followed by the subjugation of Poland and Austria), the British Cabinet endorsed Chamberlain's change of policy, which was based on his realization that "no reliance could be placed on any of the assurances given by the Nazi leaders." As Kershaw puts it, "The old policy of trying to come to terms with dictatorships on the assumption that they had limited aims was no longer possible. The policy had shifted from trying to appease Hitler to attempting to deter him. In any new aggression, Germany would be faced at the outset with the choice of pulling back or going to war."[3] And so reads the history of the failed Munich process.

In response to today's "political science" approach, which sometimes reduces politics to impersonal statistics, it should be noted that Chamberlain and Lord Runciman bear *personal* responsibility for abetting Hitler's conquest of Czechoslovakia. As William L. Shirer recorded in his important *Berlin Diary*, they "sold the Czechs short" by ingratiating the Nazis, continuously pressuring the Czechs to give in to Nazi demands and failing to pressure German leaders. Chamberlain even displayed solidarity with Hitler by appearing publicly with him after agreeing to *personally* convey Hitler's demands to Czech Prime Minister Benes. (The propaganda value of such gestures should not be underestimated.) Shirer's September 30, 1938, entry from Munich reads as follows:

> It's all over. . . . Thus the two "democracies" even assent to letting Hitler get by with his Sportpalast boast that he would get his Sudetenland by October 1. He gets everything he wanted, except that he has to wait a few days longer for *all* of it. His waiting ten short days has saved the peace of Europe—a curious commentary on this sick, decadent continent. So far as I've been able to observe during these last, strangely unreal twenty-four hours, Daladier and Chamberlain never pressed for a single concession from Hitler. They never got together alone once and made no effort to present some kind of common "democratic" front to the two Caesars. Hitler met Mussolini early yesterday at Kufstein and they made their plans. Daladier and Chamberlain arrived by separate planes and didn't even deem it useful to lunch together yesterday to map out their strategy, though the two dictators did. Czechoslovakia, which is asked to make all the sacrifices so that Europe may have peace, was not consulted here at any stage of the talks. . . . Their protests, we hear, were practically laughed off by the elder statesman [Chamberlain].[4]

There is another lesson beneath the well-known (but increasingly overlooked) lesson of "appeasement at Munich." A lesson that emerges from a deeper look is the futility of negotiating without possessing enough force to gain leverage and enough conviction to have a line not worth crossing. As Professors Norrin M. Ripsman and Jack S. Levy demonstrate, French political leaders wanted to take a firmer stand against Germany in the crisis over the Rhineland in 1936 and over Czechoslovakia in 1938—even at the risk of war. England itself, they show, was not simply naïve about German intentions.[5] But, England's weak military position fostered "the logic of appeasement," for the disarmament England and the West had enthusiastically embraced after World War I had weakened England's negotiating hand: "British leaders were unwilling to confront Germany in either crisis because they believed that Germany had already surpassed Britain and France in military strength, that Britain was particularly vulnerable to an attack from the air in 1938, and that consequently a war would be too costly. They believed, however, that the underlying trends in military power, which could be accelerated by British rearmament, pointed to both a reversal in the balance of power and enhanced British security against an air attack within a few years."[6]

This is not to excuse Chamberlain. He not only failed to challenge and confront Hitler, he enabled him. Still, Ripsman and Levy remind us that Chamberlain's government didn't simply accept Hitler's territorial advances. British leaders hoped to *forestall* German aggression through disarmament negotiations and through redressing some of Germany's grievances. They hoped that negotiating from a relatively weak position would buy them time to negotiate from a stronger position, thus thwarting the threatening growth of German power.

But it was Germany, not Britain, that knew how to use negotiations to buy time. While England placed hopes in negotiations, Hitler negotiated not out of hope but out of a calculated assessment that talking would buy precious time. By encouraging the deception that Germany was amenable to some ultimate compromise, negotiations lessened the urgency and gravity with which Germany's rearmament and expansionism were seen. By the time England realized compromise never had been in the cards, it was too late: Austria and Czechoslovakia had been subjugated and Germany's military had strengthened to the point that Germany was poised for its next act of war.

■ ■ ■

Today, we must ask: Did Iran's occasional willingness to negotiate regarding its nuclear program have the same calculated end? We shall see that the preponderance of evidence supports this conclusion. When we look at the history of Germany then and of Iran today, we are justified in asking: Are some regimes so radicalized and bent on control of their populations, so mired in deception and propaganda, and so opportunistically determined to expand power that negotiation, for them, is *necessarily* a ruse—unless, that is, opposing power is aligned so overwhelmingly against them that they have no existential choice but to compromise? Are we Americans, war-weary ourselves from involvement in Afghanistan and Iraq, allowing ourselves to be deceived by duplicitous authoritarian leaders?

These questions beg another: Are some leaders so fanatical that, even when it is irrational and ultimately self-defeating, they relentlessly pursue a destructive course? The picture of Hitler facing a clearly lost war, holed up in his bunker and about to commit suicide, and yet ordering eleven-year-olds to the battlefield and calling for the execution of any German who surrendered, is not one of a man willing to face the realities of power. So much for the popular academic assumption that even fanatical dictators are "rational actors" who can be led by the "international community" toward constructive compromise.

Hitler might not have been a "rational actor" when it came to his lust for personal power and German glory and his hate-filled fanaticism, but Hitler was a very clever man. He played Western guilt and the Western longing for peace for all they were worth. The Treaty of Versailles had left the West, especially Britain, with a guilt complex. Hitler used the language of democracies to deceive democracies, and to weaken their resolve. Negotiating not only gave Hitler time to build German armaments, mobilize German armies, and unify the German people behind the Nazi cause. It also gave him the opportunity to extend his masterful powers of persuasion outward. Hitler claimed Germany's rearmament and invasion of foreign soil were only right given the wrongs of Versailles and used lies and fervor to back his claim.

As political science professor Stacie Goddard shows, Hitler skillfully and successfully used rhetoric that appealed to such accepted democratic concepts as "collective engagement."[7] Using our own precepts to lure us in, Hitler insisted Germany was only seeking "self-determination" for German ethnic groups and "appropriate reconciliation" in Czechoslovakia. All Germany was asking for was "equality," "justice," and, yes, "peace." Indeed, Hitler argued that the Versailles Treaty made Germany unequal and promised that rectifying the imbalance would lead directly to peace. I would add that Hitler also used such rhetoric to assure war-weary Germans that obedience to Hitler's Reich would not translate into assent to war. Witness, for example, Hitler's March 17, 1935 proclamation:

> In this hour the German government renews before the German people and before the entire world its assurance of its determination never to proceed beyond the safeguarding of German honour and the freedom of the Reich, and especially it does not intend in rearming Germany to create any instrument for warlike attack, but, on the contrary, exclusively for defense and thereby the maintenance of the peace. In so doing, the Reich government expresses the confident hope that the German people, having again obtained their own honour, may be privileged in independent equality to make their contribution towards the pacification of the world in free and open co-operation with other nations.[8]

Kershaw describes the powerful effect Hitler's propaganda had on England: "Trapped in the rhetoric of collective security, many Britains saw Churchill's calls for alliances and rearmament as 'unrealistic' and 'unfair.' Enough Britains were fooled by Hitler's rhetoric that the British government was put on the defensive. Cabinet and parliamentary members themselves had a very hard time not falling for the rhetoric. Thus, it was an amiable visit to Germany by Lord Halifax in 1937 that confirmed in Hitler's mind that Britain would do nothing in response to German action against Austria. Thus, weeks of anti-Czech propaganda convinced not only most Germans but many Britains to believe that the issue was 'the despicable persecution of the German minority,' not the military destruction of Czechoslovakia."[9]

The tragic truth is that duplicitous Hitler had revealed his real opinion about "democratic rules" in *Mein Kampf* and earlier speeches. For example, in Munich on September 18, 1922, he had asserted, "Ideas such as Democracy, Majority, Conscience of the World, World Solidarity, World Peace, Internationality of Art, etc. disintegrate our race-consciousness, breed cowardice, and so today we are bound to say that the simple Turk is more man than we are."

We must see that, today as then, oppressive regimes expend massive energy and resources spreading certain ideas through propaganda and stamping out others through repression. It is no small fact that Nazi Germany had a "Minister of Propaganda" and that Hitler rose to power on his credentials as a propagandist. (Similarly, Kim Jong-il of North Korea proved himself capable of succeeding his father by working in the propaganda department in his youth.) After the First World War, Hitler engaged in propaganda work for the short-lived socialist government in Munich. His track record in propaganda and "anti-subversive activity" was recognized by Captain Karl Mayr, so that when Hitler switched to the anti-Bolshevist side, Mayr appointed him Reichswehr Propagandist and Informant.

Mayr made a brilliant choice. Hitler drew larger and larger crowds in the beer halls, proving to be a fiery, charismatic, and inspirational speaker. Hitler saw ideas as "tools of mobilization" and expertly excited his listeners with extreme nationalism combined with anti-capitalist tirades, which included the demand for punishment of "profiteers and speculators." Increasingly, in his inflammatory rhetoric, the sins of profiteers became equated with the sins of Jews. But Hitler knew enough about the human nature Nazis were so determined to re-create to know he had to make evil look like a justifiable means to a good end. While he mobilized the masses by stirring up hatred against the "other," he also promised national redemption and national unity. He railed against the corruption and inefficiency of party politics and proclaimed his way *the* way to efficient government and a strong economy. Jews and others, he claimed, were intentionally holding Germany back from a glorious, idyllic, and peaceful future.

Hitler's skill in rallying the German people toward the Nazi cause was so great that he was voted in as chairman of the National Socialist Party; from then on, his dictatorial power was widely welcomed and accepted. Where it was not accepted, it was imposed through intimidation and brutality. The Führer cult and the rapid rise of the Nazi Party were fueled by a propaganda machine so "total" that it enveloped all of German society.

A reading of Karl Dietrich Bracher's *The German Dictatorship* shows, however, that Hitler knew that even well-indoctrinated revolutionaries often turn against their leaders.[10] Hitler's strategy for preventing those who had joined his revolution from turning against him was to so pit the German people against each other that they opposed each other more than they opposed him. He made sure that for every person who wanted to destroy him, there was another who would weaken that person before he could act. Embracing contradictions as ways to confuse and divide the populace, German propaganda *simultaneously* touted unity and redemption, hate and division.

Because of Hitler's success in rallying the German people to his fanatical cause, postwar thinkers urged us to focus not only on the danger of appeasement, the folly of negotiating from a position of weakness, and the need for a strong defense, but also on *the power and the danger of ideas themselves*. In the buildup to the war, very few in the West had taken Hitler's extremist words seriously; they preferred to focus on his *other* words, of peace and unity. As Michael A. Ledeen points out in his book *Accomplice to Evil*, there were even academic debates about what Hitler really meant by the word "elimination" in reference to the Jews. He also observes, as have others, that in the 1930s and 1940s, President Franklin Roosevelt's foreign policy team, the *New York Times*, and the State Department all did more to downplay German atrocities than to expose them.

The same willingness to downplay atrocities was granted the Japanese. Although nine out of ten Americans who were captured by the Japanese were subjected to marches, imprisonment, torture, or execution, survivors were encouraged to remain silent about their ordeal. In addition, powerful people in the State Department silenced reports of Soviets capturing our POWs and taking them to horrible fates, never to be heard of again. As if we today need any more evidence that bureaucracy can sometimes suck the soul out of people, the Soviet Union's horrific treatment of Cossacks, anti-communists, POWs, Poles, Ukrainians, and even of kidnapped US soldiers were all covered up by our own bureaucracy during the war, and downplayed after the war.[11]

What most frustrated postwar thinkers about this was that, again, truth was being sacrificed on the altar of hope and fear: hope that radical regimes would be reasonable if presented with the right diplomatic openings, and fear that, if we "insulted" hostile powers, we might make the situation worse. This hope and fear, which too often guides American foreign policy today, denies the power of truth when it is raised up against propaganda, and denies the power of ideas themselves.

Modern intellectual trends support this mind-set. Many view ideas as "merely" subjective opinions, but view history as a strong, impersonal, mechanistic force. Speaking out against tyranny and tyrannical ideas is thereby demoted, while accommodation—even with those whose ideas are radically antidemocratic—is promoted. History, in this view (which stems from Marxism), is an inevitable march toward progress, even if radical regimes throw an occasional wrench in the system. Such determinism might be implied when Hillary Clinton proclaims that this or that person is (or is not) on the "right side of history." It is as if abstract history is more important than in-the-flesh humanity, and belief in progress more important than the choices and statements human beings actually make.

Would "history" perhaps have been different if people in the West, not to mention in Germany itself, had called Hitler's hate-filled ideas and rhetoric just what they were—if human beings had actively argued against and resisted Hitler's inhumane world view? The reply that by the time people understood Hitler's intentions it was "too late" is inadequate. For, as skillful as Hitler was at making bad look good, he also provided ample evidence of just how bad his plans were. *Mein Kampf* saw history as an all-out struggle in which the Aryan was being undermined by the "parasitic Jew." Jews were depicted as the sinister force behind both the Bolshevism and the capitalism Hitler despised. By 1922, Hitler had written a second book in which he laid out both the German quest for "lebensraum" (living space, which provided the excuse for the invasion of foreign soil) and the mandate of destroying "Jewish Bolshevism." In public speech after public speech, Hitler promoted both anti-Semitic and expansionist goals, while portraying nationalism and socialism as fused engines of a new, all-powerful German state. What we now call central planning was to replace every independent entity and idea throughout the Reich.

Hitler very nearly succeeded in these domestic and foreign goals. Most Germans moved in cult-like fashion "toward the Führer" and toward the state, which had become one; the Führer *was* Germany. Hitler and his propaganda machine successfully indoctrinated "the masses" with the help of the anti-individualist segment of European philosophy that exalts the state, promotes the militarization of civil society, glorifies obedience and authority rather than freedom and autonomy, and rejects everything the American polity at heart stands for: individual rights, the rule of law, pluralism, peaceful relations between states, and the sanctity of human life. As Karl Dietrich Bracher shows, the anti-individualist philosophy was already especially popular in Germany and was embraced by the German intelligentsia—by professors, writers, teachers, civil servants, and industrialists "who were more readily seduced by the siren of antidemocratic, anti-individualist and irrational ideologies than were their counterparts in other countries." By the time Hitler became chancellor, agreement with and complicity to his malevolent ideas was strong throughout German society, and was just as strong among average Germans as among party, industry, and cultural leaders.

It is important to emphasize, however, that, although totalitarian movements fed upon and inflamed cultural biases and resentments, totalitarian movements were defined by *rejection* of cultural, legal, societal, and religious norms—by the rejection of inherited truths, whether those truths were biblical or civilizational. The past was irrelevant. It was the idyllic future that mattered, and whatever brutal means it took to achieve the ever-elusive utopia were justified by the idea that the only truth that mattered was the new one. As Vladimir Tismăneanu demonstrates in his powerful book *The Devil in History*, both fascism and communism, both Hitler and Stalin, used an atheistic, nihilistic, anti-moral, anti-human rights worldview to spurn God the Creator and to become creators themselves—of new men, new societies, new international world orders.

In sum, Hitler's rise owed itself not only to the ruthless consolidation of power, but also to the successful dissemination of a hate-filled ideology, which made it acceptable to devalue human life and not only to disregard human suffering but to revel in inflicting it. Hitler's conquests of foreign peoples, in which soldiers were instructed to cast aside notions of human decency and to torture POWs, and his brutal repression of Jews, Catholics, and others, were greeted with mass acclaim.

With all this hardness and indifference to human suffering underlying Nazi successes, and at the core of fascism in general, is it any wonder that author Peter Viereck insisted upon the value not of hardheaded realism but of "softmindedness"? As Viereck saw it, the lesson of World War II was not just that we needed better defenses and geopolitical structures; it was also that we needed better hearts. He thought the lesson was clear enough that we wouldn't have to learn it again: "After enduring both world wars, Alfred North Whitehead concluded, 'The future of civilization depends on a moral approach to all problems.' 'All' includes politics and economics. Our most creative anti-communist thinkers are increasingly in accord with Whitehead's conclusion. . . . Disillusionment with the Munich-Yalta era has made the best Anglo-American social thought more receptive than ever before to a salutary softmindedness. In view of the aftermaths of both Munich and Yalta, expediency turns out to be less expedient, realism less realistic, than the old-fashioned Victorian decency of being so 'bigoted' that you feel prejudiced against murderers."[12]

Indeed, after the war, the best thinkers understood that moral concerns and power concerns were intertwined, and that giving up either or both revealed a poverty of will and a poverty of spirit. How far we are from that realization today, when so many of our political and academic leaders insist that we overlook what's going on within horrible regimes as the best way to achieve peace and harmony between nations. For every word and gesture of outreach to dictators and totalitarians by the Obama foreign policy team, there have been infinitely more moments of silence and indifference to the individuals within these regimes, who routinely suffer from repression, imprisonment, torture, disappearances, and execution. As we shall see, President Obama's version of what Viereck calls "tough-mindedness" is so great that even saying heartfelt words for the people within North Korea is rejected for the sake of the "diplomatic process" and for the one-world vision that teaches "tolerance" even of regimes that commit atrocities.

Engagement, outreach, and diplomacy are indispensable *tools* of American foreign policy, but we are paying too little attention to the political, moral, and strategic *goals* of American foreign policy. These goals are said to indicate the arrogance of American power; for the sake of a unified world, we are urged to discard them and to see the diplomatic process as an end in itself. Many of us now recoil from American attempts to influence events and ideas in dangerous parts of the world, fearing that influence will translate into military involvement. Since the Iraq War, many have succumbed to the either-or assumption that *either* we refrain from an active foreign policy *or* we'll end up with "boots on the ground." Yet, if we learned anything from World War II, it is that war is *more likely* when democratic nations bury their heads in the sand and retreat from the world stage. Scaling down our defenses and doing nothing to defend democratic principles allows the *escalation* of atrocities, weapons programs, and hostilities, and only increases the chance that we'll be forced into war by events spiraling out of control.

The in-vogue worldview places a premium on comfort, harmony, and prosperity and insists that we can have them if only we stop insulting others with "standards" and "values." (Instead, we are to emphasize "common interests," even with authoritarian regimes.) The first step toward a progressive one-world order is, in Nietzsche's terms, going "beyond good and evil." After all, there's nothing more divisive than taking a moral stand. If you believe these ideas are far-fetched, you would be surprised to know that they are widely held in our best universities and fiercely defended in academic conferences. There is a reason that President George W. Bush's Axis of Evil speech (which could rightly be criticized as inaccurate given that the three powers he mentioned were not clearly aligned) drew ridicule. Nothing provokes more antipathy from one-world advocates than the idea of evil being drawn into politics. Academicians and State Department appointees warn that taking a stand for human rights in other countries is judgmental and worse: it's the imposition of one civilization upon another. At the least, it's the attempt to impose our particular values on others who have the right to *their* particular values.

Today's progressive vision urges us to live and let live and to "coexist"—to leave each country to its own devices, and to pursue friendly relations with all countries. The irony of this one-world view is that it denies any common human strain and any singular humanity. It pushes under the rug the fact—yes, the fact—that all human beings, unless they have been thoroughly indoctrinated, are desirous and deserving of a certain degree of freedom, and of dignity. Although relativists justify generous economic deals and major political and strategic compromises with brutal regimes as only befitting an enlightened world that accepts cultural differences, they have to ignore the fate of people within those regimes to justify their policies. They have to ignore human nature and human longing. For, regardless of the culture one lives in—regardless of race, nationality, or religious creed—no one wants to see their mother raped, their children conscripted, their father or husband tortured, or their family held hostage to totalitarian dictates and methods.

Properly understood, rights are particular in that they apply to each one (that is, to each individual), but they are also universal in that they apply to everyone. Cultural relativists do not believe in the underlying idea of the American founding that individual rights are human rights; that rights are inherent, God-given, and universal—that they are not granted by government, nor does any government have any "right" to take those rights away. Relativists are therefore free to ignore the fate of the people within the countries they bargain with.

If we were honest about our one-world aspirations, we would admit that it is not ignoring human suffering for the sake of "coexistence" that is most likely to create a more unified world. It is, rather, recognition that all humans deserve a dignified life. Furthermore, it is not a matter of respecting other cultures when we fail to speak out about atrocities, for, as the most influential country in the free world, our saying nothing does positive harm. Yes, extremist-Islamist ideas are being propagated through indoctrination throughout the Muslim world, but at the same time movements for political freedom have taken root in the Muslim world. Why, in such conditions of flux, would it be better to be silent about civil society and human rights than to defend them? There is no reason to remain indifferent to merciless repression and no enduring benefit to be gleaned from doing so. Indeed, World War II taught us that indifference comes back to haunt us.

Through Hitler's astonishing successes, we learned that totalitarians *use* our indifference to buy time and to lull us into further complacency. They use our Western politeness and tolerance to evade public judgment. Conversely, when we shine light into dark regimes by exposing their crimes and revealing that bad is bad (that their ruthless policies do not, as their rhetoric insists, create "unity" or "equality"), dictators view that as an existential threat. Why, otherwise, would they expend massive energy on the dissemination of lies—on suppressing the truth? They know that truth about their rule is the biggest threat *to* their rule. (Just look at the suppression of truth in Germany, Japan, and the Soviet Union then and in Iran, North Korea, and Venezuela today.) Why would we want to prop up such regimes by going along with their deception? Saying foreign policy should be conducted without interfering with the opaqueness that shields brutal governments and facilitates their human rights violations is like saying foreign policy should be conducted by machines. For why do we have minds but to discern the truth, and hearts but to care, and voices but to speak?

No wonder political science refers to people as "actors" and places groups of people into statistical categories. It is part of the attempt to make domestic and foreign policy impersonal and nonjudgmental. But people are not actors, and groups of people are not so uniform as statistics imply. People are individual and they're human, and we'll make better policy decisions if we acknowledge this fact. When we look at individuals as actors and people as statistical clusters, it's easier to put unwise faith in the ability of central planners to pacify and unify the world. The "experts" supposedly look at the "evidence" and efficiently guide the rest of us down an enlightened path. While we forsake our ideals and our humanity for the sake of our hot pursuit of a new world order crafted by progressive experts, others who are not so progressive seek to impose their ideals and their interests on us. The moral and political vacuum created by our indifference creates space that others are only too eager to fill—as we will particularly see when we examine the cases of Syria, Iran, and Russia. This is yet another reason to speak up for universal rights and democratic values.

One of the fascinating findings revealed by digging into the history of fascism is that it was not just the *presence* of fascist ideology, but also the *absence* of a countervailing philosophy, which allowed whole populations to become slavish and cruel. Journals and diaries of those who endured and participated in Hitler's plans show that it was not just fascism and Nazism that numbed, stupefied, and radicalized entire populations; it was also the absence of the idea that human rights are inalienable, universal, and worth fighting for. The throngs of Germans,

Poles, Lithuanians, and others who enthusiastically joined in the humiliation, round up, and murder of Jews so lacked a philosophy of universal
rights that they were able to convince themselves that Jews were less
than human. In the words of Lithuanian mathematician and Holocaust
survivor Simcha Brudno in his interview with scholar George Anastaplo, "The average German behaved this way because they could see
a human being and decided that it was not a human being. They had
a tremendous sense of obstruction: when you see a human being, you
have to consider it a human being." Of his time in Dachau and Stutthof,
Brudno stated, "I had been completely made not a human being."[13]

Germans and the many Europeans who collaborated with them
failed to see human worth as pertaining at once to everyone (human
rights) and to each one (individual rights). Europe was mired in the
"group think" to which many Americans now seem willing to surrender.
Although Germany had managed after World War I to form the framework of civil society in the Weimar Republic, it lacked the structural
stability and political principles to make civil society strong. The
majority viewed life not in terms of individuals who were part of a
common whole, but in terms of national, ethnic, religious, and cultural
groups that were fundamentally different. In today's parlance, they were
ethnocentric—except that they didn't see cultural, ethnic, and national
differences as cause for celebrating diversity. To the contrary, they took
it to mean that some groups were superior to others and saw it as cause
for oppression of minorities and even war, if that was what it took to
preserve or enhance the position of one's own group. The view that
some groups—their own—were fundamentally better than other groups
provided the stew in which German (and, for that matter, Japanese)
fascism thrived.

We had better be careful: The line between those then—who
accepted atrocities because they emphasized ethnic, national, religious,
and cultural differences—and those now, who insist that for the sake of
respecting cultural, religious, ethnic, and national differences, we must
tolerate everyone, even the world's worst regimes, might not be as rock
solid as we'd like to believe. Theories that prioritize groups instead of
individuals inevitably end up, on the one hand, vilifying certain groups
and, on the other hand, whitewashing the misdeeds of others. This is
because looking at people as mere cogs in the wheel of group experience

allows us to vastly simplify human experience. Today, President Obama tells tales of exaggeration about "the wealthy," "Republicans," and even "Congress," but he does not say a word about the North Korean children who are forced to scour urban streets looking for scraps of food because their father has been murdered by the state and their mother is in a "reeducation camp," where she is routinely tortured.

Another fascinating aspect of the study of fascism's rise is learning that even many European Jews before the war embraced what we now call "group think" and that this might have something to do with the passivity with which many Jews succumbed to Nazi tyranny. In that compelling interview referred to above, Simcha Brudno struggles to understand why he and his fellow Lithuanian Jews didn't do more to resist German oppression or to escape from German hands. Why, interviewer Anastaplo asks, didn't they rise up to overcome German guards or escape—even when the opportunity was there and the odds were overwhelmingly in their favor? Even when they were in cargo trains on the way to what all knew would be their demise in concentration camps, and when the trains stopped at night, and the very few, vastly outnumbered guards got drunk and fell asleep and left the doors insecure, the hundreds of Jews on those trains did not rise up, seize the guards' weapons, and flee. Why? (Israelis struggled with similar questions regarding Jewish passivity during the trial of Holocaust mastermind Adolf Eichmann and on other occasions.)

Although never coming to a conclusion, Brudno answered that, if they had escaped, there would have been nowhere to go; surrounding citizens were either too sympathetic to the Nazis or too terrified of the Nazis to help. Anastaplo pressed further, asking if taking an unlikely chance at escape wouldn't have been better than the certain horrors that awaited them. Brudno reflected that Lithuanian Jews, before Hitler, generally kept to themselves and generally felt themselves superior to the *goyim*;[14] they were better scholars, more successful, better at taking care of their families, less prone to drunkenness, and had more "control" of themselves. This view fed into passivity. The common Lithuanian Jewish assumption was, "We've always been victims and we always will be because 'they' can't stand how good and successful we are." In addition to the level of resignation that this implies, it suggests that Lithuanian Jews fought less hard against the Nazis because they didn't have a strong philosophy of individual rights and personal responsibility to guide them.

Brudno's most painful memories of the ghetto are of the day Germans ordered adults to collect children and hand them over for "exchange with prisoners of war" and of the day when that exchange actually took place. There were only a "couple" guards to oversee the exchange, while there were hundreds of Jewish adults, but the adults obediently handed their children over. In the face of such horrible memories as these, Brudno posits that Jews and other victims of Nazi atrocities were victims not only because they were ruthlessly targeted, but also because of the "law of least resistance." German soldiers and SS guards, vastly outnumbered in the ghettos and camps they devised, could not have done what they did without "cooperation" that included cooperation "on the inside" among the people who were being persecuted.[15] This is not in any way to say that the persecuted share the blame for Nazi horrors. The blame for evil rests firmly on those that perpetrate or encourage it.

■　■　■

The world wars, the rise of totalitarianism, and the lessons these events taught led America down its twentieth-century path. Cataclysmic events and sinister new methods of oppressing whole populations made it clear that America had to become intricately involved in the world—but our postwar leaders were determined that we become involved on our own terms, in terms of our democratic tradition. Stories of passivity and complicity in the face of tyranny made it clear that, with our emphasis on individual rights and human dignity, we had something valuable to offer. The Soviet Union's brutally efficient subjugation of Eastern Europe after the war, and its expansionist campaign to destabilize and revolutionize the Middle East, Africa, and Latin America meant we also had something to fear.

Thus, unlike after World War I, after World War II, America faced its democratic responsibilities head on. The United States gave massive aid to war-ravaged, emotionally scarred Europe, created the National Security Council and the CIA, and engaged in those European alliances George Washington had warned our young, vulnerable country to avoid. Americans also faced up to unfulfilled domestic responsibilities after the war, using imperfectly realized standards of the Declaration of Independence and the Constitution to improve upon their country: No longer would a Jim Crow South, the subtle anti-Semitism that tainted much of American society, or unequal opportunity for women be considered nonurgent matters.

Before moving on to focus on the worldview and foreign policy of Barack Obama and Hillary Clinton, let's turn to the president who understood and translated into policy the geopolitical, moral, and ideological lessons of World War II better than any other: Harry S. Truman. Let's then briefly look at the presidencies between those of Truman and Obama so that we can better understand how the stage was set for a president and secretary of state who would reject the American foreign policy tradition, downplay and overlook human rights, and overhaul and weaken our national security strategy and structure.

As the first post–World War II president, a passionate student of history, and a man with common sense and a moral core, Truman saw clearly what was at stake and what needed to be done. He knew that we might win the war but lose the battle if we failed to focus on the principles of political liberty and human worth. It was thus that the masterful architect of "containment" of Soviet expansionism and his skilled foreign policy team worked as hard at de-radicalizing and reeducating Germany and Japan as they did at demilitarizing them. It was thus that efforts such as the Marshall Plan, and generous trade agreements, loans, and technical missions, were designed as much to demonstrate the advantages of our way of life as they were to strengthen our allies. In his *Memoirs*, Truman reflected, "The assistance we gave, which averted stark tragedy and started progress toward recovery in many areas of the world, was in keeping both with the American character and with America's new historic responsibility. To help peoples in distress was not only a tradition of our country but was also essential to our security. By rebuilding Europe and Asia, we would help to establish that healthy economic balance which is essential to the peace of the world."[16]

Truman freely admitted that our generosity had a self-serving aspect in that it helped bring others to our side, but he insisted that it would be a "misrepresentation of the American people" to suppose that self-interest, "even wise and enlightened self-interest," was the only cause for America's concern for the outside world. According to Truman,

American principles of generosity, fair play, and equal rights, of anti-imperialism and "freedom and justice for all," sustained us as individuals within a community and as a community in relationship with the rest of the world. Without these principles, he counseled, we were but one power among others. With them, we were the embodiment of a particular vision with universal appeal and validity.[17]

The Nazi war had been an immoral war and it had also been an antidemocratic one. Truman believed that democracy held precisely those moral and political precepts that were an antidote to the recent vicious extremes of politics. His approach, which culminated in the Reagan presidency, was to respond to Soviet internal oppression and external aggression with two weapons: the strategy of containment and the projection of American ideals. Truman was never willing to view the principled aspects and the geopolitical aspects of our foreign policy as separate, but taught that our power had to be part of our mission. Refusing to define containment in merely negative and reactive terms, he insisted upon defining it as part of a larger American purpose.

As an example, the "Truman Doctrine," which was designed to prevent further Soviet expansion in Europe by drawing a line at the eastern Mediterranean, was defined by Truman in terms of the contrast between two ways of life: "One way of life is based upon the will of the majority, and is distinguished by free institutions, representative government, free elections, guarantees of individual liberty, freedom of speech and religion, and freedom from political oppression. The second way of life is based upon the will of a minority forcibly imposed upon the majority. It relies upon terror and oppression, a controlled press and radio, fixed elections, and the suppression of political freedoms."[18]

While Truman meticulously constructed what came to be called a sphere of influence in Western Europe to counter and contain the Soviet sphere of influence in Eastern Europe, he saw any valid and lasting influence within our sphere as tied to our willingness and ability to do good. Moreover, limited containment policies pointed toward less limited long-term goals, and a bigger purpose. The Clifford-Elsey Report, an analysis of postwar Soviet relations commissioned by Truman, shows that the Truman administration hoped containment would lead not only to an end to Soviet aggression but also, by frustrating the communist cause, eventually to a change in Soviet philosophy and society.[19]

Containment meant both the contraction of communism and the protraction of freedom and peace.

As the United States entered World War I, President Woodrow Wilson had declared, "The world must be made safe for democracy." Toward the end of the war, Wilson had delivered the Fourteen Points address that sketched his ambitious ideas for an international postwar order. While wisely backing away from the expansiveness of Wilsonianism and paying more attention to grand strategy, military alliances, and defense, Truman built upon Wilson's idea that the protection and enhancement of liberty required our "entanglement" in the world's problems. World War II had proven something Wilson had preached: that indifference is one of the seeds from which extremism grows. Even Truman's most evident departures from Wilsonianism—the balance of power strategizing, the buildup of the military power of the free world, and the assumption of leadership in NATO and other alliances—were infused with the Wilsonian idea that we could not protect our principles or our interests without also living up to our responsibilities in the world.

Many in the world had come to the same conclusion. Efforts toward international law and international standards of human rights were invigorated after World War II in response to the monstrous crimes against humanity committed during that period. The Nuremberg and Tokyo military tribunals, the Universal Declaration of Human Rights, the UN Convention on the Prevention and Punishment of the Crime of Genocide, and the Geneva Conventions all emerged in the late 1940s. Although international law rightly faces limitations due to concerns regarding national sovereignty, and due to the certainty that one-world government would eventually become one-world dictatorship, and although the UN Human Rights Commission today has been commandeered by some of the world's worst human rights violators, the spirit that animated postwar human rights structures deserves applause.

Truman repeatedly emphasized the universal desire to be free. When he argued that the rights and struggles of all peoples transcended the superficial divisions of the Cold War, he suggested that we could never "win" that war through strength alone. The only true victory, the only one that would have the stability that comes from the people's satisfaction, was a victory of moral, democratic principles over oppression and wrongdoing. On January 7, 1953, just before Truman left office, he insisted, "Our ultimate strength lies, not alone in arms, but in the sense of moral values and moral truths that give meaning and vitality to the purposes of free people. These values are our faith, our inspiration, the source of our strength and our indomitable determination."[20]

Intricately thought out, principled, sensible, and successful, Truman's foreign policy path lacked the shortcomings of the paths chosen by many of his successors. Nixon, Ford, and Kissinger's realpolitik approach, Carter's humanitarian approach, and Clinton's globalist approach—all (to varying degrees and in different respects) fall short of the approach of Truman. They lack the depth of his understanding of America's mission and power.

The presidents who drew the United States into the war in Vietnam—Eisenhower, Kennedy, and Johnson—all subscribed to the domino theory and agreed with Truman that the spread of communism was a threat not just to American power and influence but to American ideals and the democratic way of life. The wrenching fear that if Vietnam fell to the communists, other countries would fall one after the other too, had to do not only with the negative geopolitical consequences of such an eventuality, but also with the negative consequences for individual rights and the rule of law.

In standing up to communism in Vietnam, however, these presidents made some un-Truman-like decisions. When the French and the Vietnamese communists reached a ceasefire agreement known as the Geneva Accords, President Dwight Eisenhower disregarded the accords and encouraged Prime Minister Ngo Dinh Diem of the South to refuse to submit to elections. The formation of the Vietcong guerrilla movement was *in part* a response to this decision. By the time John Kennedy was president, there was reason to believe Diem might win an elective contest, and yet Kennedy inexplicably made no attempt to get back to the Geneva Accords by encouraging free elections. As is well known, missteps regarding our own principles and missteps regarding military strategy increased under Lyndon Johnson, thereby decreasing chances for American success.

It is important to note, however, that for the first time in American history, the American press took an active role in undermining the American side in a war. We now know, from declassified Pentagon archives, Vietnamese testimony, and other sources, that stories of American atrocities were grossly exaggerated and sometimes fabricated, while Vietcong atrocities were often whitewashed. Historian Paul Johnson observes, "The heavy incidence of combat in civilian areas was the direct result of Vietcong tactics in converting villages into fortified strongholds, itself a violation of the Geneva agreement. And it was the restrictions on American bombing to protect civilian lives and property which made it [American bombing] so ineffective."[21]

Both popular-domestic and internal-governmental forces, which included the "force" of American ideas, prevented the American side from simply surrendering to an "end justifies the means" philosophy in Vietnam. Would the Vietnam War have seemed such an outrageous extreme to so many Americans if they had not been taught that self-determination, the peaceful settlement of disputes, and the general concern for individual and human rights were an essential part of American identity? The American people, even if inadvertently, have used American ideals to respond to (and criticize) the events of American politics. Although American ideals are sometimes egregiously violated, such violations have rarely occurred without backlash. Slavery, an entrenched institution before the founding of our country, was the gargantuan exception to this rule until the abolition movement rose against it. Now obvious and self-evident is the moral and political catastrophe that this extreme violation of our own principles entailed. The context of American principles has often been a context with which the public has judged presidential policy, and has often been a context with which presidents have presented policies to the public. But, in the attempt to embrace European-style foreign policy after Vietnam, American leaders generally deviated from this tradition.

The architects of détente responded to the heated aftermath of Vietnam with a realpolitik approach designed to give the world a cooling-off period. "Engagement" with the Soviet Union, nuclear arms reductions, and the easing of relations with China were hallmarks of the Richard Nixon and Gerald Ford presidencies. Universal rights and American principles were generally downplayed in favor of Henry Kissinger's balance of power tactics and treaties. Skillfully crafted agreements reaped tangible rewards but had less positive long-term consequences. While part of the rationale for the new relationship with China was offsetting Soviet power, China would use that relationship, and all the commercial deals and military and technology transfers it ultimately led to, to vastly increase its military might and economic leverage.

More damaging was the new message America was sending about its priorities. We had fought an excruciating war in Vietnam for both geopolitical and ideological reasons, but now we were lending credence to those who claimed principles *never had* been part of American foreign policy. Testimony to Truman's understanding that our principles had to maintain the offensive in the Cold War, America's reputation in the world continued its downward slide. On the world stage, "American imperialism" became the focus. Even though America had a stronger anti-imperialist tradition than any other world power in history, the term was widely accepted and used, at home and abroad.

In the meantime, communists seized power all over Indochina with brutal programs of social engineering and the mass murder of civilians. As the Khmer Rouge inflicted unimaginable atrocities on the people of Cambodia, American leaders said little. Worse, it became the norm for some Americans to criticize other Americans for "provoking" total-itarian states like Cambodia by drawing attention to their policies of repression and extermination. Just when communism was showing its true, bloody colors to the world, increasing numbers of Americans became sympathetic to it. From 1973 to 1979, the Khmer Rouge system-atically killed—through execution, imposed starvation, and forced labor—an estimated two million Cambodians, almost a fourth of the country's population. Countless others languished in concentration camps, where they slept on boards with no covers and ate only what they could find in surrounding fields. Just at this time, American universities and many American political and cultural institutions were revamped in order to accord a greater voice to Marxism and to foster greater "under-standing" of communist states.[22]

When it came to Mao's brutal reign in China, which created a climate of raw terror and resulted in an unbelievable thirty million lives lost, there were plenty in the West who not only criticized those who worried about Mao's atrocities; they excused the atrocities. Here was the beginning of that cultural relativism combined with fondness for socialism (with which we are still faced today) that consciously excuses communist repression. As author James Mann puts it, "At first it was suggested that Mao Zedong's regime really did reflect the overall wishes of the Chinese people, even if there were no elections to substantiate this claim. China was said to be different, in cultural terms from the West; there was no need for the formalities of voting or ballots or polling stations."[23]

The apologetics for China's human rights abuses continued on after Mao was gone. As documentary journalist Philip Pan shows, at the very time when the West was giving China credit for capitalist advances, China was issuing new laws to wipe out all history of the mass murder and atrocities Mao inflicted upon the Chinese people and was continuing on with lesser, though still grave, human rights abuses.[24] Given that China had turned from totalitarianism to authoritarianism, it made sense to pursue positive relations—but we should also have given human rights dissidents our passionate American voice.

President Jimmy Carter rejected détente on the grounds that it downplayed human rights and over-relied on military and strategic alliances. In a speech entitled "A Foreign Policy Based on America's Essential Character," he declared, "We can no longer separate the traditional issues of war and peace from the new global questions of justice, equity, and human rights . . . It is a new world that calls for a new American foreign policy—a policy based on constant decency in its values and on optimism in our historical vision."[25]

But Carter went too far in dismantling containment in order to prove US commitment to cooperation and peace. His disparagement of the post–World War II power structure and of NATO certainly did nothing to strengthen the unity of democratic states and only encouraged the Soviets toward territorial aggrandizement and domestic oppression. Moreover, Carter had a soft spot for communist states that made his focus upon human rights selective, and often hypocritical.

Noting analogies with Obama, *Wall Street Journal* columnist Bret Stephens says that Carter took office "on diplomacy and peace-making, an aversion to the use of force, the selling out of old allies."[26] Stephens argues that such policy did nothing to increase America's standing. In 1979, Iranian radicals seized the US embassy in Tehran after Carter had refused to bail out the Shah of Iran and after Carter's UN ambassador had described the Ayatollah Khomeini as "somewhat of a saint." Shortly thereafter, radicals in Saudi Arabia seized Mecca's Grand Mosque and held it until the Saudis were able to wrest it back at the cost of several hundred lives. Pointing to Yaroslav Trofimov's book on the subject, Stephens observes, "Yet throughout the Muslim world, the Carter administration was viewed as the main culprit. U.S. diplomatic missions in Bangladesh, India, Turkey and Libya were assaulted; in Pakistan, the embassy was burned to the ground. He [Trofimov] asks, 'How could that happen to a country whose president was so intent on making his policies as inoffensive as possible?' "[27]

When the Soviet Union invaded Afghanistan in December 1979, President Carter was forced to reassess his conciliatory approach (and deserves credit for doing so). American power and ideals would have served national security and human rights better than accommodating assurances of our desire to get along. *Neither geopolitics divorced of attention to principle nor advocacy of human rights divorced of attention to the importance of American power represent the best in our political tradition.* The American mission as Truman understood it comes between these approaches in saying that merely selfish goals are wrong, but that relativist thinking is wrong also. Both forget that the democratic way of life, and the respect for individual liberty and national sovereignty that it implies, is still our best hope. They forget the "universal rights of man." Truman saw his awesome responsibility as president in terms of upholding, protecting, and championing those democratic principles which, he rightly believed, were a challenge to all forms of political oppression and an inspiration to those desiring to be free.

Ronald Reagan's revival of containment combined with his Evil Empire speech revealed a Truman-like determination to enhance freedom's realm and to stymie the Soviet threat. The Soviet Union had indeed consolidated an empire and held it together by means of force and intimidation, the suppression of political and social liberties, and the financial sponsorship of countries and individuals committed to its perpetuation. Even as he constructed a powerful strategy to isolate and pressure the Soviet Union, Reagan insisted that our democratic principles were what distinguished us and made our power important. Like Truman, he passionately promoted those principles in his speeches; he knew full well that exposing the lack of scruples in Soviet practices could only enhance American power. Beneath his work to strengthen alliances and build our defenses was his fervent desire for peace and his hope that all peoples could eventually enjoy the liberty that we enjoyed.

His remarkable relationship and fruitful diplomacy with Mikhail Gorbachev, which reaped dramatic reductions in nuclear arms, show how far he was willing to go in reducing tensions as long as he could "trust, but verify." At the same time, like Truman, Reagan realized that in order to be effective, and in order to respect the sovereignty of other nations, our national security policy should not overextend its reach or its resources. Like Truman, he believed that our democratic principles placed restrictions on the use of power (as opposed to the buildup of power) to promote democracy. It was in Nicaragua where, in the view of many, he took those restrictions less seriously, that Reagan crossed his own line.

Reagan knew that the Soviet Union's Eastern Bloc was economically and morally bankrupt, that citizens no longer believed in the lies and promises upon which brutal communist rule was sanctified, and that brave dissidents were mobilizing. Reagan personally contributed to the Soviet Union's unraveling by spending money on our defense, which the Russians were forced to spend in turn when they couldn't afford it, and by repeatedly emphasizing the right of individuals behind the Iron Curtain to live free and dignified lives. He, like Truman, knew that ideas matter and that words are powerful and that American leaders should not miss a good opportunity to speak for freedom. Although the State Department and the West German government tried to discourage Reagan, he insisted on going ahead with his Berlin Wall speech. As Council on Foreign Relations member Romesh Ratnesar puts it, "the speech was as much an invitation as it was a challenge."[28] Reagan urged, "There is one sign the Soviets can make that would be unmistakable, that would advance dramatically the cause of freedom and peace . . . General Secretary Gorbachev, if you seek peace, if you seek prosperity for the Soviet Union, if you seek liberalization: Come here to this gate! Mr. Gorbachev, open this gate! Mr. Gorbachev, tear down this wall!"

Typifying today's simplistic and polarizing analysis, Reagan's presidency has been subjected to caricature. His accomplishments have been left out of history books while his role in the demise of the Soviet Union has been downplayed and denied. Deftly combining containment with moral appeals against communism, recognizing both the exigencies of power and the power of a good speech, Reagan contributed brilliantly to the unraveling of the Soviet Union.

In a 1990 speech at the UN, President George H. W. Bush showed traditional American enthusiasm for freedom's march and celebrated the "breeze of freedom" that had, by then, swept across Eastern Europe and "touched almost every corner of the globe." He pronounced, "That breeze has been sustained by a now almost universal recognition of a simple, fundamental truth: the human spirit cannot be locked up forever.... And people everywhere want much the same things: the chance to live a life of purpose; the chance to choose a life in which they and their children can learn and grow healthy, worship freely, and prosper through the work of their hands and their hearts and their minds. We're not talking about the power of nations but the power of individuals, the power to choose, the power to risk, the power to succeed."[29]

In spite of occasional stirring speeches like these, Bush had more in common with the "pragmatists" of his party than he did with the passionate Ronald Reagan. In *A World Transformed*, Bush recalled that his main objective was "encouraging, guiding and managing change without provoking backlash and crackdown."[30] In keeping with this objective, President Bush responded mildly to the fall of the Berlin Wall, later citing the desire not to gloat. His tepid response to the massacre at Beijing's Tiananmen Square is less understandable. He did not want to jeopardize improved US-Sino relations by "overreacting to events," and he refused calls from both sides of the political aisle to significantly retract relations. Although he agreed to impose limited sanctions, he sent National Security Adviser Brent Scowcroft and Deputy Secretary of State Lawrence Eagleburger to China to try to repair the damaged relationship he believed the sanctions had caused.

Bush had been America's top diplomat to China in the mid-1970s, and he deeply valued his personal relationships with Deng Xiaoping and other Chinese leaders. Sometimes he allowed these relationships to deflect his attention away from the brutal policies these men pursued. A particularly notable and jarring example of this is seen in an October 29, 1975, letter to Tom Lias reprinted in his 1999 memoir, *All the Best*. Bush wrote, "The Kissinger visit went well. . . . Meeting Mao Tse Tung was a thrill of a lifetime. He is old and has a ghastly speech problem, but still sharp. The adulation on the face of the Chinese in the room was unbelievably worshipful." In an interesting case of irony, in the same letter he wrote, "China thinks we are falling apart—a paper tiger (not quite), a country whose principles are hazy and whose discipline and order are in chaos."[31]

The Bush foreign policy team struggled to define what Bush called a "new world order." They saw the fact that the United States and the Soviet Union stood together in denouncing the Iraqi invasion of Kuwait as symbolizing a "hopeful new spirit" and believed that the division that had defined the Cold War was coming to an end. Similarly, many Americans saw the new horizon in post-ideological terms; they insisted that economic relations would now define the world and frequently exhibited a willingness to overlook human rights for the sake of economic profit.

Reflecting both the narrow economic concerns of "globalism" and the critique of America inherent in "anti-globalism," during the presidency of Bill Clinton, the United States backed away from traditional national security procedures and from traditional American principles. President Clinton largely ignored weapons proliferation by communist countries and, in his speeches, moved toward moral equivalence between democratic and socialist states. Although the 1994 treaty with North Korea is cited as evidence of concern for proliferation, the terms provided the North Koreans with more loopholes and economic benefits than restrictions.

Syndicated columnist Charles Krauthammer dissected the treaty terms. He noted that it offered North Korea an end to our joint military exercises with South Korea, and even offered North Korea assistance with technology and materials that would supposedly go toward a peaceful nuclear program in exchange for North Korea agreeing that the International Atomic Energy Agency (IAEA) could conduct a one-time inspection of seven declared nuclear sites and that it would "freeze" operation of its nuclear facilities. The United States agreed to help North Korea obtain "proliferation-resistant light water reactors for producing electrical power" and in the interim to provide heavy fuel oil for free. This in spite of the fact that North Korea was already violating the Treaty on the Non-Proliferation of Nuclear Weapons it had signed and that that treaty already required regular inspections. Krauthammer intoned, "The IAEA, if it goes along with this sham, is corrupted beyond redemption."[32] From today's perspective, we appear the unwitting victims of North Korea's deception.

Although President Clinton at first issued an executive order linking human rights conditions to China's acquiring "most favored nation" trading status, he quickly rescinded this position. A bill granting China permanent normal trade relations with the United States was pushed through by the administration and the Senate without consideration of the hard line China had recently taken in political and military matters. Supplemental legislation that would have required the president to conduct annual reviews of China's missile technologies and proliferation of WMD, and would have penalized China for violating nonproliferation treaties, was rejected. Arguing against the bill, Senator Fred Thompson asserted, "If China is going to be one of our trading partners, it's not too much to require them to stop providing weapons of mass destruction to countries who might someday use them against us."[33]

The mantra successfully employed in Clinton's presidential campaign—"It's the economy, stupid"—implied that the United States didn't stand for anything terribly important in the world. Accordingly, on his 1998 trip to China, Clinton apologized for America's imperfect realization of universal rights and praised the communist government for "reform." (Some aides even indicated that part of the reason for the trip was to improve American impressions of China, too many Americans being influenced by Tiananmen.)[34] In addition, the president repeatedly made the point that the US "does not support independence for Taiwan" or "two Chinas" or Taiwan's membership "in any international bodies whose members are sovereign states." Among the many Chinese dissidents expressing dismay at Clinton's remarks was Ye Ning, a human rights activist tortured by the Chinese government for his pro-democracy activities. He lamented, "Clinton has given the image to the world, especially to the Chinese people and opposition forces, that the government of the United States strongly and unconditionally supports the Chinese mainstream communist leaders."[35]

The two weeks following the president's visit were described by a Hong Kong monitoring group "as one of the government's toughest crackdowns on democracy activists in recent years." As arrests and detentions escalated, freedom fighters struggled to hold onto their dreams.

The administration's nonresponse to the Rwandan genocide was a low point. At the time working as a journalist, current US ambassador to the UN Samantha Power gathered documents and studied the situation. In a 2001 article for the *Atlantic*, she concluded: "U.S. officials did not sit around and conspire to allow genocide to happen. But whatever their convictions about 'never again,' many of them did sit around, and they most certainly did allow genocide to happen." The US, she said, "did much more than fail to send troops . . . It led a successful effort to remove most of the UN peacekeepers who were already in Rwanda. It aggressively worked to block the subsequent authorization of UN reinforcements. It refused to use its technology to jam radio broadcasts that were a crucial instrument in the coordination and perpetuation of the genocide. And even as, on average, 8,000 Rwandans were being butchered each day, U.S. officials shunned the term 'genocide' for fear of being obliged to act."[36]

After the genocide, many in the West, including Clinton himself, regretted their silence and inaction; some became activists drawing attention to the tragedy. The same might be the case once today's Syrian bloodbath is finally over. But, sympathy after the fact doesn't do much good.

Insofar as he emphasized both globalism and relativism, President Clinton was light years away from President Truman, who sought with his very being to raise the morale and the defenses of the *free* world and who saw moral principles as a vital part of American foreign policy. In this sense, the Clinton years set the stage for the Obama-Clinton-Kerry years. Truman stood for America's unique kind of "openness," not for the openness of today which causes many to disparage or ignore Washington, Jefferson, and Lincoln, and to believe that we can learn little more from them than we can from other political leaders in other times and places. American openness, Truman advised, should not be allowed to degenerate into randomness. Neither the narrow pursuit of our interests nor our openness to other cultures should overshadow the significance of our principles. Defending those principles as they relate to both domestic and foreign policies would, he believed, be both our own and the world's greatest opportunity for peace.

Still, President Clinton was not as far away from President Truman as would be President Obama. Behind the scenes, Clinton skillfully brokered peace between the hostile sides in Ireland. His emissary, former senator George Mitchell, worked tirelessly on the agreement. Clinton intervened in Bosnia to prevent genocide, although the method of doing so caused many civilian deaths. (It is of note that Clinton's globalist gestures were punctuated with acts of unilateralism; many European leaders felt that both the timing and the method of dealing with the Bosnian crisis were simply imposed upon them.) Moreover, Clinton applied repeated pressure on the regime of Saddam Hussein. Significantly, given the later evolution of partisan politics, he expressed particular outrage and disdain for Iraq's oppressive, WMD-producing regime, even going so far as to express the opinion that Saddam would eventually have to be "forced out." In February of 1998, President Clinton warned that if Iraq reneged on its commitment to open suspected chemical and biological weapons sites to inspection, the consequences would be "very very serious." This was considered by the press a "backing down" from his previous, more direct threat to take military action.

George W. Bush came to power with an initial focus on domestic issues, and, in his 2000 campaign, defined America's role in the world narrowly, in terms of the "national interest." Thanks to scholar Melvyn P. Leffler's exhaustive survey of memoirs from the Bush administration, it is clear that, aside from renewed focus on missile defense, the administration's early priorities were education reform and tax cuts.[37] Bush administration officials generally agree that foreign policy was not a top priority, and that they paid too little attention to emerging threats, including intelligence warnings that even America was vulnerable. Leffler writes, "Nowhere in these memoirs is there any indication that Bush, Cheney, Rumsfeld, Powell, Ashcroft, or Rice assigned high priority to a prospective, terrorist attack, an omission that would come to haunt administration officials, and no one more than Rice."

9/11 changed everything. President Bush and his team from then on lived with the horrible specter of that day, and with the enormous responsibility of preventing another attack. Memoirs highlight "the fear, anxiety, and uncertainty in which officials operated in the days, weeks, and months after 9/11." The terrorist attacks brought about hypervigilance regarding potential threats, and exponentially increased the seriousness with which those threats were seen. It wasn't just WMD that concerned policymakers; it was WMD in the hands of fanatics and the fact that traditional strategies of deterrence didn't work with fanatics. As Georgetown professor Robert Lieber explains, "The gravity of the danger was amplified by two additional factors. First, the cold-blooded willingness to slaughter thousands of innocent civilians without the slightest moral compunction raised fears about potential use of WMD. . . . Second, in view of the fact that nineteen terrorists in the four hijacked aircraft committed suicide in carrying out their attacks, the precepts of deterrence were now called into question."[38] Indeed, the United States of America had entered a whole new world.

Nevertheless, who could have predicted that a few years later America would be caught in the crossfire in Iraq, in a war that unleashed unanticipated hardships for the Iraqi people and American troops, and provided unanticipated opportunities for Iran? And who could have predicted that partisan Democratic leaders would be so determined to undermine President Bush that even during steps forward in Iraq, such as the tremendously popular 2005 elections there, they would continue to seek microphones to denounce "Bush's failed policy"? Some of this is to be expected in a democracy. But what was striking during the Bush years was the exclusive focus of numerous Democratic Party leaders on America's own faults and America's own setbacks combined with their whitewashing of the faults and setbacks of America's enemies. It amounted to the in-time rewriting of history and was facilitated by a press mostly willing to mimic their interpretations of American foreign policy.

As one example: The idea that "Bush lied" in order to force America to war is itself a distortion. The administration declassified pieces of intelligence in order to build the case for presenting Iraq with an ultimatum. Part of the evidence turned out to be exaggerated, while another part turned out to be based on the misleading testimony of a terrorist. The assumption that Iraq had an active WMD program turned out to be wrong once American troops went into Iraq to hunt for the evidence. (We cannot confirm, however, that there were no WMD materials inside the truck convoys that ferreted supplies from Iraq to Syria just before the US invasion.) But it is not true that most of the evidence presented was exaggerated, and it is not true that the administration "knew" the threat was not as bad as their argument indicated. To the contrary: In spite of internal disagreements over how to present the evidence, the administration believed Saddam Hussein had weapons of mass destruction and believed he threatened the peace. So did everyone else. Most Western powers and most Middle Eastern powers believed Saddam Hussein had WMD and that he was cruel and aggressive enough to use them. He had resisted agreed-upon inspections at every turn and, when he had permitted inspections, had played a very successful cat-and-mouse game with inspectors. Countless lethal weapons were unaccounted for; there had been no real inspections in four years.

The world knew for a fact that Saddam Hussein had in the past used his own chemical and biological weapons on his own people—the Kurds. It knew he had developed uranium enrichment and bomb-making factories and wanted to do so again. In *No Higher Honor*, Condoleezza Rice reminds us: "It was the unanimous view of the U.S. intelligence community that he had reconstituted his chemical and biological weapons programs. All but one agency believed that he was reconstituting his nuclear device in one year if he got foreign help, by the end of the decade if he had to go it alone."[39]

Although not in itself a reason for America's ultimate decision to go to war, there was wide concern regarding the regime's extreme cruelty to the Iraqi people and Saddam Hussein's expansionist thirst for power. The Iraqi president was considered to be exceptionally inhumane and aggressive—even by twentieth-century standards. Rice notes his "established pattern of recklessness, particularly in failing to anticipate the international community's strong response to his 1990 invasion of Kuwait and his 1993 attempt to assassinate former President George H. W. Bush."[40]

Despite the later critical take on the Bush administration's fearful assessment of Saddam Hussein, many intellectual and Democratic Party leaders had expressed similarly serious concerns. Articles in *Newsweek*, *Time*, the *Atlantic Monthly*, the *New Republic*, and even the *New York Times* had made the case against Saddam Hussein. For instance, in October 2001, the *New York Times* featured a book by Iraqi dissident and former leading nuclear physicist Khidir Hamza. Hamza recounted that he and a team of scientists had nearly built a nuclear device and stated his belief that Saddam Hussein had resuscitated the program.[41] In May 2002, the *Atlantic Monthly* ran an incriminating cover story titled "Tales of the Tyrant: The Private Life and Inner World of Saddam Hussein." As

Professor Frank Harvey shows, Bill Clinton and Al Gore were among the most concerned about Hussein's excesses and potential to do harm.[42]

Although Iraq was not connected with the 9/11 terrorists, notorious terrorists had been harbored in the country. As it was debating and considering what to do about Iraq, the White House was alarmed to learn that Abu Musab al-Zarqawi, a terrorist affiliated with al-Qaeda, was operating a lab in the Zagros Mountains in northern Iraq. The administration was urgently concerned about the nexus of WMD and terrorism, and believed Saddam would proliferate WMD if it suited his purposes.

In addition to all of this, the administration was frustrated and very concerned—given the security implications—that it still had not convinced Saudi Arabia to cease its financial sponsorship of terrorism. As George Friedman of Stratfor Global Intelligence shows, our invasion of Iraq was considered leverage to pressure the Saudis and others.[43] The calculation that an American presence in Iraq would increase American leverage in the region proved partly correct. After the United States went into Iraq, both the Saudis and the Libyans ceded many US demands, the latter by halting its WMD program and reaching out to the West.

As we shall see, however, there was far too little calculation about the effect of the Iraq War upon Iran. Our presence in Iraq was a boon to Iranian plans for destabilization and dominance in the region: Iran poured money, weapons, and training into anti-American forces in Iraq and skillfully incited terrorism and sectarian violence. The United States also failed to predict the reaction of Syria. With Iraq its close neighbor, and with Iraqi refugees streaming across its border, the hated Bashar al-Assad regime used the American occupation to drum up nationalist loyalty and to further justify emergency laws. Seizing the opportunity to hurt the United States and to fortify their regimes, Iranian and Syrian leaders strengthened their alliance.

Iran predicted that it would not be hard to outlast the Americans who, in their opinion, lacked the toughness and tenacity that the war in Iraq required. It was, in fact, the very time when US strategy in Iraq showed signs of success that American domestic criticism of the Iraq War and Bush's "failed policy" rose to a fever pitch. In late 2003, the program of buying American intelligence was working, while some guerrilla offensives had provided valuable intelligence insight into Shiite warfare tactics. The conclusion of the Ramadan campaign by exhausted Baathist forces marked the beginning of a more successful US strategy against Sunni insurgents as well; US forces were conducting targeted raids against Baathist strongholds. In addition, by 2004, almost all Islamic governments except Iran had lined up with the United States. Perhaps most significant, in January 2005, Iraq held elections that saw a massive turnout by citizens who appeared jubilant as they exercised their right to vote.

US policy mistakes—foremost among them the very consequential failure to reach out to defeated Sunnis, or to prepare for an insurgency, or to give adequate attention to post-invasion stability operations—would contribute to a reversal of US gains. But it is reasonable to ask if the level of criticism of the Bush administration and its war—by those within American centers of power—did not also contribute to the reversal. By accenting American mistakes and highlighting the desire to end the war as quickly as possible, America's own political leaders relayed to Iran that their assumptions about American tenacity were probably right.

When General David Petraeus forged new strategy centered around a "surge" in American troop levels (which proved highly successful), House Speaker Nancy Pelosi and Senate Majority Leader Harry Reid opposed the initiative publicly and often, saying surge strategies had "already failed." The new strategy included increasing pressure on Syria to stop the flood of terrorists across its borders. But, as if to demonstrate how divided American government was, Speaker Pelosi insisted upon leading a bipartisan delegation to Syria to discuss "security issues"— this at a time when Syria's active assistance to Iraqi terrorists had been proven and when Syria's ruthless dictator Bashar al-Assad was under intense domestic pressure. Through the Freedom of Information Act, governmental watchdog group Judicial Watch exposed a memo in which the Pentagon had urged Pelosi not to take the trip, saying it would "send Syrians and the world the wrong message."

Pelosi met for three hours with President Assad, afterward announcing that she and her delegation had urged him to stop support for militants and jihadists, but adding, "We came in friendship, hope, and determined that the road to Damascus is a road to peace."[44] In his book *In the Lion's Den: An Eyewitness Account of Washington's Battle with Syria*, Andrew Tabler describes Pelosi's visit as "the diplomatic bombshell that

Syria was waiting for. . . Pelosi's visit, combined with America's failing prospects in Iraq and the 2006 Lebanon War, strengthened the idea in Syria that Bashar was once again a political horse worth betting on."[45] With refreshing impartiality, the *Washington Post* ran an editorial accusing Pelosi of falling for Assad's "propaganda" and "attempting to introduce a Middle East policy that directly conflicts with that of the president."[46]

I am not arguing here for or against the Iraq War, and it should be clear that I take the war's unforeseen consequences very seriously. I *am* arguing that partisan arguments against the war created a false impression: that the Bush administration intentionally led the United States to war for purposes it knew were false. Many of those making this argument knew *their own* claims were misleading. This is upheld by the fact that so many people outside the Bush administration (some of whom would later lead the charge that "Bush lied") had themselves previously made the case for finding some way, perhaps war, for dealing with the Iraqi leader and regime.

In 2002, Kenneth M. Pollack published the positively received *The Threatening Storm: The Case for Invading Iraq* with the Council on Foreign Relations. The book jacket states, "Examining all sides of the debate and bringing a keen eye to the military and geopolitical forces at work, Pollack ultimately comes to this controversial conclusion: through our own mistakes, the perfidy of others, and Saddam's cunning, the United States is left with few good policy options regarding Iraq. Increasingly, the option that makes the most sense is for the United States to launch a full-scale invasion, eradicate Saddam's weapons of mass destruction, and rebuild Iraq as a prosperous and stable society . . . Pollack explains why other policies intended to deter Saddam ultimately pose a greater risk than confronting him now, before he gains possession of nuclear weapons and returns to his stated goal of dominating the Gulf region."[47]

Pollack is a Yale graduate and MIT PhD. He was a top Persian Gulf analyst for the CIA and director of national security studies for the Council on Foreign Relations. Respected foreign policy scholar Fareed Zakaria praised Pollock's book, saying, "It is intelligent, balanced, and measured, a model of fair-minded analysis on a topic that rarely gets any." But, as the war unfolded, Bush's domestic critics portrayed the president as a cowboy extremist who was completely out of touch with the *intelligent* class in his assessment of Saddam Hussein's Iraq and in his decision to issue the ultimatum that led to war.

While drawing international attention to our own troops' egregious misdeeds at Abu Ghraib, most Democratic leaders and most of the press now ignored the vastly greater cruelties that had been inflicted at that same prison and other prisons by the regime of Saddam Hussein. Even though the US occupation revealed that the human rights situation in Iraq had been even worse than feared, after the occupation, mention of Saddam's atrocities vanished into thin air. History was again being rewritten—this time, by simply leaving very recent history out.

That history included newsworthy accounts of recently freed prisoners, which added to the grim accounts about living under Saddam Hussein already told by exiles and escapees. Those who cared enough to listen were appalled to learn of all the sadistic ways Saddam's henchmen had found to inflict harm and pain. They learned of fingernails being pulled out, teeth being knocked out, ankles being drilled, limbs being severed, ears being removed, and genitals being electrocuted. They learned of chemical baths, beatings, and of prisoners being hung upside down while pain was inflicted. As if this were not already too much to comprehend, they learned that some inmates were "refrigerated naked," that some were forced to sit on broken bottles until they bled to death, and that others—allowed to "live"—were electrically shocked by prods and wires attached to sensitive parts of their body. They learned of squalid prison conditions where forty to fifty prisoners lived "in one room with rats, bugs and bats," and of "rape rooms" where branding irons, cattle prods, and manacles were used against emotionally and physically destroyed women.[48]

As journalists toured the notorious Abu Ghraib prison, a former Iraqi guard told a correspondent with the British newspaper the *Independent*, "Millions of people were killed here." Other men explained to reporters that after prisoners were shot, "the relatives would only get the bodies if they paid for the bullets." If not, "the government would bury the bodies in graves with up to 50 other prisoners."[49]

As Bush's own account and the accounts of those who know him reveal, these human rights abuses were never far from his mind. After 9/11, the Bush administration tried to forge foreign policy that combined defense strategy with the advocacy of universal democratic principles. It is significant that in a document entitled "the National Security Strategy of the United States of America," the president asserted, "People everywhere want to be able to speak freely; choose who will govern them; worship as they please; educate their children—male and female; own property; and enjoy the benefits of their labor. These values of freedom are right and true for every person, in every society."[50]

Although many focused on the "preemptive" character of the Iraq War, which they said made it unprecedented and unique, the preemptive aspect of the war echoed Woodrow Wilson's assertion that the United States had to enter World War I to *prevent* that war from endangering and engulfing us. Still, in the case of Iraq, we *made* war, which is very different from joining a war in progress.

■ ■ ■

The American tradition provides a basis for vigilance regarding how battles with extremism are conducted, and for caution. War is war and always includes tragedy and horror. Ventures affecting foreign people and measures affecting the American people, especially measures calling for war, must be judged not only according to desired results but also according to their own merits and our own ideals. In evaluating the Iraq War, the Patriot Act, enhanced interrogation, and other policies of the Bush era, both those arguing for these policies and those arguing against them should remember the heavy call of our democratic legacy. There are certain important points about the American foreign policy tradition that Americans forget at their own peril.

First, there is a deep and abiding moralism in the American worldview. It is based upon a belief in the dignity of the individual, and in his and her right and ability to govern him and herself. It is underlain by a belief that the good impulses of human beings are more powerful than the bad. In spite of the pragmatic tendencies which, some claim, have dominated all of American politics and in spite of institutionalized checks and balances in American government, there is an underlying moral axiom: Each person is so worthy that not only is it not any person's or nation's "right" to dominate another; it is "not right" for any person or nation to dominate another.

Second, there is the belief that real power not only should reside but *does* reside with the people. In the natural law tradition that influenced the American founding, individual rights, although codified in our Constitution, are innate and natural and prior to government. Only governments that are properly limited—that recognize these rights—can thrive in the long term. Recurring throughout our history is the idea that evil men and evil governments are doomed to failure; that governments that do not take the peoples' wishes into account will eventually suffer from the lack of energy, creativity, and resolve of their citizens, if not from actual rebellion. Freedom, in this view, is a driving and motivating force.

Third, there is the belief that, as a divinely bestowed privilege and opportunity of the human condition, freedom comes with serious obligations. It must be supported by spiritual principles and moderate political precepts lest it degenerate into mere license. At the same time, it must be fortified by power and determination large enough to protect it. As Vladimir Tismăneanu states, "No century witnessed and documented so much atrocious suffering, organized hatred, and devastating violence as the twentieth."[51] In that bloody century, the American tradition was faced with terrible obstacles, and it took political, moral and military will to overcome them.

In a world where totalitarian ideas and imperial schemes continue to threaten liberty, such resolve still matters. Unwavering attention to geopolitics and constant assessment of emerging strategic threats are essential. Wishful thinking and naïve belief in the words and promises of dictators are pitfalls to be avoided.

Our position of prominence in the free world, our power and our influence, means that we must take our principles, our interests, and our responsibilities seriously. Our profitable economic interaction with the world should not cause us to ignore the cruel and dangerous misdeeds of governments. Our superior military might should not cause us to dismiss the unique aspirations of other people, nor to forget that our power was built "for freedom." We cannot be the "world's policeman." On the other hand, we should not allow those who would benefit from our loss of power to lead us down a self-destructive path, toward an enervating complacency. Looking at how the Munich Agreement failed to prevent war, and at how strong American leadership in the Cold War helped to keep the European peace, we must avoid the traps of isolation and appeasement.

The fact that our nation is so rigorously scrutinized and so often criticized means that our foreign policy must be carefully construed. However, we should not be so apologetic for our stature that we accept false portrayals of our policies or the propagandistic rewriting of our history by hostile groups. Our ideas have attracted and liberated many. Our power has often been used for good. The American foreign policy tradition, while clearly imperfect, is vitally important.

CHAPTER 2

CHANGE COMES TO AMERICAN FOREIGN POLICY

Abandoning Friends, Abetting Dictators, and Demoting Democracy

Candidate Obama rode to power on promises of hope and change, on claims he knew how to fix a broken political system and create a peaceful world order, and on pledges to replace the bitter partisan divide with national unity and national redemption. He promised change so thorough that it would transform, not just restore America's political system, and that it would overhaul, not just improve upon American foreign policy.

In one of many campaign speeches filled with the word *change*, in St. Paul in June 2008, Obama urged, "Let us unite in common effort to chart a new course for America. . . . America, this is our moment. This is our time. Our time to turn the page on the policies of the past. Our time to bring new energy and new ideas to the challenges we face. Our time to offer a new direction for the country we love!"[1] In prepared remarks delivered in Colorado Springs in July 2008, Obama avowed, "Loving your country must mean accepting your responsibility to do your part to change it. If you do, your life will be richer, and our country will be stronger. . . . We need your service, right now, at this moment— our moment—in history. I'm not going to tell you what your role should be; that's for you to discover. But I am going to ask you to play your part; ask you to stand up; ask you to put your foot firmly into the current of history. I am asking you to change history's course." In his nomination acceptance address, Obama asserted, "We need a president who can face the threats of the future, not keep grasping ideas of the past. . . . If John McCain wants to follow George Bush with more tough talk and bad strategy, that is his choice—but that is not the change America needs."[2]

Change is one promise President Obama and his administration have very clearly kept. Previous American foreign policy approaches were rejected for the sake of a dramatically new approach, untried and unproven. Swiftly upon coming to power, the new president discarded the foreign policy ideas and strategies of previous American presidents. In a favorable article in the *American Prospect*, Spencer Ackerman declared, "Obama is offering the most sweeping liberal foreign policy critique we've had from a presidential contender in decades."[3]

Although some on the left feared that President Obama's foreign policy, unlike his domestic policy, would echo that of George W. Bush, this fear was unfounded. It is true that he temporarily increased troop commitments in Afghanistan, but this fit with the Democratic Party line that the unjust war, Iraq, was a distraction from the "necessary" war in Afghanistan, which was portrayed less as war than as police action against "criminal" terrorists. It is also true that he did not immediately withdraw our forces from Iraq but rather waited two years to do so, and that he did not shut down Guantanamo as he promised. Beyond this, the similarity between the Obama and Bush foreign policies and between Obama's approach and the approaches of previous American presidents ends. We must take seriously the distance Obama himself created with his predecessors. In one of many critiques of the Iraq War, in a campaign address entitled "the Past versus the Future," Obama decried "politics that uses 9/11 to scare up votes; and fear and falsehoods to lead us into a war in Iraq that never should've been authorized and never should've been waged."[4]

Without hesitation, Obama enacted historic ideological and tactical change, and sought policy advisors and State Department appointees who believed in his ideas and his goals—whose opinion of America's hitherto role in the world was low, and whose desire to impose their own worldview upon the American system was high. The new president sought the advice of and/or included in his foreign policy team such individuals as Valerie Jarrett, Anthony Lake, Charles Freeman, Robert Malley, Samantha Power, Anne-Marie Slaughter, Leon Panetta, and, of course, Hillary Clinton. To varying degrees, all believed and stated that the United States had recently, and often in history, overstepped its reach, placed too much emphasis on its own democratic principles and way of life, failed to appreciate and accommodate other cultures and political systems, poured too much money and effort into military alliances and defense, failed to recognize the benefits of engagement with our adversaries as well as our friends, and been "arrogant" in the use of power.

Samantha Power, who was a senior advisor to Senator Obama at the time, and would become a senior director in President Obama's National Security Council and (then) Ambassador to the UN, lamented in a 2003 article for the *New Republic* that American foreign policy had been so harmful to people around the world that the problem could only be remedied through self-criticism, deference to international institutions, and admission of guilt. She went so far as to draw a not so subtle analogy between Germany's past and our own: "U.S. foreign policy has to be rethought. It needs not tweaking but overhauling. . . . Instituting a doctrine of mea culpa would enhance our credibility by showing that American decision-makers do not endorse the sins of their predecessors. When [then German Chancellor] Willy Brandt went down on one knee in the Warsaw Ghetto, his gesture was gratifying to World War II survivors, but it was also ennobling and cathartic for Germany. Would such an approach be futile for the United States?"[5]

Power is a human rights scholar who has taken a strong stand against genocide, and has been a uniquely principled voice in the administration on Syria.[6] Yet, at times she conveys a version of realism similar to that advocated by John Mearsheimer and Stephen Walt, which downplays the internal practices of regimes and emphasizes the role of Israel, and the Israel lobby, in what it sees as America's overzealous policies. In a 2008 op-ed for *Time* magazine entitled "Rethinking Iran," Power argued for engaging with Iran's repressive leaders and implied that fears about Iran's nuclear program were overblown.[7] In a 2008 speech at Columbia University, Power commended Obama's campaign statement that he would negotiate with rogue regimes without preconditions, seeing it as a positive turning point in the Democratic primary.[8] In a 2007 interview at Harvard's Kennedy School, in which she called for more regard for international institutions and less deferral to special interests, Power stated, "America's important historic relationship with Israel has often led foreign policy decision-makers to defer reflexively to Israeli security assessments, and to replicate Israeli tactics, which, as the war in Lebanon last summer demonstrated, can turn out to be counterproductive."[9]

Obama's closest confidante and most influential advisor, Valerie Jarrett, who spent her early years in Iran, told author David Remnick that she and Obama "shared a view of where the United States fit in the world, which is often so different from the view people have who have not travelled outside the United States as young children."[10] Remnick writes that Jarrett views America as "one country among many, rather than as the center of all wisdom and experience."[11] Although most of Jarrett's work is behind the scenes, it is clear that she endorses activism in the construction of policy. She supports policy directives that forbid linking the concept of terror to Islamic extremism and is widely assumed to have influenced the 2011 decision to grant ISNA (the Islamic Society of North America), which both the Department of Justice and the FBI had found tied with the Muslim Brotherhood, a role in reviewing who and what are used in "countering violent extremism" training for US military, law enforcement, and intelligence personnel.

It is also clear that Jarrett leans far to the left. She supported giving activist-leftist Van Jones the position of "green jobs" czar, an assignment that was ultimately rescinded due to congressional objections. Jarrett interviewed Jones for the role and exuded at the Netroots Nation conference, "We were so delighted to be able to recruit him into the White House. We were watching him . . . for as long as he's been active out in Oakland. And all the creative ideas he has. And so now, we have captured that, and we have all that energy and enthusiasm in the White House."[12] From the 1990s to the present, Jones has worked with movements that believe in foundational political change. These include STORM (Standing Together to Organize a Revolutionary Movement), Color of Change, Social Equity Track (for the UN World Environment Day), Green-Collar Jobs Campaign, and the Center for American Progress.

Along comparable lines, Homeland Security Secretary Janet Napolitano appointed Republican intelligence expert and activist Mohamed Elibiary to the Homeland Security Advisory Council. Elbiary advocated a more positive US view of, and relationship with, the Muslim Brotherhood, and had written supportively about the work of leading Brotherhood figure Sayyid Qutb even though Qutb viewed Sharia law as the sole basis for governance and society, and was an inspiration for jihadists in Egypt and elsewhere. Although he later said he had been unaware of the conference's extremist nature, Elbiary spoke at a December 2004 conference honoring the life and works of the "Great Islamic Visionary" Iranian Ayatollah Khomeini.[13] In addition to his work with the advisory council, Elibiary would sit on the DHS committee responsible for reviewing counter-terrorism training materials. The committee issued guidelines that restricted education about the ideology and political tactics of the US Muslim Brotherhood.[14]

In appointing Charles Freeman head of the National Intelligence Council (an appointment ultimately overturned by Congress), Obama touted the "new perspective" Freeman would bring to this important and powerful position. Indeed, his perspective would have been "new" for, as observers from Frank Gaffney to Alan Dershowitz to Bret Stephens pointed out, Freeman is a man with "strong and profoundly troubling views."[15] While in the Foreign Service, Freeman forged close ties with governments and interests hostile to the United States and demonstrated sympathy to their views. He was an apologist for the Saudi, Iranian, and Chinese regimes, and Hamas. He fawned over Mao Zedong, one of the most murderous dictators in history, who forced young and old alike into communist indoctrination programs, and terrorized the Chinese people.[16] His financial ties with the Saudi Arabia and China lobbies were one of the main obstacles to his confirmation.[17]

Secretary of State Clinton, while not embracing change as radical as Freeman or President Obama himself, and while more willing to pay occasional homage to American-democratic achievements, nevertheless indicated in both her presidential campaign and in her early initiatives as leader of the Obama foreign policy team that she too believed in dramatic change. In an article praising her new approach, *Washington Post* columnist David Rothkopf asked, "Amid all the distractions, what is Clinton actually doing?" He answered, "Only overseeing what may be the most profound changes in U.S. foreign policy in two decades—a transformation that may render the presidencies of Bill Clinton and George W. Bush mere side notes in a long transition to a meaningful post–Cold War worldview." He elaborated, "The secretary has been quietly rethinking the very nature of diplomacy and translating that vision into a revitalized State Department, one that approaches U.S. allies and rivals in ways that challenge long-held traditions. And despite the pessimists who invoked the 'team of rivals' cliché to predict that President Obama and Clinton would not get along, Hillary has defined a role for herself in the Obamaverse . . . Clinton is leaving behind old doctrines and labels. She outlined her new thinking in a recent speech at the Council on Foreign Relations in New York, where *she revealed stark differences between the new administration's worldview and those of its predecessors*: The recurring themes include 'partnership' and 'engagement' and 'common interests.' "[18] (italics mine)

Clinton often joined the chorus of disdain for the "failed Bush policy" that supposedly ruined America's reputation in the world. She had voted to authorize the use of force in Iraq, but had stated, "My vote is not, however, a vote for any new doctrine of preemption, or for unilateralism, or for the arrogance of American power or purpose—all of which carry grave dangers for our nation, for the rule of international law, and for the peace and security of people throughout the world." Clinton was the first high-profile Democrat to break from the post-9/11 standard of bipartisan unity in order to criticize President Bush. On May 16, 2002, she arrived onto the Senate floor waving a *New York Post* article with the headline "Bush Knew." She demanded, "The president knew what? My constituents would like to know the answer to that and many other questions."

Clinton often derided the "arrogance" that supposedly prevented American leaders from "engagement" with those whose values and cultures are different from our own and stressed the "interests" all nations have in common. As a presidential candidate in 2008, she made remarks such as the following: "I have been absolutely amazed, even shocked at the arrogance and incompetence that marks this particular administration" and "when I'm president, I'm going to send a message to the world that America is back—we're not the arrogant power that we've been acting like for the last six years."[19]

As secretary of state, Clinton joined Obama in calling for a "reset" in our relations with potential enemies, for toning down our words and actions in support of democracy, and for embracing diplomacy and "outreach" as the best tools for dealing with extreme regimes such as North Korea, Syria, and Iran. In January 13, 2009, remarks to the Senate Foreign Relations Committee, Clinton stated that she and Obama believed "foreign policy must be based on a marriage of principles and pragmatism, not rigid ideology." But it was immediately clear that the marriage of principles and pragmatism they sought was distinct from the kind of marriage of principles and pragmatism sought by so many previous presidents and secretaries of state. For, Clinton implied that our principles could sometimes be a form of "prejudice," while "emotion" (perhaps for democracy?) got in the way of diplomacy.

Her remarks in context are as follows: "Foreign policy must be based on a marriage of principles and pragmatism, not rigid ideology. On facts and evidence, not emotion or prejudice. Our security, our vitality, and our ability to lead in today's world oblige us to recognize the over-whelming fact of our interdependence. . . . We must use what has been called 'smart power,' the full range of tools at our disposal—diplomatic, economic, military, political, legal and cultural—picking the right tool, or combination of tools, for each situation. With smart power, diplomacy will be the vanguard of foreign policy." She added, "The president-elect has made it clear that in the Obama administration there will be no doubt about the leading role of diplomacy. One need only look to North Korea, Iran, the Middle East and the Balkans to appreciate the absolute necessity of tough-minded, intelligent diplomacy—and the failures that result when that kind of diplomatic effort is absent."[20]

(In a candid exposition of just what smart power *meant* in her deal-ings with adversaries such as Iran, Clinton would say in Georgetown on December 3, 2014, "This is what we call smart power—using every possible tool and partner to advance peace and security, leaving no one on the sidelines, showing respect, even for one's enemies, trying to understand and insofar as psychologically possible, empathize with their perspective and point of view. Helping to define the problems, determine the solutions.")[21]

As precursor to this theme, in an October 2007 speech at DePaul University, Obama had asked, "How are we going to turn the page on the failed Bush-Cheney policy of not talking to our adversaries if we don't have a president who will lead that diplomacy?" He insisted, "It's time to make diplomacy a priority. Instead of shuttering consulates, we need to open them in the tough and hopeless corners of the world. Instead of having more Americans serve in military bands than the diplomatic corps, we need to grow our foreign service. Instead of retreating from the world, I will lead a new chapter of American engagement."[22]

Of course, it was convenient myth that the Bush-Cheney foreign policy team had rejected diplomacy and cooperation with other states or enacted a policy of shutting down consulates! Official Bush-era documents stated the need for "working with others to defuse regional conflicts" and for "developing agendas for cooperative action with other main centers of global power." Although Bush did refuse to personally engage with tyrants, and his administration did offend European leaders by consulting with them too little, behind the scenes, diplomats worked feverishly . . . to pressure Hosni Mubarak to institute democratic reforms in Egypt, to pressure Syria in regard to its occupation of Lebanon, to facilitate peace between Israel and the Palestinians, to get food and medical aid to people instead of regimes in Africa and to fight AIDS, to strengthen NATO, and to welcome new Eastern Europeans into the alliance. They also labored to enhance cooperation with Japan, South Korea, Australia, India, the Philippines, Indonesia, and Thailand, and to craft agreements that would verifiably reduce nuclear proliferation and ease tensions between the United States and potential enemies. What did distinguish Bush from some of his predecessors was not his rejection of diplomacy, but his post-9/11 enthusiasm for active democracy promotion.

The national security document upon which the Bush administration most relied stated, "Today, the United States enjoys a position of unparalleled military strength and great economic and political influence. In keeping with our heritage and principles, we do not use our strength to press for unilateral advantage. We work instead to create a balance of power that favors human freedom."[23] Bush strategists saw short-term balancing and containment policies as supporting the longer-term goal: It was the "policy of the United States to seek and support democratic movements and institutions in every nation and culture, with the ultimate goal of ending tyranny in our world." Strategists paid homage to history that taught that the tyrannical character of regimes makes regimes more likely to make war, to threaten our way of life, to sponsor terror, and to proliferate weapons: "The goal of our statecraft is to help create a world of democratic, well-governed states that can meet the needs of their citizens and conduct themselves responsibly in the international system. This is the best way to provide enduring security for the American people."

The ideas in this Bush-era document were not new. Since World War II, most American presidents and their foreign policy teams had made the connection between regime type and the behavior of states, and had seen efforts at nudging the world in a more democratic direction as serving both worldwide human rights and American security and power. (There were, of course, great arguments about how much nudging America could do before it violated its own democratic principles.) But President Obama eschewed the idea that working to "create a world of democratic, well-governed states" was a legitimate goal for American statecraft. He believed instead in compromising with all regimes, seeing compromise as most urgently needed in relation to regimes we differed with the most.

He and Hillary Clinton stressed the imperative of finding "common interests" with our adversaries, and advocated generally overlooking their internal practices to do so. He implied that we weren't much better than the regimes we traditionally tried to reform. Too often "unilateralist" and too often unwilling to find common ground with our opponents, we exuded the exaggerated pride of place so often found in very powerful nations. Indeed, the United States, according to President Obama, placed too much emphasis on power itself, pouring too much money into military defense, military alliances, and nuclear weapons; a country as powerful as ours had the luxury of taking the unilateral lead in disarmament.

Previous American foreign policy approaches, Obama said, especially the approach of George W. Bush, had contributed to our unpopularity and served not only to alienate other countries but also to inflame terrorists. He and Secretary Clinton laid out a vision for a "smarter" foreign policy that would see the United States as but one power among many, that would tone down America's ambitions, and that would rely more on international institutions for direction and on diplomacy as the best way to deal with hostile regimes.

Before turning to the major policy changes President Obama and his first-term foreign policy team actually enacted, let's look at the evidence that he actually rejected the American foreign policy tradition and examine how he conveyed that rejection. This will help us to understand President Obama's vision for a "new world order" and to understand where his worldview, and his policy initiatives, came from.

The new president often downplayed the differences between the United States and other nations, even brutal regimes, and often brought attention to American mistakes. In statements and speeches to domestic and foreign audiences alike, he sought to level the playing field between the United States and other countries and regions, seeing this as requisite for the creation of the (ever-elusive) "international community." In describing the American past in terms of American mistakes, he went a long way toward rejecting the idea of the "shining city on a hill" and replacing it with something much less inspiring:

In a January 27, 2009, interview with *Al Arabiya*, Obama stated, "My job to the Muslim world is to communicate that the Americans are not your enemy. We have sometimes made mistakes. We have not been perfect."[24] In an April 3 speech in Strasbourg, France, Obama stated, "In America, there's a failure to appreciate Europe's leading role in the world. Instead of celebrating your dynamic union and seeking to partner with you to meet common challenges, there have been times where America has shown arrogance and been dismissive, even derisive."[25] In an April 6 speech before the Turkish parliament, Obama volunteered, "The United States is still working through some of our own darker periods in our history."[26] In an April 17 talk at the Summit of the Americas, Obama asserted, "While the United States has done much to promote peace and prosperity in the hemisphere, we have at times been disengaged, and at times we sought to dictate the terms."[27]

So too, Obama rejected the "war on terror" and its assumptions about radical Islam. The Bush-era national security document referred to above reflected and warned, "The 20th century witnessed the triumph of freedom over the threats of fascism and communism. Yet a new totalitarian ideology now threatens, an ideology grounded not in secular philosophy, but in the perversion of a proud religion. Its content may be different from the ideologies of the last century but its means are similar: intolerance, murder, terror, enslavement, and repression."[28] Obama hailed a significantly different perspective.

President Obama's Cairo speech delivered "to the Muslim world" on June 4, 2009, was seminal. Never before had an American president defined America's place in history in such negative terms to a foreign audience. Obama declared, "The relationship between Islam and the West includes centuries of coexistence and cooperation, but also conflict and religious wars. More recently, tension has been fed by colonialism that denied rights and opportunities to many Muslims, and a Cold War in which Muslim-majority countries were too often treated as proxies without regard to their own aspirations. Moreover, the sweeping change brought by modernity and globalization led many Muslims to view the West as hostile to the traditions of Islam."[29]

As Georgetown professor Robert Lieber points out, Obama "suggested Western sources for the region's problems and downplayed local causes such as authoritarianism, corruption and internal obstacles to social and economic progress."[30] As he referred to Islam's "proud tradition of tolerance" and asked Muslim nations to show tolerance to their own people, Obama also referred to instances of supposed American intolerance to Muslims, such as "rules on charitable giving" that "made it harder for Muslims to fulfill their religious obligation." Stated he, "That is why I am committed to working with American Muslims to ensure that they can fulfill *zakat*."[31] Never mind that wayward Muslim "charities" were one of the sources of funding for the 9/11 terrorist attacks on the United States.

Strangely for a president who wanted to improve rather than diminish America's reputation in the Muslim world, Obama seemed to create moral equivalence in the Cairo speech between the United States of America and the repressive Islamic Republic of Iran, stating, "In the middle of the Cold War, the United States played a role in the overthrow of a democratically elected Iranian government. Since the Islamic Revolution, Iran has played a role in acts of hostage-taking and violence against U.S. troops and civilians."[32]

Handing Iran not only a propaganda coup but words that it would use as weapons against the United States, he offered his "understanding" of those who protest that some countries have nuclear weapons while others do not. He expressed the view that "any nation—including Iran—should have the 'right' to access peaceful nuclear power if it complies with its responsibilities under the Nuclear Non-Proliferation Treaty." In the Czech Republic, in April 2009, Obama had declared Iran's "right to peaceful nuclear technology," and had reemphasized his position in a BBC interview.[33] From that moment on, the cruel and mendacious president of Iran, Mahmoud Ahmadinejad, would refer to Iran's "right" to "peaceful" nuclear technology while brazenly accelerating a nonpeaceful program designed to humble and hurt enemy "infidels" America and Israel.

Of major note, given America's historic relationship with Israel, is the fact that Obama went on in the Cairo speech to refer to "Palestinians who have suffered in pursuit of a homeland" and to "the legitimate Palestinian aspiration for dignity, opportunity, and a state of their own" and to Israeli "obligations to ensure that Palestinians can live, and work, and develop their society." He additionally asserted, "The United States does not accept the legitimacy of continued Israeli settlements." Almost as an aside after all of this, Obama asked the Palestinians "to recognize Israel's legitimacy." He then repeated the call for a Palestinian state.[34] Thus, *in advance of Israeli-Palestinian negotiations*, for which Obama and Secretary of State Clinton hand-picked brutal Syrian dictator Bashar al-Assad as intermediary, the president preemptively gave away every bargaining tool Israel could possibly hold. He asked nothing in return other than recognition of the long-established democratic state of Israel's right to exist!

Even all of this contrition and all of these sacrificial offers to the new world order were not enough. Obama brought up "the controversy about the promotion of democracy in recent years," adding, "much of this controversy is connected to the war in Iraq." Implicitly repudiating both democracy promotion and the Iraq War, he declared, "So let me be clear: no system of government can or should be imposed upon one nation by any other."[35]

Asserted columnist Jonah Goldberg, "No statement better encapsulates how unidealistic and unrealistic the New Liberalism is. Men *should* not murder other men, but they most certainly *can*. The story of international relations has been the story of domination and imposition, often for ill, occasionally for good. Any foreign policy that doesn't recognize this cannot be called realistic. And, in an important respect, any foreign policy that thinks America has neither the power nor the moral authority to impose its will when our conscience moves us cannot be called idealistic either." What good is multilateralism, Goldberg asked, if "the Taliban throws acid in the faces of little girls trying to read" and the multilateralists themselves "are never willing to point that out?"[36]

Behind the scenes, too, President Obama and the Clinton State Department cast doubt upon the American tradition and upon their

predecessors. After Obama's meeting with the president of Kazakhstan, Mike McFaul of the National Security Council reported that
Obama "explained" to the leader of the oppressive country that we
too were working on perfecting our democracy. Assistant Secretary of
State Michael Posner reported that in discussions with China about
human rights, the US side brought up Arizona's immigration law "early
and often." Obama and Clinton quickly overturned the Bush policy
of bypassing the UN Human Rights Council as hopelessly corrupt
and antithetical to genuine human rights purposes. This is the same
"Human Rights" Council that includes Saudi Arabia, Cuba, China, and
Russia in its ranks. The council today focuses less on protecting human
rights than on steering attention away from the world's worst human
rights violators and forcing attention instead onto the United States
and Israel.

Stating the desire to create "a more perfect union in a more perfect
world," the White House even voluntarily prepared and submitted a
report on our own domestic laws and policies to the Human Rights
Council in 2010. This report, too, criticized Arizona's immigration
law, implying that Arizona was violating human rights with a law that
had "generated significant attention and debate at home and around
the world." While acknowledging the freedoms provided in the Constitution and the successful work of minorities to move toward a more
just society, the report gave a favorable nod to a "national mandate" for
universal voter registration and urged the combating of "deceptive practices" which, it claimed, were designed to deter legitimate voters from
voting. It frequently praised Obama's proposals for new regulations and
laws to move the United States toward greater fairness and equality. It
emphasized the sexism, intolerance, and discrimination that supposedly
still plague America. All of this should come as no surprise, given the
lineup of activists and left-leaning "experts" the administration chose
to review our human rights record. Among them were Stephen Rickard
and Wendy Patten of George Soros's Open Society Institute, Ron Scott
of the Detroit Coalition Against Police Brutality, and Dawud Walid of
the Council on American-Islamic Relations (CAIR). The submission of
the report marked the first time the US subjected its laws to international review and censor.[37]

With statements and gestures such as these, and with policies designed to support these statements, Obama succeeded in putting the idea of American exceptionalism under pressure. When asked whether he believed in American exceptionalism, Obama famously replied, "I believe in American exceptionalism, just as I suspect that the Brits believe in British exceptionalism and the Greeks believe in Greek exceptionalism."[38] Intoned Jonah Goldberg (in the article referred to above), "This is a profound rejection of both reality and ideal. One doesn't have to be jingoist to appreciate what everyone from Tocqueville and Marx to Werner Sombart and Seymour Martin Lipset recognized as the unique nature of America's origins and character. When Obama says America is exceptional to Americans just as Greece is exceptional to Greeks, what he is really asserting—beyond the idea that no nation is really exceptional—is that exceptionalism is a kind of superstition. . . . Obama seems to think it his mission to help us get over fairy tales of America's unique status."[39]

■ ■ ■

President Obama's September 2009 speech at the UN is informative and important because it implicitly rejected both the idea that the United States has done anything exceptional for political freedom, and the idea that political freedom is an appropriate priority for US foreign policy. The speech instead emphasized shared "interests" and "collective action"; indeed, the words *interests* and *collective* appeared again and again. In explaining why "many around the world had come to view America with skepticism and distrust," he opined, "Part of this was due to opposition to specific policies, and a belief that on certain critical issues, America has acted unilaterally, without regard to the interests of others. And this has fed an almost reflexive anti-Americanism, which too often has served as an excuse for collective inaction." He went on, "Now, like all of you, my responsibility is to act in the interest of my nation and my people, and I will never apologize for defending those interests. But it is my deeply held belief that in the year 2009—more than at any point in human history—the interests of nations and people are shared. . . . We must embrace a new era of engagement based on mutual interest and mutual respect, and our work must begin now."[40]

What is the "interest" to which President Obama referred that the world supposedly has in common? Might it have anything to do with the universal longing to be free? No—he pointed to peace and prosperity instead, asserting "it is not simply peace, but our very health and prosperity that we hold in common."

At this point in the speech, it became clear that what is sometimes referred to as the "freedom agenda" of American foreign policy stood in the way of this common interest: "No world order that elevates one nation or group of people over another will succeed. No balance of power among nations will hold. The traditional divisions between nations of the South and the North make no sense in an interconnected world, nor do alignments of nations rooted in the cleavages of a long-gone Cold War."[41]

Obama urged a shedding of "old habits" and "old arguments" that were "irrelevant to the challenges faced by our people," and again implied that the new approach would emphasize shared interests of peace and prosperity (instead of human rights and individual rights): "That is the future America wants—a future of peace and prosperity that we can only reach if we recognize that all nations have rights, but all nations have responsibilities as well. That is the bargain that makes this work. That must be the guiding principle of international cooperation." *So it is a "bargain" with other nations, even brutal ones, that "works" and it is the "rights" of nations, not of human beings, that must be our "guiding principle."*

In the next part of the speech, Obama attempted to steer his UN audience toward common work on what he called the "four pillars" of global society: nonproliferation and disarmament, peace and security, the preservation of the planet, and a global economy that advances opportunity. Again, peace and prosperity mattered most. Obama never gave the impression that certain human rights are so fundamental that they are worth sacrificing and even fighting for.

Having promised American commitment to "global interests" and his "four pillars," Obama managed to find one remaining opportunity for "American leadership" and it had to do with rectifying our environmental sins: "And that is why the days when America dragged its feet on this issue are over. . . . And those wealthy nations that did so much damage to the environment in the twentieth century must accept our obligation to lead." Wealthy nations, he added, must "extend a hand" to those with less while opening their markets to more goods.

The president went on to say of North Korea and Iran that, even though they threatened to take us down "a dangerous slope of proliferation . . . we respect their rights as members of the community of nations."

For all his emphasis on interests and all his de-emphasis on democratic principles and human rights, Obama did not, in this speech or any other, *define American interests*. Beneath his emphasis on interests lies his determination to focus only on those interests we can find in common with other regimes, including fanatical, repressive ones. Thus, although he embraces the pragmatic deal-making of détente, the deal itself is more important to Obama's one-world ambitions than the interests the deal serves. If we have to overlook some of our own interests for the sake of a deal, so be it.

Finally, at the very end of the UN speech, Obama paid lip service to democracy and human rights. But, a close reading reveals that democracy and human rights were now subordinate to other goals. After stating that "real change can only come through the people we represent," Obama explained: "That's where we will build consensus to end conflicts and to harness technology for peaceful purposes, to change the way we use energy, and to promote growth that can be sustained and shared. I believe that the people of the world want this future for their children. And that is why we must champion those principles which ensure that governments reflect the will of their people. These principles cannot be afterthoughts—democracy and human rights *are essential to achieving each of the goals that I've discussed today*."[42] (italics mine)

The problem is that in this speech, as in countless others, democracy and human rights *are* afterthoughts. They do not rank nearly as high as the admonition to tone down our American selves, to apologize for our sins, to negotiate at all costs, and to embrace multilateralism. They take second place to the pursuit of a global consensus regarding environmental and economic progress, and to world peace and disarmament. They take second place to Obama's own efforts and to the administration's own unique priorities. Tellingly, he suggested, "For those who question the character and cause of my nation, I ask you to look at the concrete actions we have taken in just nine months."[43] So much for the character and cause of the nation itself!

■ ■ ■

Given that President Obama depicted the American project as flawed and viewed American exceptionalism as false, it makes sense that he valued negotiation and compromise for their own sake. For it was, in that case, only fair that we compromise, even at the expense of our geopolitical position; even at the expense of our moral position; even at the expense of the promotion of human and individual rights. And here I must assert that the real heart of American exceptionalism is the idea that rights are not exceptional—they are universal. The very thing that makes us exceptional is that we, in our very institutions and laws, and even in the formation of our foreign policy, recognize the universality of those rights. For America at its best, individual rights and human rights are one and the same. As I stated in the previous chapter, they are particular in that they apply to each one, but universal in that they apply to everyone.

Our country was founded upon this very revolutionary principle— that was a threat to oppression anywhere it would be found, even when it existed within, as in the case of slavery. "We the people" believed men everywhere had a right to self-government and that legitimate government rested upon the consent of the governed. We declared perfect government and perfect governance to be impossible and formed a new "system of politics" in which governmental power would be strictly limited. We turned radically away not only from autocracy, tyranny, and divisions of society based on class, but also from divisions in the world based on imperial domination. We stood against militarism and colonialism and against entanglements with militaristic, colonial powers. Instead of imposing our way on others, we hoped our experiment in democracy would set a shining example, an example so compelling that the world would peacefully be drawn into our fold. Insofar as the United States had a mission it was this: Rather than engage in wars of conquest or greed, it should stand as a paradigm of liberty, democracy, and justice. We were to be one nation in which foreign as well as domestic policy was to *include* the consideration of what is right.

I emphasize the word *include* because the early definition of the US role in the world did also address concerns of power. Early American statesmen believed that avoiding the power struggles of Europe would give us time to perfect our union and to grow more powerful before pursuing stature and influence on the world stage. Moreover, they saw that the magnetic pull of our freedom would serve not only our democratic cause but also our worldwide influence, i.e., power. In addition, social contract theory as reflected in the Constitution held that the primary duty of government was the preservation of its people; the government could not protect the rights of individuals if it did not protect their very existence. Hence, any foreign policy decision had, *in principle*, to include the consideration of power. The founders thereby set the stage for a foreign policy tradition that would continuously seek the proper mix of power and principles, and that was unique in the world in that it *did* include democratic principles.

In a 1970s article, scholar Whittle Johnston worried that the dual forces of Kissinger's détente and revisionist interpretations of American history were leading us to forget our noble, albeit never perfectly achieved, attempt to synthesize principle and power. He identified a growing tendency to focus narrowly on power and "will" and economic interests instead. Said Whittle of Kissinger, "He has become less concerned to get what is right than to depict as right what he can get. The morally legitimate becomes less the criterion of the diplomatically possible than the diplomatically possible the criterion of the morally legitimate."[44] Said Whittle of revisionist William Appleman Williams's critical economic interpretation of American history, "The Statue of Liberty tells us more of the promise of America than does Williams' tract of its tragedy. Moreover, the [American] openness was never merely a commercial charter reckoned by the existence of the dollar sign. It was rather an expression of that confidence in the existence of universal moral standards which had been America's inheritance from the past and was to be her bequest to the future."[45]

To those who depended on an American foreign policy tradition that includes concerns for liberty and democracy and for what is right, and for those who looked to the United States for guidance and inspiration in the struggle against dictatorship, the United States was clearly not at its best under President Obama. Upon his March 1990 visit to the Voice of America, Václav Havel, the last president of Czechoslovakia and the first president of the Czech Republic, had stated: "You helped bring about the peaceful revolution which has taken place in Czechoslovakia. Now, you will have to inform us about how to create democracy, because we are beginning to build it, to renew it, after many long decades, and we have a lot to learn."[46] Two years after Obama came to power, Lech Walesa, the leader of Solidarity who helped forge Poland's liberation from the Soviet Union, would lament, "The United States is only one superpower. Today they lead the world. Nobody has doubts about it, militarily. They also lead economically but they are getting weak. But they don't lead morally and politically anymore. The world has no leadership. The United States was always the last resort and hope for all other nations. There was the hope, whenever something was going wrong, one could count on the United States. Today, we lost that hope."[47]

In rejecting so many important strands of the American foreign policy tradition, Obama was preparing our nation for big change. Within his first year as president, this much was already evident: His approach is not in the spirit of Wilsonian internationalism because it does not sanction spreading or promoting democracy. It is not idealistic in the sense of Carter's human rights initiatives because it willingly tries to buy peace and security at the price of cooperating with dictators who brutalize their own people. Although it embraces the pragmatic deal-making of Kissinger's realism, it forgets Kissinger's emphasis upon power-as-leverage in diplomacy and for the sake of the interests of the free world; it assumes that engaging and talking with the world's worst dictators will convince them to change their course, and hopes that reducing our own defenses will inspire hostile regimes to do the same. President Obama's ideas and policies definitely do not resemble the policies of presidents who were neither "idealistic" nor "realistic" but rather, in a uniquely American way, combined the two: Truman, Eisenhower, Kennedy, and Reagan particularly exemplify this approach.

Recall that these presidents strove to undercut the realism/idealism dichotomy. They considered both the moral worth and the practical consequences of their foreign policy decisions and, in the spirit of the American tradition, saw the two as inseparable. They are interesting for the extent to which they tied America's self-interest to its moral interests. When Truman argued that the rights and struggles of all peoples transcended the superficial divisions of the Cold War, he suggested that we could never "win" the war through strength alone. The only true victory, the only one that would have the stability and longevity that comes from the people's satisfaction, would be a victory of moral, democratic principles over tyranny and oppression.

Some American foreign policy initiatives, such as détente on the one hand and humanitarian aid to the developing world on the other, have emphasized one or the other—tactical concerns *or* American ideals. But no great American foreign policy initiative has emphasized neither. Moreover, while some presidents have made limited deals with dictators in an effort to ward off or contain what they perceived to be greater threats, no president has so ingratiated the world's worst extremists. And yet, this is precisely what President Obama and his foreign policy team have done. They have rejected it all. They reject American idealism for the sake of a relativist doctrine that views all cultures and ideals as "valid" and deserving of "tolerance." They reject American realism for the sake of an accommodation that makes little distinction between enemies and friends. And, they reject both the pro-democracy spirit and the defensive alliances of containment—a foreign policy initiative which stands, perhaps, as the most brilliant and successful of the twentieth century.

■ ■ ■

If the realist school says we should ignore the internal shortcomings of other countries, focusing instead on order and equilibrium between countries, Truman, Eisenhower, and most post–World War II presidents viewed *that* as unrealistic. They insisted that internal problems quickly became external threats, and made the connection between internal democratic government and external harmony among states. It was widely observed that democracies were much less likely than other forms of government to invade the territories of their neighbors and to pursue weapons for non-defensive purposes. These presidents therefore viewed the enhancement of American power and the invigoration of American principles as the *only* response to modern problems such as imperialism, Bolshevism, fascism, and "total war." The fact that Europe and Asia had submitted to the disastrous consequences of *their ideas* meant that we had to project and promote our democratic alternative. If we were to live up to our mission and our character, we had to accept increased moral and strategic responsibilities in the world.

It is often assumed that the advent of active American participation in European geopolitics during the Cold War stifled or halted the flow of ideas regarding America's original principles. It is as if there can't be both: the continuance of principles and the reevaluation of our position in the world. It is as if geopolitics and ideals cannot exist at the same time. And yet, their coexistence is nothing new. There have been few, if any, American presidents who considered power to the exclusion of ideals or ideals to the exclusion of power. Even those who heralded a new age of morality in foreign affairs did so partly because they thought that simply being "America," that beacon of hope, was the best way to increase our influence. Even those who viewed geopolitics as inferior to the American dream used power in pursuit of the dream. Even those who spoke out for a "harder" foreign policy did so as a way of preserving and defending not merely the American nation, but also American principles. The realism/idealism dichotomy is inadequate even as we seek to understand such presidents as Carter and Reagan. Although the latter was obviously more "realistic" in his (pessimistic) assessment of leftist dictators, he certainly did not shirk ideals for the sake of power. It was ideals to which Reagan appealed when he urged Gorbachev to "tear down this wall."

It is true that the harsh nature of the choices the United States has had to make as a powerful member of the modern world has complicated and sometimes sullied its position. As two world wars compelled it to compete with other nations and ideals, its mission was tested and strained. As Soviet-inspired communism became of paramount concern and active defensive strategies became essential, we had to decide how far we would go and what methods we would use to "contain" communism. Some were tempted to reject power politics altogether in search of a more simple, pristine world. Others were tempted to do anything to increase the power of the United States. Even if the reasons they gave were idealistic, e.g., "the struggle against the opponents of freedom," a disregard for methods stands glaringly against the regard for individual rights. It does not suffice to say that our mission depends upon our power, in that we must first stand (we must be safe) before we can enunciate that which we *stand for*. For, the very notion that our security is prior to our principles provides an excuse for the abuse of power; it allows the end to justify the means.

Thus, the active pursuit of national security leads to a kind of involvement in the world that does complicate our role in the world, and that role is all the more complicated in a world with terrorism and fanaticism. For that very reason—in order to remember what it is we're fighting to secure—it is ever important to keep our ideas alive.

■ ■ ■

What greater symbol and demonstration of this is there than Obama's response to the Berlin Wall in comparison and contrast to the response of John Kennedy? President Kennedy had stood at the wall and famously declared, "Ich bin ein Berliner." But that is not all Kennedy said. Listen to Kennedy's inspiring words:

> There are many people in the world who really don't understand, or say they don't, what is the great issue between the free world and the Communist world. Let them come to Berlin. There are some who say communism is the wave of the future. Let them come to Berlin. And there are some who say, in Europe and elsewhere, we can work with the Communists. Let them come to Berlin. . . . While the wall is the most obvious and vivid demonstration of the failures of the Communist system . . . we take no satisfaction in it; for it is, as your mayor said, an offense not only against history but an offense against humanity, separating families, dividing husbands and wives and brothers and sisters, and dividing a people who wish to be joined together. . . . Freedom is indivisible, and when one man is enslaved, all are not free. When all are free, then we can look forward to that day when this city will be joined as one and this country and this great Continent of Europe in a peaceful and hopeful globe.[48]

Like Obama, Kennedy dreamed of a peaceful, unified world. But he was not willing to purchase it at the price of political prisoners and political oppression, at the price of mollifying nations who granted their people no rights, or at the price of appeasing nations that enslaved other nations. The one-world vision was, for Kennedy, subordinate to a greater vision, one that insisted upon the right of each and every person to political freedom. "All free men, wherever they may live, are citizens of Berlin, and, therefore, as a free man, I take pride in the words *Ich bin ein Berliner*." Not only Reagan, but many other presidents repeated the theme. As one example, George H. W. Bush delivered a historic address in Mainz, West Germany, in 1989, calling for a "Europe whole and free."

Now, let us turn to what President Obama said when he came to the
Berlin Wall as a candidate in 2008. Yes he acknowledged the "dream of
freedom" in "this city, of all cities." Yes, he acknowledged our country's
historic partnership with West Germany and the "greatest alliance ever
formed to defend our common security," NATO. And, yes, he acknowledged that the fall of the Berlin Wall "brought new hope." But to what did
he attribute that success? To the willingness to take a stand for freedom,
the contagious idea of liberty, the efforts of Kennedy and Reagan and
other American presidents, the tenacity of Germans who never gave up
on the idea of a free and whole Germany? No, he attributed it to the
world finally realizing that unity was better than division. "People of the
world—look at Berlin, where a wall came down, a continent came together,
and history proved that there is no challenge too great for a world that
stands as one. . . . While the twentieth century taught us that we share a
common destiny, the twenty-first has revealed a world more intertwined
than at any time in history. . . . The walls between the old allies on either
side of the Atlantic cannot stand. The walls between the countries with
the most and those with the least cannot stand. The walls between races
and tribes and natives and immigrants, Christian and Muslim and Jew
cannot stand. These are now the walls we must tear down."

Obama pointed to "new dangers" that imperiled the hope created
by the fall of the Berlin Wall. What were the dangers? Did they have
to do with political systems and ideologies that still posed a threat to
liberty? Not only were they not that—Obama seemed to imply some
sort of moral equivalence between the danger posed by terrorists and
the dangers posed by free governments: "The terrorists of September
11th plotted in Hamburg and trained in Kandahar and Karachi before
killing thousands from all over the globe on American soil. As we speak,
cars in Boston and factories in Beijing are melting ice caps in the Arctic,
shrinking coastlines in the Atlantic, and bringing drought to farms from
Kansas to Kenya." Other dangers he emphasized included the heroin
trade in Afghanistan, genocide in Darfur, and poorly secured nuclear
material. Dangers conspicuously absent were those posed by Iran, North
Korea, Syria, Venezuela, and other repressive, hostile regimes.

At the end of the speech, Obama finally talked about what might
define the unity he values, as he put unity in the context of the United
States' own striving "to form a more perfect union." But, the definition

comes in the way of an afterthought, and lacks all passion for freedom itself; it seems to have more to do with multiculturalism and with being helped by government (from fear and want): "Our allegiance has never been to any particular tribe or kingdom—indeed, every language is spoken in our country; every culture has left its imprint on ours; every point of view is expressed in our public squares. What has always united us, what has always driven our people; what drew my father to America's shores—is a set of ideals that speak to aspirations shared by all people: that we can live free from fear and free from want; that we can speak our minds and assemble with whomever we please."[49]

In the face of this lack of passion for freedom, we are justified in asking: How successful would containment have been (and would the Berlin Wall have come down) if it had not included the passionate appeals of Truman, Eisenhower, Kennedy, and Reagan, and if it had ignored the hopes and dreams of the people behind the Iron Curtain, for the sake of unity and peace? The brave and principled Czech president Václav Havel understood the answer all too well. In an interview in which he was asked what he thought about Obama's decision to postpone meeting with the Dalai Lama, he reflected, "We know this much from our modern history. When [French prime minister Edouard] Daladier returned from the Munich conference, the whole nation was applauding him for saving the peace. He made a miniscule compromise in the interest of peace. But it was just the beginning of a chain of evil that subsequently brought about many millions of deaths. We can't just say, 'This is a small compromise that can be overlooked. First we will go to China and then perhaps talk with the Dalai Lama.'"[50]

As if to punctuate his lack of admiration for the historic achievement marked by the fall of the great symbol of communist oppression, Obama tellingly, significantly, declined the invitation to attend the twentieth anniversary celebration of the fall of the Berlin Wall. Perhaps because of the wide criticism he was already receiving over the decision, he did, in the address he sent in place of his presence, pay nice tribute to Kennedy's words and to the end of tyranny and "affirmation of freedom" that the fall of the wall represented.

To say that President Obama made outreach and multilateralism the cornerstones of his foreign policy because he thought they would work is to deny the possibility that he also embraced outreach and multilateralism because he didn't care if America's power and democratic stature went down a good notch. Many have documented Obama's worldview, which relies on theories of colonialism and imperialism to explain the world and has real sympathy for the idea that the United States is now the world's most influential imperial power. This was the view of his father, and Obama had frequently stated agreement with his father's positions. It was also the view of Reverend Jeremiah Wright and other friends who touted "liberation theology" as a way of imposing collectivism on developing nations. And it is the view of those administration advisors who see the world in terms of socialist claims on "privileged" nations. Even mainstream Democrats believed at the start of the Obama presidency that America should convey more conciliation and less strength and that we should find middle-of-the-road compromises with opponents rather than use our superior power as leverage.

When it came to military power, our superiority was willingly surrendered by the Obama White House. It began by eliminating $350 billion in weapons programs. It then proposed a new Strategic Arms Reduction Treaty (START) by offering specific reductions to our own nuclear arsenal before negotiations even began. In 2011, it initiated and negotiated with Congress $450 billion in military budget cuts through the year 2021. In January 2012, President Obama made a rare appearance at the Pentagon, flanked by his four service chiefs and Secretary of Defense Leon Panetta. He announced that it was time to cash in on the "peace dividend" and unveiled plans for a significantly reduced military. The plan included up to a trillion dollars in cuts to the defense budget over the next ten years. We will see that more defense cuts, which went against the requests and requirements of the US military, would follow.

What an inappropriate time to assume peace. Iran was threatening to close the Strait of Hormuz, and all our efforts to "engage" hostile powers had failed. The murderous Assad was annihilating the Syrian people and pressuring Lebanon, while Egypt was turning away from its peace treaty with Israel. Russia occupied a fifth of Georgia's territory (since its 2008 invasion) and was applying intense pressure on Georgian President Saakashvili. It was targeting human rights officials in Georgia and elsewhere with a campaign of terror. Russia had managed to install a pro-Russian leader in Ukraine and was forcefully inserting air, naval, and army bases in Abkhazia and South Ossetia. Moreover, the bipartisan

Quadrennial Defense Review panel had found "a growing gap between our interests and our military capability to protect those interests in the face of a complex and challenging security environment."

In an article entitled "Obama's Defense Drawdown," the *Wall Street Journal* observed, "This self-inflicted attack on defense comes at a strange time. True, the U.S. cut deeply after World War II, Korea, Vietnam and the Cold War—and in each case came to regret it soon enough when new threats emerged. But peace doesn't characterize our time. Mr. Obama yesterday wielded his familiar line that 'the tide of war is receding,' which will please his anti-war base but will come as news to the Marines in Afghanistan or the Navy ships patrolling the tense Strait of Hormuz."[51] It wasn't just arms we were reducing; it was our capacity to lead: "The real message to the world is that the Administration wants to scale back U.S. leadership. This was part of the rationale behind the White House's reluctance to take the initiative in the Middle East last year, as well as the attempts to mollify Iran's mullahs and Russia's Vladimir Putin. Now the Administration plans to draw down troops and America's profile in Africa and Europe. The Navy can easily match Iran's threats in the Persian Gulf now, but what about in ten years?"[52]

In his important February 2009 Munich speech, Vice President Joe Biden heralded just such a combination of American conciliation and withdrawal of leadership. The speech must have sent a chill down Eastern Europe's collective spine. Nile Gardiner, director of the Margaret Thatcher Center for Freedom at the Heritage Foundation, analyzed the speech, describing it as "one of the weakest projections of U.S. leadership on foreign soil in recent memory." He noted the following: Biden offered Iran a quid pro quo, "the kind the European Union has offered for several years with absolutely nothing to show for it except spectacular disaster" and lacking "any explicit statement of consequences."[53] Biden did not appeal to European Union countries to tighten their sanctions on Tehran nor call upon Russia and China to strengthen UN Security Council sanctions. He offered "little evidence" that the Obama administration intended "to adopt a tough line toward Russian aggression in its 'Near Abroad' or attempts to bully and intimidate its neighbors in the Caucasus as well as Eastern Europe." He did not express US support for Georgian and Ukrainian membership in NATO, nor did he express disagreement with Russia's brutal invasion of Georgia the previous summer. The vice president avoided any reference to the war on terror, and called for a "new way forward" in the Muslim world "based on mutual interest and mutual respect." Concluded Gardiner, "It was an address that tried to be all things to all people, lacking in concrete policy prescriptions and cloaked in vague statements designed to cause minimal offense in foreign capitals, including those of America's worst enemies. Biden's address was above all a celebration of 'soft power,' cynically re-branded by the Obama administration as 'smart power.'"[54]

To gain a better understanding of President Obama's and Secretary Clinton's "smart power" approach, we must pause to consider their academic background and the broader intellectual forces behind their ideas: The doctrines of moral relativism and of historical inevitability are very much alive on American college campuses and within the White House today. Yes, fascism fell, and so (it appeared in the late 1990s) did communism. Unfortunately, the concepts of historic inevitability and moral relativism they both contained did not fall with them. More often than not, these ideas exist side by side with the contradictory ideas that socialist societies are *better* than capitalist ones and that everything in political and cultural life can be "constructed." (Too few in the academic world are willing to point out these contradictions.) Whether we "construct" history or go along for the ride of its inevitability—either way—the belief in God-given and innate rights becomes impossible. So too, whether we embrace moral relativism or statist-socialism, the idea that individual and human rights are fundamental and prior to government can't hold.

With all this "constructing" going on, rights become something that government grants and something government can take away. On the other hand, if progress in history is inevitable, regimes can crush human rights while hiding behind the claim that they're on the relentless path to progress. Every totalitarian leader of the last century, and this one, has enlisted "progress" on his side (usually in some socialist form). In the meantime, the idea of inevitable progress allows America and the West to remain quiescent in the face of world atrocities; at least we know that what Hillary Clinton calls the "right side of history" will eventually have its way.

As if these dominant but contradictory academic trends were not enough to make heads spin, there is also, in today's academic world, the coexistence of the *one-world* vision that devalues individual rights (so that we can embrace "central planning," even on a global scale, and so that we can "coexist" with regimes that don't acknowledge these rights) and the *particularist* idea that other countries and peoples are not "ready" for the freedoms we enjoy in the West or are "incapable" of forming democracies (so that we don't interfere with regimes that deny their people freedom). Either way—whether because of a one-world vision or because of an elitist Western attitude—there is a de-emphasis on human rights.

All of these trends lead in the same direction. Whether it is reliance on central planners and social scientists to solve our problems; or belief in historical inevitability, socialist progress, and cultural relativism; or insistence that the United States is an aggressive, colonial power, all paths lead away from liberty. Thus, we see the popular academic idea (so popular that I have heard it expressed in many academic conferences) that taking a stand for human rights is the same as "imposing one civilization upon another." Thus, we see the popular academic effort to take diversity training to a global scale, and we see how that effort ultimately explains away human rights violations and atrocities as "cultural differences." Thus, we see academic enthusiasm for "autocratic models" in Asia and elsewhere, and social-scientific praise for the way they "efficiently" pursue economic plans; their model is contrasted to our "inefficient" government, which is supposedly "burdened" by the separation of powers, checks and balances, and the two-party system. Thus, we see the idea that history will mechanically "forward" removing all passion for liberty.

The Obama administration's generous gestures to oppressors and adversaries and its conscious distancing of the United States from friends and allies can be seen in the light of all these trends. These trends form the academic environment with which President Obama and Secretary Clinton are familiar and in which they are rooted.

Antipathy for the Bush administration and its post–9/11 emphasis upon American-democratic ideals, which were seen as "biases," was so great in academia that it often clouded clear thinking. Regarding a typical academic report by the American Political Science Association's 2009 "Task Force on US Standing in World Affairs," Robert Lieber observes that, among other indications of its skewed assessment of American standing, "In the 'Regions' section, there is insufficient recognition that U.S. standing in East Asia, large parts of South Asia, and in

Africa was actually rather positive in recent years." In addition, "Reference to 'the legacy of Iranian hostility toward the United States' is cited without taking into account that the bulk of Iran's population is so alienated by the repressive rule of the mullahs, their armed cronies in the Iranian Revolutionary Guard Corps, and the Basij militia that it has now become much more favorably disposed toward the United States, the regime's major adversary."[55]

It should come as little surprise, then, that Obama and Clinton took the transnational movement toward more political freedom and reversed it, denouncing not only the means to regime change (perhaps understandable, given the Iraq War), *but also the objective.* And this at a time when democratization was an ascendant principle and goal in the Middle East and elsewhere (as we shall see in the next chapters). This is not to deny that there were strong countervailing forces in the Middle East that wanted Sharia law and/or advocated militant Islam, and that hoped to subvert democracy movements for their own purposes. It is simply to point out that, given the strength of the democracy movements, and given the suffering of the people under repressive and corrupt regimes, it was both unwise and unprincipled to do nothing to win Middle Eastern hearts and minds. We will see that American indifference only made it easier for Islamist opportunists.

The reputation of democracy had not suffered so severe a blow from the Bush administration as we were led to believe. To the contrary: Pro-democracy resistance movements had strengthened, not weakened, during the Bush years, in Syria, Iran, China, Egypt, Tunisia, and elsewhere. Ukraine's Orange Revolution and Georgia's Rose Revolution occurred in 2004 and 2005, well after the United States invaded Iraq. (Large crowds greeted Bush on his 2005 trip to Tbilisi, in which he proclaimed Georgia a "beacon of liberty.") By the end of Bush's second term, Turkey had embraced some market and political reforms and was increasingly cooperative on strategic matters. With the moral and political support of the United States and France, Lebanon was emerging from Syria's grasp. Across the African, Asian, Eastern European, and Arab worlds, discontent with repressive government and disenchantment with centralized/socialist policies was growing like never before.

The world was, by all accounts, on a trajectory toward more political and economic freedom when Obama and Clinton took over. In addition, the world's worst human rights violators were under the spotlight and under pressure. Remarkably, that momentum toward freedom has been hurt by the American government itself.

Instead of nourishing this promising environment, in which democracy movements were simmering everywhere, and in which the worst regimes lived in mortal fear of these movements, Obama and Clinton announced that they wanted to negotiate with the likes of Iran, Syria, and North Korea without preconditions. Obama quickly indicated his willingness to meet with the Iranian president, sent him deferential messages addressing him as "Supreme Leader," and made it crystal clear that Iranian regime change was not a US goal. Secretary Clinton indicated that the United States would focus on economic issues rather than human rights in discussions with China and on weapons issues rather than human rights in discussions with North Korea. In addition, Obama and Clinton signaled their unwillingness to label Hamas, Hezbollah, or the Iranian Revolutionary Guards terrorist organizations. They embraced a new policy of working with "moderate" elements of the Taliban in Afghanistan.

In a major shift of policy, Clinton announced that the US would send two envoys to Syria for "preliminary conversations" and reopened our embassy there. And, in a move that is simply inexplicable, even in the light of the trends I've highlighted, the administration picked Syria's brutal Bashar al-Assad as key mediator in Israeli-Palestinian negotiations. Inexplicably as well, Obama cancelled funding for democracy programs in Iran that had begun in 2004 and that went toward programs such as Persian broadcasts of the Voice of America and Radio Free Europe.

It has been said by others, and my research for this book convinces me that it is true: President Obama's and Secretary Clinton's words and actions frequently rewarded our enemies and punished our friends. They degraded our alliances, diminished and insulted our allies, and catered to and ingratiated those who have no respect for our way of life and/or would like nothing better than to do us harm. At the least, they had as their aim a leveling of the playing field, for the first step toward a one-world vision is, in Nietzsche's words, moving "beyond good and evil." The leveling compulsion was preponderant in American foreign policy during the first Obama administration and continued on in the second. It allowed some within the White House to see our preferences as "prejudices" and our power as an "unfair advantage." It fueled the impulse to make successful democratic states and alliances a little less powerful and to turn a blind eye to an increase in the power of nondemocratic governments. Leveling the playing field depends upon moral neutrality, while moral neutrality depends upon a de-emphasis on democracy, freedom, and human rights.

Some saw the writing on the wall. In an article highlighting the suffering and genocides of the twentieth century, one writer lamented, "So far, on these matters, Barack Obama has gone in precisely the wrong direction. Instead of attempting to show that there are consequences for eliminationist murdering and expulsions, his administration has taken a soft line toward [al-Assad], one of the worst eliminationists and mass murderers of our time. In doing so, the administration is broadcasting a simple message around the globe, a message being heard by other dictators contemplating similar assaults: You will get away with it."[56]

Israel was not treated so generously. Obama publicly and repeatedly called on Israel to freeze settlements as a prerequisite to negotiations, while asking nothing concrete of Hamas, Hezbollah, and the Palestinians. He surrounded himself with such anti-Israel friends and advisors as Howard Gutman, Rashid Khalidi, and General Tony McPeak. If, in spite of this, he really wanted to support Israel as he claimed, he wouldn't have continually emphasized and stated how much we had "already" helped Israel; he would instead have explained to the American people why Israel still needed our help. If the administration really viewed Israel as a valued ally, rather than officially condemning the 2010 Israeli decision to build homes in eastern Jerusalem as an "insult" and "affront" to the United States, it would have acknowledged that the decision was in accord with Israel's unilateral concessions to the administration the prior year: Under pressure from the Obama administration, Israel had agreed to a ten-month freeze on Jewish construction in Judea and Samaria, but the agreement explicitly allowed construction in Jerusalem. Israeli prime minister Benjamin Netanyahu had also agreed to announce his support for a Palestinian state.

The thanks Israel got for these concessions was a four-part ultimatum, issued by Hillary Clinton in March of 2010: She demanded that Israel prohibit construction in Jerusalem; cancel permits for housing in the Ramat Shlomo section of East Jerusalem; and make "gestures" to the Palestinians, the suggested ones being releasing hundreds of Palestinian terrorists from Israeli prisons and negotiating on all substantive issues. If Israel didn't accept the demands, the US threatened to boycott Netanyahu and his ministers when they visited the United States. Adding insult to injury, in May 2011 Obama suggested that Israel use 1967 borders as a starting point for negotiations. Intoned American-Israeli journalist Caroline Glick, "Rather than reward Netanyahu for taking a risk for peace, in the model of Yasser Arafat and Mahmoud Abbas, Obama has pocketed Netanyahu's concessions and escalated his demands. This is not the behavior of a mediator. This is the behavior of an adversary."[57] I would add that it is possible at the same time to express concern for the human rights of Palestinians and to make support for the sovereign state of Israel unmistakably clear.

Contrary to assurances given to Israel, President Obama made a deal with Islamic states at a 2010 meeting of parties to the Nuclear Non-Proliferation Treaty, and agreed to help convene a 2012 conference, a move which Israel had argued against due to its reliance on nuclear deterrence. It is true that Obama continued our close military and intelligence relationship and our security assistance and technology transfers. But he did not support Israel the way one supports a close ally.

Also notable was the administration's periodic downplaying of anti-Semitism. In one such instance, Ambassador Howard Gutman, who was chosen to give a speech at the 2011 "Conference on Fighting Anti-Semitism in Europe," used the occasion to redefine anti-Semitism and to dismiss the historical magnitude of the problem. Said he, "There is and has long been some amount of anti-Semitism, of hatred and violence against Jews, from a small sector of the population who hate others who may be different or perceived to be different, largely for the sake of hating. Those anti-Semites are people who hate not only Jews, but Muslims, gays, Gypsies, and likely any who can be described as minorities or different. That hatred is of course pernicious and must be combated. . . . I have not personally seen much of that hatred in Europe, though it rears its ugly head from time to time."[58]

The list of unfriendly regimes treated generously and friendly regimes treated ungenerously goes on. At a time when the Chinese human rights situation was deteriorating gravely and increasing evidence of Chinese complicity in Iran's acquisition of weapons was surfacing, Obama chose to host Chinese leaders at the White House in very elaborate fashion. Meanwhile, the administration initially showed little interest in nourishing our relationship with India, a relationship that had dramatically improved in recent years and had led to India serving as a counterweight to China. When British leaders first came to town, they, unlike the Chinese who received a lavish and warm welcome, received a strangely cold reception, with Obama finding little time for discussions. Adding to the bizarre treatment of our closest World War II, Cold War, and post-9/11 ally, the administration "returned" the bust of Churchill which the British had sent as a gift to the White House after 9/11 as a show of camaraderie and support. While it was "returning" gifts to England, it was providing some dictators with arms. Freedom House and other human rights organizations questioned why the Obama administration insisted upon moving forward with arms sales to Bahrain at the very time that it was using imported arms to brutally suppress protestors.

Just as the Venezuelan people were recoiling from the realization that Hugo Chavez would never permit free elections and that oppression and economic decline were the consequences of his rule, Secretary Clinton suggested exchanging ambassadors. While attending the Summit of the Americas, she made the suggestion and defended it by asserting, "the Chavez relationship . . . is a result of eight years of isolating Chavez. We've isolated him, so he's gone elsewhere. And I don't think we believe it's worked very well. I mean, he's a very sociable guy."[59] More startling was Obama's warm greeting of Chavez at the summit. The propaganda value was unmistakable. The Venezuelan government released photographs of the two men smiling and of Obama putting a hand on Chavez's shoulder. As the *Telegraph* put it, "The bonhomie continued as Saturday's summit meeting started. Mr. Chavez presented his US counterpart with a book, *The Open Veins of Latin America*, by the left-wing Uruguayan writer Eduardo Galeano. Mr. Obama accepted the gift with a smile."[60]

The *Jerusalem Post* questioned why Obama would "smile broadly" to Chavez when the State Department had documented his "unchecked concentration of power, political persecution and intimidation" and when the Center for Strategic and International Studies said his government engaged in "arresting opposition leaders, torturing some members of the opposition (according to human rights organizations) and encouraging, if not directing, its squads of Bolivarian Circles to beat up members of Congress and intimidate voters—all with impunity." The *Jerusalem Post* also puzzled over Obama's bow before King Abdullah of Saudi Arabia at the G20 Summit. The administration denied it was a bow, but it sure looked like one. At the very least, noted the *Post*, it was a sign of great deference.[61]

Of course, all of the outreach to Chavez and other dictators achieved the opposite of intended goals. Instead of responding to our generous gestures in kind, dictators became more intransigent. Instead of creating a more stable, peaceful world, lopsided engagement policies enabled and emboldened destabilizing and aggressive regimes. As Charles Krauthammer wryly observed, the result of all this appeasing of fanatics and tyrants is that "those who hated us still do; those who put hopes in us no longer do." Chavez continued to rail against the United States and continued to work with the likes of Iran and North Korea, going so far as to lavishly host Mahmoud Ahmadinejad. By April 2010, Latin American experts were warning of an escalating Chavez threat, citing ties with Iran and Hezbollah and other terrorist groups.

In Russia—where the administration hoped that if we sought friendship and got over our own Cold War mentality, Russia would seek friendship and get over *its* Cold War mentality—things didn't turn out any better. We will explore Russia's response—as well as the Iranian, Syrian, North Korean, and Chinese responses to our attempts to conciliate and engage with these regimes—in the next chapters. For now, it suffices to note that they responded to US engagement policies with a refusal to cooperate on regional, security, and weapons proliferation matters, with incitement of other nations to do the same, with heightened repression of their citizens, with regional aggression, and with sponsorship of terror.

In one of countless setbacks for US engagement policies, on June 11, 2011, Aleks Tapinish of Agence France-Presse reported, "Iran's President Mahmoud Ahmadinejad on Wednesday joined the Chinese and Russian leaders in a rare encounter at a summit in Kazakhstan, where he launched a new attack on the 'slavers and colonizers' of the West."[62]

In regard to North Korea, President Bush and Secretary of State Condoleezza Rice had responded to heated criticism of the Axis of Evil speech by deciding to give engagement and negotiations a try. But, neither calling North Korea evil and intensifying sanctions, nor scaling back sanctions and actively pursuing negotiations bore much fruit. It is clear that removing anti-totalitarian rhetoric did not inspire the regime to move in our direction. We will see in chapter 7 that North Korea's seeming willingness to negotiate with the Obama administration over the dismantling of its nuclear program, which was widely attributed to US retraction of criticism of the regime and willingness to engage without conditions, turned out to be yet another cover for proceeding apace with the program. Soon, the North Koreans would undermine the negotiation process itself, refusing to adopt even the pretense of willingness to "talk" and compromise.

Aside from the failure of engagement to help progress on weapons issues, it is only right to question the decision to unconditionally engage with a country wherein the people endure ubiquitous, omnipresent repression and routinely suffer unimaginable horrors. The cruelty of the North Korean leadership and the suffering of the North Korean people seemed not to have worried President Obama and Secretary Clinton.

Perhaps here, too, they took their inspiration from academia. I have attended two separate panels on North Korea at the American Political Science Association. At one, panelists agreed that an emphasis on human rights would constitute an arrogant attempt to "impose" one civilization, the American, on another "civilization," the North Korean. The other panel's conclusions can only be described as delusional at best and sinister at worst. Panelists described North Korea as a "fear regime" and asserted that this fear explained North Korea's hostile posture. What was North Korea supposedly afraid of? The United States. If only we stopped criticizing their form of government, urged one panelist, relations would improve. "They have no choice" for their behavior, said she, given United States unwillingness to "accept" their form of government and given US "insults." Did she really believe, if the border opened up between North and South, as it had between East and West Berlin, that terrorized and starving Northerners would choose not to flee out of "fear" of the US-aligned South Korean government? I doubt it.

CHAPTER 3

THE RUSSIAN RESET
Obama, Clinton, and Kerry Reach Out

The Russian "reset" will long be remembered as a cornerstone of Obama/Clinton foreign policy, a sign of the times as it were. It represented a period in American foreign policy when outreach to adversaries and likely adversaries, and the attempt to elicit their cooperation and partnership through dialogue and largesse, held unique sway. It should be noted, however, that if that had been the principle motivation for resets with those who opposed American/western values, we would have stopped those policies once their unwillingness to work with us was impossible to deny. But there was more to it than that—there was the belief that traditional democratic priorities and ideals weren't so special anyway. Only this explains why, once Russia and others shunned and brazenly defied us, we *kept on* with our outreach policies.

It wasn't just the cooperation and partnership of adversaries *with us* that the Obama administration sought; President Obama and the Clinton and Kerry State Departments wanted to teach Americans how to cooperate *with them*—how to be patient and compromising, and willing to accommodate and listen to those with whom we, as Americans, were inclined to disagree. It is thus that the administration went along with NATO's weak and ineffective response to Russia's actions in Ukraine, and went along with Russian plans and "peace conferences" for Syria long *after* it saw Russia's true colors. The administration was disappointed in Russian behavior, but it was also frustrated by American outspokenness against it.

As President Obama began his first term, there *was* reason to engage with Russia. On the other hand, there was reason to maintain strong

policies of deterrence and to enunciate principles of human rights, political freedom, and the rights of weaker nations to live free from imperial
domination by stronger powers.

In favor of the former course was the fact that Russia was indeed no
longer the Soviet Union; it was a weakened state with major economic,
regional, and demographic challenges. Although Russia had, ever since
the later part of Russian president Boris Yeltsin's term, increasingly
pulled away from the West as it sought to regain the power and prestige it had lost at the end of the Cold War, that trend was interrupted
by post-9/11 cooperation in which the next president, Vladimir Putin,
offered America support in its antiterrorism campaign and its operations in Afghanistan. For a while, President George W. Bush saw the
two countries as moving toward a "new level of partnership." He looked
into Putin's eyes and found him "straightforward and trustworthy."
Even though Russian cooperation was short-lived, the US did need to
consider Russia's previous assistance and its current concerns about us,
which included our apparent disregard for Russia's role in world affairs,
and the American-Western expansion of NATO into the Soviet Union's
traditional sphere of influence. Discussions with Russia on issues such as
nuclear proliferation and relations with Russia that increased economic
and cultural ties and allowed us to encourage democratic reforms were,
in this light, warranted.

Arguing for the latter were the Soviet Union's dark history and
Russia's recent actions and pronouncements, which indicated a desire
to return to Soviet-era predominance. As Russian chess master and
activist Garry Kasparov argued in a book that came out just as I finished
this one, a major problem with post-communist Russia was that it
had not atoned for its past, and thus built the new Russia on morally
compromised foundations, which among other things, "left the roots of
the powerful Russian security apparatus intact." He continued: "After
decades of genocides, mass relocation and imprisonment, and totalitarian repression, it was decided to let bygones be bygones and move
into the bright new future without recrimination."[1] It is of no small
significance that Putin was part of that still-formidable security apparatus, a KGB man through and through.

Putin served as a mid-level agent in the KGB's foreign intelligence wing, rising to the level of lieutenant colonel, from 1975 until

communism's collapse. From 1985–1990, he worked as a spy in East Germany; he saw the Berlin Wall come down and worked against that eventuality. In the run-up to his election as president of Russia in 2000, he served as director of the Federal Security Service, a successor to the KGB. The man at Russia's helm, and in charge of Russia's foreign policy, was thereby an expert at subterfuge, repression, and propaganda.

Making matters worse, foreign policy in contemporary Russia is personalized as opposed to institutionalized. Putin's own outlook and priorities therefore had to be taken very seriously. From the time he was elected president in 2000 through his time as prime minister to his reelection as president in 2012, this popular Russian leader emphasized his commitment to reestablishing Russia as the preeminent regional power and a major power on the world stage. Although post-communist Russia had flirted with a free-market economy and closer political ties with the West, by the time Obama came to power, Putin's Russia had firmly embraced the centrality of the state, was moving in an authoritarian direction, and was rejecting the West and its institutions.[2] Putin declared in 2005 that "the collapse of the USSR was the greatest geopolitical catastrophe of the century" and, at the 2006 Munich Security Conference, issued a broad attack on all aspects of American foreign policy. Russia made good on Putin's words with an increasingly aggressive posture toward its neighbors, which included using control of energy as a means "to 'influence' former Soviet republics to change political positions that they had or to follow Moscow's policy lead."[3]

In Chechnya, post-Soviet Russia had shown its capacity for major, systematic human rights violations, including disappearances. In Georgia, Russia showed its capacity for imperial-style aggression when it launched a full-scale invasion of the country in 2008. Georgia's "Rose Revolution" was one of multiple pro-democracy "color revolutions" in the first decade of the new century. Although the United States did not intend to bring down the government of Georgia president Eduard Shevardnadze, exchange programs and financial and technical support for civil society organizations were, according to author and expert Lincoln A. Mitchell, a "necessary, but far from sufficient" condition for Georgia's revolt, especially since civil society leaders led the movement for more accountable government. The people who overthrew Shevardnadze "did it through democratic means, and saw democracy as the key to the success of post-Shevardnadze Georgia."[4] But Russian leaders saw both the pro-NATO and pro-democracy orientation of Georgia as a threat. When Georgia decided to take a military stand against the ongoing provocations of Russian forces in South Ossetia, the Russian response was severe; Russia carried out an air and ground assault on Georgia as a whole, killing hundreds of civilians and hundreds of servicemen and displacing tens of thousands of citizens.

President Bush stated, "The territorial integrity and borders of Georgia must be respected, just as those of Russia or any other country. Russia's action only exacerbates tensions and complicates diplomatic negotiations." NATO secretary-general Jaap de Hoop Scheffer expressed "serious concern" about "the disproportionate use of force by the Russians and the lack of respect for the territorial integrity of Georgia." British prime minister Gordon Brown asserted, "There is no justification for continued Russian military action in Georgia, which threatens the stability of the entire region and risks a humanitarian catastrophe."[5] Nevertheless, Russia's easy military victory and the lack of tangible costs gave it reason to assume that the price for such actions was negligible and probably "created a temptation for Russia to reproduce its triumph."[6]

All of this, along with Russia's worsening domestic repression, targeting of journalists and human rights activists, and intimidation of other Eastern European democracies—and given that Russia was still a major nuclear power and was reinstituting its war-fighting capacities—meant that attempts to engage with Putin's Russia should, at the very least, have been balanced with attempts to contain Putin's Russia. Those attempts, had they been made, should not have been merely for reasons of power, but also for reasons of principle. As the de facto leader of the free world, it behooved the United States to ask, as it sought to create a "cooperative and constructive" relationship with Russia, the following cautionary questions: At whose expense? In accordance with or defiance of what principles? At the risk of sending what signals to, and creating what openings for, ideological and geopolitical opponents?

Engagement and compromise are no replacement for policymaking. "Strategic dialogue" does not in itself create a secure and peaceful world, and it does not substitute for a strong moral and strategic position. A broad-based policy that some in the foreign relations field termed "selective engagement and selective containment" would have been far preferable to a policy that relied so heavily on engagement, and that did so little to promote traditional American-democratic priorities.

President Obama has not worked to invigorate American ideals or enhance the defenses of the free world; he has diluted our principles and deemphasized our power in order to make them acceptable to the "international community." With his belief in moral equivalence, his deconstruction of American national security strategy, and his "shedding" of the idea of American greatness, he bears little resemblance to his collective predecessors. And that, apparently, given all of his insistence upon fundamental change, is what he wants.

Obama and Clinton adopted a new kind of "realism" that sees little place for grand strategy. Their form of realism bears little resemblance to the traditional school, as it demotes military power and balance-of-power tactics and favors global initiatives and outreach to opponents. Such an approach was said by them to be the "smartest" way to reach "practical consensus."

So too, Obama's and Clinton's version of idealism, if they can be said to have one, is new in that it distances itself from morality because morality is seen as too judgmental. In its place is a striving for one-world harmony and peace that relies upon compromises with totalitarians, dictators and authoritarians. The Obama foreign policy team rejected both America's post–World War II acknowledgement of the exigencies of power, and America's historic inclination to see foreign policy in human as well as strategic terms.

In an astute August 2008 editorial, foreign policy scholar Robert Kagan asked, "Where are the realists?" He asserted, "When Russian tanks rolled into Georgia, it ought to have been their moment. Here was Vladimir Putin, a cold-eyed realist if there ever was one, taking advantage of a favorable opportunity to shift the European balance of power in his favor. . . . Why, then, the non-response by today's realists? Why didn't the smart-power pragmatists in the White House attempt to balance Russia's power moves?" Asserting that today's realists would be "unrecognizable to their forebears," Kagan observed:

> Rather than talk about power, they talk about the United Nations, world opinion and international law. . . . Power is no answer to the vast challenges we face, they insist, and, indeed, is counterproductive,

because it undermines international consensus. . . . Leading realists today see the world not as Mr. Morgenthau did, as an anarchic system in which nations consistently pursue "interest defined as power," but as a world of converging interests in which economics, and not power, is the primary driving force. Thus Russia and China are not interested in expanding their power so much as in enhancing their economic well-being and security. If they use force against their neighbors, or engage in arms buildups, it is not because this is in the nature of great powers. It is because the United States or the West has provoked them.[7]

Noting that we had just come through "the most destructive century in all the millennia of human history," Kagan asked whether mankind had really come so far and whether it was sensible to make such assumptions. He suggested, "We could use a little dose of the old realism now, at least the part that would recognize a great grab for power like Mr. Putin's and understand that it will take more than offers of cooperation and benevolent tutelage to address Russia's revived appetites." With a question we can now answer in the negative, Kagan concluded: "The only question now is whether the United States will play its part, and with the appropriate blend of realism about the world as it exists and idealism about what a strong and determined democratic community can do to shape it."[8]

■ ■ ■

President Obama's and Secretary Clinton's initiatives vis-à-vis Russia and Eastern Europe show just how little respect they had for their predecessors' containment policies, and for containment's structures and assumptions. If they occasionally gave a nod to that policy's successes, they put much more energy into denying it had current relevance. In doing so, they built upon a theory espoused in the 1990s that held that, as the world's only remaining superpower, we no longer had to worry about existential and ideological threats and could focus instead upon "the economy, stupid." In political scientist Francis Fukuyama's famous prediction (with which many in government and academia agreed), the collapse of the Soviet empire meant that the worldwide spread of democracy would take care of itself. Some, however, Robert Kagan among them, saw the folly of complacency. In a 1996 article Kagan had warned,

The most difficult thing to preserve is that which does not appear to need preserving. The dominant strategic and ideological position the United States now enjoys is the product of foreign policies and defense strategies that are no longer being pursued. Americans have come to take the fruits of their hegemonic power for granted. During the Cold War, the strategies of deterrence and containment worked so well in checking the ambitions of America's adversaries that many American liberals denied that our adversaries had ambitions or even, for that matter, that America had adversaries. Today the lack of a viable threat to U.S. vital interests or to world peace has tempted Americans to absentmindedly dismantle the material and spiritual foundations on which their national well-being was based. They do not notice that potential challengers are deterred before ever contemplating confrontation by their overwhelming power and influence.[9]

Of course, 9/11 forced America back, for a time, into the business of grand strategy and the promotion of American ideals. But, complacency ultimately prevailed, as the generally lighthearted reaction of American pundits and intellectuals to the Obama administration's foreign policy during his first term shows.

In the spirit of casting aside Cold War strategies and ideas, President Obama and Secretary Clinton declared a "reset" in relations with Russia. In advance of her March 2009 meeting with Russian foreign minister Sergei Lavrov, in which she ceremoniously handed him a "reset button," Secretary Clinton said in an NPR interview, "We're going to hit the reset button and start fresh." She explained that, unlike "the last administration," the Obama administration would "believe in arms control and nonproliferation as a core function of our foreign policy" and would "work with the Russians on the START treaty and the nonproliferation treaty and other matters of great concern."[10]

Obama and Clinton projected little concern about those Eastern Europeans who had recently thrown off the Soviet yoke and who looked to America for support in resisting the Soviets, who were showing renewed interest in subjecting them. They declared their commitment to finding areas of "mutual interest" with Russia, and before even finding such areas, preemptively offered Russia a generous "bargain" regarding nuclear weaponry that hurt both our geopolitical position and our moral stature. They did this without asking anything in return, beyond vague assurances that Russia would be more helpful vis-à-vis Iran.

At Cairo, Obama had broadcast his belief that "no single nation should pick and choose which nations hold nuclear weapons," and in his dealings with Russia he moved quickly to make good on that claim. In September 2009, President Obama became the first American president to preside over a United Nations Security Council summit-level meeting, underscoring the importance he placed on the meeting's purpose: The UNSC unanimously sponsored Resolution 1887 calling for "a world without nuclear weapons." In his Prague address, Obama described nuclear weapons as dangerous relics of the Cold War, called for a world free of nuclear weapons, and pledged commitment to new START, test ban, and nonproliferation treaties. While pointing to the threat an Iran with nuclear weapons would constitute, he again took a generous stand for Iran's so-called nuclear "rights." Declared the American president, "We want Iran to take its rightful place in the community of nations, politically and economically. We will support Iran's right to peaceful nuclear energy with rigorous inspections. That's a path the Islamic Republic can take. Or the government can choose increased isolation, international pressure, and a potential nuclear arms race in the region that will increase insecurity for all."[11]

To emphasize US commitment to the elimination of its own nuclear weapons, Hillary Clinton attended the Conference on Facilitating the Entry into Force of the Comprehensive Nuclear Test-Ban Treaty. As Theodore Kalionzes and Kaegan McGrath of the Monterey Institute of International Studies point out, Washington had not sent a representative to this conference in nearly a decade, and had never sent an official of such stature.[12] In a summit meeting in Moscow in July of 2009, President Obama and Russian president Dmitry Medvedev agreed on the basic structure of a new START treaty and committed to reducing their countries' strategic offensive arsenals. After meeting again with Medvedev in London, Obama instructed his team to include warheads and delivery vehicles in negotiations. He then made ratification of the new START agreement and Comprehensive Nuclear Test Ban Treaty top priorities, stating, "After more than five decades of talks, it is time for the testing of nuclear weapons to finally be banned."[13] The administration attempted to move quickly, while its political capital was high.

Secretary Clinton urged Congress to approve the treaty "immediately" during the lame duck session and insisted, "This is not an issue that can afford to be postponed."

President Bush, too, had worked for nuclear arms reductions, announcing his intention to reduce the US's operationally deployed nuclear warheads by some two-thirds and inviting Russia to do the same. President Putin had accepted the offer. The Bush administration launched the Global Threat Reduction Initiative, which secured more than six hundred vulnerable nuclear sites around the world and helped convert fifty-seven nuclear reactors in thirty-two countries from highly enriched uranium to low-enriched uranium, thereby removing enough weapons-grade material for more than forty nuclear bombs. In May 2008, President Bush had approved a new START agreement and transmitted a "presidential determination" recommending it to Congress for review. But, when Russia invaded Georgia, Bush rescinded the determination, stating that if circumstances changed, a new one would be issued.

Unlike his predecessor, President Obama was unwilling to allow Russia's violation of Georgia's sovereignty and human rights to get in the way of START. In his May 2010 message to Congress recommending the agreement, Obama noted Bush's position and clearly indicated that START ratification would no longer be tied to Russian behavior. Obama stated: "1) that the situation in Georgia need no longer be considered an obstacle to proceeding with the proposed Agreement, and 2) that the level and scope of U.S.-Russia cooperation on Iran are sufficient to justify resubmitting the proposed Agreement to the Congress for the statutory review period of 90 days."[14] These words handed Russia nice cover for its resurgent plans. Just as Putin was truculently pressuring Eastern European countries to submit (as in the Cold War days) to Soviet authority, Obama announced that the plight of Georgia, the country where Russia was asserting the *most* pressure, would not be an obstacle to improved relations. Even though Russia had not provided one ounce of help with Iranian proliferation, Obama praised the "level and scope" of Russia's cooperation on the matter.

Some conservatives seemed to forget that Ronald Reagan negotiated the first START treaty, and did so with sincere commitment to a world free of nuclear weapons, when they criticized Obama's efforts at drastic nuclear reductions. But others expressed more specific concerns regarding inadequate verification and why we would preemptively offer lopsided concessions at a time when Russia needed an arms control agreement much more than we, and when Russia was turning darkly away from the opening it had experienced under glasnost and, in addition, was harassing and intimidating fledgling democracies in Eastern Europe while actively supporting Syria and Iran. The treaty required greater US reductions than Russian, stipulating that the US reduce its arsenal by 265 warheads and that Russia reduce its arsenal by 189. Moreover, Russia was not required to cut the number of its deployed strategic launchers, while the United States was required to destroy several hundred. The treaty gave real advantages to Russia.

Kim Holmes of the Heritage Foundation pointed out that the new treaty suffered from "the inability to verify the number of actual warheads in Russia's arsenal," which meant Russia could conceivably "load more warheads onto each launcher and exceed the total warhead number that the treaty allows without getting caught." The biggest problem was Obama's misreading of Russia's intentions. Holmes explained, "Russia's nuclear and conventional weapons arsenals are declining faster than ours, due to age and funding, so of course they want to bring our levels down to theirs. But Mr. Obama doesn't seem to realize he is playing right into the Kremlin's strategy of relying more, not less, on nuclear weapons over conventional ones. . . . Why? Because with this treaty the Russians are trying to constrain our advantage in conventional (non-nuclear) 'strategic' weapons, including missile defense, in order to accentuate the power of their nuclear arsenal."[15]

The treaty implicitly elevated Russia while demoting NATO. For the corollary Nuclear Posture Review failed to make a clear commitment to defend the United States and its allies. *Investor's Business Daily* complained, "While Obama envisions a world without nuclear weapons and moves steadily toward unilateral disarmament of our nuclear arsenal, we envision a world without tyrants and thugs willing to use them against us. We do not fear nuclear weapons in the hands of Britain or France, countries that share our love of freedom and democracy."[16]

An announcement made in 2010 drew more widespread concern, even among some Democrats and liberal commentators. In a preemptive and completely unnecessary announcement that could only be joy to the ears of weapons proliferators and terror sponsors, Obama issued a nuclear doctrine that Defense Secretary Robert Gates admitted "includes significant changes to the US defense posture." He explained, "Under the new doctrine if a state attacked us with chemical or biological weapons, but that same state was in compliance with the [Nuclear] Non-Proliferation Treaty," the US pledged not to use or threaten to use nuclear weapons against it.[17] Charles Krauthammer observed, "Under the old doctrine supported by every president of both parties for decades, any aggressor ran the risk of a cataclysmic U.S. nuclear response that would leave the attacking nation a cinder and a memory. . . . Credible? Doable? No one knows. But the very threat was effective."[18] David E. Sanger and Peter Baker noted in the *New York Times* that the Bush policy, while arguing for a rethinking of nuclear deterrence, "reserved the right to use nuclear weapons to deter a wide range of threats, including banned chemical and biological weapons and large-scale conventional attacks."[19] They rightly described Obama's new strategy as "a sharp shift from those of his predecessors."

It was yet another bargain vis-à-vis Russia that drew the most concern not just domestically but also internationally. Although Reagan's promotion of missile defense technology as a modernized defense strategy was widely viewed as a long shot and derided by many, by the time Obama came to power, missile defense was so much a reality that smaller nations viewed it as a valuable protective shield and as a way to enhance their own stature, while Russia and Iran viewed it as a hindrance to hegemonic authority and regional influence. The Bush administration had installed missile defense interceptors and radars in Alaska and California and had proposed a third site in Europe as defense against the growing threat of ballistic missile attack there. The Polish and Czech governments had agreed to allow the installment of these missile defenses on their soil. They had then based much of their future security policy on the assumption that they would get missile defenses from the United States; this helped to allay deep fears regarding a future military threat from Russia. They valued the agreement both as a means of increasing their security and as a way of strengthening their allegiance with the United States and its NATO allies.

As political columnist Frank Gaffney notes, they also saw the agreement "as a tangible expression of the U.S. commitment to their security in the face of assiduous Russian efforts to reassert a sphere of influence that would turn the clock back, reestablishing in some form their unhappy status under the Kremlin's thumb." Gaffney added an important point: "It was precisely in the interests of advancing that ambition that the Russians assiduously opposed the deployment of the Third Site."[20]

It was thus a profound insult to Eastern Europeans and a boon to Russia when Obama offered to dismantle the missile shield program. In fall of 2009, he announced his decision to "overhaul" the Bush-era missile defense shield for Europe by scaling back the Airborne Laser and Kinetic Energy Interceptor programs, which could be rapidly deployed to counter unexpected threats, and the Multiple Kill Vehicle program, which was intended to attack incoming missiles in midcourse. He also deferred more funding for the space-based "sensor constellation," which was to provide warning and detection. (Never mind that these decisions violated the terms of the Declaration on Polish-American Strategic Cooperation and other supposedly binding agreements.) In exchange for eliminating an important program for reducing the threat posed by Iran's development of missile technology, the United States supposedly received verbal assurance from Russia that it would be more helpful in pressuring Iran to relinquish its non-peaceful nuclear program.

Time has already told the tale that could have been anticipated: Russia has demonstrated no particular helpfulness to the United States on this or any other issue. The helpfulness of Poland and the Czech Republic, which was very much in evidence before the momentous decision to dismantle missile defense, was ruined by this move. Stunned at being shamed on the world stage, and abandoned by their best ally, Poland and the Czech Republic retreated from their previous support of the United States. And who can blame them? "This is a catastrophe for Poland" declared a spokeswoman for the Polish Ministry of Defense. "I would consider it a dirty trick if the Czech Republic and Poland would end up unprotected," Alexandr Vondra, a former deputy Czech prime minister and one-time ambassador to the United States, told the Associated Press.[21]

In the *Bulletin of the Atomic Scientists*, Marek Madej described the fallout, observing that the missile defense agreements "were politically costly for Poland as they damaged Polish-Russian relations and adversely affected Poland's image among some European allies."[22] He pointed out that the agreement to host missile defenses had been attached to the US-Polish Status of Forces Agreement, which stipulated that the United States place troops in Poland, and was seen as a prerequisite to the deployment of Patriot missiles on Polish soil. "So now the [Polish] government can be criticized on two fronts: by those who supported missile defense in Poland but believed the government demanded too much and by opponents of the system who believed that in the long run, negotiations would bring more losses than benefits for Polish security. Many in Poland simply believe that Obama's decision is a 'betrayal' aimed at making Moscow more cooperative regarding Iran and in future disarmament talks. . . . But the announcement also was widely viewed as another sign (in addition to a lack of appreciation for Polish involvement in Iraq and the denial of U.S. visa waivers for Polish citizens) of U.S. ingratitude for Polish support in international politics."[23]

Russia watched with canny satisfaction as the cards unfolded to its advantage. The president of the United States had not only chosen to ignore its invasion of Georgia the previous summer; its intensifying bullying of Ukraine and Chechnya; its continuing aid and arms sales to the world's worst regimes; its threats of military retaliation against the Poles, Balts, and Czechs for standing with the US on missile defense; and its refusal to join in pressuring Iran—the administration had offered to dismantle missile defense as well.

But this was not all! The Obama administration next promised to "listen" to Russian ideas about security architecture and to delay a push for Georgia and Ukraine to join NATO. From Moscow, a reporter from the *Foundry* reported, "A senior Russian official half-jokingly told me that the US steps are 'birthday presents for President Medvedev and President Putin'. . . . When I asked why President Obama needed to provide all these goodies while getting nothing in return, Lavrov and Putin said that they did not view US 'reset' measures as concessions. 'They corrected mistakes that the Bush Administration made,' said Lavrov."

The *Foundry* reporter of course saw through the prevarications on both the American and the Russian sides: "Unilateral concessions by the Obama Administration are interpreted as a sign of weakness, from Moscow to Teheran to Caracas. Blaming the Bush Administration and making unrequited concessions is bad policy, especially when dealing with the Russian geopolitical chess masters, or those who invented chess—the Iranians."[24]

Such US decisions have had serious consequences for the balance of power in Europe and for the political and military position of

NATO. The military equilibrium and democratic principles that have kept major nations in Europe and Asia at peace since World War II had been compromised. So too had the reputation, the influence, and the democratic standing of the United States. Bartosz Weglarczyk, columnist for the Polish newspaper *Gazeta Wyborcza*, wrote, "I have no doubt that under the new administration, Washington has neglected relations with Poland and with Central Europe as a whole. Some say, and I count myself among them, that it is a mistake, and that someday Washington may pay dearly for it."[25]

On March 6, 2009 (before the announcement on missile defense), Stratfor Global Intelligence reported on a NATO meeting that revealed that the administration's indifference to the problems of Eastern European democracies was so great that it was pressuring Western European nations toward similar indifference. Stratfor observed, "The real revolutionary change lies in the U.S. administration's plans for dealing with Russia. When the NATO meeting began Thursday morning, Lithuania—on behalf of the Baltic states—tried to block a resolution that would restore ties with Moscow . . . [and] along with Estonia, Latvia and Poland, has made it abundantly clear to Washington that it does not trust the Russians. These countries are all relying heavily on the planned U.S. ballistic missile defense (BMD) systems in Central Europe to guarantee their security against a resurgent Russia. By early afternoon, however, Lithuania's protest had been swept aside and NATO states voted unanimously—in line with the wishes of Washington and other heavyweights—to restore ties with Moscow."[26]

At this same meeting, Hillary Clinton broke the news to the Georgia delegation "that the United States needs some space in their relationship." Stratfor saw the ramifications of this break with previous policies: "This means Tbilisi will more or less have to fend for itself the next time Russia starts rumbling in its neighborhood. In other words: The Georgians should forget about NATO membership for now, because the Americans have bigger problems to work on with the Russians."[27]

The administration continued to place roadblocks in front of Georgia's and Ukraine's efforts to join NATO and continued to give Georgia the cold shoulder. Ukraine and Georgia had had their "Orange" and "Rose" revolutions and, in so doing, had wrested their countries from the Soviet sphere. But the liberation they had waited for so long and still worked hard to achieve was likely to be lost, and the United States seemed to indicate indifference. As if to emphasize that indifference, Obama refused outgoing Georgia president Mikheil Saakashvili's request for a one-on-one meeting during the nuclear nonproliferation conference of April 2010. Instead, he met with the new pro-Kremlin leader of Ukraine, Viktor Yanukovich.

Further reinforcing its lack of concern for the position of Eastern European democracies, the administration sent the US National Security Advisor to Poland for the important seventieth anniversary commemoration of World War II. This was widely viewed as a snub to Poland, which had expected Secretary of State Hillary Clinton or Vice President Joe Biden. Vladimir Putin, French prime minister François Fillon, and British foreign secretary David Miliband all attended. Regarding the messages Washington was sending Poland's way, commentator Lukasz Kwiecien wrote in the national daily *Dziennik*: "They don't want us. They don't care about us. We are paying for our blind love for America."[28]

The dismantling of containment and the disparagement of the ideas behind it, and the abandonment of countries that feared some kind of return to Soviet rule, did not end there. Harry Truman and his followers accepted "spheres of influence" in Europe, but at the same time showed with actions and words that they cared deeply about the people behind the Iron Curtain. They built military alliances, the nuclear umbrella, and eventually missile defense while at the same time taking a moral stand for political liberty—for human rights and the rights of weaker nations to live free from the imperial domination of major powers. President Obama and Secretary Clinton spurned all of it for the sake of an "international community" that has no room for strong strategic alliances, for they are viewed as too divisive for the one-world unity that community requires.

Nor does the international community have room for strong principles. After all, what is more divisive, and contrary to a grand one-world compromise, than a moral stand? Obama and Clinton hoped to purchase harmony at a price. And that price has been paid not just by the United States, but by its allies and admirers.

In exchange for ignoring Russian expansionist designs and actions in Chechnya, Georgia, and Ukraine, for overlooking Putin's crackdown on dissidents and the press, for scaling down plans for missile defense, and for preemptively offering drastic reductions in nuclear weapons, we expected Russia to reassess its need for a revived sphere of influence in Eastern Europe and to cooperate with our efforts to constrain North Korea and Iran. But, by 2012, it would be clear that our willingness to negotiate away or give away our strategic advantage had reaped no reward. Instead, President Putin and his government worked both publicly and privately to diminish American standing and obstruct American policy.

In May and June of 2012 alone: Putin announced that he would skip the G8 Summit at Camp David, further dashing hopes of Russian cooperation on Syria and other matters. Russia's top military officer threatened to deploy new rockets to carry out a preemptive strike on US-led NATO missile defense facilities in Eastern Europe if Washington proceeded with already scaled-down plans toward a missile shield. In spite of all the diplomatic efforts to convince it to do otherwise, Russia continued its support of the brutal Syrian and Iranian regimes, going so far as to supply Syria with attack helicopters that it used to exterminate and terrorize the innocent. In October, it got worse: Russia announced it was backing out of its twenty-year deal with the United States to dismantle WMDs in areas controlled by the former Soviet Union.

In addition to its aggressive foreign policy posture, Russia's internal choices revealed a government with amoral, antidemocratic priorities. Arrests of peaceful demonstrators and detentions of pro-democracy activists escalated. The Kremlin disqualified serious opposition candidates from presidential elections and appointed ministers in defense, finance, and foreign relations that adhered to Putin's authoritarian and expansionist worldview. Reported the *Wall Street Journal*'s Alan Cullison from Moscow, "One new appointee to the ministry of culture is a high-level official from Mr. Putin's United Russia party, who has lately called for the government to play a greater role in producing patriotic films and literature. 'Stalin knew a lot about ideology and brainwashing,' the official, Vladimir Medinsky, told a regional newspaper in February. 'Now everything is left to chance, and efficiency has of course gone through the floor.'"[29]

■ ■ ■

The half-measures that the US administration took against Russian aggression in Ukraine during the Obama/Kerry period were offset, on the one hand, by unwillingness to give significant assistance to Ukraine or to impose strong sanctions on Russia and, on the other hand, willingness to acknowledge Russia's point of view. This dynamic was manifest in a March 1, 2014, State Department press statement. Secretary of State Kerry did criticize Russian actions:

> The United States condemns the Russian Federation's invasion and occupation of Ukrainian territory, and its violation of Ukrainian sovereignty and territorial integrity in full contravention of Russia's obligations under the UN Charter, the Helsinki Final Act, its 1997 military basing agreement with Ukraine, and the 1994 Budapest Memorandum. This action is a threat to the peace and security of Ukraine, and the wider region. . . . The people of Ukraine want nothing more than the right to define their own future—peacefully, politically and in stability. They must have the international community's full support at this vital moment.

Yet, even though Russia's stated concern for Russian minorities in Ukraine was mere pretense for its aggression, Kerry also praised Ukraine for committing to protect "all Ukrainians" and for showing restraint, and himself gave voice to Russia's supposed concerns:

> We also urge that the Government of Ukraine continue to make clear, as it has from throughout this crisis, its commitment to protect the rights of all Ukrainians and uphold its international obligations. As President Obama has said, we call for Russia to withdraw its forces back to bases, refrain from interference elsewhere in Ukraine, and support international mediation to address any legitimate issues regarding the protection of minority rights or security. From day one, we've made clear that we recognize and respect Russia's ties to Ukraine and its concerns about treatment of ethnic Russians. But these concerns can and must be addressed in a way that does not violate Ukraine's sovereignty and territorial integrity, by directly engaging the Government of Ukraine.[30]

Kerry recommended such Ukrainian magnanimity even though he himself, three days later at the US Embassy in Kyiv (while referring to Russia's "legitimate interests" in Ukraine), showed recognition that Russia was relying on myths to support its actions:

> The Russian Government would have you believe that the Ukraine Government somehow is illegitimate or led by extremists, ignoring the reality that the Rada, representing the people of Ukraine, the elected representatives of the people of Ukraine—they overwhelmingly approved the new government, even with members of Yanukovych's party deserting him and voting overwhelmingly in order to approve this new government. . . . And today, the Rada is the most representative institution in Ukraine.
>
> The Russian Government would also have you believe. . . . that somehow these streets of Kyiv are actually dangerous, ignoring the reality that there has been no surge in crime, no surge in looting, no political retribution here. The Russian Government would have you believe, against all the evidence, that there have been mass defections of Ukrainians to Russia, or that there have been mass attacks on churches in eastern Ukraine. That hasn't happened, either.
>
> They would have you believe that ethnic Russians and Russian bases are threatened. They'd have you believe that Kyiv is trying to destabilize Crimea or that Russian actions are legal or legitimate because Crimean leaders invited intervention. And as everybody knows, the soldiers in Crimea, at the instruction of their government, have stood their ground but never fired a shot, never issued one provocation, have been surrounded by an invading group of troops and have seen an individual who got 3 percent of the vote installed as the so-called leader by the Russians.
>
> They would have you believe that Kiev is trying to destabilize Crimea, or that somehow Russian leaders invited intervention. Not a single piece of credible evidence supports any one of these claims—none.[31]

Secretary Kerry held out the promise of better relations with the United States and better international standing if Russia took reasonable steps. In the latter statement he said, "It is diplomacy and respect for sovereignty, not unilateral force, that can best solve disputes like this in the twenty-first century. . . . Russia can choose to comply with international law and honor its commitments under the Helsinki Final Act under the United Nations Charter." In the former, he said, "Unless immediate and concrete steps are taken to deescalate tensions, the effect on US-Russia relations on Russia's international standing will be profound." Russia, of course, failed to take such steps, but the "profound effect" on US behavior never materialized.

Let's look, then, at the trajectory of US policy after Russian incursions into Ukraine made it humiliatingly clear that the Russian reset was a one-way street, and that Russia simply didn't care about international law, diplomatic solutions, and better relations with the United States.

Under pressure from Russia, in November 2013 President Viktor Yanukovych of Ukraine backed off from his tentative agreement to initial a trade association agreement with the European Union. Protests erupted and grew, and Yanukovych used increasingly violent methods to suppress dissent. In February 2014, in the face of overwhelming opposition, he fled the country and an interim, pro-EU government was formed.

In what could not help but remind of Hitler's annexation of Czechoslovakia under the pretense of protecting German minorities, pro-Russian "separatists" claiming to be an oppressed minority and backed by covert Russian troops began to seize and occupy government buildings in eastern cities, while moving to annex Crimea. (Critics of the comparison pointed out that Putin was no Hitler, but those noting the parallel weren't equating Putin and Hitler in the first place.) In March, self-appointed officials backed by armed, undercover Russians, held a referendum for Crimea's secession from Ukraine. After the vote for secession, Russia moved quickly toward annexation.

The West's response was minimalist. While new sanctions levied by the Obama administration made the news, the weakness of those sanctions could only embolden Putin, who knew how to read between the lines. The United States "levied new sanctions on *seven Russian officials* and *17 companies* with links to Putin's inner circle. The US also revoked licenses for *some high-tech items* that could be used by the Russian military." (italics mine) Lamented Nile Gardiner:

> At a time when American leadership is badly needed, Obama has been AWOL on the Ukrainian front. Not only should U.S. sanctions be dramatically increased against Moscow, but a whole host of measures should be implemented, including: the immediate U.S. withdrawal from the New START Treaty, the bolstering of NATO allies bordering Russia (including the establishment of a permanent U.S. military presence in the Baltic states of Estonia, Latvia and Lithuania), the lifting of restrictions on the export of natural gas to U.S. allies in Europe with the goal

of reducing energy dependency on Moscow, and a firm commitment to a robust and swiftly implemented missile defense system in Europe.[32]

In an open letter to President Obama, fifty-six former US government officials and foreign policy experts signed a bipartisan document recommending "imposing real costs" on Russia, enhancing the deterrence posture of NATO, and aiding Ukraine by, among other measures, expanding "the scope and scale of US military assistance available to the government of Ukraine, including intelligence sharing, training, and other support for Ukrainian forces, in coordination with NATO and the European Union."[33] At the same time, the House Foreign Affairs Committee passed the Ukraine Support Act introduced by Republican Chairman Ed Royce and Democratic Representative Eliot Engel to "promote Ukraine's sovereignty and democratic institutions" and sanction "those who have sought to undermine Ukraine's independence and stability."

In April, the Ukrainian military initiated operations against pro-Russian separatists in Luhansk and Donetsk. In May, these separatists—led mostly by Russian citizens before changes in leadership that summer—held a rigged referendum and, as in Crimea, announced independence.[34] Top commanders of the rebel movement during this time included Russian agents Igor Strelkov and Igor Bezler, and as many as 80 percent of the combatants consisted of Russian paramilitaries.[35]

After Russia cut off all gas supplies to Ukraine in June, the new pro-Western president Petro Poroshenko, who had won a clear mandate from the Ukrainian electorate, declared a ceasefire based on Russian offers for negotiations. But separatists continually violated the ceasefire, leading to renewed fighting and the Ukrainian government taking the offensive. Still withholding substantive aid to Ukraine, the EU announced stiffer sanctions that targeted Russian state banks, as well as energy and defense sectors.

In June testimony to the Foreign Relations Committee, Steven Pifer of the Brookings Institution asked, "Why should the United States care about Ukraine?" and answered:

> First, Ukraine has been a good international partner of the United States for more than two decades. When the Soviet Union collapsed in 1991, Ukraine had on its territory the world's third largest nuclear

arsenal ... all designed to strike the United States. Ukraine agreed to give up that arsenal, transferring the nuclear warheads to Russia for elimination and destroying the ICBMs and bombers. . . . In 2003, following the downfall of Saddam Hussein, Kyiv responded positively to the U.S. request for contributions to the coalition force in Iraq. . . . And in 2012, Ukraine transferred out the last of its highly enriched uranium as part of the U.S.-led international effort to consolidate stocks of nuclear weapons-usable highly enriched uranium and plutonium.

This kind of partnership merits U.S. support when Ukraine faces a crisis.

Second, as part of the agreement by which Ukraine gave up its nuclear weapons, the United States, Britain, and Russia committed in the 1994 Budapest Memorandum on Security Assurances to respect the sovereignty and territorial integrity of Ukraine and not to use or threaten to use force against Ukraine. Russia's illegal seizure and annexation of Crimea constitute a gross violation of its commitments under that document, as does Russia's ongoing support for separatists in eastern Ukraine. The United States and Britain should meet their commitments by supporting Ukraine and pressuring Russia to halt actions that violate the memorandum.

Third, Russia's actions constitute a fundamental challenge to the post-war order in Europe. The illegal seizure of Crimea is the most blatant land-grab that Europe has seen since 1945. The United States and Europe need to respond adequately and ensure that Russia faces consequences for this kind of behavior. Otherwise, the danger is that Mr. Putin may pursue other actions that would further threaten European security and stability.[36]

Indeed, Russian action in Ukraine and the inadequate consequences Russia incurred, which emboldened Russia and demoralized America's actual as opposed to hoped-for "international partners," did threaten the postwar order in Europe. In July, a Malaysian airliner was shot down in separatist-held territory, and it was widely believed pro-Russian forces were responsible. In August, Russia moved in more "volunteers" and artillery. A Ukrainian military spokesman announced that Russia had "begun an enormous buildup of armored vehicles, aircraft, and personnel at the Ukrainian border." On August 27, two columns of Russian tanks entered Ukrainian territory in support of the pro-Russian separatists in Donetsk and Luhansk, and engaged Ukrainian border forces.

Brigadier General Nico Tak, a top NATO official, told reporters that the ultimate aim of Russia was to stave off defeat for the separatists and turn eastern Ukraine into a "frozen conflict" that would destabilize the country "indefinitely." With estimates of one thousand to four thousand Russian troops in Ukraine, NATO estimated that another twenty thousand Russian troops were right over the Russian border. President Obama said Russia had "repeatedly and deliberately violated the sovereignty and territorial integrity of Ukraine," but he and other administration officials refrained from calling this an invasion.[37]

In spite of all of this, the United States and Europe decided against severe financial sanctions against Russia, and against providing Ukraine with arms, military equipment, and training, with the US promising an economic assistance package instead. Although Ukraine had seized the offensive, Russia escalated military activity and launched a new offensive in southeast Ukraine, thereby opening up a second front. NATO members met in September in Wales, where rather than raise the costs to Russia for violating agreements and continuing its actions, they broadcast their moral and strategic ambivalence. They agreed to a new "rapid reaction" spearhead force of four thousand troops, but again declined Ukraine's urgent requests for antitank and antiaircraft weapons, and failed to announce new sanctions.

Under relentless pressure within, and with only minimal support from without, Poroshenko reached a cease-fire agreement with Putin in Minsk. Only one day after the Minsk agreement, the shelling of Mariupol began. Former Polish prime minister Donald Tusk tweeted, "once again, appeasement encourages the aggressor to greater acts of violence." Under siege, Ukrainians nevertheless voted overwhelmingly for pro-Western parties on October 26. Given this, and given Russian escalation and continual violation of cease-fire agreements, you might have thought Europe and the United States would have considered increased defense spending, significantly elevated intelligence measures, Truman-esque and Reagan-esque speeches for freedom, military and energy assistance to Ukraine, and strong financial and energy sanctions on Russia. Instead, in February 2015, Germany and France brokered new cease-fire in talks in Belarus. Predictably, Russia again violated the cease-fire, and hostilities and casualties escalated further.

European requirements for Russian natural gas, and the degree to which the European and Russian economies were tied, inhibited Europe's response. Then, as Robert Kaplan observed, there was the fact that Europe remained a "semipacifistic geopolitical space." Kaplan suggested, "Putin knows that NATO's ultimate power is a reflection of the size of the defense budgets of its member-states. And with a few exceptions, NATO member-states are not even willing to have their defense budgets equal 2 percent of their gross domestic products."[38] The *Washington Post* editorial board observed that the administration was "hiding behind the Europeans, saying it cannot move unless and until they do." This, they pointed out, "makes U.S. credibility contingent on accord among 28 nations, including Cyprus, Greece and several others friendly to Russia."[39]

European weakness paired with Russia's own economic and geopolitical difficulties made the US response all the more significant in Putin's calculus of costs and benefits of subversion in Ukraine and elsewhere in Europe. Calculations about the relative strengths and weaknesses, resolve or ambivalence, of opponents played a role in Ukraine just as they had in Georgia in 2008. As Peggy Noonan sagely put it,

> Mr. Putin doesn't move because of American presidents, he moves for his own reasons. But he does move when American presidents are weak. He moved on Georgia in August 2008 when George W. Bush was reeling from unwon wars, terrible polls and a looming economic catastrophe that all but children knew was coming. (It came the next month.) Mr. Bush was no longer formidable as a leader of the free world.
>
> Mr. Putin moved on Ukraine when Barack Obama was no longer a charismatic character but a known quantity with low polls, failing support, a weak economy. He'd taken Mr. Obama's measure during the Syria crisis and surely judged him not a shrewd international chess player but a secretly anxious professor who makes himself feel safe with the sound of his voice.[40]

In December, Congress passed The Ukraine Freedom Support Act, which sought to increase US assistance to Ukraine and to increase sanctions on Russian defense and energy sectors. It authorized, but did not mandate, $350 million in military aid, which would include military training and defense items such as anti-tank weapons, counter-battery radars, and surveillance drones. Stated the bill's co-sponsor, Robert Menendez, "This legislation sends a very direct message to President Putin who must change his calculus in Ukraine and abandon his disruptive path."[41] President Obama signed the bill, but stipulated, "Signing this legislation does not signal a change in the Administration's sanctions policy, which we have carefully calibrated in accordance with developments on the ground and coordinated with our allies and partners. At this time, the Administration does not intend to impose sanctions under this law, but the Act gives the Administration additional authorities that could be utilized, if circumstances warranted."

Russian aggression in Ukraine thereby highlighted the unwillingness of the Obama administration and the Clinton and Kerry State Departments to engage in convincing policies of deterrence and convincing displays of moral conviction, or to assume the leadership role that would make either one possible. Putin saw that the time was right to act on his revanchist desires and did not limit his actions to Ukraine.[42]

He pressured Bosnia, Moldova, Macedonia, Estonia, and Montenegro, inserted intelligence officers in the Czech Republic and elsewhere, repeatedly violated Baltic airspace with Russian warplanes, and exploited divisions and economic vulnerability in Europe and the Caucasus. Whether with petrodollars and threats of withholding Russian natural gas and oil, or with provocative military exercises and war planning, Russia demonstrated renewed desire for a sphere of influence and aggressive opposition to neighbors that were attempting to bridge the Cold War–era divide by moving closer to NATO and the West.

Yet, Putin's own ambitions and power plays reached beyond Eastern and Central Europe. Putin's Russia shunned the US-orchestrated Nuclear Security Agreement of 2014, in which thirty-five signatories agreed to implement guidelines meant to prevent nuclear and radioactive materials from falling into the hands of terrorists. Russia announced in February 2014 that it was negotiating with eight governments around the world for access to military facilities, and to extend its long-range naval and strategic bomber capabilities. In November 2014, a Russian nuclear ballistic submarine test-fired a missile in the Barents Sea, underscoring its mission of establishing a foothold in the energy-rich Arctic region. In September 2015, Russia tested a ground-launched cruise missile in violation of the intermediate-range nuclear forces treaty. All of this, along with Russia's staunch support of the Syrian and Iranian regimes, flagrant mistreatment of those within its orbit, and increased strategic cooperation with China and Pakistan, should have made containing Russia and countering Russian propaganda an American foreign policy priority.

Defense and strategy expert Michaela Dodge highlighted the seriousness of the situation and suggested the following:

> Given Russia's repeated violations of the INF Treaty and the U.S.'s inability to bring Russia back into compliance, it is time for the U.S. to withdraw from the treaty. . . .
>
> A continuation of the status quo will allow Russia, which has made nuclear threats against NATO, to gain an advantage across an entire class of weapons.
>
> The U.S. therefore cannot allow Russia to gain a strategic advantage in Europe that it can use to cow NATO and reassert its influence. . . .
>
> In addition to withdrawing from the INF Treaty, the U.S. should take further steps to counter the Russian nuclear threat: modernizing its nuclear arsenal and committing to developing a comprehensive layered missile defense system.
>
> The U.S. nuclear arsenal is aging, and no yield-producing tests have been conducted in over 20 years. The U.S. must modernize its arsenal in order to maintain a credible deterrent. Furthermore, the U.S. must develop missile defense systems capable of responding to new threats. U.S. missile defense programs have suffered under the Obama administration. This trend must be reversed.[43]

Instead, echoing Hillary Clinton, President Obama said Putin was on the "wrong side of history," while John Kerry said Putin's behavior was "nineteenth century behavior in the twenty-first century." In response to the question, "Does the Ukraine crisis mark the beginning of a new Cold War?" Obama answered, "The United States does not view Europe as a battleground between East and West, nor do we see the situation in Ukraine as a zero-sum game. That's the kind of thinking that should have ended with the Cold War."[44]

Our president and secretary of states thereby broadcast their refusal to believe that Cold War dynamics might resurface, and that Cold War–style containment policies might be required. As Michael Doran put it, "The president is partially correct. Unlike the Soviet Union, Russia has neither the intention nor the capability to challenge the entire European

order, and it is certainly not mounting a global revolutionary movement. Nevertheless, it is a revanchist power, and its appetites are much
larger than the president cares to admit. That Russian President Vladimir Putin sees Ukraine as a zero-sum game seems obvious. Somewhat
less apparent is the fact that his revisionist aspirations also extend elsewhere, and most saliently to the Middle East."[45] Russia's incursion into
Syria, would, of course, prove Doran more than right.

While the United States downplayed deterrence and Western/demo-
cratic ideals, Putin's Russia, Assad's Syria, Kim Jong-un's North Korea, Xi
Jinping's China, and Ali Khamenei's Iran all poured economic and military resources into increasing their geopolitical reach and controlling
the ideological and historical narrative.

When Russian militias take over Ukrainian towns, they seize television towers and switch them to Kremlin channels. RT, formerly Russia
Today, has become a worldwide vehicle for Russian propaganda and
psychological operations. RT relies upon conspiracy theories to foster
dependency on the Russian state, and manipulates the news to support
Russia's foreign policy agenda. Russia has an army of Internet trolls who
spread propaganda online and dispute reports that contradict Russian
claims, especially regarding Ukraine. Russian media exploits the West's
relativism by delivering "news" that causes the West to question its own
findings. Central and Eastern European countries, bombarded with
Russian propaganda and facing NATO's weak response to Russian
aggression, are increasingly vulnerable. NATO's Supreme Allied
Commander Europe, General Philip Breedlove, has called the Kremlin's
media campaign in Europe "the most amazing information war blitz-
krieg known in history."[46]

The Voice of America (and similar programs) is, therefore, literally
and figuratively, as essential today as it was when FDR founded it, and
when Cold War presidents from Truman to Kennedy to Reagan relied
upon it. Chairman of the House Foreign Relations Committee Ed Royce
proposed legislation to reverse the post-Cold War "hollowing out" of
US broadcast services like the Voice of America, Radio Free Europe, and
Radio Liberty. In an April 2015 *Wall Street Journal* editorial supporting
the move, Royce noted that these services "helped Russians, Eastern
Europeans and countless others shed tyranny by providing the truth
about events in their own countries, and showed them a world outside

the prison of Soviet propaganda."[45] In a *Washington Times* editorial, I said, "Royce is right. The VOA tradition is a proud one of bringing truth and hope into places of darkness and repression."[48]

In a classic case of "too little/too late," the Obama administration gradually woke up to the fact that "talks" and the lure of becoming a respected member of the "international community" weren't convincing Russia to alter its policies, and therefore incrementally altered America's own course. In June 2015, the administration pledged to add troops, arms, and intelligence assets to the NATO rapid response plan and, in September, announced that it would send long-range counterbattery radars to Ukraine. In a fascinating admission that Cold War dynamics weren't dead after all, in Mainz, Germany, Secretary of Defense Ashton Carter criticized Russia for trying "to reestablish a Soviet-era sphere of influence." Said he: "We do not seek a cold, let alone a hot war with Russia . . . We do not seek to make Russia an enemy. But make no mistake: we will defend our allies, the rules-based international order, and the positive future it affords us. We will stand up to Russia's actions and their attempts to re-establish a Soviet-era sphere of influence."[49]

But, with continued willingness to go along with Russian plans and "peace conferences" for Syria and quiescence in the face of Russia's proliferation of weapons and arms sales to Iran and its defense of the Iranian and Syrian regimes, the administration showed that it would only go so far in reassessing its engagement policies. (US accommodation of Russian plans for Syria, and Secretary Kerry's defining role in that accommodation, is discussed in detail in Chapter 6.)

As if to emphasize that the United States would only go so far, Secretary Kerry met for extensive talks with President Putin and Foreign Minister Lavrov in May 2015, emerging from the talks with pledges of "closer cooperation" on Ukraine and Syria but without any "major break-throughs" on major differences separating the powers.[50] Kerry and Lavrov promised to work hard to convince both sides in Ukraine to adhere to a February cease-fire and to implement a 2012 US-Russia strategy for "transitional government" in Syria. In what reporters Matthew Lee and Bradley Klapper called a "surprising moment," Kerry and Lavrov also issued warnings to Ukrainian president Poroshenko not to seek the "liberation" of the Donetsk Airport from rebels in eastern Ukraine.[51] Asserted Kerry, "We would strongly urge him to think twice not to engage in this kind of activity," saying this would jeopardize the cease-fire. Indeed this was a surprising moment, and an incredible one for an American secretary of state. Standing next to Lavrov and pressuring Ukraine not to "engage in this kind of activity" was quite the show of camaraderie with Russians whose own militants had a track record of violating cease-fires, and who were the true aggressors in the conflict.

■ ■ ■

In an article in March 2015, by which time Syria was a cataclysm and ISIS was a formidable threat, I said "forging strategy to battle ISIS without *also* forging strategy to thwart Syria, Russia and Iran is a terrible mistake."[52] When nation states escalate weapons programs and atrocities, foment regional chaos and war, and plot against the United States and its allies, history tells us to take it seriously. We must, therefore, take Russia, Iran, and Syria, and the collusion between them, seriously. With the apparatus of the state at their disposal and the backing of each other, they are, potentially, an even greater threat than ISIS. Moreover, because they are terror sponsors and supporters, WMD in their control means WMD out of control, susceptible to being sold to fanatics who can afford the price, or are willing to work for the desired cause. Although the president now bemoans the "brutality" of the Islamic State, he still whitewashes the brutality of *established states* Russia, Syria, and Iran, and still ignores the need for "grand strategy" to deal with them.

Worse, the White House plan for fighting ISIS plays right into their hands, for it revolves around *their* plans—plans which include allowing Assad to stay in power after all, plans which allow Russia to keep orchestrating Syrian "peace conferences" which buy Assad time, plans which accommodate the Iranian nuclear program in exchange for Iran's ever-elusive "cooperation," plans which give Iran the lead in the battle against ISIS in Syria and Iraq. Since the beginning of Assad's reign of terror on the Syrian people, the administration has succumbed to "Russian plans" and Iranian schemes.

Looking at how badly this approach fared can serve as fair warning of the horrors that lie ahead if we do not get our moral and strategic priorities right.

CHAPTER 4

MIDDLE EASTERN DEBACLE
Engagement with Iran Goes Nowhere

Modern approaches to history are often underlain by the assumption that, since there is no objective truth (truth being redefined in each time and place), no society can claim to have a better understanding of the cultural or political good than another. But this means that all cultural ideas and political movements are valid. Terrorism and other modern atrocities render such suppositions absurd. For, whether it is Iranian, Syrian, Sudanese, or al-Qaeda forces asserting their will to power, no human beings want their children conscripted, their parents imprisoned, their sisters raped, or their spouses tortured. No one wants to be treated as less than human for the sake of a political cause.

The fact that people and nations don't agree on the truth need not mean that there *is* no truth. It just as easily means that some people are closer to grasping the truth (i.e., regarding justice) than others. It just as easily means that some countries have moved farther toward a lawful and free society than others. This, in turn, means that Americans must know what they stand for and why. As Truman and Eisenhower and Kennedy and Reagan understood when facing the Cold War, we will not win the battle with tyranny through strength alone, but also through the power of American ideals.

Those ideals still have revolutionary potential. That is why dictators are so terribly afraid of them, and that is why oppressive regimes expend so much material and intellectual capital spreading certain ideas through propaganda, and stamping out others through suppression. While President Obama and Secretary Clinton subjected our ideals to what John Kerry called the "litmus test" of international opinion and institutions, others intently sought (and continue to seek) to impose their ideals upon us. Thus, to say nothing or do nothing unless the UN endorses it is not only a surrender of national sovereignty; it a relinquishment of moral and political influence.

Al-Qaeda, Islamic State, hardliners in the Iranian government, and groups like Hezbollah provide us with deadly evidence of the perils of *their* ideas. In their worldview, the rights and the lives of other groups can be discarded so long as their "righteous" group prevails. In an article entitled "Are Human Rights Universal?" (written before September 11, 2001), international law expert Thomas Franck made a cogent connection between the Taliban and others who define politics in terms of group authority instead of individual rights: "In taking a stand against global human rights, the Taliban have made common cause not with tired nationalist defenders of state sovereignty, but with a powerful and growing subset of cultural exceptionalists. These include some traditional indigenous tribes, theocratic national regimes, fundamentalists of many religions, and surprisingly, a mixed bag of Western intellectuals who deplore the emphasis placed by modern human rights rhetoric on individual autonomy."[1] The founding American idea, which is a better idea, is that rights are particular in that they pertain to each one, but also universal in that they pertain to everyone. Here, I again assert that human rights are individual rights and that individual rights are human rights. Everyone deserves political freedom, and everyone, in one way or another, longs for a better life.

The aggressive pursuit of the interests of groups, whether imposed within nations or exerted upon other nations through force, has historically led to oppression and injustice. In Hitler's and Stalin's atrocities, we saw the horrible reality of groupthink taken to extremes. In the inhumane treatment of the "other"—the Jew, the Cossack, the capitalist, the POW—fascism and communism had much in common. Indeed, the Nazi-Soviet Non-Aggression Pact was based upon the mutual agreement to subjugate and divide Poland; the fate and the wishes of the Polish people themselves were inconsequential to the decision.

As the examples of Germany and Japan in the 1930s and 1940s showed, "self-determination" for particular groups easily became the excuse for bellicose nationalism and domestic cruelty. Moreover, between the world wars, Eastern European "nationalities" and ethnic groups sought to "determine" their destinies by dominating and exploiting others. During and after these wars, European powers exploited those ethnic rivalries in order to gain the upper hand. More recently, atrocities in the Balkans, Africa, the Middle East, and elsewhere prove the cataclysmic results of ethnic, nationalist, and religious rivalries run amok.

If the concept of self-determination is to stand for something positive in the world, it should no longer be equated with the "right" of cultural, religious, or nationalist groups to forcefully unite with their compatriots, or to violently "fulfill" their "historic" destiny. Self-determination must be reoriented away from group identity and toward the idea of consent as it relates to each nation's internal and external politics. And *this* is best done by promoting the rights of individuals to freedom from oppression by their own governments and the right of nations to freedom from imperial domination by outside powers.

Even within the United States, the prevalence of groupthink degrades our traditions. When ethnocentric, religious-extremist terrorists attacked America on 9/11, many reassessed the popular definition of *culture*, which emphasizes the distinct history and uniqueness of so-called "cultures" within American society. Perhaps, the idea of the melting pot had not been so bad after all. For, it is only when individuals find common ground in universal rights that pluralism and mutual respect come together. The American tradition is no threat to diversity so long as it stays firmly grounded in the belief that *every* person has inalienable rights and that it is *no* person's right to violate the rights of another. Like it or not, our greatest recourse against degeneration into interest groups with nowhere to go but apart is our mutual assimilation to the principle of liberty, equality, and justice for all.

In addition, our greatest influence in the world will come from the combination of abundant power, restraint in the use of it, and the projection of the ideas of individual and human rights. Dictators and totalitarians respect little else than power when it comes to outside forces, but they also recognize the potential threat to their rule in an alienated populace excited about the prospect of freedom.

In an important April 2009 speech in Chicago, former British prime minister Tony Blair emphasized the power of ideas themselves. Said he, "We should not revert to the foreign policy of years gone by, the supposedly sensible practitioners of caution and expediency, who think they see the world for what it is, without the illusions of the idealist who sees what it should be. We should remember what such expediency led us to, what such caution produced . . . The ideology we are fighting is not based on justice. And worldwide these groups are adept, certainly, at using causes that indeed are about justice, like Palestine. Their cause, at its core, however, is not about the pursuit of values that we can relate to; but in pursuit of values that directly contradict our way of life. They don't believe in democracy, equality, or freedom. . . . They are not pluralist. They are the antithesis of pluralism. And they don't think that their own community or state should be like that."[2]

Compare and contrast Tony Blair's worldview with that of President Bill Clinton's national security advisor, Sandy Berger, who gave his own important talk at about the same time. In a May 2009 appearance at the Council on Foreign Relations, Berger explained the Obama-Clinton approach to foreign affairs as follows: "There is a greater willingness for dialogue with our friends and adversaries. Some have described his [Obama's] willingness to talk to Iran and Syria and Cuba as a sign of weakness. President Obama clearly believes that negotiation does not mean concession, that it's a way of seeking common ground, and, failing that, of laying the groundwork for tougher collective action if negotiations fail. . . . We've seen a much more pragmatic, less dogmatic policy. *No more rhetoric about democracy as the defining purpose of American foreign policy, no more discussion of ending tyranny in the world.* This is America as problem-solver rather than crusader. And there's been a willingness to be self-critical; again, criticized by some as unhelpful. . . . So, all in all, it's been, I think a new chapter of American engagement."[3] (italics mine)

The idea that America should stop crusading for democracy, either by projecting its ideals or by using its leverage, has had particular effect in the Middle East. It was one thing to oppose the Iraq War; the idea that the US was using war for democracy promotion clearly created resentment among Middle Easterners and probably made some reformers more nationalistic. (Nationalism was a way for reformers to assert that they did not want democracy imposed by an outside power—namely the United States.) But it was also clear that the majority of Middle Easterners longed for more freedom, both economically and politically. They were tired of the stagnation, corruption, and repression of centralized authoritarian regimes and sought democratic alternatives to those regimes. The Iraq War did not stem the tide of discontent; instead, democracy movements grew during the Bush years.

If the Iraq War caused resentment, so did realpolitik policies that had led the United States to form reluctant alliances with Middle Eastern dictators. Indeed, claims that the United States supported governments that denied their people rights caused many Middle Easterners to turn to Islamic political movements as opposed to more secular/Western ones. Claims of US collusion with authoritarian governments had been one of the selling points of al-Qaeda itself.

It was thus Westerners, not Middle Easterners, who were upset by the Bush administration's focus upon the Middle East's "freedom deficit." Sentiment against the freedom deficit was overwhelming in the Middle East itself by the time Obama and Clinton took office. Critics of the Iraq War who insisted they wanted to improve America's reputation in the world should, then, have wanted the United States to place more emphasis on democracy and human rights, not less.

Instead, after the United States invaded Iraq, many American progressives asserted that Iraq and most other Middle Eastern nations were not "ready" for democracy because they had no democratic traditions. Moreover, being culturally different from the West, they might never "want" it. Cultural relativism caused many academics to claim or imply that antidemocratic regimes were just as valid as democratic ones. In response to the first claim, Condoleezza Rice pointed out that if democratic traditions were prerequisite for the formation of democracy, post–World War II Germany and Japan certainly defied that logic; these democratic allies had "traditions" that were far from democratic. In response to the latter claim, a group of Middle Eastern scholars at a panel I attended in 2008 disagreed. Said one, "Most Muslims want freedom." Said another regarding the Pakistani military, "They refuse to learn that democracy is the only game in town." A third panelist showed that most Muslim countries in Africa tended to be just as democratic as non-Muslim countries. These scholars had an attitude of hopefulness at the end of the Bush years.

True to their predictions and an utter surprise to the Obama administration, the Middle East soon thereafter erupted with democracy movements. What a pity that the administration was unprepared for the situation and incapable of nurturing or positively influencing it. You would think that the same people who downplay American exceptionalism and democracy's advantages for the supposed reason of "respecting" other cultures would at least demonstrate respectful sympathy and moral support to other peoples fighting for respect within their own societies.

Unlike American intellectuals, Arab intellectuals who contributed to the first post-9/11 Arab Human Development Report pushed the idea of democracy, stating, "There is a substantial lag between Arab countries and other regions in terms of participatory governance. The wave of democracy that transformed governance in most of Latin America and East Asia in the 1980s and Eastern Europe and much of Central Asia in the late 1980s and early 1990s has barely reached the Arab states. This *freedom deficit* [in the Arab region] undermines human development and is one of the most painful manifestations of lagging political development. While de jure acceptance of democracy and human rights is enshrined in constitutions, legal codes, and government pronouncement, de facto implementation is often neglected and, in some cases, deliberately disregarded."[4] 9 (italics mine) The report highlighted two decades of failed central planning and developmental decline and blamed many of the problems in the Middle East on Middle Eastern forms of governance, even asserting that poverty can exist not just in terms of lacking income but also in terms of lacking freedom.

Sentiment for more freedom was not limited to intellectuals. As Shibley Telhami of the University of Maryland shows in his analysis of public opinion polls, Arab sentiment, while objecting to the invasion of Iraq and seeing the Bush administration's emphasis upon democracy as insincere, overwhelmingly favored human rights and democratization. Stated Telhami regarding the Arab Spring, "It was hardly surprising to discover Arabs were angry with their rulers. In fact, every year, after conducting the Annual Arab Public Opinion Poll in Egypt, Saudi Arabia, Morocco, Jordan, Lebanon, and the United Arab Emirates, the question that leapt from the findings was not, 'When will Arabs have reason to revolt?' but 'Why haven't Arabs revolted yet?'"[5]

Thus, nowhere has the Obama administration's rejection of human rights and democracy in the formation of foreign policy been more devastating than in the Middle East, where it has led to indifference to human longing and human suffering and to the enabling of some of the world's worst regimes. Obama and Clinton said nary a word in support of Iranian dissidents languishing in notorious Iranian prisons. They did nothing to encourage Egyptian ally Hosni Mubarak to embrace democracy and very little to encourage his Islamist successors toward toleration of Christians and moderates. They came very close to ignoring the bloodbath in Syria and did ignore it at first. They said nothing about Syria's brutal occupation of Lebanon. They were impassive in the face of Sudan's oppression of its own people and its abetting of rape and genocide in Darfur.

Obama's outreach to Muslim leaders, at times, devolved into outright obeisance, as it did when he addressed the Turkish parliament in February 2009. He not only said, "The United States is not and never will be at war with Islam. Our partnership with the Muslim world is critical in rolling back a fringe ideology that people of all faiths reject." He also said, "America's relationship with the Muslim world cannot and will not be based upon opposition to al-Qaeda. Far from it, we see broad engagement based upon mutual interest and mutual respect."[6] One might have expected the president of the United States to say a word for democracy in Turkey, which had a tradition of secular government but was moving in a more Islamist direction, and which had instituted reforms and was in the process of internal soul-searching and debate regarding whether to move in a more or less democratic direction. Instead, what we got from our president was not only explicit support for the status quo, but also implicit support for Turkey's possible devolution toward a less secular, less tolerant regime.

On the rare moments when Obama and Clinton spoke for human rights or democracy in the Middle East, their words lacked conviction. One exception is a May 19, 2011, speech in which President Obama spoke (after the fact) for the people in the Middle East who had "risen up to demand their human rights" and against "the relentless tyranny of governments that deny their citizens dignity."[7] (President Obama almost never says the words *human rights* and never says the words *individual rights*.) Another exception is Hillary Clinton's December 14, 2009, speech at Georgetown University in which she spoke of the need to define human rights "broadly" in terms of both freedom from tyranny and freedom from want, adding, "People should be free from tyranny in whatsoever form, and they should also be free to seize the opportunities of a full life."[8]

Generally, Obama and Clinton were careful to tone down objections to tyrants and tyranny for fear of being too American: too moralistic, too democracy-promoting, too proud. In Chapter 2, I said that never before had a president and secretary of state so rejected not only idealism and realism but the uniquely American combination of the two. Here, I add that never before had a president and secretary of state so abandoned all attempts to influence the worst human rights violators or to stop the worst atrocities. All too often, they stood idle as terrible events unfolded, as if the United States were the least influential country in the world.

It is true that America has at times abandoned its own principles in its interactions in the Middle East. But Obama and his friends point mostly to our transgressions and never to acts of generosity—to risks taken and blood shed to support the sovereignty of Middle Eastern nations or efforts made to improve the living standards and political status of Middle Eastern people. They point to our mistakes. For the sake of learning from history, those mistakes should be recorded and acknowledged. Three of the biggest mistakes were working with England to oust and replace the communist-leaning but nevertheless democratically elected leader in Iran in the 1950s; supporting the Taliban in an effort to oust the Soviets from Afghanistan in the 1980s; and sporadically and tentatively working with Saddam Hussein in order to curtail the ascendancy of the Iranians. (Some would add, and not without good reason, American collusion with the antidemocratic House of Saud.) At a realpolitik low point, the US government decided on silence about Iraq's mass execution of the Kurds in 1988.

Another egregious case of untempered "realism" occurred in the 1990s: With its sponsorship by the Soviets evaporating, Syria joined the American-led alliance to oust Iraqi forces from Kuwait in apparent exchange for the United States' tacit consent for Syria to use its forces in neighboring Lebanon to implement the National Reconciliation Accord, also known as the Taif Agreement, to end Lebanon's civil war. Syrian control in Lebanon would of course have terrible implications for the Lebanese people, who had for so long been exploited by outside powers.

These actions were both wrong and counterproductive, as they made our enemy's enemy our friend and, in the end, emboldened extremists in Afghanistan, contributed to anti-American sentiment in Iran and elsewhere, and gave Saddam Hussein and Bashsar al-Assad an exaggerated sense of inculpability. The history of American relations with the Middle East is a long one, however, and an honest look reveals a much more complicated picture.

As Michael Oren documents in *Power, Faith, and Fantasy: America in the Middle East—1776 to the Present*, as early as the Revolutionary period, restless Americans travelled to "Arabia" in search of new goods and adventure. In the eighteenth and nineteenth centuries, Americans continually landed on Middle Eastern soil. The main reasons they endured the arduous journey were curiosity due to romantic and mythical conceptions about Arab society, the missionary and charitable impulse, and the search for trade and the next "frontier." Among these, the charitable and missionary impulses ranked high. Whether one agrees or disagrees with missionary work, letters and documents reveal that naïve and headstrong Americans believed they were doing good. They found a world much more brutal and dangerous than they expected, but saw the good they might do as worth the hardships they endured. By the late 1800s, the American government was investing very large sums of money in the missionaries and their schools, and infrastructure and agriculture projects.

The US government, of course, hoped all this missionary work and trade would lead to a greater opening up and even eventually to the democratization of the Middle East. In the words of Oren, "Most Americans still looked forward to the day when the Middle East would be freed from despotic rule and made to resemble the United States."[9] (In contrast to the refrain of many in the West today, they did not claim that the Arab world and Arabic people were "incapable" of democracy or "unsuited" to freedom.) Teddy Roosevelt, the first twentieth-century American president, broke from the nineteenth-century standard when he toyed with "gunboat diplomacy" and declared Egypt "not ready" to govern itself. It was the time of imperialism of the great powers, and the United States was temporarily tempted to become like Europe. The United States tried out imperialism with its occupation of the Philippines in the 1890s, but soon rejected imperialism on the basis that it was un-American, undemocratic, and more trouble than it was worth. (The US did not, from then on, refrain from interfering in the internal affairs of Latin American countries, but it did reject colonial occupation.)

Woodrow Wilson, William Howard Taft, and most twentieth-century presidents not only spoke out against European imperialism in the Middle East, but also took concrete steps to make it harder for Europeans. Nothing placed so great an obstacle in the way of imperialism as Wilson's pleas for "self-determination," his insistence upon making "the world safe for democracy," and his famous Fourteen Points address. Wilson opposed all attempts to use the upheaval caused by World War I as an excuse to divide the Middle East into de facto colonial outposts. As Oren puts it, "Arabs, Jews, Armenians, Kurds, and even the Turks were ecstatic about the Fourteen Points and profoundly grateful to their author."[10] From the time of Wilson on, imperialism was on the defensive, but "the absence of American input for planning for the postwar Middle East meant that Wilson could not effectively apply his principles of democracy to the region."[11]

Although lacking geopolitical influence in the Middle East between the world wars, the United States continued to assert moral influence. When the ambassador to the Ottoman Empire, Henry Morgenthau, was asked why he, a Jew, would worry about Christian victims of the Armenian massacre, he replied that he acted not "in the name of any race or religion, but merely as [a] human being."[12]

After World War II, the European powers lost their grip on their colonial territories, and the United States led the way in pressuring Europeans. The concept of "mandates" enabled a compromise between Americans and Europeans, through which various powers were given temporary control over former enemy territories in order to prepare them for self-rule. While doing little to support Jewish independence, Franklin Roosevelt did appoint Patrick J. Hurley to map out ways to seek "free governments and free enterprise" and to put an end to "exploitation and imperialism" in the Middle East and developing regions. Truman both decided to support the creation of a Jewish state in Israel and stated his belief that the peoples of the Middle East were "deserving of postwar political independence." Eisenhower and his secretary of state, John Foster Dulles, went so far as to support Egyptian president Gamal Abdel Nasser against the Europeans—even after Nasser shocked the world by announcing Egypt's nationalization of the Suez Canal. When English and French planes bombed Egyptian airfields in response, the United States condemned the assault.

But the United States would not be rewarded for support of Egypt. Increasingly under the sway of Soviet power and extremist ideology, many post–World War II self-determination movements, including Nasser's, were starting to define themselves less in terms of political freedom than in terms of Soviet-style "liberation" from capitalist Western powers, including the United States. By the time Kennedy came to office, postcolonial regimes in Syria, Egypt, and Iraq had devolved into dictatorships. Still, Kennedy opposed imperialism, supported nationalism, and worked to improve relations throughout the region.

I have already touched briefly upon more recent history of US involvement in the Middle East, which included the continuation of financial aid and infrastructure and agriculture projects, but also included decisions that compromised American ideals. Some are so bold as to argue that, in spite of alleged American antipathy to Islam, most of America's recent involvement in the Middle East has been intended to help Muslim people. Asserts Robert Lieber, "Remarkably, most of the post–Cold War American military interventions abroad have been to save Muslim populations from starvation, ethnic cleansing, civil war, invasion, and oppression—as large numbers of Kuwaitis, Somalis, Kurds, Bosnians, Kosovars, Iraqi Shiites, and the people of Afghanistan, especially women, can attest. Moreover, the absorptive character of the United States has made it far better than any of the countries of Europe or Asia in accommodating and integrating Muslims."[13]

A history that began with missionary zeal for improving the lot of Arab people and with the hope of eventually inspiring them toward democracy—and that continued the quest for democracy even as it intermittently compromised democratic principles—has, with the Obama administration, turned full circle. No longer concerned with the people themselves nor with oppressive governments, the administration has abandoned the American tradition and replaced it with coldhearted "engagement" with brutal regimes. Nowhere is this more evident than in its generous treatment of the cruel, repressive, and hostile Islamic Republic of Iran.

Lest anyone doubt that the Iranian regime is cruel and hostile, numerous books and documents tell the story. Among them are the detailed reports of Human Rights Watch and the Iran Human Rights Center, and the books *A Time to Betray* by Reza Kahlili and *Accomplice to*

Evil: Iran and the War Against the West by Michael A. Ledeen. Ledeen notes that Islamic fundamentalism owes much of its inspiration to fascist and communist regimes, particularly those of Hitler and Stalin. "There was no European totalitarian movement or regime with which the jihadis were unwilling to collaborate. . . . In keeping with their embrace of some of the main themes of European and Russian totalitarianism, blended with the revealed truths of the Koran and the Hadith, the leaders of the Islamic Republic are quite outspoken about the nature of the apocalyptic struggle in which they are engaged. They believe that the final battle will be fought between the followers of the Twelfth Imam and the Jews and their followers, in Israel, America, and the West."[14]

Iran actively supports, with weapons and money, Hezbollah, Hamas, extremists in Egypt, and terrorists in Iraq, Syria, and Yemen. It strengthened support of the brutal Assad regime just as the regime responded to the Syrian rebellion by terrorizing the Syrian people with atrocities and bombardment. It indoctrinates and trains men from all over the world with its ideology and methods of terror. Intelligence documents declassified in 2008 reveal that Iran, more than any other factor, contributed to destabilization and terrorism in Iraq. Iran brought Shiite Iraqis into training camps in Iran, then sent them back to Iraq to disrupt elections, intimidate citizens, and wreak terror.

The Ayatollah Khomeini came to power in 1979 promising what dictators always promise: All Iranians and "not the specific few" would enjoy the "people's share" of wealth and an improvement in their material life. He attributed victory to the "unity of voice of all Muslims" and to the "unity" of all the parts of Iran. All were supposedly united around religious and economic rebirth and strict Islamic values. As Reza Kahlili perceives, language and ideology, not weapons, were the biggest forces in the Iranian Revolution.

Ideas matter. They matter so much that they cause seismic shifts in history. Extremist ideas foster revolutionary fanatics so beholden to ideology that attempting to "balance" them or use negotiations to contain them can be like placing a Band-Aid on an open wound. The attacks of 9/11 and other acts of Islamist terror upended previous notions of deterrence; you can't simply "deter" someone who doesn't care if he dies as he inflicts terror, or dies in the punishing response to it. You also have to work to counter the ideology that leads him to devalue his own life and the lives of innocent others. It's time we ended the habit of restraint in the expression of ideas regarding democracy, decency, human rights, and the value of human life. And it's time we reembraced the noble American tradition of speaking out for freedom.

Instead of countering Iranian words and ideas with words and ideas of our own, the American intelligentsia has typically whitewashed the truth about revolutionary Iran, while the American government has typically remained silent. President Obama and Secretary Clinton went beyond silence and toward, in effect, offering to ignore Iran's extremism. In his first television interview as president, with al-Arabiya, Obama explained his new approach to the Muslim world, saying, "We are ready to initiate a new partnership based on mutual respect and interest" and to "set aside some of the preconceptions that have existed and have built up over the last several years." In her Senate confirmation hearing, Secretary Clinton said she would build a world with "more partners and less adversaries," and that she and Obama were committed to a fresh approach with Iran, which involved more willingness to talk, and might include the opening of a US diplomatic office for the first time since the overthrow of the Shah in 1979.

On her Latin America tour, Secretary Clinton went so far as to proclaim in response to a question about relations with hostile regimes like Hugo Chavez's Venezuela, "Let's put ideology aside; that is so yesterday."

Of course, high and escalating rates of arbitrary detention and executions, discrimination against women and minorities, and extensive restrictions on expression, the press, and association give the lie to Khomeini's unity. A report entitled "Rights Disregarded: Prisons in the Islamic Republic of Iran" documents the imprisonment of successive generations of activists, human rights defenders, journalists, and other citizens. It highlights the targeting of political prisoners and prisoners of conscience, and the chronic abuse of prisoners by authorities. It shows that the situation within Iranian prisons is grave, with Iran not endeavoring to hold up either the international "Standard Minimum Rules for the Treatment of Prisoners" of its own domestic prison regulations.[15]

Reza Kahlili was a member of the Iranian Guard who later defected and agreed to spy for the CIA in hopes of helping the Iranian people. He was heartbroken by what was happening in his country and desperate to bring Western attention to political, cultural, and religious oppression and grave human rights violations. This is what he witnessed: In Evin Prison and in other fortresses of the Republican Guard, anyone who failed to adhere to even minor Islamic rules, anyone "suspicious," anyone who dared to suggest disagreement with the regime, anyone who had sympathized with the Shah, was brutally tortured. Children were among the tortured, often being raped and beaten for months on end, until they died. Kahlili's friend received a letter from a teenage friend describing interrogations: While others were being raped or beaten, "they would line up the rest of us and make us hold one leg up for a long time. If you got tired, they would lash you on the tired leg and make you stand on it. All of us were crying. Some would faint from the bleeding."[16]

In the Islamic Republic of Iran, atrocities are routine. So is the cruel mistreatment of women. The regime treats women like second-class citizens and like property and encourages Iranian men to do the same. The Stone Age punishments inflicted for the most minor deviations from strict religious laws are generally well known.

It is true, as historians William Cleveland and Martin Bunton and Iranian-American scholar Nikki Keddie point out, that the Iranian government is not simply united around fascist-Islamist ideas and that the 1990s saw some brave governmental efforts for reform. After Ayatollah Khomeini's death in 1989, his successor, Ali Akbar Hashemi Rafsanjani, privatized some companies that had been nationalized under the Islamic Republic and tried (with little success) to slow down the radical Islamization of society. He is known for partial attempts at an economic opening with the outside world. Less well known is that he worked with radicals to suppress Iranian citizens, violated agreements with the West, and actively supported assassinations and terrorist activities abroad.

In the elections of 1997, Rafsanjani was replaced by Mohammad Khatami, whose platform for reform was more genuine. Khatami won with a large majority and was strongly supported by youths and by women looking for greater equality, opportunity, and freedom. But, the undemocratic structure of government institutions and the undemocratic dictates of the country's constitution stifled Khatami's reforms. At every turn, he was opposed—by Supreme Leader Ali Khamenei, chairman of the Guardian Council Ayatollah Ahmad Jannati, and others.

When Khatami nevertheless was reelected in a landslide victory in 2001, hardliners in the regime responded with arrests, newspaper closures, and the encouragement of vigilante violence against democracy advocates. Intense protests spread throughout Iran, but as Reza Kahlili says, "Guards and Baijis brutally crushed the demonstrations. . . . And once again, the world looked the other way."[17]

The failure of reform and the crackdown on reformers lent credence to the idea that regime change was necessary. Cleveland and Bunton explain, "Khatami's moderate approach began to lose its appeal, especially among university students. Outspoken student leaders claimed that the regime could not be changed from within, as Khatami was seeking to do, because it was authoritarian at its core and would not be willing to submit to a reduction of its power. In making these claims, the student spokespersons revealed the existence of a wide gap between the popularly elected president and the Maijlis, on the one hand, and the closed, self-selective circle of ulama who controlled the central levers of power and determined the official policy of the state, on the other."[18] Cleveland and Bunton also note that the 2004 elections "dashed any hopes that this gap could be successfully bridged by political change from within the system."[19] Hardliners in the Guardian Council forcefully retook control by disqualifying more than two thousand reformist candidates. The extremists' takeover of Iran's institutions culminated in the victory of Mahmoud Ahmadinejad in the 2005 presidential elections.

Cleveland and Bunton point to the Bush administration's tendency to simplify Iran and the Middle East by, for example, failing to acknowledge the conflicting forces within the Iranian government. I would argue that Obama's Iran policy also rested upon simplification. Instead of seeing the Iranian government that spoke and acted for Iran as a distortion of the country, Obama chose to ignore most of the struggling reformers within the government—and especially among the Iranian people themselves—in favor of dialogue and engagement with Iran's dictators. *His words and actions implied that respect for Iran as a whole meant respect for Iran's most repressive leaders.* We will see that he went so far as to publicly criticize the goal of Iranian regime change and to promise the leaders not only acceptance but also respect for their internal policies.

President Obama didn't just reach out to the new President Ahmadinejad. He catered to him, flattered him, and handed him the words he needed to succeed. We've already seen how he offered up Iran's "right" to "peaceful" nuclear technology, thus handing the Iranian president just the words he needed for Hitler-like verbal deception. We've seen that he rejected preconditions for direct, personal negotiations with Iranian leaders even though he presented Israel with preconditions in regard to negotiations with the Palestinians. (He explicitly offered to meet and talk with Iran with "no preconditions.") We've seen, too, that Obama and Clinton quickly made it official US policy to ignore human rights violations for the sake of engagement.

But Obama went further than this in courting the Iranians. He offered Iran a "new beginning" which promised an end to the policy of seeking regime change. To emphasize the point, he sent an unprecedented Persian New Year message to the people and leaders of Iran in March 2009, in which he repeatedly referred to the "Islamic Republic." Stipulating that Iran had to meet its international responsibilities, he stated, "The United States wants the Islamic Republic of Iran to take its rightful place in the community of nations."[20]

He also sent a personal letter to "Supreme Leader" Ali Khamenei, who holds ultimate power and has continuously, personally, been one of the main obstacles to reform. Charles Krauthammer fumed, "Where to begin? 'Supreme Leader'? Note the abject solicitousness with which the American president confers this honorific on a clerical dictator."[21] The respect was not mutual. Shortly after Obama's message, in what *Newsmax* described as a "nasty slap in the face for President Obama," Iran arrested and sentenced to eight years in prison a journalist of dual Iranian-American nationality, Roxana Saberi.

Then it got worse. Millions of Iranians took to the streets to protest rigged elections in June 2009, marking the largest anti-regime demonstration Iran had seen since the final days of the Shah in 1979. Sixteen Iranian Revolutionary Guards Corps officers publicly pledged to join the movement, signaling that the once-solid support of the corps for Ahmadinejad was starting to crack. Many of the protestors shouted, "Death to the Dictator!" We citizens of the United States had to witness the sickening spectacle of young and hopeful protestors being crushed by the regime—and of our president and secretary of state responding by saying . . . nothing. For anyone who cared at all about the American tradition and/or about human rights, the silence was painful. The protestors cried out in disbelief, "Obama are you with us?" But not a word.

After days of silence, days when brave young Iranian men and women were beaten, killed, and sent to horrible places like Evin Prison, Obama finally expressed a passionless request that the "violence" stop, the word *violence* implying moral equivalence between the two sides. Even then, he stipulated that he would continue his policy of dialogue with the Iranian regime. Stunning and dismaying the dissidents, he said, "It's not too late for the Iranian government to see there is a peaceful path that leads to legitimacy in the eyes of the Iranian people."[22] Worse, he said the difference in the disputed election between Ahmadinejad and Mir-Hossein Mousavi "may not be as great as has been advertised" and called on other nations to "recognize the government of Ahmadinejad as a legitimate government." Note that Ahmadinejad was *so* extreme that even the extremist Khameini sometimes stepped in to downplay his hateful, anti-Semitic rhetoric.

Thanks in part to Obama's unctuous support, it was, indeed, "not too late" for the Iranian government or for Ahmadinejad himself. Many questions arise from Obama's indifference to Iranian youths longing for freedom. We will see that one is why he so consistently ignored their plight, while being so quick to embrace the youths of Tahrir Square who would rally against detested Egyptian leader Hosni Mubarak. Egypt was an American ally in desperate need of domestic reforms; Iran was a declared enemy of America, so fanatical that reform would never be enough. Why support for Egyptian youths, but not Iranian youths?

Stepping back a bit in time punctuates the tragedy in this scenario. In 2006, the Bush administration announced it was shifting US Iran policy toward a two-pronged approach that involved concerted international pressure to deter Iran from seeking nuclear weapons and, on the other hand, pressuring the Iranian regime by working to "support the aspirations of the Iranian people for freedom in their own country."[23] By then, the majority of Iranians did have such aspirations, for they had suffered long and hard under the Islamic Republic. Condoleezza Rice asked for seventy-five million dollars to increase TV and radio broadcasts and to fund dissident groups. By the time Obama took power, the regime's domestic reputation had deteriorated further and a strong and widespread student opposition movement had again formed. In a December 2008 article in the *New York Post*, Amir Taheri noted the strength and popularity of the movement and asked, "Could this develop into a nationwide movement that could upset the regime's calculations before the June election? Is Iran entering a pre-revolutionary phase that could threaten the Khomeinist regime?"[24]

Iran had recently suffered a setback in its attempt to dominate Iraq when Iraqi prime minister Nouri al-Maliki had signed the Status of Forces Agreement with the United States. With technology in their hands and the majority of citizens on their side, students across Iran were mobilizing. But they did not believe they could change the regime alone; they were counting on US support.

What might that support have looked like? Continuing, rather than discontinuing, Voice of America and similar broadcasts. Continuing, rather than discontinuing, Bush's successful campaign to get foreign banks to stop doing business in Iran. Doing everything possible to get the technology of communication, and perhaps funding, into student hands. Stringently sanctioning US companies that sold technology used for repression and materials used for Iran's uranium enrichment program. Shining light into the darkness by insistently drawing attention to the truth about the suffering of Iranians and the fanatical goals of Iranian leaders. Leaving it up to the people themselves to foment revolution, being careful not to dictate terms. As Ledeen points out, similar strategies worked to strengthen Poland's Solidarity movement. In sum, it would have meant doing the opposite of what the Obama administration has done in its relations with Iran.

The plight of Iranian youths apparently did not move President Obama. In his December 2009 speech in Oslo accepting the Nobel Peace Prize, he said that relations with repressive regimes were important even when engagement "lacks the satisfying purity of indignation." Lamented Human Rights Watch's executive director Kenneth Roth in an interview, "Engagement without pressure is read by authoritarian governments as capitulation."[25]

Even when dealing with matters of nuclear proliferation, it does not make sense to cast aside concerns about the kind of regime we're dealing with. As Ledeen put it in 2009, "If Iran were not actively killing Americans and did not call for our destruction, the prospect of a nuclear Iran would not be so threatening." [26] In April 2012, India successfully test-fired a long-range ballistic missile capable of carrying a nuclear warhead. The reason India's missile launch did not garner the same attention and concern as the North Korean missile launch is obvious; it is the difference between a regime that is likely to proliferate nuclear weapons and to use them aggressively and a regime that values nuclear weapons as defensive shields and harbingers of regional influence.

Still, we can ask, apart from concerns regarding the kind of regime we're dealing with, how did the policy of engagement with the Islamic Republic fare during Obama's first term? Was progress made in regard to the advancement of Iran's nuclear weapons program or weapons proliferation? By most accounts, engagement did not go well. Let's look at the series of steps and missteps in the attempt to get Iran to give up its nuclear program.

President Obama and Secretary Clinton hoped engagement and cooperation with Iran would reap fast rewards in nuclear negotiations. They were not the first to try diplomacy with Iran; they were simply the first to keep negotiating in the face of Iranian intractability and intransigence. At some point, every administration since Carter's had attempted to negotiate. This includes the Bush administration, which, in spite of the impression we were given by Democratic presidential candidates in the 2008 campaign, did try diplomacy. The repetitious story is of Iran refusing to negotiate when offered the chance, or of agreeing to negotiate, then violating the negotiated agreements by moving ahead with its covert nuclear program, weapons proliferation, and sponsorship of terror.

Sometimes, Iranian hardliners don't bother to be covert. In January 2009, at precisely the moment of Obama's outstretched hand, Ahmadinejad's adviser for press affairs, Ali Akbar Javanfekr, said that, despite overtures from the United States, Iran had "no intention" of stopping its nuclear activities. When asked about a UN resolution calling for suspension of Iran's uranium enrichment, Javanfekr replied, "We are past that stage." Shortly thereafter, Ahmadinejad himself would state that Iran's nuclear program was like "a train without breaks." [27]

Secretary of Defense Bill Gates seemed to have a better grasp on the likely outcome of more negotiations than the rest of the administration, noting that "the Iranian leadership has been consistently unyielding over a very long period of time in response to repeated overtures from the

United States about having a better and different kind of relationship."[28] Significantly, as early as May 2009, the *Wall Street Journal* reported that not only Israel but also key Arab allies had "voiced concerns about the usefulness of diplomacy with Iran." Noted the *Journal*, "The U.S. point man on Iran policy, Dennis Ross, was greeted with skepticism from Arab allies during a tour this month through Egypt and the Persian Gulf countries, said U.S. officials. Saudi Arabia and the United Arab Emirates in particular have expressed alarm over Iran's nuclear activities and its moves to support militant groups operating in Lebanon, Iraq and the Palestinian territories. Israel believes Tehran could be far enough advanced in its nuclear work by early next year to make protracted negotiations moot."[29]

■ ■ ■

The Obama administration hoped the promise of better standing in the international community and the offer to reduce our own nuclear arsenal would soften Iran's stance and provide a disincentive for continuing its pursuit of nuclear weapons. But there were early signs that this hope was misguided. In September 2009, Obama had the unpleasant task of having to announce to the Group of 20 Summit in Pittsburgh that Iran was building a secret nuclear fuel plant underground near the city of Qom. The IAEA (International Atomic Energy Agency) voted overwhelmingly for a resolution requiring Iran to stop this activity, but Iran's chief delegate to the IAEA Ali Asghar Soltanieh defiantly contested the resolution.

In October, in direct talks in Geneva, the United States and its allies offered Iran nuclear fuel for a civilian nuclear reactor in Tehran, which produces radioisotopes for medical procedures. In exchange, Iran was to ship low-enriched uranium to Russia, where it would be enriched and then sent to France and converted into fuel rods for Tehran's reactor. By most accounts, this was a good deal for Iran. Having lied about the Qom facility for years, the Iranians had plenty of time to clean the facility before inspections. Previously, the US had required a freeze on enrichment as precondition for talks; now Iran simply had to *promise* to freeze enrichment. Not only that, the agreement actually enhanced Iran's access to uranium. All that was required was the commitment to use it for peaceful purposes!

According to the *Financial Times*, the semiofficial Fars News Agency noted that Iran had the "upper hand" in the talks. Iran initially agreed to the deal but then reneged, showing that it did indeed have the upper hand. Iran remained in utter defiance of multiple Security Council resolutions that demanded total suspension of enrichment activities. As if to emphasize that it was in the driver's seat, in January of 2010, Iran set its own one-month deadline for its counterproposal to the UN and warned that if its requirements for "peaceful" nuclear technology were not met, it would produce reactor fuel at a higher level of enrichment on its own.

One cannot help but be reminded of the North Korean agreement of the Clinton presidency, which was similar in many ways. In a September 2009 article in *Foreign Policy*, Blake Hounshell put it this way: "Now put yourself in the minds of Iranian leaders. Despite some major remaining technical hurdles, you're inching closer to achieving your nuclear goals. You've been watching the North Koreans very closely, noticing that even after they tested a nuclear device one, two times, the regime is still in power and, if anything, the carrots they've been offered have only become more generous. And you're willing to bet that once you've got the Bomb, you'll be able to sort out all those issues like your frozen bank accounts and airplane spare parts with the Great Satan."[30] Along the same lines, the Associated Press stated, "There is no doubt that Iranian leaders have taken careful notice of neighboring Pakistan. First came international pressures and outcry over Pakistan's nuclear arsenal—and then reluctant acceptance. Iran's foreign minister was the first to visit Islamabad, saying Muslims are 'happy' that an Islamic nation had the capabilities to counter Israel's suspected nuclear-armed military."[31]

Keeping engagement as a goal, while pushing new sanctions in the UN (supported by the US and others), Turkey and Brazil negotiated a new tripartite deal with Iran in May 2010. But, in the words of John Limbert of the Tehran Bureau, "the last-ditch diplomacy ended up a classic case of bad timing." The timing was bad because it was late. Iran's program was, by then, much farther along: "Terms acceptable in October 2009 were not acceptable in May 2010. In the intervening seven months, Iran had enriched more uranium. The original deal called for Iran to transfer 1,200 kilograms, which then represented an estimated 80 percent of its stock. By May, the same amount was only about one-half of its stock.

Nor did the new agreement deal with the 20 percent enriched uranium Iran had produced in the interim."[32]

President Obama and Secretary Clinton decided to turn to Britain, France, and Germany, the three countries that had initially led diplomatic efforts with Iran, in pursuit of a new sanctions package. Tellingly, the United States also pushed for a generous incentives package for the Iranian regime. The administration was continuing on with its policy of offering economic aid and technical assistance in exchange for a more proliferation-proof Iranian nuclear power industry. The agreed-to sanctions led to Security Council Resolution 1929, which was passed on June 9, 2010. This required UN members to block the transfer of technology related to either missiles or nuclear weapons and to cut off access by Iran to uranium mining for nuclear production in their territories. It also imposed restrictions on travel by Iranian officials involved in proliferation and called on member nations to block new branches of certain Iranian banks. At the same time, the House and Senate passed the Comprehensive Iran Sanctions, Accountability, and Divestment Act, which Obama signed into law. The title of the bill was a misnomer; penalties and costs to Iran were not "comprehensive."

This combination of incentives and disincentives produced no significant change in Iran's course. Iran continued to accelerate its nuclear program and intensified its anti-Western activities and rhetoric. In November 2011, the IAEA issued a report saying Iran had carried out tests related to "development of a nuclear device."

In the face of the ineffectiveness of existing sanctions, in December 2011, Congress passed additional sanctions that targeted financial institutions that do business with the Central Bank of Iran, but made exceptions in clear cases of humanitarian need. Inexplicably, the administration worked behind the scenes to weaken the congressional sanctions bill, which became known as the Kirk-Menendez Iran Sanctions Amendment. Even more inexplicable, the White House then suddenly, publicly, announced its *opposition* to the bill and worked to obstruct it, arguing, among other things, that including sanctions against the Iranian central bank would interfere with the foreign relations of US allies.

This reportedly infuriated several senators. Democrat Robert Menendez said he "regretted working with the administration on the issue" and that perhaps he should have just agreed to Republican Mark

Kirk's original Iran sanctions amendment, which was more severe and provided the administration with less room to maneuver than the compromise amendment.[33] (Senator Kirk of Illinois had sought a US declaration that Iran's telecom and technology sectors were "zones of electronic repression," and wanted to make them off-limits to US firms. In spite of Hillary Clinton's later claims to the contrary, both the White House and the Clinton State Department had opposed Kirk and Menendez's efforts to add an amendment to the annual National Defense Authorization Act that would have blacklisted several of these sectors.)

Mark Dubowitz and Toby Dershowitz of the Foundation for Defense of Democracies cited the urgent need for revisiting Kirk's proposals, writing, "In Iran's telecom and technology industries—as in its energy and financial sectors—there is little distinction between the Iranian government and the Revolutionary Guards. The Guards have used their control of TCI and their dominant role in the security establishment to take extraordinary measures to cut Iranians off from one another and from the outside world. . . . Unfortunately, foreign companies have sold the Guards the technologies they need to make this oppression possible."[34]

French president Nicolas Sarkozy pressed for a total embargo on Iran's oil exports and central bank, but he, too, came up against a lack of Obama administration support. In December, the *Wall Street Journal* reported that the European Union (EU) and the Obama administration were "yet to fully embrace" Sarkozy's proposal. The EU and the United States did ultimately decide to impose an embargo on the purchase of Iranian oil, in early 2012. And, in May, the Senate did finally approve measures requiring companies that trade on the US stock exchange to disclose Iran-related business to the Securities and Exchange Commission. Congress also expanded penalties for energy and uranium mining joint ventures with Iran.

As with the other sanctions, Obama and his foreign policy team claimed full credit for them, once they had no choice but to go along. They pointed to the "unprecedented sanctions regime" in response to critics that accused them of being too slow and too minimalist in their response. They failed to mention that the Treasury Department was actively issuing exemptions to thousands of companies wishing to do business with Iran.

In *Commentary*, Alana Goodman noted that even after Senator Kirk suffered a stroke, Obama never mentioned his role in constructing sanctions. "It's not that Obama should have to give Kirk a nod every time he mentions the sanctions. But a brief acknowledgement for the man who had the foresight to fight for them—even when the president was reluctant to support them—would be the classy thing to do."[35]

In another take on giving credit where credit is due, in a May 2015 article in the *Daily Beast*, Josh Rogin exposed Hillary Clinton's attempt to rewrite history by claiming she was responsible for tough sanctions on Iran.[36] Speaking at the American Jewish Committee in May of 2014, Clinton claimed, "We went after Iran's oil industry, banks, and weapons programs, enlisted others to cut Iran off from global commerce." To the contrary, Rogin shows, the Clinton State Department "often worked hard against many of the measures she's now championing" and "repeatedly opposed or tried to water down an array of measures that pushed into law by Democrats and Republicans in Congress." Examples he cites include the White House and State Department opposing the passage of gasoline sanctions in 2009; Undersecretary of State Wendy Sherman expressing "strong opposition" to sanctioning the Central Bank of Iran in 2011; and the White House and State Department opposing Congressional efforts to bar Iranian financial institutions, including Iran's Central Bank, from doing business with SWIFT, the global financial clearinghouse. (Rogin notes that Clinton does deserve credit for lining up votes for UN Security Council sanctions on Iran, and urging European countries to levy their own sanctions.)

It was not until February of 2012 that President Obama signed a bill that encouraged American institutions to freeze assets related to the Central Bank of Iran. And, in an executive order, he announced that the US was freezing Iranian government assets held or traded in the United States. The president stipulated, however, that he "reserved the right to treat the provisions as non-binding." Although noting the evolution in policy from "olive branch" to "sanctions hammer," Tabassum Zakaria and Caren Bohan reported: "Obama is still open to an Iranian overture for serious negotiations on its nuclear program officials say. Indeed, that is the ultimate goal of the pressure. . . . But with Iran announcing it has begun enrichment at the protected underground site near Qom, and Israel not ruling out a unilateral strike on Iran's nuclear sites, time might be short."[37]

As early as the fall of 2011, it was clear to most observers that President Obama's "outstretched hand" had done nothing to improve relations. Just look at Iran's behavior from the time President Obama took office until then. In February 2009, Iran announced it would increase its blocking of the Internet and tightened pressure on dissidents. In that same month, it bulldozed the mass graves of political victims. In September 2009, Ahmadinejad and Hugo Chavez of Venezuela agreed to strengthen ties and to stand together "against the United States." In early 2010, Ahmadinejad travelled to Syria to meet the brutal Bashar al-Assad, where the two announced the strengthening of "strategic ties." After the meeting, Assad expressed support for Iran's nuclear activities. Also in 2010, arms control expert Jeffrey Lewis stated that "Iran is enriching uranium faster than we can swap it." In the summer of 2011, a plot was foiled in which Iran had plotted to kill a Saudi diplomat in the United States. After the disclosure, Iran's "Supreme Leader" warned the US of a "resolute response" to any reprisals. In addition, he invited the leaders of Afghanistan, Pakistan, and Iraq to Tehran to discuss regional affairs and to argue for an accelerated exit of American forces from the region. In September 2011, Ahmadinejad delivered a speech at the UN which amounted to a stinging attack on the US and other "militarist, imperialist" powers.

The Iranian regime continued to foment terrorism in Iraq, Palestine, Yemen, and elsewhere and turned to Afghanistan, where it supplied and assisted Taliban and al-Qaeda terrorists. Iranian leaders issued warnings to Sunni Arab Gulf kingdoms and tried to incite their Shiite populations. They bolstered extremists in Egypt. They threatened to close the Strait of Hormuz and warned allies of Israel of possible retaliation for that alliance.

In response to the potentially devastating and destabilizing closing of the Strait of Hormuz, the United States, England, and France agreed to run a flotilla through the Strait in January 2012 as a show of resolve. In a situation highly insulting to our British ally, it was only after the intervention of Sarkozy that the Obama administration "agreed" to allow a Royal Navy frigate to join the flotilla. Stratfor Global Intelligence reported that the administration quietly "reached out" to Iran in an attempt to resolve the Hormuz crisis.

By almost all accounts, late 2011 and 2012 were very bad times for the US government's long-term goals of preventing a nuclear Iran and diminishing Iran's regional influence. During that time, the IAEA confirmed that Iran had rapidly expanded its nuclear work, and the Institute for Science and International Security confirmed that Iran had concealed a key atom center. The IAEA announced that inspectors had located radioactive traces in an underground Iranian bunker. It then announced the discovery of traces of uranium enriched to higher purity levels than previously found, "sparking fresh fears that Tehran is moving closer to possessing materials for atomic weapons, even as it engages in diplomacy with global powers."[38] Khameini announced that Iran's atomic program was a "pillar of national dignity," while Ahmadinejad reiterated Iran's "nuclear rights." Liberals and conservatives alike acknowledged that it was now only a matter of time until Iran could make and use an atomic bomb. Middle Eastern expert Walid Phares asserted that the Iranian quest for nuclear weapons was "not stoppable," but also urged confronting the Iranian regime before it actually obtained such weapons.

None of this deterred Obama administration officials and their UN cohorts from giving negotiation and outreach another try. White House press secretary Jay Carney explained, "Our approach right now is to continue to pursue the diplomatic path that we've taken, combined with very aggressive sanctions. . . . There is time and space to pursue the policy we have been pursuing since the president took office."[39] But the US and its P5+1 partners then offered to *ease* sanctions that barred the export of US-made spare aircraft parts to Iran's national carriers and offered aid for Iran's "development of nonmilitary applications for nuclear power."[40] In return, the group proposed that Iran "freeze" (not halt or dismantle) production of nuclear fuel enriched to 20 percent purity and ship its stockpile to a third country. Iran balked at the offer, once again dashing hopes for a diplomatic breakthrough and once again revealing that it was *using the diplomatic process to buy time, cover—and eventually de facto acceptance—of its nuclear program.*

Reported the *Washington Times* in May 2012, "Iran's nuclear chief said [Sunday] there are no reasons at the moment for his country to halt production enriched to 20 percent, a key demand of world powers, and Iran is planning two new reactors. The West is concerned that the 20-percent enrichment could quickly be turned into nuclear weapons-grade material. Iran insists its nuclear development program is for peaceful purposes."[41] By November, the nuclear chief would pronounce, "Despite sanctions, we will most likely see a substantial increase in the number of centrifuge machines this year. We will continue enrichment with intensity."[42]

Indeed, Iran *was* continuing its enrichment program with intensity, and with increasing stridency. Iran accused UN inspectors of spying and sabotage, and threatened to restrict UN access to Iranian nuclear facilities. In November, the IAEA reported that Iran had completed work on an underground factory for making enriched uranium that could someday be used to make a nuclear bomb. UN inspectors also documented a sharp rise in Iran's stockpile of a more purified form of enriched uranium that could potentially shorten the country's pathway to becoming a nuclear-weapons state. The Institute for Science and International Security said Iran's total output of low-enriched uranium since 2007 could potentially be used for six or seven nuclear weapons if refined much further.

■ ■ ■

In the meantime, Iran funneled new weapons, including long-range rockets, to anti-American forces in Iraq and Afghanistan. Analysts predicted (and that prediction became a reality) that Iran would exploit the power vacuum as the US withdrew from the two countries. As Michael Scott Doran showed in an excellent piece in *Foreign Affairs*, the underlying anarchic nature of Arab politics remained, to the point that there was difficulty finding distinction between "domestic" and "foreign" in some Arab countries. Therefore, "transnational movements hold unusually powerful sway in the Arab world" while the "porousness of Arab politics" gave movements like al-Qaeda and the Muslim Brotherhood great opportunities. Today, there is little counter to pernicious "influences"—particularly Iran—that are trying to make the region hostage to their causes and plans. In addition to moving rapidly toward nuclear weapons, Iran had developed "a credible deterrent to any conventional attack against its nuclear infrastructure, thanks to a diverse set of covert and overt capabilities in Lebanon, Gaza, Iraq, the Persian Gulf and Afghanistan."[43]

As Doran pointed out, in Iraq and elsewhere, Iran has proven its capacity for destabilizing vulnerable regimes. In fact, with Iran arming and funding Shiite radicals and its ally Syria arming and funding Sunni radicals, the two nations managed to keep civil warfare going in Iraq. They not only directly encouraged Sunnis and Shiites to unite against the regime, they also indirectly encouraged Sunnis and Shiites to fight against each other so as to achieve maximum destabilization, which in turn met their goal of humiliation of the United States. Through fomenting turmoil and violence in the Middle East, which translates into high costs for Westerners involved there, Iran's geopolitical and ideological "grand strategy" is to wear the United States down. As Doran puts it, Iran "does not think it can compete with the United States—but it does believe that it can exhaust it. . . . The shadow war in Iraq was thus a prelude to an impending regional contest."[44]

Even before the Arab Spring, this was a very big problem for the United States. Regardless of what the Arab revolts were originally about, Iran and its proxies were eager to hijack them. The United States, on the other hand, lacked eagerness for its strategic alliances and its democratic principles. In the words of Doran, Iran, Syria, Hezbollah, and Hamas bear a "ruthlessness and intensity of focus that the United States—a distracted Gulliver—cannot match."[45] This "lack of focus about our interests and clarity about our purpose" translates, he argues, into a foreign policy that is absent "grand strategy."

Indeed, the Obama administration made minimal effort to maintain or project American influence after its decision to withdraw forces from Iraq. In announcing the end of combat operations on August 31, 2010, President Obama seemed to go out of his way to indicate the finality and completeness of our withdrawal. He said, "So tonight, I am announcing that the American combat mission in Iraq has *ended*. Operation Iraqi Freedom is *over*, and the Iraqi people now have lead responsibility for the security of their country. . . . This *completes* a transition to Iraq of responsibility for *their own* security."[46] (italics mine) Is it any wonder that the Iraqi government has, since then, so often succumbed to Iranian demands? Is it any wonder that al-Qaeda, and now the Islamic State in Iraq, have made such gains?

An October 2012 Associated Press story by Qassim Abdul-Zahra enti-tled "Officials Warn Al-Qaida Making Comeback in Iraq" elaborated: "During the war and its aftermath, U.S. forces, joined by allied Sunni groups and later by Iraqi counterterror forces, managed to beat back al-Qaida's Iraqi branch. But now, Iraqi and U.S. officials say, the insur-gent group has more than doubled in numbers from a year ago—from about 1,000 to 2,500 fighters. And it is carrying out an average of 140 attacks a week across Iraq, up from 75 attacks a week earlier this year, according to Pentagon data."[47] Kenneth Pollack had argued forcefully in *Foreign Affairs* that, regardless of one's position on the Iraq War—perhaps more so because of the hardships unleashed by the war—Iraq still needed our support. His assessment is important and worth quoting at length:

> Iraq remains devastated by thirty years of Saddam Hussein's misrule, three foreign wars, a dozen years of comprehensive international sanc-tions, and an intercommunal war. As a result, Iraq needs all the help it can get. Its armed forces continue to rely on the U.S. military for combat and logistical support, and Baghdad has an ongoing desire to purchase large amounts of American weaponry and to retain U.S. training for its still-nascent armed forces and internal security services. The Iraqi economy is a basket case, and Iraqis from across the political spectrum recognize a need for American assistance in rebuilding the country's bureaucracy, infrastructure, agricultural sector, educational system, and industrial base. Iraq must also be helped to integrate into the global economy, overcome a series of lingering diplomatic prob-lems, and avoid excessive intervention by any of its neighbors. Many Iraqis even recognize that their fragile democracy would benefit from a continued American military presence in the country—if only to restrain predatory indigenous politicians and neighboring states alike.[48]

Pollack argued that all of this Iraqi need for things we could offer gave us leverage, which he said we should use to encourage the building of a strong democracy.

Our choosing *not* to exert leverage meant that Iranian leverage was greater than it otherwise would have been. With the vacuum left by American forces, and with the Obama administration's political acqui-escence, the al-Malaki government (which the Bush administration had also misguidedly enabled) became increasingly beholden to Iran, and yet more sectarian and intolerant of Sunnis. The government's worsening repression and slide toward authoritarianism stoked the radical-Sunni flame, and spurred the rise of ISIS.[49]

Iran's influence became particularly strong in southern Iraq, which has abundant oilfields, and in Yemen, where the Gate of Grief is a chokepoint for oil. Iran's strategy in Yemen has been similar to the one it employed in the 1980s to build Hezbollah into the leading political power in Lebanon: Iran created partnerships with Yemini separatists—not only with Shiite Houthis, but also earlier on when it suited its destabilization purposes, with (Sunni) al Qaeda. With Iranian weapons, money and training, the Houthis were able to take significant territory, ultimately seizing Yemen's capital Sena and ousting the pro-American government, which had been an essential partner in the war on terror. Al Qaeda in the Arabian Peninsula (AQAP) has, in turn, taken advantage of Yemen's anarchy.[50] Iran has also forged increasingly close military ties with Sudan, as evidenced when it dispatched a naval task force to Sudan just days after a widely reported airstrike by Israel against a missile base run by Tehran in Khartoum.[51] Both Saudi Arabia and Israel see Iran's rising influence in Iraq, Yemen, and Sudan as a credible threat.

In a November 2012 blog for Ricochet, I argued:

> As the news out of the Middle East goes from bad to worse, we have no choice but to learn—once again—what a mistake it is to ignore (unlearn) the lessons of history. Take the case of Iran. Iran is the main source of the 200 missiles a day Hamas has recently been firing at Israel. Both the new *Fajr-5 missiles* and the new *Ayub drone* that are being devastatingly used to destabilize the Middle East are the result of Iranian technology. Iran still actively supports, with weapons, money and training, terrorists and terror-sponsoring regimes. Human rights violations within Iran are severe. . . . Last week, Iranian Vice President Rahimi <u>declared</u>, "We will break [the] grasping hands of Obama and we will be successful in bypassing sanctions." This is the thanks Obama gets for engaging in obsequious outreach to Iran's repressive leaders; for his non-response to the cries of brave young Iranian protestors for support; for speaking up for Iran's "right" to peaceful nuclear technology; for acknowledging Ahmadinejad as the *legitimate, elected*

leader, even after his brutal crackdown on massive protests against rigged elections; for relentlessly pursuing negotiations no matter how many times Iran obfuscated and deceived; and for pursuing a minimalist response to the Iranian nuclear program.[52]

This is the thanks we always get for placating extremist dictators. This is our history.

Israel viewed the prospect of a nuclear-armed Iran with greater urgency than the rest of the world, seeing it as a threat to its very survival. A March 2012 meeting between President Obama and Israeli prime minister Benjamin Netanyahu showed clearly where the men differed. Obama urged for more time to allow a mix of negotiations and economic pressures to work. Netanyahu said Israel must be the "master of its own fate" and indicated it could not sit by and allow the emergence of a nuclear-armed Iran.

Powerful leaders in Iran justify Israel's annihilation with Islamic Law. Michael Rubin cited an article in the state-sanctioned Iranian press that summarized Khamenei's views, saying, "The first Qibal of Muslims has today fallen into the hands of Israel, this cancerous tumor in the Middle East.... Every Muslim has the obligation to equip himself against Israel. I have been warning about the dangers of international Zionism for about 20 years ... All our troubles are due to Israel!"[53] Ahmadinejad's calls for Israel's destruction were even more explicit than Khamenei's, and more public, as they were sometimes issued through speeches. The United States Institute of Peace points out that this ideology (not just the problem of weapons proliferation) makes peaceful relations with Iran difficult. Since Khamenei's foreign policy is driven by animosity to the United States and Israel, "it is unclear whether he could abandon this position without undermining the raison d'être of the Islamic system."[54] Again, ideology and regime type matter. When will "political science" pay more attention to the ideas behind "who does what, when, where and how"?

Acknowledging both the ideology and the nuclear ambitions that make up the Iranian regime's "reality," Israel had to decide whether to take preemptive action against Iran in the form of missile strikes on Iranian nuclear facilities. In the face of talk of a military crisis in the region, and the possibility of an Israeli airstrike, Iran "agreed" in 2012 to new negotiations with the West. Secretary Clinton herself saw the opportunism in Iran's offer and expressed doubt that Iran had any intention of negotiating a solution. She warned that Iran's "window of opportunity" for creating a peaceful solution would "not remain open forever." Words out of the mouths of Iranian leaders themselves indicated the futility of more discussions: "Iran's right for uranium enrichment is nonnegotiable," said Iranian lawmaker Ali Aghazadeh. "There is no reason for Iran to compromise over its rights. But Iran is open to discussions over concerns about its nuclear program."[55]

In relation to the crisis between Iran and Israel, the administration—strangely—seemed to work harder to prevent Israel from acting militarily than it did to prevent the possibility of having to deal with a nuclear Iran. In the *Daily Beast*, Leslie Gelb went so far as to suggest that the Obama administration and the Islamist regime were pursuing a "common tactic" as well as a "shared goal" vis-à-vis Israel: Reentering "the charade of substantive negotiations" was the best way to pressure Israel to maintain the peace and to prevent Israel from taking preemptive military action, Gelb posited.

Negotiation is obviously an indispensable tool of American foreign policy, but it is sometimes used by our opponents as their own tool for deception and stringing us along. In "Taking Tea With the Taliban," Michael Rubin documented the Bill Clinton administration's persistent policy of engagement with the Taliban and the determination of the administration to hold onto that policy in the face of Taliban aggression and obfuscation. Diplomats met with the Taliban every few weeks and "what resulted was theater . . . The Taliban would stonewall on terrorism but would also dangle just enough hope to keep diplomats calling and forestall punitive strategies." Engagement allowed the Taliban a reprieve so that they could better prepare and arm for an attack. They played to our cultural relativism by talking about the traditions of Afghan custom. "They engaged not to compromise but to buy time."[56]

Iran has learned the lessons of history better than we. Iran agrees to negotiate, then violates negotiated agreements and refuses to negotiate, then—when the international response is about to get strong—agrees to negotiate again. Although, in welcoming the negotiations Iran offered to stave off an Israeli airstrike, Secretary Clinton said the "window of opportunity" would not remain open forever, that window remained open for a perilously long time. Even though *those* talks fell apart, the administration swiftly expressed its desire to resume diplomacy.[57]

In a sobering, chilling reminder of the mentality that allowed Hitler to march forward with his plans and deceive the West, Shahram Chubin, senior associate in the Nuclear Policy Program at the Carnegie Endowment for International Peace, had recommended the following in 2011: "To be sure, there are risks that Iran could use negotiations to string along the international community, seek to divide the United States and Europe with counterproposals, and deflect further sanctions. But a U.S. initiative could counter these Iranian moves. A generous offer that meets Iran's minimum demand—for some enrichment—would reassure the international community and transfer the responsibility for any failure to the Iranian regime itself. This would put an end to the narrative of a vengeful, arrogant U.S.-led coalition dictating terms as a substitute for forcing a regime change and put responsibility for the prolonged crisis and its consequences where it belongs, thereby signaling that the nuclear dispute is about not Iran's rights but the regime's insistence on keeping control at home by ensuring continual crises abroad."[58]

In the face of being so obviously outplayed by the Iranians, some commentators noted a subtle but evident shift in the goals of the administration. Did the White House give up, they asked, on stopping the event of a nuclear Iran and decide instead to try to "contain" it? It behooves us to ask: Was there some willingness all along to accept a nuclear Iran if negotiations didn't work? (As early as December 2009, Robert Lieber and Amatzia Baram observed that "a number of influential policymakers and foreign policy analysts appear much too complacent regarding the prospects of a nuclear-armed Iran.")[59] Had the administration mapped out alternative policies for the day when Iran would be close to possessing a nuclear bomb?

Dictators use negotiations to buy time and to proceed on with their weapons programs and military buildup. They use words like *rights* and *equality* and *progress* to legitimize their regimes, and they also use such words to figuratively and literally "disarm" us. Worst of all, they use our silence regarding their atrocities and their oppression to keep their people in the hellish night of political prisons, rape rooms, torture chambers, and internment camps.

In March 2012, the UN released a report describing "a striking pattern of violations of fundamental human rights" in the Islamic Republic.[60] It noted that Iranian laws allowed human rights violators to act with impunity and cited an "alarming increase" in executions. It cited harassment and repression of students and imprisonment of dissidents and journalists. Declared Sarah Morgan and Andrew Apostolou of Freedom House, "Washington will only neutralize Iran by exploiting the regime's main vulnerability: its false claim to legitimacy. The ayatollahs' hold on power is inherently unstable because they have no popular mandate. Since staging a rigged election in 2009 to keep Iranian President Mahmoud Ahmadinejad in power, they have relied on repression and brutality to silence opposition, jailing journalists, torturing detainees, and executing critics (both real and imagined). Highlighting these crimes on the world stage and actively supporting Iran's dissidents, the United States can place a new more effective kind of pressure on Tehran and support the movement for democratic change from within. Focusing on human rights violations will allow the United States to expose the hypocrisy of the regime and remind Iran of its domestic troubles as it tries to expand power and influence."[61]

In addition to highlighting Iran's human rights abuses on the world stage, Saaed Ghasseminejad and Sara Akrami suggested the following measures in a November 2012 article entitled "Time for Regime Change in Iran": increasing sanctions on Iranian officials and their families through prohibiting travel and blocking bank assets; a Voice of America-type media program; an Internet-freedom project; isolation of Iran in the international arena; and efforts to unite Iranian opposition groups. Of course, it also would have been prudent: to confirm that containment (rather than prohibition) of an Iranian nuclear program was not acceptable by showing cohesion with our ally Israel; to make our resolve credible by not agreeing to negotiate every time Iran backed out of *previous* agreements; and to make our power formidable by exerting leverage in Iraq and Syria, strengthening our military alliances, and maintaining rather than decreasing our defense spending.

That this would have been the prudent course was borne out as Obama's second inauguration approached. In December 2012, the P5+1 powers got their hopes up again as they prepared for possible new talks with Iran amid signs that Iran's leaders might be willing to discuss scaling back nuclear activities in return for future sanctions relief. Even though Iran had rejected a similar deal earlier in the year (see above), the six powers agreed on new incentives for cooperation.

But the latest package of inducements did no good—it didn't even get Iran to the negotiating table. In January 2013, Iran told UN nuclear officials that it planned to add potentially hundreds of next-generation centrifuge machines to its main uranium-enrichment plant. The move would dramatically boost its ability to produce the fuel used in nuclear power plants and, possibly, in nuclear bombs. This did not stop the administration from getting its hopes up yet again. Next, the White House offered that it was open to *direct* talks with Iran. (Previously, the White House sought talks via the P5+1 group so as not to elevate a hostile Iran by offering one-on-one negotiations.) Iran slyly indicated that it *might* be open to direct talks.[62]

Thus, although Iran was now openly and unambiguously defying the 'international community' upon which the Obama administration pinned its hopes, the administration's response was to offer Iran one-on-one negotiations that bypassed the international community. Was the administration resorting to the 'unilateralism' it consistently decried for the sake of getting some agreement—any agreement—with Iran? At about the time of the second inauguration, it appeared that even this offer had backfired: Iran was seeking to acquire tens of thousands of highly specialized magnets used in centrifuge machines and was getting ever closer to a nuclear bomb.[63]

President Obama's actions (and his inaction) during his first term often seemed inexplicable in the light of supposed US goals. He verbally legitimized the Iranian regime and chose a gradual, minimalist approach to sanctions. He declined to speak out for human rights, choosing an approach that came at the expense of the Iranian people. He weakened our relationship with Israel and backed away from our strong geopolitical posture.

President Obama's approach to Turkey is also difficult to understand in light of supposed American-democratic purposes. In Obama's first years in office, Turkey remained a relatively moderate Arab state and an invaluable ally, but Turkey was backing away from recent democratic advances and its recent more moderate stance toward Israel and was allowing more Islamic influences in its secular government. Although

Turkey maintained a pragmatic rather than extremist foreign policy, in 2010, it voted "no" to a new round of UN sanctions against Iran.

Yet, Obama and Clinton did little, if anything, to encourage Turkey to turn back the other way. Instead, it was Turkey that influenced the Obama administration, for example, in its decisions not to include an Israeli warship in a NATO-run flotilla patrolling the Mediterranean, and not to invite Israel to NATO's May 2012 summit in Chicago. In an editorial, Jonathan S. Tobin puzzled over why President Obama emphasized his "friendship" with Turkish leader Recep Tayyip Erdogan at the very time that Turkey was jailing journalists and opponents of the ruling party, abandoning its long-standing alliance with Israel, and refusing to support the West on isolating Iran.

According to Jackson Diehl of the *Washington Post*, Obama expended more effort talking to the Turkish Prime Minister than to any other ally. In an interview with *Time* magazine, Obama told Fareed Zakaria that Erdogan was someone he had become friends with and with whom he had forged "bonds of trust." If Obama was using his friendship with the Turkish leader to encourage democracy and promote American interests, there wasn't evidence of it. In a nuanced article, Omer Taspinar of the Brookings Institution suggested: "It is still too early for a clear account of how the Arab Spring will affect Turkish foreign policy. In the new Middle East, Turkey will remain an important and able player. . . . Washington can help with stronger support for normalization of Turkish-Israeli relations and better coordination with Ankara on issues related to Iraq, Syria, and Libya."[64]

■ ■ ■

Although the Iranian regime successfully squashed Iran's own democracy movement, Iran faced a grave challenge in the Arab Spring—strategic, political, and ideological. By mid-2012, the Assad regime was under such pressure that it appeared, in the NATO secretary general's words, to be "approaching collapse." Iran was hated throughout most of the Sunni Arab world for its support of the Syrian butcher, and Assad's setbacks gave moderate Arabs hope. Even Hamas, utterly dependent upon Iranian funding, and Hezbollah, Iran's reliable proxy, were distancing themselves from Syria and Iran. Daniel Byman of the Brookings Institution wrote, "In the eyes of Al Qaeda and local Sunni

Jihadist groups, Iran is very much on the wrong side of this [Syrian] war. They tie Iran, correctly, to Bashar al-Assad's regime in Syria and the Nuri al-Maliki regime next door in Iraq . . . Throughout the Arab world, Iran's malevolent role is decried—a painful reversal for a regime that has long tried to lead this region."[65]

Although Iran used the Iraq War and the precipitous withdrawal of American forces—both of which neutralized Iraq's counterbalancing power—to dominate Iraq and the Persian Gulf, the rise of the Islamic State of Iraq and Syria (ISIS) was a wrench in Iran's plans. Especially frustrating to Iran was the fact that ISIS grew in part out of al-Qaeda groups Iran had at times supported in order to destabilize Iraq. Although it is Shiite, Iran backs Sunni extremists when it serves its larger goal of undermining Sunni, Israeli, and Western governments. Let us not forget that Shia Islam is a minority religion in the Middle East, with Sunni Islam the decided majority; this gives Iran an inherent disadvantage.

In a March 2012 interview with the *Atlantic*'s Jeffrey Goldberg, President Obama himself described Iran's predicament and even spoke positively of the impulse toward freedom: "Well, look there's no doubt that Iran is much weaker now than it was a year ago, two years ago, three years ago. The Arab Spring, as bumpy as it has been, represents a strategic defeat for Iran, because what people in the region have seen is that all the impulses towards freedom and self-determination and free speech and freedom of assembly have been constantly violated by Iran. [The Iranian leadership] is no friend of that movement toward human rights and political freedom. But more directly, it is now engulfing Syria, and Syria is basically their only true ally in the region."[66]

■ ■ ■

Obama's second term, and the inauguration of the new secretary of state, John Kerry, therefore provided a promising time frame for the United States to apply pressure on Iran regarding its support of Assad, sponsorship of terror, regional aggression, and steadily advancing nuclear program. Instead, complacent American policies smoothed the road for Iran. While continuing on with a minimalist response to Iran's nuclear program, the administration reaffirmed the domestic legitimacy and international standing of the Iranian regime. Obama and Kerry began the term with new outreach to Iran, which, as the term went on, increasingly included willingness to listen to Iranian ideas about how to solve Middle Eastern problems, and deferral to Iran on Syria.

By February 2013, Deputy Secretary of State William Burns, foreign policy advisor Jake Sullivan, National Security Council staffer Puneet Talwar, State Department nonproliferation advisor Robert Einhorn, and Ambassador to the United Nations Susan Rice were all directly engaging with their Iranian counterparts. In September, John Kerry and Iranian foreign minister Mohammad Javad Zarif met at the UN, marking the highest-level meeting between the United States and Iran in many years. President Obama, whose request for a personal meeting with the new Iranian president Hassan Rouhani at the UN was rebuffed, nevertheless exchanged letters with Rouhani, and followed up by telephoning him for the first direct contact between leaders of the two nations since before the 1979 Iranian revolution and takeover of the US embassy.

As the United States placed hope in engagement, outreach, and half-hearted sanctions, Iran expanded its nuclear enterprise. We have seen that by the end of Obama's first term, it was clear that Iran was playing a terribly clever game, and was using the negotiating process (more accurately, the promise of negotiations) to buy time, and cover, for its nuclear program. The IAEA reported that Iran was enriching uranium at a pace that would bring it to Israel's "red line" in just over seven months.

On human rights, the Iranian regime wasn't any more malleable. An August 2013 report by Amnesty International entitled "Iran: New President Must Deliver on Campaign Promises" would fall on deaf ears. Calling for basic freedoms and reforms, it noted that arbitrary arrest, torture, and other ill-treatment; impunity for human rights violations; and use of the death penalty remained prevalent. It pointed to President Ahmadinejad, in May 2013, signing into law revisions to the Islamic Penal Code of the Islamic Republic of Iran which "maintained cruel, inhuman and degrading punishments such as flogging, as well as stoning" and that accorded women inferior status before the law.[67] Human Rights Watch issued a similar plea. The International Campaign for Human Rights in Iran observed that Iran had significantly ratcheted up its efforts to repress minorities, and that the Revolutionary Guard Corps' latest crackdown marked a new phase in the regime's repression of Christians.

Nevertheless, during the second term, the administration continued to turn a blind eye and remained silent regarding the intensifying persecution of Christians in the Middle East. By then, it was widely suggested that the administration's determination to strike a nuclear deal and develop a cooperative relationship with Iran trumped everything else. In a November 2014 editorial in the *Daily Beast*, Senators Marco Rubio and Mark Kirk urged, "As the United States and its partners attempt to finalize a nuclear deal with Iran, we believe that the United States and other democracies must do more to stop and reverse these abuses."[68]

New "deadlines" for negotiations surpassed old deadlines, rendering the word meaningless. Extensions of deadlines were extended further. And Iran, not the United States and its allies, benefitted and prevailed. With Secretary Kerry and Foreign Minister Zarif engaging in diplomacy on the sidelines, Iran finally sat down to the negotiating table with the P5+1 powers and, in November 2013, signed a six-month interim agreement known as the Joint Plan of Action. In an incisive article, Michael Doran described the makings of the deal and noted that, in spite of assumptions to the contrary, the "moderate" Rouhani had little to do with it. It was, rather, a result of relatively minor Iranian concessions paired with significant US concessions:

> In April 2013, the Americans and their P5+1 partners met with Iranian negotiators in Almaty, Kazakhstan, where they offered to relieve the sanctions regime in exchange for the elimination of Iran's stockpiles of uranium that had already been enriched to 20 percent. This was concession number one, bowing to the longstanding Iranian demand for economic compensation immediately, before a final agreement could be reached. Even more important was concession number two, which permitted the Iranians to continue enriching uranium to levels of 5 percent—this, despite the fact that six United Nations Security Council resolutions had *ordered* Iran to cease *all* enrichment and reprocessing activities.
>
> Iranian negotiators rejected these two gifts—or, rather, they pocketed them and demanded a third, the one they coveted the most. Hailing the proposals by their counterparts as a step in the right direction, they criticized them for failing to stipulate the Iranian "right to enrich." There was a difference, they argued, between temporarily *permitting* Iran to enrich uranium to 5 percent and recognizing its

inalienable *right* to do so. If Obama wanted a deal, he would have to agree to shred the Security Council resolutions by offering, up front, an arrangement that would end the economic sanctions on Iran entirely and that would allow the Iranians to enrich uranium in perpetuity.

Obama's acceptance of this condition, the third and most important American gift, is what made the Joint Plan of Action possible. The American negotiators transmitted the president's acceptance to the Iranians in the backchannel, and then John Kerry sprang it on his hapless negotiating partners in November.[69]

The agreement restricted components of Iran's nuclear program and required new inspections while granting the right to enrich uranium and billions of dollars of sanctions relief. Domestic opponents questioned why we would lift sanctions for a deal that fell well short of stopping Iran's nuclear program when sanctions brought Iran to the negotiating table in the first place. Senators Menendez and Kirk prepared legislation that would impose sanctions-in-waiting if Iran failed to negotiate an acceptable final agreement. In a significant *Wall Street Journal* editorial, Senator Kirk and Congressman Eliot Engel argued:

> We believe the U.S. must exhaust all nonmilitary options to prevent Iran from achieving critical capability. Our most effective tool for avoiding a military strike is enacting harsher sanctions.
>
> In 2011, Congress implemented sanctions targeting Iran's central bank and oil exports. A year later, the U.S. blacklisted Iran's shipping, shipbuilding and energy sectors. The result? Since December 2011, Iran's currency lost more than two-thirds of its value while the regime's oil revenues were cut in half. So sanctions are working. But loopholes remain, and the pressure is nowhere near maximum levels.
>
> Iran continues to access billions in foreign-exchange reserves held in banks around the world. It continues to export more than a million barrels of oil per day to China, India, South Korea and Japan— by far, the regime's single greatest remaining source of revenue. And it continues to reap immense profits from mining, construction and engineering.
>
> American resolve is critical, especially in the next few months. By bringing the regime to the verge of economic collapse, the U.S. can convert that leverage into a diplomatic solution, forcing Iran to

comply with all international obligations, including suspending all enrichment-related and reprocessing activities.

We can go a long way toward achieving that goal by taking the rest of Iran's oil exports off the market, cutting off access to its overseas reserves, and blacklisting strategic sectors of the Iranian economy. [70]

The Obama administration announced its opposition to such sanctions, and actively strode to prevent them.

Israeli prime minister Benjamin Netanyahu called the deal a "historic mistake." Most Sunni Arab nations reacted with notable silence. Saudi prince Alwaleed bin Talal, who occasionally speaks for the royal family when issues are too sensitive for direct statements, called Iran a "huge threat" and said, "The Persian empire was always against the Muslim Arab empire, especially against the Sunnis. The threat is from Persia, not from Israel."[71] Hezbollah considered the deal "a great victory for Iran." Leading Arab officials voiced concerns about allowing Iran to maintain its enrichment program. Members of Saudi Arabia's royal family, including Prince Turki al-Faisal, said that Riyadh could seek to develop or buy nuclear weapons if more wasn't done to stop the program.[72] Indeed, as if tacitly acknowledging the advantage to an aggressive Iran the latest agreement constituted, under the direction of General James Mattis, the United States was allocating renewed military resources to the Persian Gulf, including F-22 stealth fighters dispatched to the United Emirates, missile defenses planned for Qatar, and deployment to the Middle East of the USS *John C. Stennis* aircraft carrier strike group.

Events in December 2013 were revealing. On December 3, Jay Carney called any new sanctions on Iran "bad faith," while a spokeswoman for the National Security Council indicated potential American willingness to allow Iran to *retain* an enrichment program as part of a final agreement. On December 19, a bipartisan group of thirteen Republicans and thirteen Democrats in the Senate formally introduced the Nuclear Weapon Free Iran Act of 2013. "Current sanctions brought Iran to the negotiating table and a credible threat of future sanctions will require Iran to cooperate and act in good faith at the negotiating table," said Senator Menendez. President Obama threatened to veto the bill.

Within the administration, optimism about Iran becoming a cooperative member of the international community and desire to develop "constructive partnership" with the Islamic Republic prevailed. When, in a February 2014 interview with CNN, John Kerry was asked why he didn't back more sanctions, he replied, "I believe it's a mistake now to break faith with a negotiating process when you're in the middle of the process. The United States of America agreed, together with our P5+1 allies—with Russia, China, France, Great Britain, Germany—all of them agreed that during the time we're negotiating we would not increase sanctions."

In March 2014, President Obama commemorated the Persian New Year by sending a short video to the Iranian people expressing hope that ongoing nuclear negotiations would "resolve the world's ongoing concerns with the Iranian nuclear program" and (as he had before) offering Iran a "new beginning" which would include a "better relationship with the United States and the Iranian people, rooted in mutual interest and mutual respect." Secretary Kerry sent his own message expressing hope that the Iranian people could "fulfill their aspirations" and suggesting additional educational exchanges between our countries. At least these messages did express concern for the Iranian people.

Contrary to these hopes, Foreign Minister Zarif said, "I can tell you that Iran's nuclear program will remain intact." Supreme Leader Khamenei said, "None of the country's nuclear achievements can be stopped, and no one has the right to bargain over it." President Rouhani said that Iran would accept "no limits" on its nuclear technology. Indeed, on May 12, The UN released a report that detailed extensive efforts by Iran to evade sanctions and illicitly obtain materials for its nuclear and missile programs. Just then, with the interim accords set to expire in July, on May 14 the P5+1 talks resumed. But parties to the talks reported no progress.

In June, the US tried another approach, once again holding bilateral talks with Iran. Again, no progress was reported. In an editorial in the *Washington Post*, Kerry said both sides were negotiating seriously, but that the July 20 deadline was "fast approaching." Acknowledging a discrepancy "between Iran's professed intent with respect to its nuclear program and the actual content of that program to date," Kerry reasonably asserted, "Iran's claim that the world should simply trust its words ignores the fact that the International Atomic Energy Agency has reported since 2002 on dozens of violations by Iran by its international nonproliferation obligations, starting in the early 1980s. The U.N. Security Council responded by creating four resolutions under Chapter VII, requiring Iran to take steps to address these violations. These issues cannot be dismissed; they must be addressed by the Iranians if a comprehensive solution is to be reached."[73] For his part, Rouhani said he doubted whether the United States had "adequate good will" to resolve the nuclear dispute, and even acknowledged that Iran violated sanctions saying, "Yes, of course, we bypass the sanctions. We believe they are illegal and crimes against humanity."[74]

In spite of Kerry's editorial, it was clear that Iran was using US eagerness to develop a good relationship to gain concessions on its nuclear program and, conversely, was using US eagerness to strike a nuclear deal to gain acquiescence to its moves in Iraq and Syria. In the meantime, Iran used the partial sanctions relief it had been granted increase its Middle East influence, fund terror and proliferate weapons. In September 2014, Iran announced that it was ready to cooperate with the United States against ISIS in exchange for a loosening of US demands regarding its enrichment program. In the same month, Reuters reported that the United States told Iran in advance of its intent to strike ISIS in Syria.

The United States would, from then on, treat Iran as a partner in the battle against ISIS, often simply handing Iran the lead. Iran would take that lead and run with it, steadily building its base in Syria and Iraq, and using the battle against ISIS as the excuse to further aid and defend Assad. While responding passively to the Assad regime's slaughter, the administration mostly accepted Iran's insertion of militias, weapons, and terrorists into the Syrian war. Instead, Iran's backing of terror groups in Syria, Iraq, Lebanon, Yemen and elsewhere; its uncompromising pursuit of nuclear weapons and ballistic missiles; its regional adventurism and worsening human rights violations, should have made containing Iran and stopping its nuclear program an *American foreign policy priority*.[75]

US coordination and information sharing with Iran in the battle against ISIS was egregiously shortsighted, as evidenced in Iran's predominance in Syria and Iraq. Although the United States maintains a strong security relationship with the Gulf States, America's cooperation with Iran and its anemic reaction to Assad's atrocities and Vladimir Putin's aggression gives them less reason to trust the United States and more reason to fear Iran—in itself a positive development for the Islamic Republic.

To Iran, our generous gestures only confirmed our cowardice and naïvete. Although the recurring assumption was that Iranian compromise was just around the corner if only we compromised ourselves, what recurred instead was the steady progress of Iran's nuclear program. Attempting to call Iran's bluff on the purely peaceful purpose of its nuclear program, on October 1, 2014, 354 House members sent a letter to Secretary Kerry stating that Iran must disclose the possible military dimensions of its program as part of a final agreement.

On October 16 and 17, the P5+1 held talks in Geneva, in which Iran again showed unwillingness to compromise on major issues. Yet the administration sanctioned Congress, not Iran, with a senior US official saying the White House would seek to bypass Congress in its implementation of any deal with Iran. "We wouldn't seek congressional legislation in any comprehensive agreement for years," he said. Handing Iran another advantage, the administration reportedly said it would allow the regime to possess 4,000 centrifuges, up from its earlier proposed limit (itself a concession) of 1,300.

Then, in November, against the promise it had made to allow negotiations toward a final deal (after the interim deal) to go on for only a finite period, the administration agreed to extend the talks beyond the November 24 "deadline" . . . all the way to June 30, 2015. Secretary Kerry and Vice President Joe Biden defended both that decision and the decision not to pass new sanctions at the Saban Forum on Middle East issues in Washington. They dismissed the idea that the lifted sanctions and the corollary increase in Iranian funds made it easier for Iran to stall in negotiations, and to advance its nuclear program and sponsorship of terror.

Evidence, however, pointed in that direction. The Foundation for Defense of Democracies and Roubini Global Economics said in a joint report that Iran's economy was expected to grow in 2014–2015 by 2.5 percent, after having fallen by 1.9 percent in 2013–2014 and 6.6 percent in 2012–2013, when full sanctions were in place.[76] An advocacy group called United Against Nuclear Iran noted that Iran had a sufficient stockpile of low-enriched uranium for as many as seven nuclear weapons, and that its stockpile continued to grow. The former head of the Department of Safeguards at the IAEA declared that Iran could have up to five thousand advanced-model IR-2 centrifuges, five times as many as it claimed to have. Stated the Foreign Policy Initiative, "These developments are particularly worrisome when one considers the extraordinary lengths to which Iran has gone to stall U.N. inspections of its nuclear program."[77]

Iran's status as a formidable regional power, which had seemed at risk in 2012, was now higher. Iran, Iraq, and Syria were cooperating in the battle against an increasingly fearsome ISIS, and, along with Russia, were employing propaganda to position the Assad regime as the only viable alternative to Islamist extremism. Russia announced that it would reverse an earlier ban and send S-300 missile defense systems to Iran. Iran unveiled new military hardware in the form of missiles, warships, and torpedoes. The Iranian Navy displayed new vessels equipped with cruise missiles and other rockets. In March 2015, when Iraqi forces and Shia militias tried to recapture the city of Tikrit from ISIS, the leadership role of Iran became clear. Militias confirmed that General Qasem Soleimani, the commander of Iran's Revolutionary Guards Quds Force, was personally orchestrating the operation. Notably, Human Rights Watch documented "ruinous" abuses by the militias following the recapture of Tikrit, which included looting, torching, and blowing up civilian houses and buildings in Tikrit and neighboring towns.[78]

Iran and its proxies were also decisively and forcefully influencing events in Syria, Yemen, and Lebanon. In expectation of sanctions being lifted altogether, Iran boosted weapons shipments to Hamas and Hezbollah. Clearly, as I argued in a March editorial, Iran's star was rising:

> Although Shiite Iran faces a formidable challenge in the rise of Sunni extremism in Iraq and Syria, Iran finds itself with unprecedented freedom to advance its aims. The Islamic Republic's chances for regional supremacy, global influence, and the spread of Shia Islam increase by the day. It is poised for a level of geopolitical and theological leverage that, only a couple years ago, looked highly unlikely. The exponential progress of Iran's nuclear and ballistic missile programs shifts the balance of power in the Arab world and beyond. China and Russia have strengthened their strategic relationship with Iran, while key ally Syria has been saved by Iran and its proxies. The United States has handed Iran the de-facto lead in the battle against ISIS, and has publicly rebuffed Iran's declared enemy Israel. Iran has thereby gained status not only in the charge against Sunni extremism, but also in the jihad against the Jewish state. With Assad's rising fortunes, Iran

has been able to reassert authority over Hezbollah and Hamas. Then, there is Iran's success in fortifying and installing friendly regimes by sponsoring terror and inciting sectarian violence. As Lee Smith puts it, "Iran now controls four historic Arab capitals—Baghdad, Damascus, Beirut, and Sana'a."[79]

As the Iranian regime's geopolitical position ascended, the Iranian people's situation deteriorated. The execution rate was escalating significantly under the "moderate" Rouhani. The International Campaign for Human Rights in Iran showed that nine government ministries under the direct authority of Rouhani were themselves responsible for ongoing human rights abuses. Human rights defenders and their families were being harassed, imprisoned, and tortured as part of a concerted strategy to silence dissent. Trumped-up charges and the systematic use of both physical and psychological torture in prisons continued. Discrimination against and persecution of women, ethnic minorities, and Christians continued as well. Women in prisons suffered horrible abuse and sexual assault. Amnesty International reported a "sharp rise in arrest, prosecution and imprisonment of independent journalists in Iran." In March 2015, the United Nations released a report documenting Iran's extensive and pervasive human rights abuses against its own people.

Then there were the 2011–2014 arrests and imprisonment of four Americans in Iran: former Marine Amir Hekmati, *Washington Post* Iran bureau chief Jason Rezaian, Christian pastor Saeed Abedini, and ex-FBI Agent Robert Levinson, who had yet to be released when the United States and its P5+1 "partners" signed the nuclear deal with Iran, and whose release was not a prerequisite for the deal.

In May 2015, six senators sent a letter to Secretary Kerry requesting information about the ongoing delay of the annual *Country Reports on Human Rights Practices*, which, by law, should have been released in February. In July, the State Department finally issued the incriminating reports, which critics suggested had been delayed to avoid embarrassing Iran during the nuclear negotiations. In brief remarks on the release of the report, Secretary Kerry stated, "The message at the heart of these reports is that countries do best when their citizens fully enjoy the rights and freedoms to which they are entitled." But Kerry's characteristic relativism was on full display:

The discomfort that these reports sometimes cause does more to reinforce than to undermine the value and credibility of these reports. Truth cannot successfully be evaded or dented or defeated, not over time. . . . And so my advice to any leader who is upset by these findings is really to examine them, to look at the practices of their country, and to recognize that the way to alter what the world thinks and the way to change these judgments is to alter what is happening in those countries. That is the advice that we also give to ourselves. There is nothing sanctimonious in this. There is zero arrogance. And we couldn't help but have humility when we have seen what we have seen in the last year in terms of racial discord and unrest. So we approach this with great self-awareness. But we also understand that when human rights is the issue, every country, including the United States, has room to improve.[80]

In spite of hopes and expectations that a breakthrough in Iran nuclear negotiations was imminent, June came with still more obstacles. Iran remained unwilling to consider a deal that lifted international sanctions in stages instead of all at once, or that allowed inspectors open access to military sites. Moreover, Iran was balking on its agreement to freeze or scale back much of its nuclear program in the next decade. Although President Obama said he was prepared to walk away from a deal unless Tehran accepted a tight monitoring regime, the United States and the five other powers negotiating with Iran agreed to extend talks past the (itself extended) June 30 deadline. Kerry stated, "If hard choices get made in the next couple of days and made quickly, we could get an agreement this week. But if they are not made, we will not. . . . We have our own sense of deadline."

Chairman of the United States Senate Committee on Foreign Relations Bob Corker was one of many within Congress, and without, who voiced strong concerns. Senator Corker pointed out that negotiators had moved from seeking a twenty-year agreement to a ten-year agreement that would allow Iran to continue developing an advanced ballistic missile program and research and develop advanced centrifuges. "I am alarmed by recent reports that your team may be considering allowing the deal to erode even further," Corker wrote. "Only you and those at the table know whether there is any truth to these allegations," he said, adding that he hoped they were inaccurate.[81]

Concerns compounded exponentially once the agreement was signed. Opponents saw the "Iran Nuke Deal" as unnecessarily advantageous to Iran: It unleashed hundreds of billions of dollars in frozen assets, and lifted the arms embargo. UN inspectors had to request written permission from Iran to inspect suspicious undeclared sites, and could be blocked from doing so for twenty-four days. US inspectors, whose technological savvy is crucial, were not permitted to take part in inspections. Yet Iran would receive American funding and technical assistance for its "peaceful" nuclear program. Uranium enrichment facilities at Natanz and Fordow, which are forbidden in multiple UN Security Council resolutions, were now merely constrained (at Natanz) and delayed (at Fordow). Iran was given an eight- to ten-year road map for research and development on advanced centrifuges, increasing its ability to build a bomb after the "sunshine period." The idea that "snapback" sanctions could be speedily enforced if Iran violated the deal had been dismissed by the Iranian foreign minister himself.

President Obama and his team initiated an all-out public relations campaign to win over Americans and pressure Congress to support the deal. In doing so, Secretary Kerry at times seemed more focused on Iranian concerns about us than on American or Sunni and moderate Arab concerns about Iran. In an interview with the *Atlantic*, Kerry complained, "The ayatollah constantly believed that we are untrustworthy, that you can't negotiate with us, that we will screw them . . . This [a congressional rejection] will be the ultimate screwing."[82]

The president went so far as to accuse congressional Republicans of finding "common cause with Iranian hard-liners" in opposition to the deal. Yet it was congressional Republicans and some congressional Democrats who questioned the administration's rapprochement with Iran's hard-line regime. They pointed to Iran's sponsorship of terror, regional aggression, intractability and duplicity in negotiations, support of the Assad regime, vilification of Israel and the United States, and repression. They wanted stronger sanctions so that the US could negotiate from strength, and opposed the lifting of sanctions in exchange for *promises* rather than *evidence* of nonproliferation. In a *USA Today* editorial, I argued:

> According to President Obama, there are only two ways of preventing
> Iran from obtaining a nuclear weapon and preventing an arms race:

this deal or war. Yet, those objecting to the deal believe *it* will make war and an arms race more likely. They predict that Iran will use the massive funds it will receive via sanctions relief to clandestinely perfect its nuclear program, to sponsor even more terror and to incite even more proxy wars. They believe that when Iran emerges from the temporary "sunshine period" it will be in a better position to build a bomb than it is today under painful economic sanctions. They are alarmed by inadequate inspections, and by last-minute concessions regarding ballistic missiles and advanced weapons, concessions the administration promised not to make. . . .

Clearly, the Iranian regime's power, influence, and capacity for regional and global troublemaking will increase. The deplorable Syrian Assad regime might regain ground as Iran, flush with cash, pours military resources into that country.[83]

Flying in the face of claims that the nuclear deal would decrease the likelihood of a Middle East arms race, President Obama (at Camp David), Secretary of Defense Ashton Carter (on a Middle East tour), and Secretary of State Kerry (in a follow-up summit with the Gulf Cooperation Council) all campaigned to reassure Middle Eastern partners nervous about Iran's growing power. They emphasized US willingness to engage in greater security cooperation and share military capabilities, including missile defenses. Saudi Arabia and other Arab states indicated that they would match Iran in nuclear capacity and ramp up defenses. Saudi Arabia also stepped up its involvement in Yemen, as a way to counter Iranian dominance. Indian defense procurements showed that it was preparing for a destabilized Middle East.

Indeed, there was reason to prepare. After the nuclear deal, Iran and Russia increased their coordination with each other and increased their military presence in Syria. Russian airstrikes on Syrian rebels threw the entire region into deeper crisis. In October 2015, Iran tested a new precision-guided ballistic missile in defiance of a UN ban. In December, the IAEA formally confirmed that Iran has repeatedly concealed, and continues to conceal, efforts to weaponize nuclear materials.

In the next two chapters, we will see that the stance of Obama, Clinton, and Kerry toward Egypt and Syria was similarly devoid of grand strategy, American democratic principles, and the humanitarian impulse.

CHAPTER 5

EGYPT AND THE ARAB SPRING
Skewed American Priorities

The Arab Spring, also known as the Arab Awakening, took many by surprise, including—perhaps especially—the Obama administration. It makes sense that an administration that based its outreach to the Muslim world on improving relations with autocratic and dictatorial regimes would be surprised by the opposition of the people themselves to those engagement policies, and by the people's own insistence upon democratic reforms.

The Arab Spring encompassed several popular movements: revolutions in Tunisia (where it all began) and Egypt; civil uprisings in Bahrain, Yemen, and Libya, the latter two resulting in the resignation of the country's longtime governments; major protests in Algeria, Iran, Jordan, Kuwait, Morocco, and Oman; minor protests in Lebanon, Mauritania, Saudi Arabia, and Western Sahara; and a peaceful revolt in Syria, which grew exponentially in reaction to the Assad regime's bloody policies. Most of these movements had in common that they arose out of opposition to repressive government, out of enthusiasm for democracy's promise of political representation, and out of frustration with the economic stagnation and lack of opportunity that are the combined result of the socialism and corruption that have long characterized Middle Eastern government.

By the time of the George W. Bush presidency, there were two currents shaking and transforming the Middle East—one toward Islamic extremism, the other toward political liberalization. Many in the West were blind to the latter. They claimed that Arabs, being culturally different from the West, didn't want democracy and wouldn't know what to do with it if they had it. They thought Middle Eastern nations were not "ready" for democracy because they had no democratic traditions. (Never mind that post-World War II Germany and Japan defied that logic; these Democratic allies had "traditions" that were far from democratic.) In addition, with cultural and moral relativism very much in vogue, influential intellectuals argued that antidemocratic regimes were just as valid as democratic ones, and that our best policy was to refrain from judgment and find "common interests."

In an article for the *Washington Post*, Elliott Abrams suggested that President Bush "had it right" in his emphasis on the "freedom deficit" in the Middle East and his understanding of the likely consequences: "While liberty expanded in many parts of the globe, these nations were left behind, their 'freedom deficit' signaling the political underdevelopment that accompanied many other economic and social maladies." Abrams asserted that the Bush administration would not have been surprised by the Arab Spring and would have reached out to the movement. He recalled what Bush said at a 2003 speech marking the twentieth anniversary of the National Endowment for Democracy: "Sixty years of Western nations excusing and accommodating the lack of freedom in the Middle East did nothing to make us safe—because in the long run, stability cannot be purchased at the expense of liberty." Bush concluded, "As long as the Middle East remains a place where freedom does not flourish, it will remain a place of stagnation, resentment and violence ready for export."[1]

Still, the United States' freedom agenda should not be over-credited with the Arab Spring. Tremendously brave Middle Easterners, who faced the likelihood of detention and torture by their regimes' dreaded security forces when they decided to insist upon free elections and democratic procedure, deserve the credit. As historian James L. Gelvin points out, "The freedom agenda took a top-down approach, assuming concessions by autocrats would, over time, lead to true reform. Hence, the attempt to get them to undertake electoral reform and hold free elections. Populations in the region, on the other hand, knew that no autocrat would make any concession likely to put him out of business."[2] Almost uniformly, Middle Eastern leaders had reneged on any promises of free elections, knowing such elections would lead to a swift end to their rule. Gelvin also points out that movements for democracy and human rights predated the freedom agenda, Syria's "Damascus Spring" in 2000 being one of the most notable.

When we look at Egypt's post-Mubarak travails, and at the crimes against humanity, rise of Islamist extremism, and cataclysmic war in Syria, we must ask whether the United States could have done more to encourage a positive strategic, political, and moral outcome. It seems safe to say that clarity of vision and purpose on the part of the United States would have helped. An enthused US stand for democratic principles, human and individual rights, and the rule of law was in order; as was an emphasis on our traditional alliance with Egypt and on the benefits to the new Egyptian government of maintaining close ties; and as was focus on Bashar al-Assad's annihilationist policies and on the geostrategic implications of the Syrian War.

Respect for sovereignty doesn't translate into doing nothing to foster political freedom or to strengthen our position in the world. Precisely because of ascendant factions in Egypt desiring Islamic rule, and precisely because of human devastation in Syria, an unambiguous stand for liberty as well as an attempt to maintain geopolitical influence were and are in order.

Turning to Egypt (and Libya) in this chapter, then to Syria in the next, we can see that no one has shown a greater interest in the Egyptian and Syrian outcomes than Iran. Iran has done everything conceivable to prop up the despicable Syrian regime. Iran immediately saw the Egyptian and Syrian upheavals as a chance to spread Islamist ideology, to disrupt the US-Egyptian alliance, and to destabilize and dominate the Levant. Unlike the Obama administration, the Iranian theocracy had planned for such an eventuality and seized the opportunity it presented.

President Ahmadinejad said Egypt's popular uprising showed a new Islamic Middle East emerging, one that would not be influenced by US and Israeli "interference." Tens of thousands of Iranians marched down Tehran's main boulevard in state-organized demonstrations, chanting in support of Egypt's revolt. Iran's state TV broadcast simultaneous live footage of events in Tehran and antigovernment demonstrations in Cairo. "Despite all the [West's] complicated and satanic designs . . . a new Middle East is emerging without the Zionist regime and US interference, a place where the arrogant powers will have no place," Ahmadinejad told the crowd.[3] Iran, of course, gave no such support to Iranian pro-democracy activists; to the contrary, it was stepping up harassment and arrests.

Once again, we are faced with the burdensome condition of the modern, interconnected world: If we do not take the lead in helping or influencing others, those who hate democracy and everything it stands for will take that lead and, in doing so, will harm the prospects for democracy and America-friendly alliances. (Our continuing challenge, and one we must pursue, is to be influential without violating national sovereignty or marginalizing the people.) While Iran worked feverishly to assert *its* influence in Iraq, Syria, Egypt, Yemen, and elsewhere, the Obama administration was careful not to promote democratic ideas and was halfhearted at best in working to keep any strategic leverage we already had in the Middle East.

During the Bush years, the national security team and State Department had worked both overtly in pressing democratic ideals and behind the scenes in pressing Egyptian President Mubarak toward democratic reform. Probably due to a combination of external and internal pressure, perhaps also reflecting differences with his father, by the time Obama came to office, Mubarak's son Gamal was promising reforms that included privatizing Egypt's economy and freeing it from the military's grip. But, the long-repressed Egyptian people didn't trust Mubarak's son and didn't want reform in the hands of Mubarak's handpicked successor. They wanted free elections and the chance to choose their leaders. Alaa Al-Aswany explained in *On the State of Egypt*, "The argument that Gamal Mubarak will be a civilian president for Egypt is [also] based on a fallacy, because what defines the nature of a regime is not the profession of president but the way in which he assumes power. . . . If Gamal Mubarak gains the presidency of Egypt, this will not put an end to military rule but merely add to it another disaster. Autocracy will be combined with a hereditary system, and after that what will there be to stop Gamal Mubarak from granting the presidency to his son or nephew?"[4]

Mubarak had stayed in power for thirty years through increasingly fraudulent elections. Asserts Shadi Hamid of the Brookings Institution, "If there was any doubt the status quo was untenable, the November 2010 elections—arguably the most fraudulent in Egyptian history—confirmed what many long suspected: reform through the existing system had become impossible."[5] Corruption and cronyism were endemic to the regime, as were detentions by the dreaded security services. The regime had particularly targeted the Muslim Brotherhood, who were subject to arbitrary arrests and disappearances.

Interestingly, Mubarak tolerated Egypt's growing number of Islamic extremists, including Salafists, many of whom had been influenced by Wahhabism while working in Saudi Arabia or had been swayed by Wahhabi broadcasts and preachers. The reason, according to Al-Aswany, is that Salafist Wahhabism actually *enables* despotic government because it urges Muslims to obey their rulers and forbids rebellion against Muslim leaders. Also interesting is the fact that, for the sake of appeasement, Mubarak periodically went along with Islamist demands to treat Christians like second-class citizens.[6]

Egypt's Christian Copts are one of the most ancient Christian communities, tracing their roots back to the Gospel writer Mark who brought Christianity into Egypt in the first century. They are also the largest Christian community in the Middle East. In the second half of the twentieth century, from the time of Nasser and through the time of Sadat and Mubarak, the Copts faced discriminatory policies which generally fell short of outright persecution. The Copts were an important part of Egyptian society even though they lacked equal rights and equal protection under the law. Scholar Edward Wakin documented the institutionalized stratification which favored Muslims, and the quotas for Christians in all areas of Egyptian life—government, education and business. Copts who dared to proselytize were regularly detained, while those who agreed not to make waves were granted certain benefits. Those Muslims who chose to harass and intimidate Christians could generally do so with immunity.[7]

Mubarak's regime was hard for Christians, but it was not at all as hard as Iran's or Somalia's or North Korea's or Saudi Arabia's. And it was not nearly as hard as it would be under Mohammed Morsi. The question that arises from a careful study of the Obama administration's Egypt policy is why—before, during, and after the revolution—it took outreach to Morsi and the Muslim Brotherhood so far.

■ ■ ■

By the time President Obama came to office, oppression of Christians by Muslim extremists had intensified, and Mubarak's government, under pressure itself, was doing little to stop it. In spite of Mubarak's often successful attempts to convince the West that Egypt was pluralistic and tolerant, numerous sources indicated that Egyptian authorities were not offering effective protection to Copts who complained of harassment, attack and rape by Muslim perpetrators. Coptic Christian complainants were often pressured by government authorities to engage in "reconciliation sessions" and were sometimes arrested themselves as a way for the government to avoid prosecuting alleged Muslim assailants. In *Persecuted: The Global Assault on Christians,* authors Paul Marshall, Lela Gilbert, and Nina Shea point to a 2010 letter written by eighteen bipartisan members of Congress to Hillary Clinton's State Department concerning allegations that Coptic girls were being subjected to "fraud, physical and sexual violence, captivity, forced marriage, and exploitation in forced domestic servitude or commercial sexual exploitation" and that financial benefits were being granted to those who forced conversion of the victims.

Of course, where the law favors some, it cannot be relied on to protect anyone. The Australian Government's 2010 Refugee Tribunal Report cited evidence that *both Coptic Christian students and Muslim Brotherhood students* were the subject of regular discrimination and mistreatment by government authorities.

In spite of the rise of Islamist extremism in Egypt, the majority of Muslims in Egypt were moderate compared to the extremists. They longed for political and economic reforms which would allow them more opportunity and a better life. Indeed, in the lead up to the revolution, Muslim youths, Christian youths, the educated class, women and secularists were all fed up with the lack of political freedom and the economic malaise that resulted from the Mubarak government's authoritarian policies. Given the wave of discontent throughout the Arab world, and given the inherent dangers to Christians in any revolutionary situation, it would have been an excellent time for the US government to take a principled stand for religious and political freedom; to speak out for limited government and human rights.

Protestors in Tahrir Square and other sites across Egypt demanded human rights and democracy, an end to the hated emergency law that had been in place since Anwar Sadat's assassination in 1981, and free and fair elections. Different groups and individuals, including the Muslim

Brotherhood, Christians, and secularists, came together in support of this cause. The April 6 Youth Movement, which initiated the revolt in Cairo, made explicit demands regarding democracy and human rights. Although some have attempted to rewrite history by defining the revolutions that began in Tunisia in terms of Islamic-extremist goals, this is misleading. James Gelvin delineates distinctions between the goals of the Arab Spring and the goals of organizations like al-Qaeda:

> Although protesters in various countries found inspiration and learned from protests elsewhere in the Arab world, each uprising was a national uprising, targeting a specific government against which protestors held specific grievances. Al-Qaedists believe that the Crusader-Zionist conspiracy against Islam obligates every Muslim to engage in "defensive jihad," which, for them, means armed struggle. Yet from Tunisia to Egypt to Bahrain, protesters embraced the tactic of nonviolent resistance. Finally, al-Qaedists believe that Muslims should obey the rule of God, not the rule of man, and that true freedom lies in obedience to Islamic law and freedom from the materialism and oppression of the West. Yet the central demands of the protesters include democratic governance—rule by the majority, not by the word of God—and respect for internationally accepted norms of human rights. These are certainly not al-Qaeda's ideals.[8]

Daniel Byman notes that the Arab uprisings actually removed one of al-Qaeda's reasons for being. Al-Qaeda won recruits by denouncing despotism and pitching itself as a revolutionary alternative to repressive Arab governments.[9]

Still, there was reason to fear that the Egyptian revolution, like so many before it, would take a radical turn. There are two things about the Egyptian revolution that those inside the US government would have immediately seen that the rest of us did not. First, the Egyptian military had a vested interest in the revolution because the military was vehemently opposed to succession of power to Mubarak's son Gamal, who was promising to free the economy from military control. The military influenced all aspects of Egyptian civil society, including the economy, and its oligarchical power was threatened by the prospect of reform. Second, although the revolution included a mix of various parts of Egyptian society, including youths eager for Western-style freedom, the best organized among them was the Muslim Brotherhood. Evidence indicates that most Brotherhood demonstrators were genuine in their desire for free elections. On the other hand, their philosophy and history were cause for concern over how committed to reform they would be once they achieved a higher place in Egyptian politics and society.

There was perhaps reason to engage with the Brotherhood since they were more moderate than other organized Islamist/Egyptian groups and since they occupied a strong position in the movement for reform. But there was also reason to fear and mistrust the Brotherhood and to put all kinds of provisos on any support we gave them. On the positive side, unlike the more radical Salafists, the Brotherhood had eschewed violence as a way of achieving its goals. Revolution against Mubarak, for the Brotherhood, was also revolution against the repressive political system that had denied them political opportunity.

Yet, both the long-term goals of the Brotherhood, and the ideological trajectory of the Brotherhood at the time of the Arab Spring should have given the United States major concerns about what the Brotherhood would do when and if it actually came to power. (The rising persecution and harassment of Egyptian Christians at the time should have added to these concerns.) The Brotherhood has always been clear about its goal of a global Muslim caliphate in which the Quran is the source of all law. Its slogan is "Islam is the Solution." The Egyptian Brotherhood had not wavered from commitment to Sharia Law nor from its refusal to recognize Israel's right to exist.

It imposed restrictive dictates on women, made racist declarations about Christians and Jews, insisted that the Coptic population was much smaller than it was, and saw political institutions as vehicles for Islamization. In addition, the group had taken a more radical turn by the time of the Arab Spring, and was marginalizing and forcing out young reformers who were more open-minded and pragmatic than the majority. In a 2005 interview with the newspaper *Azzman*, Mohammad Habib, key member of the Brotherhood's highest official body, the Guidance Council, had stated, "The Muslim Brotherhood rejects any constitution based on secular and civil laws, and as a consequence the Copts cannot take on the form of a political entity in this country. When the movement will come to power, it will replace the current constitution with an Islamic one, according to which a non-Muslim will not be allowed to hold a senior post, whether in the state or the army, because this right should be exclusively granted to Muslims. If the Egyptians decide to elect a Copt for the presidential post, we will issue a protest against such an action, on the basis that the choice should be ours."[10]

It is inconceivable that the US government would not know that an Egypt ruled by the Muslim Brotherhood would pose a threat not only to Christians, but to any Egyptians who didn't go along with the group's religious-political vision. So too, it is inconceivable that the US government was simply naïve about Mohamed Morsi's ultimate goals when he ran for president. In his years as a parliamentarian, from 2000 to 2005, Morsi sought to make civil society, the state and the private sector more in accord with the Quran's principles. While serving as the first president of the Freedom and Justice Party, which was founded in 2011, Morsi did, in his willingness to work with other groups, reveal the "pragmatic" side that the Obama administration praised. However he also revealed his dogmatic side, as he stated that the "two-state solution is nothing but a delusion concocted by the brutal usurper of the Palestinian lands," that it was "insulting" to suggest that damage from aircraft collision brought down the World Trade Center, and that no evidence had identified al-Qaeda terrorists as the "real culprits."[11]

A *USA Today* article entitled "Egyptian President's Aims Unknown" published just after Morsi won the presidential election, cited a cross-section of expert opinion and was picked up by newspapers around the world. Keeping in mind that, if *USA Today* had access to this opinion, the US government certainly did as well, the article warrants our attention:

> But his years spent studying in America have not dissuaded him from the most doctrinaire beliefs of the Muslim Brotherhood, which has called for religious law, segregation of the sexes and scorns the influence of the West and Israel, experts say. 'If you look at his public statements over time, he tends to say provocative things about the U.S. and Israel,' says Shadi Hamid, an expert in Islamist political parties at the Brookings Doha Center. . . . As a leader of the [Muslim Brotherhood] movement, Morsi is a firm believer in *sharia,* or Islamic law, as he made evident on the campaign trail. . . . 'He was a loyal brother, an enforcer.' . . . He is 'an icon of the extremists in the (Muslim Brotherhood),' says Eric Trager, an analyst with the Washington Institute for

Near East Policy who is in Cairo. Trager says Morsi rose to the top of the Brotherhood's cult-like hierarchy by adherence to dogma at each level of his ascent. He is one of the main authors of the group's 2007 platform that said women and Christians should not be able to run for president, a stand that was later dropped, he says. Morsi is not likely to make serious concessions to liberals and Christians despite promises to do so and will not give them positions of real power, Trager says.[12]

Clearly, there was no reason for the US government to be sanguine regarding Egypt's political outcome, and many reasons for the United States to be wary.

Thus, the Obama administration was privy to very troubling information about the Muslim Brotherhood and about Mohamed Morsi himself. At best, its assessment of the group and of the group's leader should have been very mixed. Nevertheless, even before the revolution provided the Brotherhood with vastly enhanced status and unprecedented opportunities, the White House treated the Brotherhood warmly rather than cautiously, and as a mainstream political party rather than as a controversial, or at least suspect, political/religious group.

After the revolution, the Egyptian military and the Muslim Brotherhood were, in the words of Stratfor Global Intelligence, "savvy powerbrokers" in that they were careful not to pose too great a challenge to each other, since they both had an interest in marginalizing other groups. The military used recurring street violence to "divide and conquer" and to keep the army's position strong, while the Brotherhood kept its own people off the streets in those cases where a military crackdown on protests worked to its advantage, in that it intimidated those looking for a different kind of change in Egyptian society. The military, in turn, allowed elections in which Muslim Brotherhood members were fully accepted as candidates. No wonder Iran immediately, chillingly, praised the revolution, predicting that it heralded an Islamic Middle East. (Shiite Iran supports Sunni extremists when it serves its larger goal of undermining Sunni, Israeli, and pro-Western governments.)

Given all of this—given the power vacuum created by the revolution, given Iran's overt interest in the outcome, given that Egypt was the United States' best Middle Eastern ally apart from Israel, and that that alliance was essential to Israel's existential concerns, it behooves us to ask: Why didn't the Obama administration put more effort into encouraging democratic reform and moderate political forces before the revolution occurred? Why did President Obama, after days of indecision over whether to support "stability" via the maintenance of Mubarak or the "stable transition" to a post-Mubarak government, then decide to insist that Mubarak step down immediately? Why did Mubarak have to "go now" if the much worse Ahmadinejad, and the much worse Bashar al-Assad, in the face of a much more widespread collapse of support, didn't have to "go now"? Why the one and not the others? Why didn't the administration use our substantial leverage to influence the rebellion, once it ousted Mubarak, toward continued friendly relations with the United States, *genuine* democratic reforms, and continued support of the peace treaty with Israel? After all, in addition to giving Egypt $2 billion a year, the United States routinely provided Egypt with military and technical aid and humanitarian assistance. Why not use all that aid and assistance to get more cooperation?

Instead, the Obama administration's reaction to events in Egypt lacked strategic or pro-democracy direction. In the words of one conservative columnist, the approach was "apathetic" and "dilatory." In the words of one liberal columnist, it was "uncertain" and "weak." Especially disturbing, *the only consistent Egypt policy, before, during, and after the January 2011 revolution, was reaching out to the Muslim Brotherhood.* Consider the following timeline of events.

In 2009: The White House invited the Islamic Society of North America (ISNA) to Obama's inauguration and had president of ISNA Ingrid Mattson deliver a prayer at the National Prayer Service. Previously, ISNA had been named an unindicted coconspirator in *US v. Holy Land Foundation*, which concluded that ISNA and such other groups as the Council on American-Islamic Relations (CAIR) had links with and were sponsoring the Hamas, an offshoot of the Muslim Brotherhood. Since her election as ISNA president in 2006, Mattson's apologias for the radical Wahhabi sect of Islam had gained a wide audience, while ISNA had become a supporter of the Wahhabi lobby. An editorial in *Investor's Business Daily* had this to say: "Outrageously, these dangerous fronts, cloaked as they are in religious garb, still enjoy charitable tax status. The IRS exempts their funding, much of which comes from the Middle East. And they are still free to lobby Congress, Homeland Security, and the

TSA against airport profiling and other anti-terror measures. Yet none are even registered as lobbyists."[13]

Also that year, Obama invited the Muslim Brotherhood to his Cairo speech as "special guests," infuriating Mubarak. The president was urged by Egyptian Christian Copts to mention their plight, but he devoted only half a sentence to their situation, while making a strong and repeated case for tolerance of Islam. He appointed a Brotherhood-tied Islamist, Rashad Hussain, as US envoy to the Organization of the Islamic Conference (now the Organization of Islamic Cooperation). He skipped the US National Day of Prayer but recorded a special message to Muslims at the start of Ramadan.

In 2010: The administration sent envoy Rashad Hussain to meet with the Brotherhood's Grand Mufti in Egypt. Obama's former associates, Weather Underground members William Ayers and Bernardine Dohrn, and CODEPINK cofounder Jodie Evans, spent much time in Egypt. (Evans was a fundraiser and financial bundler for Obama's presidential campaign.) This led, among other things, to Evans pleading with Mubarak's wife to allow 1,400 activists to cross from Egypt into Palestine for a march with thousands of Palestinians in Gaza. Egypt finally agreed to allow one hundred activists to cross into Gaza. This, in turn, led to weeklong marches and protests within Egypt, until the protestors reluctantly agreed to the Egyptian government's limit of a hundred.

The organizer of the "Gaza Freedom Flotilla"—designed to get supplies into Gaza and to challenge Israel's blockade—was a radical group called the Free Gaza Movement. Israel maintains a blockade around Gaza that causes great hardship for Palestinians; the blockade's existential reason for being is preventing missiles and rockets from being smuggled to Palestinian terrorists and lobbed into Israel. The flotilla consisted mostly of members of Muslim Brotherhood chapters, most of whom called for Israel's destruction. When Israel raided the flotilla, causing bloodshed and international condemnation, President Obama himself proposed an "independent inquiry" into Israel's action.

In 2011: As the Egyptian revolution heated up, but *before* Mubarak's exit, the administration indicated its acceptance of the Muslim Brotherhood's participation in Egypt's "political dialogue." The White House also declared that *all opposition groups* (including the Muslim Brotherhood) should be represented in the post-Mubarak government. In an

NPR interview in January, Secretary Clinton said it was in the "best interest" of the United States to have "more democracy, more openness, more participation." She also said, "Today, we learned that the Muslim Brotherhood has decided to participate, which suggests that they are now involved in the dialogue that we have encouraged."[14]

This stance was new for the United States and was big news. Headlines across the world read, "Clinton Welcomes Muslim Brotherhood Participation." It was one thing to welcome their participation after the fact; it was another to actively encourage it beforehand. Brotherhood participation in presidential elections was so controversial that, even after Mubarak's ouster, Brotherhood leaders *themselves* promised not to run for election.

The *New York Times* reported on January 4, 2011 that the administration was seeking "closer ties" with the Muslim Brotherhood, correctly adding: "The administration's overtures—including high-level meetings in recent weeks—constitute a historic shift in a foreign policy held by successive American administrations that steadfastly supported the autocratic government of President Hosni Mubarak in part out of concern for the Brotherhood's Islamist ideology and historic ties to militants." Asserted Senator Kerry according to the *Times*, "You're certainly going to have to figure out how to deal with democratic governments that don't espouse every policy or value you have."[15]

Adding to the supportive signals the Brotherhood received from the administration, the day before Mubarak resigned, the White House sent intelligence czar James Clapper to Congress to testify that the Brotherhood was a "moderate" and "largely secular organization" that had "eschewed violence" and had "no overarching goal, at least internationally." He added, "They have pursued social ends, betterment of the political order in Egypt, etc." No overarching goal? The slogan of the Brotherhood is "Allah is our objective; the Prophet is our leader; the Quran is our law; Jihad is our way; dying in the path of Allah is our highest hope." The Muslim Brotherhood sees Israel's demise as a political/spiritual mandate.

As if to publicly dispute Clapper's claims, the Brotherhood's spiritual (not secular) leader, Sheikh Yusuf al-Qaradawi, was given a hero's welcome in Tahrir Square. The Brotherhood vowed to tear up Egypt's thirty-year peace treaty with Israel and quickly worked to formally reestablish Egyptian ties with Hamas and Hezbollah. The timing was strange, then, when Obama again demanded that Israel relinquish land to the Palestinians, and the Justice Department announced that there would be no further prosecution of Muslim Brotherhood front groups for funneling millions to Hamas. In a break from US tradition, the administration announced in June that it would formally recognize and resume diplomatic contact with the Egyptian Muslim Brotherhood. *Secularists and Christians received no comparatively supportive signals from the administration.*

A number of meetings between US Ambassador Anne Patterson and Brotherhood members ensued shortly after the revolution. Egyptian Christian human rights and religious rights activist Michael Meunier reported that the ambassador seemed to favor the Brotherhood and hardline Salafists over the secularists and Christians. In fact, she turned down requests from heads of political parties and other secularist politicians.[16] Deputy Secretary of State William Burns and Senator Kerry sent similarly supportive messages by visiting Muslim Brotherhood headquarters and talking with one of their revolutionary leaders, Khairat El Shatar, whom Kerry went so far as to publicly praise.

Still, Egypt's Brotherhood leaders publicly stated that they would not run a candidate for president and would not compete for more than a third of the seats in a new parliament. *Rather than attempting to publicly hold them to this pledge, Obama and Clinton again publicly offered support for their participation in Egyptian elections.* "It's in our interests to engage with all of the parties that are competing for parliament or the presidency" a senior US official told Reuters, on condition of anonymity.[17] The Brotherhood formed the Freedom and Justice Party for upcoming elections, with Dr. Saad al-Katatni as its leader. The new party's spokesperson noted that "when we talk about the slogans of the revolution—freedom, social justice, equality—all of these are in the Sharia" (Islamic law).

In 2012: In January, Islamists (the Muslim Brotherhood and the more extreme Salafists) won 72 percent of the seats in the lower house of Egypt's parliament. The Brotherhood itself won 235 out of 498 parliamentary seats. The Brotherhood party's deputy leader, Dr. Rashad al-Bayoumi, had said earlier in the month that the Brotherhood would not recognize Israel "under any circumstance" and that Brotherhood members would never meet with Israelis for negotiations. "I will not allow myself to sit down with criminals," Bayoumi said. He went on to say that the Muslim Brotherhood would take legal procedures toward canceling the peace treaty between Egypt and Israel.

Nevertheless, White House press secretary Jay Carney urged listeners not to "judge the disposition" of a government and parliament that was only "just beginning to take shape," while Hillary Clinton emphasized that "what parties call themselves is less important than what they do." What was important, she said, was the Brotherhood's adherence to democratic procedures. But, *FrontPage Magazine* broke the story that the State Department's special coordinator for Middle East transitions and long associate of Muslim Brotherhood apologists, William Taylor, and his office, had been giving Egyptian Islamists training to prepare for the election contests. Taylor justified this by saying assistance was available to all parties and that "sometimes Islamist parties show up, sometimes they don't."[18]

The Department of Homeland Security issued new guidelines that empowered Brotherhood members as interlocutors with Muslims in the United States and required FBI training materials to be reviewed by Muslim community leaders and interfaith groups. The White House issued its own "Strategic Implementation Plan for Empowering Local Partners to Prevent Violent Extremism" that effectively guaranteed Muslim organizations a say in its policy guidelines. The State Department announced that Deputy Secretary of State Bill Burns met with Mohamed Morsi, the head of the Brotherhood's Freedom and Justice Party, in Washington's highest-level outreach to the group and as part of a series of meetings between US officials and Egyptian political leaders. Morsi welcomed the meeting and called on Washington to adopt a "positive position concerning Arab and Muslim causes." Hillary Clinton described all of this as "reengagement in light of Egyptian developments."

She made such statements even though the marriage of convenience between the Egyptian military and the Brotherhood was very much in evidence. By January 25, 2012, the military junta and the Muslim Brotherhood had officially made their peace and formed a power-sharing agreement. Caroline Glick observed,

> This is bad news for women and non-Muslims. Egypt's Coptic Christians have been under continuous attack by Muslim Brotherhood

and Salafist supporters since Mubarak was deposed. Their churches, homes and businesses have been burned, looted and destroyed. Their wives and daughters have been raped. The military massacred them when they dared to protest their persecution. As for women, their main claim to fame since Mubarak's overthrow has been their sexual victimization at the hands of soldiers who stripped female protesters and performed "virginity tests" on them. . . . What they [the Western media] fail to recognize is that the Islamic fundamentalists now in charge of Egypt don't need a constitution to implement their tyranny. All they require is what they already have—a public awareness of their political power and their partnership with the military.[19]

Egyptians would have two choices in the spring presidential elections—one a member of the Muslim Brotherhood (Mohamed Morsi), and the other Hosni Mubarak's last prime minister and part of the military establishment. Reported Sarah El Deeb of the Associated Press, "Whoever wins after two days of voting, Egypt's military rulers will remain ultimately at the helm, a sign of how Egypt's revolution has gone astray 16 months after millions forced Mubarak to step down in the name of freedom."[20]

By May of 2012, it was clear that the lack of a new constitution and the intentional exclusion of pro-democracy groups from the new government had undermined the government's legitimacy. Morsi won the June 2012 presidential election, and indeed reneged on his promise of forming a "unity government." While other groups boycotted the election due to the collaboration between the hated military and the Brotherhood in the run-up to the election, Brotherhood activists refused to participate in the boycott.

Muslim Brotherhood leaders had themselves offered and pledged not to run a candidate for president. But that was according to the old rules—under which a party that described Sharia law and the destruction of Israel as goals was viewed with alarm. *Obama and Clinton themselves threw out the old rules.*

The Obama administration's support of the Muslim Brotherhood helped legitimize the group as the rightful representative of Egyptian people, when, actually, its popularity and place in Egyptian society was tenuous. Michael Wahid Hanna observed that the administration had given "outsized attention on the cultivation of ties with the now ascendant Muslim Brotherhood, often heedless of broader Egyptian political dynamics." He went on, "The United States cannot micro-manage Egyptian politics, but it retains real influence and it can, at the very least, attempt to staunch negative trends as opposed to reinforcing moral hazards. The current Egyptian government now believes in its own centrality and strategic significance, and it further believes that it has the uncritical support of the United States and the international community."[21]

Morsi moved quickly to use his victory to maximize Muslim Brotherhood control of Egyptian government and society. Like all would-be dictators (including Hitler, Pol Pot, and countless others as they came to power), he claimed he stood for *unity* and urged his countrymen to put aside their differences. "This national unity is the only way to get Egypt out of this difficult crisis," said he upon coming to power. Of course, unity would mean oppression of those who didn't agree with Brotherhood-Islamist goals, and the real goals of the Brotherhood would soon become apparent. Morsi issued edicts that granted him near absolute power. He tacitly accepted Brotherhood violence against and intimidation of Christian Copts. He pushed a constitution that declared Sharia law "the main source of legislation" and moved to undo the independence of the judiciary. As the military used force to intimidate civilians and Islamists demonstrated their release from Mubarak-era restraints, the position of Christians, moderates, and women in Egypt deteriorated rapidly. In spite of the huge risks incurred by expressing opposition to the increasingly thuggish government, Egyptians would take to the streets en masse in November 2012 to protest rigged elections and the "unprecedented assault" on the judiciary and its rulings.

■ ■ ■

Engagement and outreach to Muslim Brotherhood leaders in the spirit of respecting the wishes of the Egyptian people, in the attempt to encourage continued close relations between the United States and Egypt, or in the attempt to encourage moderation on the part of the Brotherhood, are one thing. But the lack of demonstrated US enthusiasm for legitimate democracy and individual rights, and the lack of demonstrated US concern for Israel's rapidly deteriorating position as

Egypt's commitment to peace wavered (and its likelihood of soon facing a nuclear Iran), must give us pause.

Where, in all of this, was the American tradition of combining geopolitical strategy with advocacy of democratic principles? Stated Human Rights First in a paper on the one-year anniversary of the Egyptian uprising, "The U.S. government should now focus on delivering a sustained clear message about its policies and goals in Egypt, one that emphasizes U.S. support for civilian democratic rule. . . . The only way to advance democracy is by implementing the democratic process and building safeguards for democratic rights and freedoms as the process moves forward."[22] But Obama and Clinton spoke up for democracy rarely, and when they did, their speech lacked direction and conviction. They did not use US leverage to safeguard the democratic process or to promote democratic principles. In addition, their foreign policy team focused far too little on the strategic consequences of the Egyptian upheaval.

This is not to say that the administration was wrong in attempting to forge relations with the elected Egyptian Muslim Brotherhood; American policy has often included trying to influence activist groups toward more moderate means and ends by forging ties with them. Moreover, we cannot support democracy in the Middle East without also accepting that voters might very well vote Islamists into power. The question is, rather, whether we should have taken our support of the Brotherhood so far, and whether we did enough to support other freedom-seeking Egyptians: those who relied on the fact that power was about to devolve away from Mubarak and had placed hope in reform, and those who had marched in rebellion against the regime itself in hopes of bringing democracy and the rule of law to their country.

Clinton insisted that it was not "who" was in power in Egypt that mattered, but "what" they chose to do. By her own logic, then, why wouldn't we have made the continuation of billions of dollars in annual aid to Egypt contingent upon the elected Brotherhood's initial promise to recognize Israel's right to exist and to perpetuate Mubarak's peace agreements, and upon an improvement in respect for human rights and individual rights? Instead, in March of 2012, the White House indicated that Secretary Clinton would use her "waiver authority" to release at least part of the $1.5 billion in aid to Egypt.

Democratic senator Patrick Leahy expressed disappointment in the decision, saying, "I know Secretary Clinton wants the democratic transition in Egypt to succeed, but by waiving the conditions we send a contradictory message. The Egyptian military should be defending fundamental freedoms and the rule of law, not harassing and arresting those who are working for democracy. They should end trials of civilians in military courts and fully repeal the emergency law, and our policy should not equivocate on these key reforms."[23] Republican Kay Granger, chairwoman of the state and foreign operations subcommittee of the House Appropriations Committee, also objected to the decision, stating, "I am disappointed by the timing of the Secretary's decision to issue a partial waiver of restrictions on FMF [foreign military financing] funds for Egypt while the Egyptian government's transition is ongoing. The State Department needs to make the case that waiving the conditions is in the national security interest of the United States."[24] David Kramer, president of Freedom House, chimed in, "The decision to waive the conditions, partially or in full, on military aid sends the wrong message to the Egyptian government—that U.S. taxpayers will subsidize the Egyptian military while it continues to oversee the crackdown on civil society and to commit human rights abuses. . . . A resumption of military aid also sends the wrong message to the Egyptian people—that we care only about American NGO workers, not about the aspirations of the Egyptian people to build democracy."[25]

Why would Secretary Clinton *not* take a clear stand for human rights and the rule of law in Egypt as did Senator Leahy, and why would she *not* use financial leverage to press for improvement in these matters, as Senator Leahy urged? I use the word *clear* because Clinton did *on occasion* speak up for democratic procedure and "rights" in Egypt and elsewhere. Such was the case in her speech to the US-Islamic World Forum at the Brookings Institution in April 2011. Clinton eloquently pointed to the "myth that governments can hold on to power without responding to their people's aspirations or respecting their rights; the myth that the only way to produce change in the region is through violence and conflict; and most pernicious of all, the myth that Arabs do not share universal human aspirations for freedom, dignity, and opportunity." She offered US partnership in pursuing democratic goals and emphasized the importance of economic reform and minority rights, including rights for women and women's inclusion in government.

It was a good speech, but troubling questions remained. Why would President Obama and Secretary Clinton do so little to support our ally Israel and so little to preserve the foundational requirements of our alliance with Egypt? And here's a particularly troubling question: Why did the administration remain mostly silent and indifferent about the persecution of Christian Copts, secular reformist groups, and women in the new Egypt? As journalists Frida Ghitis and Caroline Glick, David J. Kramer of Freedom House, Victor Davis Hanson of the Hoover Institution, and others have skillfully reported, civil society itself was imperiled by the turn of events in Egypt.

Ghitis reported on a dramatic turning point in August of 2011. Tahrir Square "became the scene of a stunning change at the vanguard of the revolution, when Egypt's Islamists shed their cloak of unity with secular liberals." She continued:

> Leaders of the April 6th movement, religious parties, and leftist groups had agreed to a demonstration of solidarity without religious banners or slogans that might divide them. But liberal groups were dumbfounded when the Muslim Brotherhood and Salafist groups started unfurling banners denouncing secularism and calling for religious law. . . . Days later, in actions one liberal blogger called "our Kristallnacht," the young idealists suffered another painful blow. When they least expected it, the army went after their last remaining sign of strength, a tent city at Tahrir. Making matters worse, everyday Egyptians pitched in to help the Egyptian army. When hundreds of soldiers started beating the protestors and shooting in the air, large crowds of Egyptians joined them, chanting, "Allahu Akbar."[26]

After the crackdown in August, Egypt's Supreme Council of the Armed Forces continued to brutally attack demonstrators. In addition, it prosecuted regime critics in military tribunals, assaulted female protestors, and maintained the hated emergency law under which Mubarak had ruled.

In October 2011, state action took an explicitly anti-Christian turn. When Christian Copts staged a peaceful protest in reaction to the torching of a church and other displays of intimidation, the police response was cruel and brutal. According to Coptic groups themselves, who produced photographs to prove it, a massacre ensued. Muslims who joined the demonstration "seemed to split between those who sided with the military and those who tried to shield the Christians."[27]

On Copticliterature.wordpress.com, we find an outcry not only against the brutality of the new Egyptian regime, but also against the small-hearted response by the US and British governments: "The responses of Britain and the United States of America were particularly troubling. Their politicians, sadly, did not match their nations in their outrage as newswires cabled and reported the bloody Sunday in Cairo. What did President of the United States of America—*that great country which the Copts love and look for as leader of the free world*—[have] to say about the massacre of the peaceful and unarmed Copts by Egypt's army? I will simply copy the White House statement on the event (it calls it 'violence' and does not mention the word 'massacre')."[28] (italics mine)

The White House memorandum that the Coptic writer went on to cite was a sickening addition to multiple instances in which President Obama described the slaughter of innocents by murderers-in-power as "violence" between two flawed sides. It stated: "The President is deeply concerned about the violence in Egypt that has led to a tragic loss of life among demonstrators and security forces. . . . Now is a time for restraint on all sides so that Egyptians can move forward together to forge a strong and united Egypt."[29] The memorandum stated the "belief" that the rights of minorities, "including Copts," must be respected, but ended by giving Prime Minister Essam Sharaf credit for calling for an investigation and appealing to "all parties to refrain from violence."

After the massacre, more violence against Christians—burning of churches, bullying on the streets, forced confessions for crimes not committed—occurred, and our president and secretary of state remained silent. This moral equivalence and indifference to human suffering—this verbal gift to tyrants by way of calling murderous crackdowns on peaceful protestors "violence"—is an affront to everything the United States stands for and has fought for. Where is the outcry from American citizens in response to this degradation of the American tradition? Yes, there was some ardor in response to the harassment and detention by the Egyptian government of our own citizens working for NGOs. But where was the passion for our fellow human beings? It would be nice if our leaders encouraged, rather than discouraged, the oft-observed American caring for the world's oppressed.

By April 2012, Egypt's Coptic Orthodox Church was announcing its withdrawal from the constitutional assembly's drafting of a new constitution, saying its domination by Islamists made Coptic participation "pointless." Other liberal parties joined in announcing their withdrawal from the assembly, seeing their hopes for representative government as already lost. Given the administration's early support for Brotherhood participation in Egypt's government, this would have been a good time to pressure the Brotherhood to make *participation* palatable to Christians and others who had been excluded and/or were threatened by the new power structure. Again, by Secretary Clinton's own logic, if it is not who rules but what they do that matters, why the silence in response to the actions of Morsi and the military? Why the nonresponse to the outcry of Egypt's real reformers?

As early as September 2011, human rights groups estimated that at least one hundred thousand Copts had left Egypt since the revolution.[30] Many remaining Copts were denied property rights and protection of the law. Coptic-owned businesses were harassed, while Christians reported that they were being publicly taunted and maligned. There was a dramatic upsurge in attacks on Coptic churches, and the Brotherhood and the Egyptian military chose to look the other way. No wonder the US Commission on International Religious Freedom asked the State Department to place Egypt on its list of "countries of particular concern" regarding the egregious violation of religious freedom. The State Department declined, saying it preferred to work with the Egyptian government to improve conditions for Christians.

At least Hillary Clinton did, in regard to the broader issue of religious tolerance, take a verbal stand—not a passionate (or consistently taken) stand, but a stand. In the release of the State Department's report on international religious freedom in September 2011, she said, "Hatred and intolerance are destabilizing. When governments crack down on religious expression, when politicians or public figures try to use religion as a wedge issue, or when societies fail to take steps to denounce religious bigotry and curb discrimination based on religious identity, they embolden extremists and fuel sectarian strife. And the reverse is also true: When governments respect religious freedom . . . they can help turn down the temperature. They can foster a public aversion to hateful speech without compromising the right to free expression. And in doing so, they create a climate of tolerance that helps make a country more stable, more secure, and more prosperous."[31] Clinton was careful to couch her plug for religious freedom in terms of its practical benefits; as usual, she was careful not to take an outright, forthright moral position.

That was perhaps the first Obama administration's most troubling flaw. It lacked a moral compass because it thought morality was the old-fashioned provenance of right-wingers. In the popular relativist view, there is no better and worse, high and low, beyond each culture's or each person's definition of these things. Morality, like all codes of ethics or laws, including the US Constitution, is "organic," evolutionary, and dependent upon the particularities of each time and place. It is something which individuals, groups, and even political factions can choose to live with or to replace. Morality is "constructed"; it has no foundation in God or permanence in objective truth.

Why, then, would progressive leaders choose to be beholden to it? Why would they be so "arrogant" as to try to hold other countries to a "subjective" moral standard? Sure, some governments are so abhorrent that, being human, American progressive leaders cannot help but object to their dehumanizing policies. But today's progressives are constrained by the view that politics at its best is political "science," and that America, if it is ever to redeem itself, must become "non-judgmental." (Never mind that the concept of redemption is itself a moral one.) They are bound by the assumption that morals are merely "norms" and by the belief that central planners, whose plans are supposedly based upon social-scientific expertise, know better than the average man or woman how to move society forward. (Never mind, that by their own logic, their own dictums are disputable and transient.)

Related to the supposed nonjudgmental tenet of progressivism is progressivism's inability to see radical Islam and its promotion of worldwide jihad against "infidels" for what it is. As Michael Youssef put it, "Americans need to realize that an extreme sect of Islam has declared war on Western civilization, on the United States of America, and on Christians and Jews. While the War on Terror is not a religious war— that is, not a war of one religion versus another religion—we must realize that religious beliefs and ideology drive the hostility at the heart of the conflict." He noted that regardless of *our* stance, "an extremist form of Islam chooses to be at war with us," and asserted, "America is losing the war of ideas."[32]

Political philosopher Leo Strauss dissected the amoral theories of mid-century American academic life and knew they would have big consequences for the American polity. Said he, "According to our social science, we can be or become wise in all matters of secondary importance, but we have to be resigned to utter ignorance in the most important respect: we can't have any knowledge regarding the ultimate principles of our choices, i.e., regarding their soundness or unsoundness; our ultimate principles have no other support than our arbitrary and hence blind preferences. We are then in the position of beings who are sane and sober when engaged in trivial business, and who gamble like madmen when confronted with serious issues—retail sanity and wholesale madness." He added, "Once we realize that the principles of our actions have no other support than our blind choice, we really do not believe in them anymore. We cannot wholeheartedly act upon them anymore. We cannot live any more as responsible beings."[33]

Today, "wholehearted" belief in American principles, or in any principles, is rare in American political circles. The biggest problem in Washington today is that the social engineers have come to town. They are in bureaucracies and think tanks, in Congress and the courts, in the State Department and the Executive Office. Too many in these positions contradictorily believe they know better than the rest of us how to achieve the betterment of society, while rejecting the very significance and meaning of the word *better* for the sake of supposed social-scientific impartiality.

Of course, the one place moral relativists are willing to stand on principle is in regard to their own interest group. Beholden to group politics that downplay individual rights but play up the importance of "who gets what, when, where, and how," they are willing to fight for their own. Thus, as secretary of state Hillary Clinton was an enthused supporter of women's issues and rights and inspired women with her powerful advocacy. In a *Newsweek* interview she said, "I have been working hard to integrate women's rights as a cornerstone of our foreign policy," adding, "They are often discriminated against, even brutally enslaved, or simply not able to contribute to society or realize their potential."[34] (If only Clinton also spoke out for other groups, like Iranian youths and Syrian civilians, who desperately needed her support.) The State Department's 2012 budget included $1.2 billion in programs specifically targeting women. During a 2009 visit to Afghanistan, Clinton unveiled the $36 million Ambassador's Small Grants Program to Support Gender Equality. Still, it must be stipulated that Clinton's support for women was tempered to the point of being weak when it came to women in places like Egypt and Iran—places the administration was determined to "engage" with. The response of the administration to the brave, principled, and intelligent Muslim women who produced the documentary *Honor Diaries*—to promote awareness about "honor killings" and persecution and abuse of women and girls in Muslim countries—was indifference.[35]

The more we look into which groups the administration chose to support and which it did not, the more troubling it gets. In a November 28, 2012 blog entitled "Obama's Response to Iran Compared with His Response to Egypt Raises Troubling Questions," I argued:

> Compare his [Obama's] response to the Green Revolution in Iran with his response to Egypt's revolt against Hosni Mubarak. Why did President Obama ignore the plight of Iranian protestors and their pleas for support while being quick to support protests against Mubarak? Egypt was an essential American ally in desperate need of domestic reform; Iran was a declared "enemy" of America, so fanatical that reform would never be enough. Why support for Egyptian youths, but not Iranian youths? *Why was Mubarak told by Obama to "go now," if the much worse Ahmadinejad, in the face of a more widespread collapse of support, was not?* . . . .
>
> As Egyptian Islamists ran for and won elections, reneged on promises of representative government, and took hostile action toward secular-reformist groups, Christian Copts, women, and Israel, U.S. supportiveness remained. . . . Obama's passivity in the face of Morsi's recent assumption of dictatorial powers continues the trend. It is significant that Obama and Clinton have not sided with protestors against Morsi, as they did with protestors against Mubarak. It is significant that they sided against Mubarak, but not against Ahmadinejad. The United States is a country that has lost its way.

And, we can ask a related question: Why was Mubarak told to "go now" if the much worse Bashar al-Assad of Syria, in the face of a much more widespread collapse of support, was not?

Speaking at the Carnegie Endowment for International Peace in July 2012, Clinton did at least indicate that she was aware of the Egyptian Christian's plight: "I heard from Christians who want to know that they will be accorded the same rights and respect as all Egyptians in a new government led by the Islamist party. . . . They wonder, will a government looking explicitly to greater reliance on Islamic principles stand up for non-Muslims and Muslims equally. Since this is the first time Egypt has been in this situation, it's a fair question."[36] Indeed, it was a fair question, which should have led to another: What could the United States do to encourage a more positive outcome? By then, Christian Copts were fleeing Egypt in even greater numbers and discrimination against and targeting of Christians were even worse.

Not surprisingly, when Secretary Clinton visited Egypt in the same month, she was met with widespread protest from Christian Copts and secular activists, who objected to what they believed was the administration's role in helping the Muslim Brotherhood consolidate power. Citing the stream of meetings between high-level administration officials and Muslim Brotherhood leaders, Michael Meunier explained frustration over US policy: "The MB used these high-level meetings to tell the Egyptian people that the US is supporting them and does not object to their rule. Many of us reached out to US officials at the State Department and complained that the US policy regarding the MB was putting the secular forces in Egypt at a disadvantage because it seemed to be propping the MB, but our concerns were dismissed. We warned of the MB's desire to impose Sharia law once in power and the grim effect it would have on the rights of the millions of Christians and moderate Muslims, and on women and children, yet all our warnings were dismissed."[37]

Those Egyptians who had hoped the new constitution would secure freedoms and buoy civil society were to be disappointed. The problem was not just that the constitution itself did not adequately protect rights of minority groups and individuals. The problem was that, in the spirit of all would-be dictators, President Morsi issued extra-constitutional decrees, placed restrictions on the press, clamped down on the opposition, and discriminated against and marginalized certain groups. Pressure upon Egyptian journalists, Christians, secularists, and human rights groups, combined with pressure upon NGOs working within Egypt for democratic reform, quickly signaled that America's "outreach" to Morsi did not translate into improvements in the lives of most Egyptians, nor into the strengthening of US/Egyptian strategic ties. When threats to American NGO workers were ultimately resolved with their release, the administration took no stand for the Egyptians themselves who were still facing criminal charges for their association with the NGOs.

In what appeared to be a positive breakthrough on the geopolitical front, in November 2012, Morsi helped broker a cease-fire between Israel and Hamas. He received lavish praise from President Obama and Secretary Clinton for doing so, with Clinton lending the occasion visibility with a brief stop in Egypt for talks with the Egyptian president. However, as Dennis B. Ross and James F. Jeffrey of the Washington Institute for Near East Policy observed, "[But] Morsi's behavior domestically the day after the ceasefire should again remind us of his basic purpose and orientation: he immediately sought to parlay his role in the ceasefire and the international plaudits he won for it by removing all judicial oversight on his exercise of power."[38] The fact that Morsi made this power grab just after personal conversations with Hillary Clinton, and that the administration did not criticize him for it, were painful reminders that the administration's policy favored "regional stability" over human rights, and did not, in the spirit of our best foreign policy traditions, work for both.

In spite of the huge risks incurred by expressing opposition to the increasingly repressive government, Egyptians filled the streets in November 2012 to protest rigged elections, the opaque process of writing the constitution, the assault on the judiciary and its rulings, and the government's failure to institute genuine democratic reforms. After a night of street fighting between Morsi supporters and secular opponents left at least six dead and 450 wounded, nine Morsi administration officials quit in protest. One of those who quit was the new general secretary of the commission overseeing the planned referendum. "I will not participate in a referendum that spilled Egyptian blood," he said.[39]

In December, Coptic nationalists announced that they would boycott the referendum on the constitution, calling it "an Islamist constitution and not an Egyptian constitution" and saying there were no assurances of "fairness and transparency." Noting that the Brotherhood and Salafist votes in previous elections were "magnified by those non-Islamist Egyptians who saw at the time that Morsi was the lesser evil compared to Shafi, who was seen as part of Mubarak's regime," they declared: "The situation has now changed: the dictatorial nature of the Islamists has been revealed to millions of Egyptians; their incompetence in managing the affairs of the country has been remarkable; and the economic situation is deteriorating while the country is approaching complete collapse."[40]

Strikingly, the United States agreed to send F-16s to the Egyptian government and to give Egypt additional aid at precisely this time of growing fallout—when Egyptians were taking to the streets en masse in protest. The message was clear: US support of the Morsi government remained. Egyptians were thus indirectly pressure by the United States itself to get behind the government and to tone down their expectations. Discussing the US decision to deliver the advanced aircraft to the Egyptian military, retired brigadier general Safwat al-Zayat told *Al-Ahram Weekly*, "It is obvious that the finalization of the deal on 11 December, which happened to be at the height of the mass demonstrations in Tahrir Square against Morsi, conveyed a political message. Between the lines, Washington was sending a message to three parties. The first was to Morsi and it states, 'We support you. Move ahead.' The second was to the army and it said, 'We are encouraging this man,' meaning Morsi. The third was to the opposition and it said the same thing."[41]

With most Christian and secularist leaders having resigned in protest, and with the Christian and secularist boycott, the constitution passed with 63 percent of the vote after its second referendum. Protests erupted again, this time against the rushed and distorted process which had enabled an Islamist-oriented constitution. YouTube videos captured gangs of men loyal to the Muslim Brotherhood beating and assaulting protestors. Around the country, Coptic Christians were being bullied, intimidated, and even raped with immunity. Sharia law was being instituted, step by step.

Significantly, however, the US administration linked its support for a massive new infusion of financial aid to cooperation with the International Monetary Fund *instead of* to progress on religious freedom and human rights. Not only that, the new loan was supported *in spite of* Morsi's Islamization of Egyptian government and society.

When, shortly thereafter, a video was released showing Morsi spewing anti-Semitic rhetoric, Shoshana Bryen of the Gatestone Institute had this to say:

> The Obama administration placed a very heavy bet on its ability to manage relations with Morsi, and the world's discovery of his virulent anti-Semitism will not change it. Key to "managing relations" with Morsi is ignoring almost everything related to the Muslim Brotherhood and everything Morsi does that defies democratic norms. This includes ignoring the Brotherhood's lie that it would not run candidates for all the seats in parliament and would not run a presidential candidate. It includes ignoring massacres against the Coptic Christian community; the hasty construction of the constitution; the dismissal of judges; the quick-and-dirty "referendum" that claims 63% of the vote without noting that less than 25% of Egyptians voted; and the December protests. It requires, then, allowing Morsi to run roughshod over the Egyptian people, much as his predecessor did.[42]

■ ■ ■

The Obama/Kerry period was little different than the Obama/Clinton period of US-Egypt relations. By March 2013, even the Center for American Progress was gently criticizing the Obama administration for not using its leverage and enunciating democratic principles with more consistency. Brian Katulis, Ken Sofer, and Peter Juul pointed to the "looming political legitimacy crisis" in Egypt and said "it remains uncertain how much leverage the United States has managed to build for itself inside Egypt." Noting that the current policy approach "with its focus on the links between security and economics, has served some US national security interests in the short term," they pointed out that this approach "has limitations, given the messy political transition process and the growing political and social divisions inside Egypt." They added that the United States should "continue to outline more clearly and consistently that it seeks to support a truly free and democratic transition in Egypt" and should "underscore that US interests and values are at stake."[43]

Even critics of American "unilateralism" and of what they saw as Bush's overly zealous Mideast policies were starting to question and criticize America's seeming indifference to the Egyptian peoples' plight and its unwillingness to pressure Morsi's government. Michael Wahid Hanna noted that "unconditional support of nominal allies will endanger the very stability that the United States prizes." His prescription for better policy centered around "conditional engagement" merits attention:

> The United States must make clear to regimes that its support cannot substitute for the support of a country's own citizens, and that the judgments of those citizens regarding their regime's legitimacy must ultimately dictate the position of the United States. This is a critical message for America's undemocratic allies in the region, and this conditional engagement represents the only plausible path forward for the United States. The uneven performance of the region's democratically elected Islamist leaders also suggests a policy approach toward states that have suppressed the forces for change—namely, encouragement of bottom-up democratization. Doing this would include taking steps such as pressing for municipal and provincial elections as a precursor to broader reforms. In pushing such a course on countries that have avoided regime change, the United States can explore anew the feasibility of more gradual reform, which has often been employed rhetorically by authoritarians to avoid actual reform. Further, an approach that seeks to impart governing responsibilities upon opposition groups will ease their potential transition to national leadership. The United States also should not make assumptions about the inevitable role of Islamists. While they remain the most organized and potent political force in many countries in the region, the United States shouldn't view the Arab world with an essentialist lens that sees in Islamist rule the natural equilibrium. Such an approach will alienate non-Islamist political forces and encourage the monopolization of power by Islamist groups. . . . Assuming Islamist predominance will also create a misplaced permissiveness with respect to religiously based repression. What might be termed the soft bigotry of Orientalist expectations would undermine notions of universal values and encourage an inherently unstable model of governance that will ill serve U.S. regional interests and undermine the prospects for peaceful and sustainable change.[44]

By spring of 2013, the situation in Egypt had deteriorated further, but there was still room for the United States to try to make a positive difference. In what Amir Taheri cautiously termed a hopeful sign, President Morsi announced fresh parliamentary elections to take place in April. He delayed the timetable of the elections by a week to meet the demands of Christian Copts that the elections not coincide with Coptic Easter. Taheri noted that Morsi had refused to issue an outright ban on political parties or to actually *close* those opposition newspapers he had pressured.[45] In perhaps another hopeful sign, the Freedom and Justice Party denounced violence that took place outside the Coptic cathedral in Abbaseya, and stressed its support for initiatives "to bridge gaps and preserve the nation."

While these were perhaps hopeful signs, there was still much room for skepticism. In *Persecuted*, Marshall, Gilbert, and Shea disclosed the "underreported fact" that Christians are the single most widely persecuted religious group in the world today—a fact confirmed by the Pew Research Center, the *Economist*, the Vatican, and other sources.[46] Gilbert asserted in an April 2013 blog on Ricochet, "Attacks on Egypt's Copts . . . have increased dramatically since the ouster of strongman Hosni Mubarak. The present Muslim Brotherhood regime makes virtually no effort to protect the increasingly vulnerable Christian community.[47]

Emphasizing the difficulties of dealing with the Muslim Brotherhood whose "values and beliefs fundamentally challenge our own," Dennis Ross and James Jeffrey acknowledged that US influence would be "along the margins." Nevertheless, they urged the use of US leverage, given Egypt's profound economic needs, to convince Egypt to maintain international obligations; to fight terror and not provide a safe haven for terrorists; to respect minority and women's rights; and to permit political pluralism.[48] To their list, I would have added religious freedom. The "free world" could have and should have done more.

There was no reason to think that the Morsi government's recent conciliatory gestures would have occurred were the government not under extreme internal pressure. On the other hand, for that very reason, there *was* reason for the United States, finally, to make its support of the Morsi government *conditional*. With enough internal *and* external pressure, that included the imposition of clear, unwavering conditions for US aid, and that included the clear, unwavering pronouncement of democratic principles and strategic priorities, the situation might possibly have improved. If it had improved enough that Christians and secularists and women and Muslim moderates actually believed enough in the legitimacy of democratic processes that they participated in them—and believed their voices would be heard and their votes would be counted—Egypt might have turned a tenuous corner toward a better future without revolution.

But the United States did not advocate political liberty and human rights and never made a move to pressure the Morsi government toward true reform. In In the *Washington Post*, Glenn Kessler aptly observed that the Morsi government "didn't have to pay any apparent price for its anti-democratic actions." Among such actions, Kessler noted, "Morsi launched more prosecutions against reporters and authors for the crime of 'insulting the president' than Mubarak, Anwar Sadat, Gamal Abdel Nasser and previous rulers put together." Kessler added, "Yet, in Tanzania, Obama said, 'Decisions [on aid] are based on whether or not a government is listening to the opposition [and] maintaining a free press.' "[49]

On June 30, 2013, millions of Egyptians emerged in solidarity onto the streets to protest President Morsi and his regime. Fed up with the regime's disregard of human rights and constitutional free-doms, disastrous handling of the economy, and failure to address the people's concerns, they shouted, "Leave, leave!" Many of the protestors carried signs with such slogans as "Obama Supports Morsi." Journalist and scholar Walid Phares explained in an interview, "Most Egyptians are—with the exception of the Brotherhood obviously—very angry, very frustrated. . . . Not with the American public; they love the American people and citizens, but with the Obama administration because it openly was supporting the Muslim Brotherhood regime."[50]

In the wake of massive protests and overwhelming Egyptian rejec-tion of the Morsi government, Egypt's army intervened in support of Egyptians rebelling against Islamist authoritarianism. When it suited its purposes, the military had opportunistically allowed and abetted violence against the very secularists, women, and Christians with whom it now claimed an alliance. Now, the military sought the endorsement of religious leaders, political leaders, and youth activists, many of whom shared the stage when General Abdel Fattah el-Sisi announced Morsi's ouster. The next day, the military announced that the chief justice of the Supreme Constitutional Court had been sworn in as president. As James Jay Carafano and James Phillips of the Heritage Foundation put it, "Egypt's secular and liberal opposition [turned to] Egypt's army in despair, angry that the Obama administration uncritically supported the Morsi regime."[51]

Not surprisingly, after Morsi's ouster, violence and chaos erupted across Egypt as Islamists protested the "coup" against their "elected president" while those who threw him out insisted that Morsi's presidency was illegitimate and violated every principle of elective government.

As Brotherhood protests grew in intensity and violence, and the military response grew in response, the Obama administration seemed to find the voice for democracy it had previously lost. Seemingly incapable of forthright speech or action for liberty and human rights when the Muslim Brotherhood was in power, the administration spoke out with conviction against the actions of the military. Secretary of State John Kerry, Secretary of Defense Chuck Hagel, and US diplomats objected to the state of emergency in Egypt energetically and often. "In the past week, at every occasion . . . we and others have urged the government to respect the rights of free assembly and free expression, and we have also urged all parties to resolve this impasse peacefully and underscored that demonstrators should avoid violence and incitement," Kerry said.[52]

Backing its words with actions, the administration hastily took the extraordinary step of halting delivery of four F-16 fighter jets to a strategic Middle Eastern ally. Although the Obama administration had been unwilling to use leverage to reign in President Morsi, it did not hesitate to use the leverage of the United States against President el-Sisi. In October 2013, it went further, announcing the decision to cut much of its military aid, with President Obama warning that "business as usual" with Egypt would not continue. It also announced it would withhold $260 million in cash assistance until the government made "credible progress" toward inclusive government.

Having been silent regarding the Morsi government's abuses, President Obama made a rare (for him) statement in defense of political liberty. He took a moral stand, which he had been unwilling to do before. He declared that the new government was embarking on a "dangerous path taken through arbitrary arrests, a broad crackdown on Mr. Morsi's associations and supporters, and now tragically the violence that's taken the lives of hundreds of people and wounded thousands more." Without a word regarding the Morsi supporters' violent attacks on Christians and secularists, Obama said, "We deplore the violence against civilians. We support universal rights essential to dignity, including the right to peaceful protest. We oppose the pursuit of martial law, which denies those rights to citizens under the principle that security trumps individual freedom, or that might makes right. And today the United States extends its condolences to the families who were killed and those who were wounded."

Oh, what Egyptian secularists, Christians, women, and Muslim moderates would have done for such displays of support from the American president. Oh, what peaceful Iranian protestors and peaceful Syrian protestors would have done for such words on their behalf. But this presidency has been defined by *not* issuing such words, by moral neutrality, and by "engagement" with the world's worst tyrants.

In the *Daily Beast*, Josh Rogin and Eli Lake observed that the Obama administration then resorted to "revisionist history," now claiming that its decisions toward Egypt were always based on advocacy of the rule of law, civil liberties, and democracy.[53] That, we know, is patently *not true*. Rogin and Lake point out, for example, that, in March, five senators had proposed changing the way the US gives aid to Egypt by placing more emphasis on safeguards of democracy, human rights, and the rule of law. But the Obama administration, led by Secretary Kerry and Ambassador Patterson, fought those changes. Not only that, Kerry delivered an additional $190 million of aid to Egypt that very month, conditioning it only on economic (not political) reform.

Egyptians went to the polls in May 2014 and handed strongman Sisi and his military regime an overwhelming victory, with 97 percent of the vote. As Eric Trager put it, "Many Egyptians [thus] came to fear the Brotherhood so profoundly that they welcomed the military's return to politics and cheered the deadly assault on pro-Morsi protests last summer." Indeed, Sisi won the election in spite of demonstrated brutality; more than 2,500 demonstrators had, by then, been killed in the post-Morsi crackdown.[54] Seeing itself in an existential battle, especially after the rise of an ISIS-related insurgency, the regime and its ruthless security forces would perpetuate the crackdown with mass arrests, due process violations, disappearances, and mass death sentences of convicted Muslim Brotherhood and Salafi activists.[55]

In Egypt, we see the deadly dynamic that now repeats itself in many countries in the Middle East and Africa: strongmen use Islamist extremism and terrorism as the excuse for repression and the withholding of political liberties. Extremists use the cruel misdeeds of dictators as the excuse for terror attacks and violence. Dictators win votes and adherents by emphasizing the dangerous world we live in. Terrorists win recruits by emphasizing the human rights violations of dictators. Thus, in Sinai and the Egyptian mainland, Islamic insurgents known as Sinai Province activated sleeper cells in 2013 after the army regained power, and successfully used anger against the government to win recruits. The growing insurgency, in turn, allowed the government to present its crackdown as the only path to Egyptian security.

All of this is another reason for the United States to resurrect its place as a "shining city on a hill" that provides a voice to victims of political violence, discrimination and oppression, who long to be free. Clearly, there are both strategic and moral reasons to do so. In a 2003 study, professors Alan Krueger and Jitka Malecková found that the only variable that was consistently associated with the number of terrorists originating from particular countries was the Freedom House index of political rights and civil liberties.[56]

In January 2015, the Kerry State Department hosted a delegation of Muslim Brotherhood–aligned leaders who sought anti-Sisi support, thereby strongly signaling that the United States was interested in maintaining engagement with the group. Stated terrorism expert Patrick Poole, "What this shows is that the widespread rejection of the Muslim Brotherhood across the Middle East, particularly the largest protests in recorded human history in Egypt on June 30, 2013, that led to Morsi's ouster, is not recognized by the State Department and the Obama administration."[57]

Increasingly concerned about the growth of murderous Islamic State, and under tremendous pressure from lobbying groups, in summer 2015, the administration decided to deliver eight F-16 fighter jets to Egypt and announced that it would relaunch its "strategic dialogue" and resume joint military exercises with the country. In the case of Egypt, the United States should not have adopted either-or policies in the first place. It could have recognized the importance of the Egyptian alliance and of Egypt's position as a secular and *relatively* inclusive government in the Middle East—which, at its best, provides a buffer for Israel—and *at the same time* pressured the Egyptian government regarding its egregious human rights violations. Such a balancing act is not easy, but what, in today's complex and violent world, is?

■ ■ ■

Balance was conspicuously absent in the Obama administration's seesawing relationship with Libya. President Obama's early relationship with Libyan dictator Muammar Gaddafi defies explanation.

Gaddafi's Libya was exceptionally brutal and corrupt. The United States had long held an adversarial relationship with Libya, accusing it of egregious human rights violations and multiple terrorist attacks, including the Lockerbie aircraft bombing in 1988 and the killing of US servicemen in a German nightclub two years earlier. After the United States invaded Iraq, Gaddafi had agreed to eliminate his weapons of mass destruction program and backed down on his intransigence, fearing Libya would be next. The US and Libya had developed a "cooperative" relationship, although President Bush and Secretary Rice still occasionally criticized Libya's "cruel, inhumane and degrading" treatment of dissidents such as Fathi el-Jahmi. The Obama administration continued the Bush administration's policy of cooperating with the Libyan dictator, but dropped the Bush administration's occasional plugs for human rights. The part of this that is inexplicable is Obama's response when Scotland and the UK considered releasing convicted Lockerbie bomber Abdel Basset Ali al-Megrahi.

On July 25, 2010, the *Telegraph* reported Scotland's First Minister saying that, while the Americans "didn't want . . . al-Megrahi's release," the Americans thought "it was far preferable" to give the terrorist "compassionate release" than to arrange his transfer to a Libyan prison by way of a prisoner transfer agreement.[58] On July 26, the *Australian* provided disturbing details: "The US government secretly advised Scottish ministers it would be 'far preferable' to free the Lockerbie bomber than jail him in Libya. Correspondence obtained by the *Sunday Times* reveals the Obama administration considered compassionate release more palatable than locking up Abdel Basset al-Megrahi in a Libyan prison. The intervention, which has angered US relatives of those who died in the attack, was made by Richard LeBaron, deputy head of the US embassy in London. . . . The document, acquired by a well-placed US source, threatens to undermine US President Barack Obama's claim last week that all Americans were 'surprised, disappointed and angry' to learn of Megrahi's release. Scottish ministers viewed the level of US resistance to compassionate release as 'half-hearted' and a sign it would be accepted."[59]

Was it behind-the-scenes signals such as this or was it the warm handshake and photo op between the two at the G8 Summit that caused Gaddafi to predict and state that his "friend" President Obama would stand by him as he brutally stamped out the 2010 rebellion? Here again, Obama's reaction is hard to understand. At first, he spoke out against the "violence," seeming to impute both those fighting for and those fighting against the regime, but did not speak out against Gaddafi—even though some in the administration, Clinton included, considered Gaddafi's latest atrocities "genocide." This response stands in strange contrast to his quick condemnation of Mubarak of Egypt after the demonstrations in Tahrir Square. (Mubarak was an Egyptian dictator who deserved to go, but who was also a desperately needed American ally in the Middle East. Gaddafi was a Libyan strongman who had supported terror operations against American interests for many years, and was much more repressive than Mubarak.) To her credit, Secretary Clinton did release a statement saying, "The United States condemns the ongoing violence and human rights violations committed by the government of Libya against its own people."

President Obama then changed his mind and decided to follow the UN Security Council toward intervention against Gaddafi. In early March, Britain and France had called for a no-fly zone over Libya. After the Arab League joined the call, the administration threw its weight behind the UN initiative that led to a Security Council vote authorizing "all necessary measures" short of foreign occupation to protect civilians under threat from the regime. Some Republicans criticized the administration's decision for reasons including failure to enunciate clear goals, deference to multilateral institutions, and insufficient consultation with Congress. Secretary of Defense Gates was against the intervention, while Clinton, along with Obama advisers Samantha Power and Susan

Rice, reportedly pushed the idea.[60] Afterward, Clinton praised President Obama for his "smart leadership," pointing also to the capture and death of Osama bin Laden and the announcement that remaining US forces would leave Iraq by year's end.[61]

In taking this act of war against the Libyan regime, our president sought neither congressional approval nor the approval of the American people. He did not make his case to Congress and he did not make a speech explaining or justifying his decision to Americans. Instead, US military action and assistance to the Libyan rebels were simply "announced." It was not reported in the press that, by the time the United States intervened, Gaddafi had almost succeeded in suppressing the rebellion. Nor was there much discussion about whether President Obama had overstepped his constitutional bounds and violated the War Powers Resolution. Nor was there due attention to the inadequate postwar planning.

Unfortunately, conditions in Libya did not improve; instead radicalism, destruction, and violence mounted. Although Gaddafi was out, war between his supporters and rebels continued; terrorists from Ansar al-Sharia to Islamic State exploited the power vacuum; foreigners living and working in Libya faced ever-increasing risk. Joint Chiefs chairman General Martin Dempsey later testified that the rising terrorist threat in Libya was well known. In December 2012, the Senate Committee on Homeland Security and Governmental Affairs released a "Special Report on the Terrorist Attack at Benghazi," wherein it was determined that in the months leading up to the attack on the US consulate, there was a large amount of evidence gathered by the US intelligence community and from open sources that Benghazi was increasingly dangerous and unstable and that a significant attack against American personnel there was much more likely. The report found that, while this intelligence was shared within the intelligence community and with key officials at the Department of State, it did not lead to an increase in security at Benghazi nor to a decision to close the American mission there, either of which would have been more than justified by the intelligence presented.[62]

The stance of Secretary of State Clinton before and after Ambassador Christopher Stevens and three other Americans were killed in a terrorist attack on the US consulate on September 11, 2012, was, therefore—similar in this sense to Obama's earlier stance on Gaddafi—puzzling.

The US embassy had made multiple requests for more security while the embassy and the CIA had made a joint recommendation to move US diplomats into the CIA's Benghazi annex. But, the State Department was strangely unresponsive. Indeed, a bipartisan report released by the Senate Intelligence Committee in January 2014 verified that the State Department under Hillary Clinton refused requests to boost security despite warnings from the CIA and the State Department's own staff about the danger of militant attacks.

After terrorists stormed the compound, the regional security office placed urgent calls to the Benghazi CIA annex and the embassy in Tripoli, saying, "We're under attack, we need help, please send help now," and a rescue was ultimately attempted. Diplomatic security service agents and regional security officers informed Washington that they were under a "terrorist attack".[63] Although personnel on the ground clearly knew this was terrorism, Secretary Clinton and others in the administration at first repeatedly implied that the attack might have been part of a spontaneous demonstration against an anti-Muslim video on the Internet. On the night of the attack, the State Department issued this statement under Clinton's name: "Some have sought to justify this vicious behavior as a response to inflammatory material posted on the Internet. The United States deplores any intentional effort to denigrate the religious beliefs of others. Our commitment to religious tolerance goes back to the very beginning of our nation. But let me be clear: There is never any justification for violent acts of this kind." Susan Rice explicitly blamed the attacks on the video on national television. Worse, Hillary Clinton did not respond energetically or decisively once word of the attacks, and pleas for help, reached Washington. And, consequences for those who perpetrated the attack were minimal.

The questions of why the administration would deny requests for heightened security, would (until it was undeniable) downplay the fact that this was a terror attack, and would respond weakly to the attack led to the suggestion that, since the administration prided itself on its "humanitarian intervention" in Libya and held it up as a successful example of international collaboration, it didn't want to draw attention to Libya's deteriorating conditions, especially in the run-up to President Obama's election for a second term. Since Clinton played a key role in the decision to attack Libya and described the action as "smart power at its best," was she trying to divert attention from postwar problems in Libya by, among other things, minimizing Benghazi? Whatever the answers to these questions, it is widely agreed that Libya is now a "failed state" and a fertile breeding ground for terrorists.

■ ■ ■

The US government must work feverishly to restore its badly damaged reputation with the Egyptian people, and to reestablish strategic and geopolitical leverage in the region, for the stakes are high. Now that it has rediscovered words like *freedom* and *rule of law* (in defense of the Muslim Brotherhood), it must show that it genuinely promotes and believes in such things. It must lend its considerable resources and knowledge to those seeking to establish civil society in Egypt. Yes, the United States should pressure the Egyptian army to live up to its promises, but it should apply similar pressure to Islamists. Our alliance with Egypt is indispensable. Our demonstration of *genuine* support for a freer political and economic system and greater opportunity for the Egyptian people should be our upmost priority—not just because it benefits us to have a stable and free ally in the Middle East, but because it is within our best foreign policy traditions. It is the right and the wise thing to do.

CHAPTER 6

SYRIAN CATACLYSM
Missed Opportunities and Heartless Policies

Nowhere are the deficits of the Obama administration's Middle East policies more evident than in Syria, where afflictions of unimaginable proportions unfold. Turning their backs on the seismic geopolitical upheaval and the dire humanitarian crisis, President Obama and his foreign policy team were idle and mute as war in Syria, and the tragic human toll, escalated out of control. In response to the slaughter, the disappearances, the systematized torture, the bombing of towns and farms, the use of heavy artillery and chemical weapons on civilians, the escalation and radicalization of the conflict, and the incursions of Russia and Iran, the United States exhibited moral and strategic detachment.

The moral and strategic stakes were and are high. Syria is a state sponsor of terror and opportunistically aligns with the world's *other* worst regimes. It has a key location in the Middle East, some of the region's largest oil reserves, and (had) *tons* of chemical weapons. The methods the Syrian regime uses to dominate the people are unprecedented and extraordinarily cruel. No child, woman, man, village, or town has been spared. Bloodshed and despair have turned many into radicals, multitudinous others into refugees. The cataclysmic war has brought chaos and violence to an entire region. Terrorists and extremists have capitalized upon the upheaval, exponentially compounding the horrors. Iran and Russia, too, have seized the day, changing the balance of power not just in Syria, but throughout the Middle East.

As in previous times in our history, complacency and apathy in the face of multiplying threats and growing atrocities comes back to haunt us. My guess is that most Americans recoil, as I do, from the horrific news out of Syria, feeling in their gut that we should at least have done *something* before things got this bad, this out of control. In tracing the recent course of events in Syria, we find that the Obama administration's Syria policy was in defiance of the American tradition, indifferent to human suffering, counterproductive to Middle Eastern struggles for democracy, and devoid of grand strategy.

■ ■ ■

Bush administration policymakers were divided between the harder line toward Syria advocated by Secretary of Defense Donald Rumsfeld and the softer line advocated by Secretary of State Colin Powell. After 9/11, the Powell approach initially prevailed. Syria provided limited intelligence on al-Qaeda; perhaps in return, the administration obstructed Congress's Syrian Accountability Act and did not object when Syria was nominated for a rotating seat on the UN Security Council. There was some sympathy for the fact that the Iraq invasion caused severe damage to the Syrian economy, and hence to the Syrian people, whose standard of living was already very low due to lack of freedom and opportunity.

On the other hand, Syria caused severe setbacks for American troops by, among other things, smuggling military equipment to terrorists, training Iraqi insurgents, and allowing Iraqi leaders and Iraqi weapons to escape through their territory. Powell and the Bush team decided to give Syria another chance to choose between "being with the US or against it." Using the time-tested tactic of its totalitarian predecessors, however, the Syrian government decided to play for time, showing some interest in regional peace processes, while refraining from actually meeting US demands on Iraq and other issues.

As attacks against US troops grew and evidence of Syrian and Iranian support for those attacks emerged, the US position hardened. In 2003, Powell started to refer to Syria's presence in Lebanon as an occupation. In 2004, the Bush administration reversed its opposition to the Syrian Accountability Act. The law demanded that Syria "halt Syrian support for terrorism, end its occupation of Lebanon, stop its development of weapons of mass destruction, [and] cease its illegal importation of Iraqi oil and illegal shipments of weapons and other military items to Iraq."

Under pressure, Syrian President Bashar al Assad agreed to return to negotiations with Israel without preconditions. But, in February 2005, Prime Minister Rafic Hariri of Lebanon was assassinated, and it was widely believed Syria was responsible. The assassination, combined with the brutal Syrian occupation and diminishing prospects for freedom, led to the Cedar Revolution within Lebanon. The assassination was also the straw that broke the camel's back for US policy; the United States and France joined together to ratchet up the pressure on Syria, particularly in regard to Lebanon.

Sanctions and international condemnation appeared to have their effect. By April 2005, Syria had decided to end its long and cruel occupation of Lebanon. Reported the *New York Times*, "Surrendering to international and Lebanese popular demands, Syria ended its 29-year military presence in its smaller neighbor on Tuesday with a farewell ceremony near their shared border, where a Syrian commander told Lebanese troops: 'Brothers in arms, so long.' The soldiers responded, 'So long.'"[1] But, with Democratic Party candidates winning the House of Representatives and the Senate away from Republican control, and with increasing discontent over the Bush administration handling of foreign policy, Secretary of Defense Rumsfeld announced his resignation.

In 2006, the Iraq Study Group recommended engaging with Syria and Iran over Iraq and the Middle East, and the new secretary of defense, Robert Gates, indicated that the United States would again give engagement a try. Still, the inflammatory actions of Iran and Syria meant that engagement would only go so far. In testimony before Congress on September 10, 2007, General David Petraeus stated regarding Iraq, "Foreign and home-grown terrorists, insurgents, militia extremists, and criminals all push the ethno-sectarian competition toward violence. Malignant actions by Syria and, especially, by Iran fuel that violence."[2]

Obama and Clinton rode to power with promises of full-fledged engagement with Syria, Iran, and North Korea (as well as other extremist regimes), and of negotiation without preconditions. Syria's state-run newspaper *Al-Thawra* ran an article saying Syria "extended its hand" to President-elect Obama and offered to "use its weight in the region to moderate the behavior of non-state players like Hezbelloh in Lebanon and Hamas in Palestine, and find solutions for the US standoff with Iran over its nuclear program." The article made it clear that, unlike the new US administration, Syria *did* have preconditions for cooperation, including an end to anti-Syrian rhetoric, rolling back sanctions, helping Syria regain the Golan Heights, sponsoring Syria's indirect peace talks with Israel, and abolishing the Syrian Accountability Act. Even though Syria had a track record of deception and violation of international agreements, and even though Syria was strengthening ties with Iran and Hezbollah at the very time it was offering to help contain them, the Obama administration responded to the Syrian offer with unmitigated enthusiasm.

After the Hariri assassination, the Bush administration had withdrawn the US envoy from Syria and severed diplomatic relations. With Obama and Clinton, this policy was quickly reversed. In March 2009, the administration sent acting Assistant Secretary of State Jeffrey Feltman and Daniel Shapiro of the National Security Council to meet with Syrian officials. The US said these talks would focus on getting Syria to close its border with Iraq and on seeking Syria's assistance in negotiating an Arab-Israeli peace. The administration did approve the renewal of sanctions passed by the Bush administration, but according to a report by the Council on Foreign Relations, on their second Syrian visit, Feltman and Shapiro asked Syria "not to pay any heed and to look at the sanctions as 'pro forma.'"[3]

In February 2010, the administration announced it was appointing an ambassador, Robert Ford, to Syria for the first time since the Bush administration had severed diplomatic ties. Senator John Kerry played a supportive role in the outreach policy, making multiple trips to Syria for discussions with Syrian leaders. In July, Obama's special envoy to the Middle East, George Mitchell, became the highest-level US official to visit Syria since 2005. Mitchell emphasized that Syria had a key role to play in forging peace in the region.

As Michael Scott Doran pointed out, insisting on Syria's role as intermediary in the Israeli-Palestinian peace process elevated Syria's prestige. Doran lamented that the administration had "chosen to treat Syria not as an adversary deserving containment but rather as a partner in the negotiations deserving of engagement."[4] Thus, even before Syrian protests began and Syrian dictator Bashar al-Assad unleashed retaliatory horrors on the Syrian people, and before the United States did indirect harm with its quiescent response, the United States did positive harm with the supportive signals it sent to the Syrian regime.

In an important policy assessment, Matthew R. J. Brodsky of the Center for Security Policy argued that it was folly to assign the role of peace intermediary to Syria, because Syria's importance in the Middle East rested on its ability to play the role of spoiler, as it had in Iraq; because Syria was a state sponsor of terror; and because Syria's intermediary role would be severely compromised by its documented and continued support for Hamas, Hezbollah, Islamic Jihad, and other organizations. Syria viewed the Iraqi insurgents as well as Hezbollah and Hamas as legitimate resistance movements, and showed its support of these groups not only through military and financial assistance but also through actively training and encouraging the jihadists.

Reported Brodsky, "As a matter of policy, the Syrian government financed, trained, armed, encouraged, and transported foreign jihadists to fight against both Coalition forces in Iraq and the fledgling army of the new Iraqi government. Once the war began in 2003, state-chartered buses transported insurgents with considerable fanfare and publicity. So brazen was Syria's support for jihad against the United States that the regime allowed volunteers seeking to fight the U.S.-led collation in Iraq to gather in front of the Iraqi embassy, located across from the US embassy, while the Syrian mufti—the most senior state-appointed cleric—formally endorsed holy war against the coalition forces. This was nothing short of a declaration of war on the United States."[5] All of this should have been enough to make clear the futility—and vacuity—of relying on Syria for leadership in creating a Middle East peace.

If this were not enough, what of the fact that Syria did not itself abide by international peace resolutions, such as those calling on Syria to respect the border with Lebanon, to stop the flow of weapons to terrorists, and to halt its pursuit of WMD? What of the fact that, given Syria's regime type, worldview, and regional ambitions, it had no reason to *want* peace between the Palestinians and Israel? (In 2000, Syria rejected Israel's final offer in US-sponsored peace talks of full withdrawal from the Golan except for a one-hundred meter strip of land along the Sea of Galilee's northeastern shore. Ever since then, it had supported Hezbollah and Hamas.) Of course, the Obama administration hoped that negotiations, discussions, and the promise of improved relations with the United States would positively influence Syria so that progress toward peace could finally be made. They also hoped improved relations with the United States would drive a wedge between Syria and Iran.

Even this goal, reasonable on the surface, is questionable upon closer examination. Syria had recently strengthened ties with Iran and continued to strengthen ties after offering to help the Obama administration with Iranian issues. Mahmoud Ahmadinejad and Bashar al-Assad had signed protocols pushing educational, economic, and cultural cooperation between the countries, and Assad had, multiple times, voiced support for Iran's nuclear program.

In fact, Andrew Tabler reveals in his first-hand account *In the Lion's Den* that, in spite of its long-time repression of Islamists and the Muslim Brotherhood, starting in 2006, the Syrian regime had turned away from secularism and accepted Iran's radical form of Islam as a way of strengthening Syrian-Iranian ties. "While Syria's deepening relationship with Iran made international headlines, the regime began to reorient its rhetoric and propaganda toward Islam. . . . On the streets of Damascus, posters with images of Assad, Ahmadinejad, and [Hezbollah secretary-general Hassan] Nasrallah, all surrounded by roses, began appearing on shop facades and car rear windows. Large banners with *Syria is Protected by God* were strewn throughout the Syrian capital. Syrian flags, with the slogan written into the middle white band alongside two stars—reminiscent of Saddam Hussein's addition of 'Allahu akbar' (God is great) to the Iraqi flag after his forces were driven out of Kuwait in 1991—hung from buildings. State-owned radio and TV repeated the slogan so many times that it quickly turned into a mantra."[6] Syria held its first competition for reading the Koran, issued a decree opening an Islamic college in Aleppo, and began to encourage Islamic instruction.

In an early indication that American outreach wouldn't translate into a change in the Syrian position, a few days after the announcement that the US would be sending Ambassador Ford to Syria, in February of 2010, Assad hosted Iran's Ahmadinejad in Damascus, announcing afterward that Syria's "strategic ties" with Iran would be strengthened. At the same time, he voiced support for Iran's nuclear activities, demanded to know why Israel's nuclear program was off-limits, and reiterated that both Syria and Iran were committed to Hamas. Thereafter, Assad became a more overt apologist for the Iranian regime.

In May of 2010, Assad hosted Dmitry Medvedev of Russia, announcing afterward that Syria and Russia, too, had strengthened ties. In a May 2010 interview with the Italian newspaper *La Repubblica*, he laid out his vision for "a new geostrategic map which aligns Syria, Turkey, Iran and Russia, which are brought together by shared policies, interests and infrastructure."

Another indicator that compromising engagement with Syria was unlikely to work was Syria's ongoing sponsorship of terror. As James H. Anderson observed in *World Affairs*, "The Assad dynasty has long matched repression at home with support for terrorism abroad. The US has designated Syria a sponsor of state terrorism for thirty straight years, ever since Congress began requiring the State Department to list such offenders. A state does not make this list for three consecutive decades because its sponsorship of terrorism is somehow tangential to its policies. On the contrary, terrorism as an instrument of state policy lies at the very core of the Assad dynasty. In addition to supplying Hezbollah with sophisticated weapons in Lebanon, Syria has long permitted Hamas, Palestine Islamic Jihad, and other terrorist groups to operate in Damascus. Assad periodically meets with these groups in public forums, something his father never did."[7]

Again, the de-emphasis on regime-type led the Obama administration astray, allowing it to think that the Syrian regime might respond, just like any reasonable regime, to negotiations that promised peace and prosperity, and to cooperation with the United States that promised to elevate Syria's reputation with the "international community." But the Syrian regime was ruthless and bellicose, not reasonable. Bashar al-Assad ruled with an iron fist, like his father. Syria was and is a police state, which stamps out freedom of expression, sees no reason for political representation, and engages in arbitrary detentions, torture of political prisoners, harassment of dissidents, and terrorism. Syria had long repressed the Muslim Brotherhood and others through mass arrests and disappearances. Syria's "emergency law" had long justified anything the regime wanted to do, including detaining and punishing civilians without charge. Syria's long-time pursuit of chemical and nuclear weapons was well known. In 2002, US Ambassador to the UN John Bolton testified to Congress that Syria was continuing to develop offensive biological and chemical weapons capability, including the nerve agent sarin that could be used on aircraft or ballistic missiles.

In July 2011, human rights activist and journalist Elias Bejjani lamented, "The world has known many brutal and bloody regimes in the Middle East and elsewhere since WWI, but none of them was more barbaric, savage and cruel than the current Syrian al-Assad dictatorship," which "shows no respect whatsoever to its own people's dignity, rights, feelings, pain, grief, safety, and welfare." Noted Bejjani of Assad's "Stalinist occupation" of Lebanon, "the Syrian regime resorted to evil tactics of murder, terrorism, kidnapping, assassination, cruelty, a policy of divide and conquer, and barbarism against the Lebanese people."[8] Regarding the ruthless crackdown on the Syrian people and Syria's reoccupation of Lebanon, and the American and Western nonresponse, Bejjani predicted, "Their cajoling and appeasing—their callous indifference to the Syrian bloodbath—will go down in history as a time of ineptitude and shame."[9]

In fact, we should not ignore the likelihood that Syria's reassertion of thuggish dominance in Lebanon in the first year of Obama and Clinton's tenure was partly the result of the signals given through the United States' outreach policies. In tragicomic symbolism of Syria's enhanced status, Syria and Lebanon reestablished "ties," and Saad Hariri—the very son of Rafic Hariri who had been assassinated (in almost all estimations by the Syrians)—visited Damascus in December 2009. The visit was one of many woeful consequences of Assad's newfound leverage in the Levant. By December 2011, Frida Ghitis was reporting in *World Politics Review* that "Assad has played a key role in the emergence of Hezbollah as the dominant power in Lebanon" and that Hezbollah chief Hassan Nasrallah had recently made "a rare public appearance" in which he expressed support for the Syrian dictator. Ghitis also reported Druze leader Walid Jumblatt's "surprise decision" to throw the support of his Progressive Socialist Party to Hezbollah, which had helped bring down the pro-Western government that had emerged from Lebanon's Cedar Revolution.

Why would Jumblatt, who had called Assad "a snake, a butcher and a liar," and Hariri, whose father had probably been assassinated by a Syrian-Hezbollah coalition, cater to the dreaded Assad? The answer is clear: The West, particularly the United States, had abandoned Lebanon and was catering to the Syrian dictator. Noting that the power situation would change dramatically if Assad were successfully ousted, Ghitis reported that Jumblatt eventually expressed support for the Syrian opposition.

None of this prevented Hillary Clinton from making what CNSNews. com called a "startling statement" in a March 27, 2011, interview with CBS's Bob Schieffer, in which she drew a contrast between Assad and his father, and between Assad and Gaddafi of Libya, and stated that US lawmakers who had recently visited Damascus considered Assad a "reformer." Stated she, "There's a different leader in Syria now. Many of the members of Congress of both parties who have gone to Syria in recent months have said they believe he's a reformer."[10] Not only was Clinton aware of the routine brutality of the Assad regime; she was also well aware that a few days prior, on March 23, Assad's security forces had opened fire on peaceful protestors in Daraa and had followed this action with what would be the first of countless mass shootings of civilians.

Although Assad had occasionally promised reform, and had enacted limited economic reforms by denationalizing some parts of the economy, it was clear that such promises were a ploy to stem the tide of discontent.

In response to the regime's ongoing corruption, ruthlessness, and repression, Syrian pro-democracy activists had mobilized under the Damascus Declaration, a powerful statement signed by a collection of pro-democracy groups that had bravely begun to organize in 2006. By 2008, the group's power and influence was growing, and the regime was cracking down. In January 2008, members of the organization's National Council were detained and charged with breaking Syria's civil code. In October, the National Council was collectively sentenced to two and a half years in prison. The Syrian people lived in constant fear.

In February 2009, Human Rights Watch issued a report called "Far From Justice: Syria's Supreme State Security Court." The court was created to back up the country's "state of emergency" and was used "to prosecute those whom the Syrian authorities do not approve of in trials that lack basic due process guarantees." Stated the report, "The SSSC consistently ignores claims by defendants that their confessions were extracted under torture and frequently convicts them on vague and overbroad offenses that essentially criminalize freedom of expression and association."[11]

■ ■ ■

The Syrian rebellion began as a peaceful movement organized by the Damascus Declaration's pro-democracy groups. Protestors only grew violent in response to Assad's atrocities. They wanted human rights, free elections, an independent press and judiciary, and an end to the hated Emergency Law. When peaceful young protestors poured into the streets of Damascus in March 2011, Assad shot them down. When the revolt grew in response, Assad initiated massacres, arrests, and torture—even of children and teenagers. When brutality further fanned the flames of rebellion, Assad employed cluster bombs, attack helicopters (and, eventually, Scud missiles and chemical weapons) on rebels and civilians alike. Torture centers amplified the regime's reign of terror, as did its tactic of blockading and starving entire neighborhoods into submission.

In a report entitled "We've Never Seen Such Horror: Crimes Against Humanity by Syrian Security Forces," Human Rights Watch described the brutality that stoked Syria's protests and sparked Syria's revolt:

> The Daraa protests, which eventually spread all over Syria, were sparked by the detention and torture of 15 young boys accused of painting graffiti slogans calling for the downfall of the regime. On March 18, following Friday prayer, several thousand protestors marched from al-Omari Mosque in Daraa calling for the release of children and greater political freedom, and accusing government officials of corruption. Security forces initially used water cannons and teargas against the protestors, and then opened live fire, killing at least four. The ultimate release of the children—bruised and bloodied after severe torture in detention—fanned the flames of popular anger. Protests continued, every week growing bigger with people from towns and villages outside Daraa city joining the demonstrations. . . . In most cases, especially as demonstrations in Daraa grew bigger, security forces opened fire without giving advance warning or making any effort to disperse the protestors by nonlethal means. Security forces deliberately targeted protesters who were, in the vast majority of cases, unarmed and posed no threat to the forces; rescuers who were trying to take the wounded and the dead away; medical personnel trying to reach the wounded; and, during the siege, people who dared to go out of their houses or to gain access to supplies. In some cases they also shot bystanders,

including women and children. From the end of March, witnesses consistently reported the presence of snipers on government buildings, targeting and killing protestors.[12]

The report, furthermore, documented arbitrary arrests and severe torture of prisoners, which included the use of metal and wooden racks, electric batons and Tasers, and executions.

Whether or not one agrees with the Obama administration's outreach to Assad, the time was right to emphasize human rights. Given that the administration was determined to hold onto its engagement policies, it could have framed human rights as integral to those policies—a way of reaching out not just to the regime but also to the people themselves.

Why should the administration have swiftly directed attention to Syrian human rights? Because the already dire human rights situation in Syria had gotten much worse, and the Syrian people were pleading for our support. Because focusing on human rights would have shown the Syrian people and even the Syrian government that we were concerned not just with our own foreign policy issues but also with Syrian issues and the Syrian people. The rationale would have been both principled and practical: Given that the Syrian democracy movement had defined itself in nationalist rather than pro-American terms due to objections to the Iraq War on Syria's doorstep and due to US support for Israel's deadly retaliations in Lebanon, emphasizing human rights would have been a way of saying "You are not just pawns in our geopolitical game." It would have allowed the administration's engagement policies to stand for something higher than dialogue with dictators. It would have honored the American foreign policy tradition rather than defiling it.

Instead, Obama, Clinton, and other administration officials mostly avoided talking about the war in Syria and, when they did, took pains to make Assad appear better than he was. As the Assad regime's slaughter of civilians turned into massacres, they never gave Reaganesque speeches condemning the regime's murderous policies. In fact, they never gave *any* speeches on the subject, preferring to issue an occasional memorandum. As if to emphasize the United States' equivocal stance, Obama said in a *written statement* of April 8, "I strongly condemn the abhorrent violence committed against peaceful protestors by the Syrian government today and over the last few weeks. I also condemn any use of violence by protestors."[13] He did go on to call for an end to arbitrary arrests and the detention and torture of prisoners (which he had not done in March), but it was again apparent: he was downplaying crimes against humanity by calling such crimes "violence" and by emphasizing the violence of *both* sides.

Making matters worse, the administration preemptively, unnecessarily, and unwisely declared that the US "would not" enter the conflict in Syria as it had in Libya. Of course, we did not want to become entangled in the conflict, but announcing the fact sent the wrong message to Assad. So did the persistence of the administration's unwillingness to speak out against Assad's horrendous acts against the Syrian people.

The crimes against humanity in Syria were and are heartbreaking. As James L. Gelvin puts it, "As if to demonstrate Lenin's maxim that 'the purpose of terrorism is to terrorize,' the government committed seemingly purposeless acts of violence, frequently against children and even infants, in an attempt to cow the population."[14] Rather than succumb to the indifference the Obama administration encourages, let us record and condemn Assad's annihilationist policies.

■ ■ ■

As atrocities intensified, President Obama and Secretary of Defense Leon Panetta pronounced, as they would many times, that we would not "intervene" in Syria, while Obama and Clinton indicated that in any action we might eventually undertake, we would "lead from behind." They *announced* that the United States would not supply the Syrian resistance with arms. They deferred to the UN Security Council, wherein they knew and the world knew Russia and China would veto every meaningful action. They *announced* that the United States wouldn't get involved without the UN Security Council's permission. "Never again"— that statement of resolute determination that arose from the horrors of the Holocaust—was the farthest thing from their minds, and they encouraged the rest of us Americans to be small-hearted as well. Such a stance surely emboldened Assad. The unbelievable Syrian cataclysm had begun.

By July of 2011, Clinton would answer an ABC news reference to her former optimism that Assad was a "reformer" by saying, "Well we had

hoped so because there was a lot at stake; we wanted to see an agreement, for example, between Syria and Israel. . . . We heard what Assad
said about what he wanted to do for reform. But when it came to it, in
the Arab Spring . . . he responded, as we have seen, very violently. But he's
not going to be able to sustain what is an unfortunately growing armed
opposition apparently fueled and maybe led by defectors from his army.
It's probably too late for him to change course, but there needs to be
change at the top of that government and there needs to be an effort to
engage in genuine dialogue and start on the path of reform."[15] Note all
the ambiguity, even in this statement. Which is more "unfortunate"—
the fact that the opposition movement, and hence the "violence," arose
in the first place or Assad's slaughter of the Syrian people? Is Clinton
saying that Assad should leave because he is slaughtering his people, or
that he should "start" the path to reform?

In an apparent answer to this question, Clinton said at an international conference on democracy in Lithuania in July that Syria's
government was "running out of time," that Assad and his allies must
"begin a genuine transition to democracy," and that she was "hurt by
recent reports of continued violence." In the meantime, the Syrian
government attempted to regain support by inviting in some foreign
journalists and allowing a group of opposition intellectuals to meet.
Journalists reported that they were accompanied by minders and several
attendees said they were subsequently threatened.[16]

For anyone with the slightest knowledge of twentieth-century
history, Assad's ploy rang a familiar bell. Hitler had "invited" journalists to Germany at precisely the moment when stories of the horrors of
Nazism were reaching Western ears. Pol Pot had courted both Western
journalists and Western diplomats by giving them carefully orchestrated
tours that hid the horrors of his extermination policies.

As Robert M. Danin of the Council on Foreign Relations asserted,
there were "more questions than answers" in Secretary Clinton's
remarks on Arab uprisings. As Syria's slaughter of demonstrators and
destruction of rebel groups and rebel towns grew ever more devastating,
Clinton continued to equivocate, pointing out, for example, that to
achieve the same goal as we achieved in Libya "we would have to act
alone, at a much greater cost, with far greater risks and perhaps even
with troops on the ground."[17] In no instance did she make a passionate

plea for the Syrian people, nor did she make an unambiguous attempt to use American power, American influence, or America's regional alliances to intimidate the murderous Syrian regime.

Obama, Clinton, and Panetta's approach to Syria has been described by various analysts as inconsistent, frigid, weak, laissez faire, inexplicable, and inexcusable. The strategy itself has been termed appeasement and failed policy. I would add that that it was indecent. Concerns of the heart and the mind converge and recoil in response to an American policy so passive and so heartless. *Assad did not deserve the benefit of the doubt he was given before the uprising against the regime, and he certainly didn't deserve it afterward.*

As reports out of Syria got even worse, the administration turned to the UN Security Council for guidance—and for cover for its own ineffective policies. As Assad's security forces targeted entire villages for annihilation; as desperate youths relayed the slaughter of innocent families, women, and children through secreted videos; as the heartbreaking toll taken on Syrian childrenemerged; as Syrians cried out to America for help, President Obama and his administration stuck with their policy of indifference. It had become official US policy to say nothing and do nothing other than, occasionally, calling for an end to the "violence." Again, the term *violence* implied moral equivalence between the sides and drew attention away from the dire humanitarian and human rights situation.

In what *Politco* columnist Josh Gerstein termed "Obama's slow burn on Assad," in August 2011, Obama finally issued a muted call for Assad's exit and announced new sanctions on Syria's energy sector. While saying Assad must "lead a democratic transition or get out of the way," Obama also volunteered, "The United States cannot and will not impose this transition in Syria." Gerstein observed, however, that "Afterward, the White House seemed eager to dispel perceptions that the timing of Obama's action fits an emerging Republican critique that the president prefers to 'lead from behind'—a phrase an unnamed Obama adviser used to describe Obama's foreign policy in an interview with the *New Yorker* earlier this year."[18]

Indeed, our government was careful not to appear overbearing in the Syrian matter, with Clinton noting that energy sanctions from the US would have little direct effect since most Syrian oil exports go to

Europe. Indicating that the US would try to get other nations to impose similar sanctions, she nevertheless again downplayed a leadership role for the US, adding "if Turkey says it, if King Abdullah says it, if other people say it, there is no way the Assad regime can ignore it."[19] Administration officials emphasized that they were urging Saudi Arabia, Turkey, and other Arab countries to play a greater role. Thus, after *tentatively* calling for Assad's ouster and imposing impotent energy sanctions, the Obama administration continued to defer to the UN, to offer that it would not "intervene," to solicit Arab leadership, and to voice its rarely stated objections to Syria's crimes against humanity in diplomatic ways.

In tandem with non-US-led efforts, Syrian massacres and atrocities intensified. Human Rights Watch, Human Rights First, Amnesty International, and other organizations again documented Syrian crimes against humanity and again pleaded for a stronger response. A meticulously documented August 2011 report by the UN Office of the High Commissioner for Human Rights detailed atrocities committed by Assad's security forces, including systematic torture, several massacres, and the routine "picking off" by sniper and helicopter fire of unarmed civilians, including children. It also included a list of more than 4,500 Syrians who were "missing." But a survey of American policies after the muted American call for Assad's exit and after the UN human rights report, both issued in August 2011, reveals that the US did very little to encourage Assad to leave and shines an unflattering light on the administration's moral and strategic position.

In October 2011, State Department spokesman Mark Toner announced the US was temporarily pulling its ambassador out of Syria as "a result of credible threats against his personal safety." CNN's headline was typical of the reporting on the issue: "US Pulls Envoy from Syria Over Safety Concerns." Notice that the State Department defined the reasons for withdrawing Ambassador Ford narrowly, in terms of the ambassador's personal security, instead of morally, in terms of objections to atrocities.

In November 2011, France pressed for harsher sanctions against Iran and for active humanitarian intervention in Syria. White House officials commended French president Nicolas Sarkozy's efforts at a leadership role, but said they were "taken by surprise" by French foreign minister Alain Juppé's calls for a "humanitarian corridor" inside Syria. They said forceful intervention could feed the civil conflict and give Damascus an incentive to crack down more aggressively on political opponents. Also in November, the Arab League, which had taken the lead on the Syrian problem as the US had urged, announced that Syria had agreed to its peace plan. The plan did not require Assad to step down, but did require the immediate withdrawal of military and security forces from the streets of Syria, the opening of the country to reporters and monitors, and dialogue with the opposition.

The Arab plan was announced on November 2. By November 12, the League was engaged in an "emergency meeting" in Cairo due to Syria's failure to implement the plan. Jordan's King Abdullah became the first Arab head of state to call for Assad to step down, and the Arab League suspended Syria's membership. Asserted Kori Schake in *Foreign Policy*, "The shame for Americans is that the Arab League, so long a repressive force in the politics of the region, has a better Syria policy than does the Obama administration. 3,500 Syrians have been killed by their government this year; during that time, our government has adjusted its position from considering Bashar al-Assad a reformer—Secretary Hillary Clinton's memorable phase—to saying 'he cannot deny his people's legitimate demands indefinitely.'"[20]

In December, observer teams from the Arab League arrived in Syria. One observer reported, "What is happening in Syria is genocide." Homs, the largest center of resistance, became a war zone as the shelling of civilians brought the death toll to over five thousand. In January 2012, the chief of the Arab League, Nabil Elaraby, expressed growing doubts about the monitoring mission's effectiveness and noted that the Syrian government was not cooperating.

As the Arab plan and Arab initiatives faltered, the administration continued to express support for them, going so far as to indicate that they were the only policies available. (As late as June 2012, Hillary Clinton implied in a Brookings Institution forum that the plan and Arab leadership were still the only options.)

UN chief Ban Ki-moon next urged the Security Council to speak with "one voice," saying casualties had reached an "unacceptable" level. He called for Assad to "stop killing and listen to his people." Human rights organizations and the UN's own Human Rights Council indicated that some nine thousand had, by then, died in the Syrian conflict, while more than ten thousand had been detained and at least several hundred had disappeared. The EU tightened its sanctions, with the US praising the move. President Obama condemned the "unacceptable violence" and vowed to scale up the international pressure on the Assad regime. With momentum for a Security Council resolution building, France, Britain, and Germany began working on a draft resolution, with the United States supporting the plan, and Russia announcing it would not support any action that included sanctions or military intervention.

Secretary Clinton did take a stronger verbal position than she had previously when she urged passage of the resolution at a January 2012 Security Council meeting: "It is time for the international community to put aside our own differences and send a clear message of support to the people of Syria. The alternative—spurning the Arab League, abandoning the Syrian people, emboldening the dictator—would compound this tragedy, and would mark a failure of our shared responsibility, and shake the credibility of the United Nations Security Council."[21] Of course, the credibility of the Security Council had already been shaken, many times, due to the fact that members Russia and China have the power of the veto and choose to use it often. Russia introduced amendments that so undermined the wording and intent of the resolution that US ambassador to the UN Susan Rice termed them "unacceptable." When a vote was taken on the original plan, both Russia and China vetoed it.

Russian prime minister Sergey Lavrov justified the move, saying the resolution "left the door open to military intervention." He also criticized the Arab League mission and defended Russian arms sales to Syria. With nothing to stop them, Syrian forces stepped up their actions against rebels and civilians, bombing districts of Homs and other cities.

At the end of January, a controversy highlighted how little the US had done to pressure the Syrian regime. It had just been discovered that a Russian ship loaded with weapons that Russia claimed was heading to Turkey had actually gone to Syria. To make matters worse, it was revealed that the Russian state arms trader Rosoboronexport had signed a contract to sell the Syrian government thirty-six combat jets capable of attacking ground targets.

In response to this situation, Human Rights First wrote a January 31 letter to Secretary of the Treasury Timothy Geithner under the header "Disrupting the Supply Chain for Syrian Atrocities." The letter pleaded with Secretary Geithner to use his authority "to disrupt the activities of Rosoboronexport and similar third-party enablers that provide material support the Syrian government needs to perpetuate its crimes," saying, "It is critical that [this] diplomacy be reinforced by a vigorous effort to disrupt the enablers of Syria's atrocities as well."[22] At the end of February, Human Rights First renewed its plea, stating, "The U.S. government should immediately halt its own purchases from Rosoboronexport and other enablers of the ongoing Syrian atrocities."[23] In March, seventeen senators joined the call for the Defense Department to cut its ties with the Russian arms dealer. In July, Human Rights Watch and Human Rights First issued new appeals that protested the Pentagon decision to go ahead with a huge purchase of attack helicopters. Although President Obama ignored the appeals, in December the Senate spearheaded a bill banning Department of Defense deals with Rosoboronexport, which would fully come into effect when Obama signed the 2013 federal budget into law.

In a January 2012 article for the *Daily Beast*, Ilan Berman noted the "deliberate minimalism" of the Obama administration's response to Syria's ever more brutal crackdown. Three rounds of sanctions had "stopped short" of comprehensive economic pressure. In addition, the administration had neglected to pressure international partners to issue harsh sanctions of their own. It had "publicly written off" the idea of using force and had taken pains to draw "distinctions" between the situation in Syria and that in Libya.[24] Indeed, in a March 7 response to Senator John McCain's calls for military assistance, Secretary of Defense Panetta spoke in a way that specifically limited American options, *thereby making it clear to the Syrian regime that costs for its behavior would only go so far.* In testimony which could only serve as a morale boost to the murderous Assad, Panetta—publicly—ruled out calls for unilateral airstrikes against Syria. Headlines around the world read, "Panetta Rules Out Strikes in Syria." Panetta did say, however, that the administration was "considering" delivering nonlethal and humanitarian aid to rebels.

Perhaps because the situation in Syria only worsened after Panetta's testimony, in April, Secretary Clinton issued her strongest warning so far to the Assad regime, threatening to invoke sanctions under Chapter VII of the UN Charter—a move that would allow the Security Council to authorize force. At about the same time, the Arab League urged the quick deployment of hundreds of UN observers in an unprecedented mission aimed at halting the killing of Syrian civilians, as the conflict had taken "another gruesome turn." Scenes of even worse destruction and chaos and more secreted videos of civilians crying for help emerged.

In response to the deteriorating situation, former UN chief Kofi Annan presented a new six-point plan calling for a ceasefire, the withdrawal of heavy weapons from population centers, humanitarian assistance, release of prisoners, and free movement of journalists. The plan did not call upon Assad to give up his presidency; instead, it called for negotiations between the sides. Mirroring Obama's morally neutral definition of the conflict, it called on both government forces and opposition fighters to end the "violence."

The US acquiesced to the Russian-backed UN plan, failing to point to the futility and turpitude of asking the Syrian opposition to negotiate with a regime that was slaughtering, torturing, and imprisoning them and that had provoked the rebellion in the first place through a brutal crackdown on civilians. In the Middle Eastern paper *The National*, Michael Young observed that it was the "understandable and laudable refusal to reconcile themselves with Mr. Al Assad, or to give him leeway to survive politically, that made them [the opposition] dismiss Mr. Annan's project." Young intoned, "To say no to a mass murderer, even if civil conflict ensues, is not always reprehensible."[25]

As for Assad himself, the Syrian backlash against his atrocities meant that any compromise would eventually entail his demise. Not surprisingly, he paid lip service to Annan's plan while ignoring it. By the time of the plan, at least eleven thousand Syrians had been killed. Disappearances haunted Syrian society. Syria had a virtual archipelago of detention and torture facilities. Many leaders of ISIS would emerge out of these facilities, hardened and filled with hatred.

After all of the equivocation on the US side and all of the horror on the Syrian side, finally, in *April of 2012*, President Obama tightened sanctions on Syria and Iran by taking aim at those who provided the regimes with technology to track down dissidents for abuse, torture, or death. In a visit to the Holocaust Memorial Museum, the president said, "These technologies should be in place to empower citizens, not to repress them." Still, the president made it clear that he favored a limited rather than comprehensive approach, choosing to limit the first application of the new sanctions to entities inside Syria and Iraq. Human rights groups observed that the moves were unlikely to have any impact since they didn't target companies that made or sold the technologies at issue.

It is reasonable to ask why these sanctions had not been imposed long before and why the sanctions weren't stronger. As if to reassure Assad that Washington wasn't serious about wanting him gone, the White House continued to publicly indicate that it was not planning to supply the rebels with communications technology or arms.

In May 2012, pro-regime Alawite forces from neighboring villages took part in the killing of 108 people, mostly women and children, in the village of Houla. In June, UN observers reported their gruesome finding that another massacre had been committed in Qubair, with a UN spokeswoman reporting the "heavy stench of burned flesh." But UN observers, whose presence was key to the UN plan, were fleeing Syria. "UN observers in Syria suspended their activities and patrols Saturday because of escalating violence in the country, the head of the mission said, the strongest sign yet that an international peace plan for Syria is disintegrating."[26] In response, Hillary Clinton met with Kofi Annan to discuss how to salvage his plan. But it was clear that the Annan plan, like the Arab plan, had already failed.

In July, the Syrian government launched an offensive to retake neighborhoods in the nation's commercial hub of Aleppo, unleashing artillery, tanks, and helicopter gunships against poorly armed opposition fighters. Also in July, as many as two hundred people were massacred in the village of Tremseh. The town was subjected to assault by helicopters, artillery, and tanks and then sacked by *shabiha* irregulars.

In spite of the regime's relentless assault, and in spite of the debility of the US/UN response, by mid-2012, the Assad regime was, in the NATO secretary-general's words, "approaching collapse." Rebels had gained significant territory and their numbers were steadily rising. Defections were increasing, and top defector Brigadier General Manaf Tiass was planning a new government. The regime had earned the hatred of so much of the populace that its overthrow seemed a matter of time. Even Syrian ally Hezbollah was distancing itself. With momentum on the rebels' side, England, France, Turkey, Saudi Arabia, and some members of Congress urged aid (short of military intervention) to the Syrian resistance—but the US avoided strong action, rejecting ideas such as a no-fly zone, a humanitarian corridor, and the supply of arms to vetted rebels.

Invigorated by the rebels' failure to procure viable international aid, and determined to keep power, Assad employed yet more extreme tools of domination. In the meantime, the chaos created by the Syrian War and the vacuum created by US and UN passivity opened the door to Syrian allies Russia and Iran, and to extremist groups eager to hijack the Syrian revolt. Among them: Iranian Quds, al-Nusra, and al-Qaeda in Iraq, soon to become ISIS. The radicalization and escalation of the conflict would suit Assad very well.

Still, the administration's position remained as ambiguous as it was weak. The Obama administration was "in 'a holding pattern,' waiting for Russia to abandon its support for Bashar al Assad, waiting for sanctions to topple the economy and waiting for an organized Syrian opposition to present a coherent vision for a post-Assad Syria."[27]

Making matters worse, reports emerged that the regime was amassing chemical weapons to use in Aleppo and elsewhere. The use of banned cluster bombs on innocents had already been confirmed. In a March 2012 article entitled "Syrian Ironies," Victor Davis Hanson had seen this coming: "The Obama State Department is quietly briefing U.S. officials and foreign governments that Syria not only has sizable stores of biological and chemical weapons, but also may be likely in fact to use both in extremis—an apparent attempt to help justify the possibility of some sort of aerial intervention or other preemptive attack. This is the liberal mirror image of the Bush administration's 2002–03 worries about Saddam's Iraq. Actually, there is a final, final irony. If that intelligence is true, and if the Assad regime in fact has such enormous WMD stores, where might at least some of these weapons have come from?"[28]

It was now more likely that a post-Assad regime would have strong Islamist influences. America's indifference to Syria's humanitarian plight meant a decrease in US and Western stature among Syrian reformers. US/UN passivity meant that there was a vacuum in Syria that others had filled. Funding and arming the rebels was left to Saudi Arabia and Qatar, while al-Qaeda, Iran, and Russia were working very hard to thwart American/Western goals. In late summer 2012, it was confirmed that al-Qaeda operatives from Iraq were streaming across the border to "help" the Syrian resistance. The escalating violence in Syria and its spillover into neighboring Turkey threatened to ignite all-out war.

Kofi Annan announced in August that he would quit his role as special envoy to Syria. This announcement should have signaled the futility of the Obama-Clinton approach to foreign affairs. Their approach rested upon finding consensus with the "international community" in order to solve post–Cold War problems. They stressed all the great things we could accomplish if only we compromised with our opponents and acted in concert with the UN. But the Syrian cataclysm showed that Obama's one-world vision was a pipedream and an excuse for moral indifference. While Syrians cried out for help and Syria became a graveyard, Kofi Annan and his supporters sought just the kind of international consensus and just the sorts of compromises Obama lauded. Stated Annan, "Things fell apart in New York. The increasing militarization on the ground [in Syria] and the clear lack of unity in the Security Council have fundamentally changed the circumstances for the effective exercise of my role."[29]

With the failure of the plan finally out in the open, the administration finally announced a plan to provide nonlethal assistance to the rebels, in the form of communications equipment and training. Was the planned assistance a response to the failure of Annan's plan or a response to the fact that failure had finally been made public?

In a fascinating August 2012 question-and-answer session at the State Department, a Mr. Arshad pressured press office director Patrick Ventrell on the administration's moral and strategic ambiguities. Ventrell admitted that "we're not surprised that the Joint Special Envoy [Kofi Annan] was at a point where, given the regime's intransigence, he thought it was the appropriate time to step down." Arshad shot back, "You spent months and months of diplomatic effort that all failed to try to promote his plan and make it a viable political transition strategy. And that has gone nowhere. So if it's not surprising, why did you spend so much time if you never—if you didn't think it would succeed in the first place?"[30] Ventrell denied that was the case. He said Clinton had recently announced that the United States might be able to provide more aid to the Syrian rebels once they controlled more territory and formed "safe zones," but Arshad pressed on: If diplomacy had admittedly failed, and the administration was now putting its hopes on the opposition gaining more ground—if the administration really wanted to hasten the day when Assad stepped down—why wouldn't it actively help rebel efforts to hold territory? He probed, "Aren't you kind of putting the cart before the horse in the sense that if you were to give them more support, they would be able to . . . capture and hold more territory? I mean, aren't you setting them up to fail when you could be helping them achieve your aim? . . . We send nominal support in terms of communication equipment, which, and some, obviously, humanitarian aid for those who have been affected. But practically, you're just going to let the Syrian opposition fight it out until Assad goes?"[31]

Administration officials, Hillary Clinton included, went public with their reservations about arming the rebels. In a February 2012 interview with Fareed Zakaria on CNN, General Martin Dempsey, chairman of the Joint Chiefs of Staff, said, "I think it's premature to take a decision to arm the opposition movement in Syria. I would challenge anyone to clearly identify for me the opposition movement in Syria at this point." In a February 2012 interview with CBS News in answer to questions about US reluctance to arm dissidents, Clinton said, "First of all, we don't know who it is that would be armed . . . what are we going to arm them with and against what? We're not going to bring tanks over the borders of Turkey, Lebanon, and Jordan." She made similar arguments in a House subcommittee hearing on February 29.[32]

In the unavoidable face of escalating destruction and war, senior officials within the administration did *eventually* propose more substantial aid to the Syrian opposition, including providing them with weapons. In February 2013, Secretary of Defense Panetta and General Dempsey testified in Congress that they supported a 2012 plan by Secretary Clinton and CIA director David Petraeus to begin arming opposition forces. But the White House would not back the plan, and it is unclear how definitively the plan was developed or promoted. Reported the *New York Times*, "Wary of becoming entangled in the Syria crisis, the White House pushed back, and Mrs. Clinton backed off."[33]

In spite of her later emphasis upon her own authorship of the plan, it seems that Clinton was less an advocate for arming the rebels than one who thought it might be worth trying since diplomacy had failed. "At the time of the Obama administration's internal debate over that decision, several officials said, Mrs. Clinton's advocacy was far less thunderous: the United States had tried every diplomatic channel with Syria, she said, and nothing else had worked, so why not try funneling weapons to the moderate rebels," reported Mark Landler in the *New York Times*.[34] "A former Obama administration official who attended White House meetings on Syria said Clinton didn't push hard on arming the rebels," reported the *Wall Street Journal*.[35]

Using Americans' understandable fear of another war as an excuse for muteness and inaction, President Obama dodged questions about why he didn't say or do more to help the Syrian people with answers such as this: "I think what you mean is why didn't we involve ourselves militarily in the conflict." Secretary Clinton bolstered the case for inaction by implying that America's cautious response had been conditioned *all along* by fears of Islamist extremism within the opposition.[36] Their excuses for US inaction sounded sensible enough, *but they were misleading.* In spite of the Obama administration disinformation campaign, which implied that radical Islam was a big factor from the start of the Syrian revolt, the goals and tactics of the Syrian opposition were originally the opposite of Islamic extremists, who want to instate Sharia law and advocate violence.

In the State Department's own testimony to Congress on December 14, 2011, Middle East Peace Office Regional Affairs Coordinator Frederick Hof had stated, "The main thrust of the Syrian opposition today remains that part of the opposition that is absolutely committed to peaceful transition in Syria. We are talking about mainly the Syrian National Council and other organizations. These are organizations that are absolutely determined to do their best to avoid civil war."[37] In his 2012 book *The Arab Uprisings,* historian James Gelvin described the two most important groups of the Syrian resistance as "the spontaneous, mostly peaceful crowds that have come together in city after city, town after town, to protest some local provocation or in solidarity with those in neighboring communities" and a "variety of pro-democracy, pro-human-rights, and social media groups," with many "tracing their roots to the 'Damascus Spring.'"[38]

As late as August 2012, newspapers across the world, including the *Washington Post,* were reporting that the National Council which had risen with the Damascus Spring was still the most significant element and leader of the rebellion. *As late as March 2013,* the new secretary of state,

John Kerry, stated in Saudi Arabia that there were moderate elements in the opposition that could be trusted to maintain custodianship of any arms they received. *As late as September 2013,* Anthony Cordesman of the Center for Strategic and International Studies asserted that our interests in Syria are "tied to the risk that *a still largely moderate Sunni rebel movement in Syria* may be driven to extremism if Assad survives."[39] (italics mine) Just as the role of Sunni Arab moderates fighting Assad has been downplayed, with their requests for arms and equipment typically stonewalled, so the valiant role of the Kurds in fighting ISIS has been little appreciated, while their requests for arms and equipment have often been ignored.[40]

Let us remember that protests grew (and grew "violent") *in response* to *human rights atrocities in the regime's own response to protests.* As one momentous example, in an assault on villages surrounding Daraa, security forces fired on and rounded up civilians, and a child named Hamza got separated from his father. A month later, Hamza's body was returned bloated, purple, and bruised from torture. In response, residents of Douma, a Damascus suburb, went out onto the streets shouting, "We are all Hamza al-Khatib!"[41] It is also important to note that, under assault, protestors *specifically pleaded for American/democratic (not Islamic extremist) help. If significant numbers in the opposition have turned toward radical Islam, it is largely because of radical Islam's active infiltration of the movement and because of the moral, political, and strategic vacuum created by American/Western policy.* While the United States prevaricated and deferred to others, others stepped in.

Let us remember that Assad's own strategy rested upon dividing the population by defining the struggle in sectarian terms, and by defining the opposition as terrorists. We thereby see that the American regime in some ways encouraged Americans to fall for the *Syrian regime's* propaganda. With its claims that it supported a "strong sanctions regime" all along, with its mischaracterization of Syria's democracy movement, with its downplaying of Assad's atrocities, with its depiction of the Syrian conflict as "sectarian," with its insinuation that it was (always) afraid to support the Syrian opposition due to the opposition's ties with terror, and with Clinton's claim that the administration practiced "people-to-people diplomacy," the administration attempted to rewrite history as it unfolded.

It is the Assad regime (not the Syrian reform movement) that has long employed terror as an instrument of state policy and sponsored terrorist groups, and that is a major threat to regional peace. While it is true that extremism is now rampant in Syria, that ISIS is now a fierce and formidable part of the opposition, and that this changes our policy options, there was a time when we *did* have better policy options. The tragic irony is that those who accept the do-nothing Syria policy of the Obama administration due to the assumption that the opposition was and is radicalized overlook how radical the Syrian *regime* is and how many radical groups it supports.

Indeed, with the apparatus of the state at their disposal, and with the backing of other states, Ahmadinejad's Iran and Assad's Syria are potentially *more* capable of planning attacks on the West, and of using WMD in the attacks, than terrorist organizations. With this reasoning, Scott Stewart of Stratfor Global Intelligence responded as follows to Hillary Clinton's 2010 statement that she considered weapons of mass destruction in the hands of an international terrorist group to be the largest threat faced by the United States, even bigger than the threat posed by a nuclear-armed Iran:

> Due to the military, financial, diplomatic, intelligence and law enforcement operations conducted against the core group it [al-Qaeda] is now a far smaller and more insular organization than it once was and is largely confined geographically to the Afghan-Pakistani border. . . . The bottom line is that a nuclear device is the only element of the CBRN [chemical, biological, radiological, and nuclear] threat that can be relied upon to create mass casualties and guarantee the success of a strategic strike. However, a nuclear device is also by far the hardest of the CBRN weapons to obtain or manufacture and therefore the least likely to be used. Given the pressure that al Qaeda and its regional and franchise groups are under in the post-9/11 world, it is simply not possible for them to begin a weapons program intended to design and build a nuclear device. Unlike countries such as North Korea or Iran, jihadists simply do not have the resources or the secure territory on which to build such facilities.[42]

Providing further food for thought, the *Chicago Tribune* ran an article the title of which says it all: "Imagine if Hamas Was Backed by a Nuclear

State."[43] To this we can add our own headline: "Imagine if Syria Provides Chemical Weapons to Hezbollah." The scenario is not far-fetched; a January 2013 United Nations report confirmed that Hezbollah is fighting for Assad in Syria.

There were countless missed opportunities to influence events in Syria during the first term and, as we are about to see, in the second. The administration assumed an indifferent posture in relation to the humanitarian crisis; passed up opportunities to develop ties with the Syrian opposition and to influence its agenda; failed to cooperate with border states to stop the flow of terrorists in and out of Syria; and rejected proposals from allies and from Congress for stricter actions such as a humanitarian corridor and a no-fly zone. In addition, according to the Arabic news portal Elnashra, at the request of the Muslim Brotherhood in her native Egypt, Obama's advisor on Muslim affairs Dalia Mogahed blocked a delegation of Middle Eastern Christians from meeting with Obama and members of his national security team to discuss the Syrian crisis. Some Syrian Christians supported Assad for fear of Islamist retaliation. Given the administration's own philosophy of engagement, this was more, not less reason, for dialogue in which Americans would have had opportunity to encourage discussions between Christian and Muslim groups and discourage Christians from accommodating the brutal Syrian regime.

In October 2012, the Associated Press posted a significant article entitled "Civil War Leaves Syrian Economy, Cities in Ruins." It stated: "In Syria's cities and towns, entire blocks of apartment buildings have been shattered, their top floors reduced to pancaked slabs of concrete. Centuries-old markets have been gutted by flames of gunfire in places like Aleppo and Homs—an irreplaceable chunk of history wiped out in a few hours of battle. And then there are the many factories, oil pipelines, schools, hospitals, mosques and churches that have been systematically destroyed in nearly 19 months of violence. Aside from the human tragedy of the many lives lost in Syria's civil war . . . there is the staggering damage to the country's infrastructure and economy."[44]

In January 2013, Senators John McCain, Joe Lieberman, and Lindsey Graham posted an op-ed in the *Washington Post* called "Syria's Descent into Hell." They asserted:

President Obama has declared that his "red line" is Assad's use of chemical weapons. Many Syrians, however, have told us that they see the U.S. red line as a green light for Assad to use all other weapons of war to massacre them with impunity. . . . For months we have argued . . . that the United States, together with our allies in Europe and the Middle East, must do more to stop the killing in Syria and to provide help to moderate forces among the opposition. Specifically, we have advocated providing weapons directly to vetted rebel groups and establishing a no-fly zone over part of Syria. Neither course would require putting U.S. troops on the ground or acting alone. Key allies have made clear again and again their hope for stronger American leadership and their frustration that the United States has been sitting on the sidelines. . . .

Most distressing of all are the swiftly deteriorating humanitarian conditions in Syria. . . . Recent visitors to Aleppo have told us they saw no sign of U.S. aid there, nor were local Syrians aware of any American assistance. . . . [This has created] opportunities for extremist groups to provide relief services and thereby win even greater support from the Syrian people. To many, these extremists appear to be the only ones stepping in to help Syrians in the fight. Meanwhile, moderates in the Syrian opposition are being discredited and undercut by our lack of support. . . . If we remain on the current course, future historians are likely to record the slaughter of innocent Syrians, and the resulting harm done to America's national interests and moral standing, as a shameful failure of U.S. leadership and one of the darker chapters in our history.

■　■　■

Secretary of State Kerry at times issued human rights statements that seemed more heartfelt than the rare human rights statements issued by President Obama and Secretary Clinton in the first term. Most of the time, however, his statements exuded moral ambivalence. The former was the case when Kerry spoke at the Preventing Sexual Violence Initiative in London, and pled for the release of kidnapped human rights activist Razan Zaitouneh: "Human rights defenders like abducted Syrian activist Razan Zaitouneh, are especially on our minds. Razan has risked her life inside Syria to care for political prisoners and call attention to human rights violations, including against women. We stand in awe of her leadership and heroism. And again today, I call for her release and the release of thousands of human rights defenders around the world. Their voices must not be silenced—their voices must be empowered."[45] The latter was the case when Kerry pushed Russian plans for Syria, and urged both sides to compromise for the sake of the Russia and US-sponsored Geneva "peace process":

> [The Geneva peace process] is the only way to bring about an end to the civil war that has triggered one of the planet's most severe humanitarian disasters and which has created the seeding grounds for extremism. . . . And any names put forward for leadership of Syria's transition must, according to the terms of Geneva I and every one of the reiterations of that being the heart and soul of Geneva II, those names must be agreed to by both the opposition and the regime. That is the very definition of mutual consent. . . . This means that any figure that is deemed unacceptable by either side, whether President Assad or a member of the opposition, cannot be a part of the future. . . . And so on the eve of the Syrian Opposition Coalition general assembly meeting tomorrow to decide whether to participate in Geneva in the peace conference, the United States, for these reasons, urges a positive vote.[46]

What better sign of moral ambiguity than the fact that the Kerry period was defined by attempts to find solutions for Syria by collaborating with Russia. American-Russian engagement must be seen not only in light of the failure of the US "reset" to elicit helpful Russian behavior, but also in light of the failure of US attempts to deal with Syria by working with Russia. American-endorsed, Russian-sponsored "peace plans" and "peace conferences" succeeded only in elevating Putin's stature and extending Assad a lifeline. They gave the Assad regime time just when time was running out.

Russia is a key ally to the Syrian regime. It runs interference for Syria in the UN Security Council, provides Syria with many of the very weapons it uses to massacre civilians, and demonizes Syrian pro-democracy groups in its own propaganda. Thus, even before Russia invaded Syria with troops, military aircraft, and tanks in 2015, it was clear that the Obama administration's deferral to Russia on Syrian matters was as unprincipled as it was unwise.

Invigorated by US and UN passivity and ineffectiveness, and determined to keep power, Assad employed even more extreme methods. In April 2013, Israel's senior military intelligence analyst said the regime used chemical weapons "repeatedly" and France and Britain wrote letters to the UN making a similar claim based on "credible evidence." The Turkish prime minister said it was "clear" chemical weapons were used. But the American president wasn't so sure and the US response, as headlines indicated, was again weak: *Bloomberg*, "US Sees No Hard Evidence of Syrian Chemical Weapons;" *Washington Post*, "US Still Evaluating Claims that Syrian Government Used Chemical Weapons."

Making matters worse, the United States and Russia touted a proposal for negotiated compromise just as evidence of chemical weapons use surfaced, and at the very time rights groups were finding clear evidence of torture facilities. In May 2013, Secretary of State Kerry and Foreign Minister Lavrov announced plans for a conference based upon the Geneva Communiqué of 2012. That communiqué, while calling for a transitional government, did not rule out Assad's participation in that government. Putin and Lavrov had stridently claimed that the communiqué did not require Assad's departure. But this did not stop Kerry from stating, along with the announcement, that US and Russian interpretations of the communiqué were "very similar." He explained that even though he couldn't see how Syria could be governed by Assad in the future, he was "not going to decide that" because "the Geneva Communiqué says that the transitional government has to be chosen by mutual consent" . . . "of the current regime and the opposition."

The vacuum created by US/UN equivocation opened the door to Russia, Iran, and Hezbollah, and to extremist groups eager to hijack the Syrian revolt. But moderates were still *fighting* jihadists, the most formidable of which was an emboldened and strengthened ISIS. Indeed, David Kenner documented sharp divisions between mainstream rebel groups and extremists and suggested that these divisions actually made it easier to vet non-Islamist, non-extremist rebels.[47] Michael Weiss asserted, "There is perhaps no better indicator of the readiness of certain rebel groups to play ball than the confidence with which top FSA commanders in Daara openly condemn Jabhat al-Nusra and the Islamic State of Iraq and the Levant."[48] But, with Hezbollah, Iranian Quds, al-Qaeda affiliates and ISIS vying for dominance, and the United States doing nothing to capitalize on these divisions, Syria was and is imploding.

In October 2013, Senators McCain and Graham wrote another editorial, which critiqued America's "abdication of a leadership role in the Middle East and its serious consequences." Nothing, they said, "highlights these failures more vividly than the abandonment of the Free Syrian Army and other moderate opposition forces in Syria." True to the senators' depiction of US policy, the administration's response to the Assad regime's August 2013 unleashing of chemical weapons on thousands of Syrians was vacillating and weak.

This time, even the Obama administration expressed "high confidence" that the regime had carried out a chemical weapons attack, which, according to Obama's "red line," should invoke US airstrikes. But Obama decided to submit the proposal for military action to Congress, clearly hoping to shift the blame and/or allow time for the crisis to pass. Smelling another opportunity, Russia commandeered another plan—this time for removal and destruction of Syria's chemical weapons by 2014 if the United States refrained from striking Syria. This gave Obama the "out" he wanted and bought Assad more time to annihilate the opposition.

It was, again, misguided to think anything good could come from a plan orchestrated by Syrian ally Russia. It was foolhardy to place faith in Russia on the issue of chemical weapons, for it was Russia that, while everyone else was confirming Assad's use of chemical weapons, denied and questioned their use. Tellingly, the US failed to persuade Russia to include, in the UN resolution that formalized the plan, invocation of Chapter VII, which would have authorized the use of force if Syria didn't disarm. Chillingly, Syria's Minister of National Reconciliation praised the agreement as "a victory for Syria that was achieved thanks to our Russian friends."

The resolution included a call for a conference to implement the Geneva Communiqué—which had become a symbol of US/Russian collaboration. Predictably, the resolution emboldened the Assad regime, which seized the offensive and retook rebel territory. By calling on both sides to compromise and confirming Assad's role in negotiations, the agreement also re-legitimized the regime.[49] How tragic-absurd that the United States adopted such policies. History tells us not to put faith in negotiations with murderous dictators; Hitler's Germany provides them with a model of how to cooperate *just* enough to buy time for their deadly aims.

Peace talks were a pipe dream. Rebels knew that if they laid down arms, Assad would crush them. And, in the absence of major military setbacks, Assad had no reason to compromise. Not surprisingly, the regime denied it had accepted the idea of transitional government, while the opposition insisted upon Assad's departure. Diplomats claimed that just getting the two sides together was an accomplishment, but was it? The fatally flawed peace process gave both the Assad regime and jihadists *time* to seize the upper hand. Indeed, by January 2014, the situation in Syria was much worse: 130,000 people had been killed in the cataclysmic war. In conservatively derived estimates, the United Nations High Commissioner for Refugees (UNHCR) cited two million external refugees (half of them children) and 4,250,000 Syrians facing severe problems.

After the "peace conference," the ruthless Assad stepped up his bombardment. Human Rights Watch reported that Syrian jets were dropping incendiary bombs with napalm-like fuel that cause horrific injuries, and that children were suffering severely. Countless souls were being psychologically and physically scarred for life; entire towns and farming communities were bombed into oblivion, and throngs of desperate children had lost both their parents and their homes. Torture and sexual abuse, starvation and disease, compounded the tragic scenario. Faced with unrelenting misery, some anti-regime residents around Damascus agreed to regime-enforced truces or "national reconciliations" with the dreaded military and security forces.

This did not stop the administration from endorsing yet another Russia-sponsored "peace-conference," in Moscow in early 2015. Before the failed Moscow conference, Kerry expressed hope that the conference would be "helpful," while, afterward, he called it "useful." Yet, even the goal of a transitional government had been dropped, benefitting Assad.

In the meantime, ISIS, in the words of General Jack Keane, had grown from "a terrorist organization" to a "terrorist army" now wreaking havoc in both Syria and Iraq, and controlling large swaths of land between Mosul in Iraq and Raqqa in Syria. Keane observed that the Free Syria Army was the only organization "truly contesting ISIS." He, like many others, suggested giving more aid to these forces so that they'd have more ammunition to fight not only the vicious Assad regime, but also the vicious Islamic State. "They have been vetted. We are now giving them missiles. We have to increase that rather robustly. ... If we increased the arms and increased the training for that, it's likely they'd be able to change the momentum. Quite frankly, we have not been doing what we should in helping them."[50]

Ironies abound. While the Obama administration justified unwillingness to give meaningful aid to Syrian rebels with fear of giving aid to extremists within rebel ranks, that stance allowed extremism within Syria to metastasize. While the administration justified American passivity with American aversion to "boots on the ground," that passivity allowed ISIS to build a stronghold in Syria and Iraq, a development so serious that it *required* a US military response. While the administration hoped that Iran's cooperation on nuclear issues would be more easily gained if the US didn't take a strong stand against Assad, Iran saw this as another sign of American weakness and proceeded with its nuclear program accordingly. While the US hoped that it could develop a constructive, cooperative relationship with Russia by working with Russia on Syria, Russia took American acquiescence to its Syria plans and ran with them—continually upping the ante in the Assad regime's favor.

Even as it began to take limited military measures against ISIS in Syria and Iraq, the administration broadcast that it wouldn't do whatever it took, thus indicating to enemies that, as in Iraq and Afghanistan, the best strategy was to wait feckless America out. In Wales, Kerry said that while the US and allies were ready to confront the Islamic State, they wouldn't send combat troops into the Middle East. "I think that's a red line for everybody here," he said. "No boots on the ground." Similarly, Obama said in his speech outlining US action against ISIL, "It will not involve American combat troops fighting on foreign soil."

Peace through strength should be our goal, but we shouldn't downplay American military resolve, nor hamstring our military leaders with prohibitive rules of engagement against terrorists. This is especially the case because Islamic State credibility increases with territorial gains; the Caliphate the terrorist group promises depends not just upon the spread of its hate-filled ideology, but also upon the wresting of land from enemy infidels. ISIS is "simultaneously a strategic threat to the region and the world and a genocidal terror movement." [51]

Nor, in the struggle against ISIS, should the US have downplayed the pernicious role of the Syrian, Russian, and Iranian regimes. In a February 2015 article entitled "Beware ISIS Strategy That Fortifies Russia, Syria, and Iran," I argued:

> Although the president now highlights the brutality and aggression of the Islamic State, he still whitewashes the brutality and aggression of *established states* Syria, Russia, and Iran, and still ignores the need for grand strategy to deal with them. When nation-states escalate weapons programs, enact egregious human rights violations, foment regional chaos and war, and plot against the United States and its allies, history tells us to take it seriously. We must, therefore, take Iran, Russia, and Syria, and the collusion between them, seriously. . . . Working with the Iranian, Russian and Syrian regimes to address Middle Eastern problems and fight ISIS is a sure way to alienate Middle Eastern moderates and traditional partners.
>
> Iran's backing of terror groups in Syria, Iraq, Lebanon, Yemen, and elsewhere; its uncompromising pursuit of nuclear weapons and ballistic missiles; its regional adventurism and worsening human rights violations, should make containing Iran and stopping its nuclear program an *American foreign policy priority*. Assad's reign of terror on the Syrian people; the opportunities for "bad actors" the Syrian cataclysm provides; the Syrian regime's use of WMD and unrepentant enactment of some the worst atrocities the world has ever seen, should make finding an end to the Assad regime an *American foreign policy priority*. Russia's staunch support of Syria and Iran; its ruthless aggression in Ukraine; and its expansionist designs in Eastern Europe, should make containing Russia an *American foreign policy priority*. Instead, much of the White House plan for combating ISIS plays right into Syrian, Iranian, and Russian hands, for it revolves around *their* plans—which include allowing Assad to stay in power, legitimizing Russian-sponsored "peace conferences" that buy Assad time and raise Putin's stature, accommodating the Iranian nuclear program, and giving Iran the lead in the battle against ISIS and in the Levant.[52]

The Assad regime and ISIS might be enemies, but ISIS is useful to the regime. Insofar as the Islamic State is part of the opposition, it lends credence to the argument Assad has made all along: that those fighting against the regime are terrorists. Insofar as the Islamic State fights other opposition groups, it hastens the demise of moderate Syrian rebels. Tellingly, the regime and ISIS often spare each other while targeting others.

Particularly revealing, in 2011, the regime released much of the current ISIS leadership from prison, hardened and radicalized from years of torture and abuse. Western intelligence sources and activists told the *Telegraph* that the regime released ISIS militants "to persuade the West the uprising is terrorist-led."[53] In turn, Russia and Iran have used the war against ISIS as the excuse for further incursions into the region and for strengthening their military relationship with each other and Assad. The US response to ISIS, meanwhile, has been inadequate, weak, and captive to the decisive actions of Russia and Iran. Adam Garfinkle put it this way:

> The Russians are flexing their military muscle as well as their mouths. The U.S. effort against ISIS, meanwhile, has been about as feckless a use of military force as one can imagine. . . . It has also remained, from the start, bereft of a coherent strategy, for U.S. policy refuses to acknowledge that the key proximate cause of ISIS is the brutality of the Assad regime's campaign against the majority Sunni population of Syria. Attacking ISIS with aerial pinpricks while leaving the source of its political strength alone—whether to avoid interrupting the appeasement of Iran en route to the July 14 nuclear deal, or for some other reason—is akin to thinking that one can affect the position of a shadow by doing things to the shadow.[54]

Just as ISIS presents itself as the only force that can achieve the theocratic goals of Islamist ideology and defeat the brutal Assad, Assad presents himself as the only force that can counteract Islamist extremism and defeat the Islamic State. In a *60 Minutes* interview, Assad said that ISIS had expanded since US airstrikes and that he was "open" to negotiations with the United States. But the enemy of our enemy is not really the enemy of our enemy. Rather, both the Syrian regime and Islamic State are enemies of *us* . . . of everything we supposedly stand for, of the liberal-democratic tradition itself.

As if to highlight its moral and strategic equivocation for all the world to see, the administration went from more definitively indicating that Assad should go, to more definitively agreeing that Assad could stay, within the course of a few months. By the spring of 2015, in spite of the advantages that Iranian and Russian assistance (and US accommodation of Russia and Iran) gave the Syrian regime, it had suffered a series of military setbacks and its reputation was at a new low. On May 11, Secretary Kerry met with Putin in a "bid to advance a stalled Obama administration goal of forcing Syria's leader from power." Although the administration dismissed calls for the establishment of "safe zones" within Syria, an administration official said, "We're going to press upon the Russians that now is the time for them to really make a 180-degree turn on their support for the regime given what's happened on the ground."[55]

Yet, when, in October, Russia brazenly sent tanks, military aircraft, drones, and troops into Syria with the goal of helping Assad, the United States steadily backed away from its anti-Assad position. While expressing concern about the fact that the Russian campaign was targeting rebels the US supposedly supported instead of targeting ISIS (the purported reason for the incursion), Kerry nevertheless volunteered that he would consider talks with Russia that would be aimed at finding "common ground," and more "peace talks" in which he said we would not be "doctrinaire" about the time or date of Assad's departure. Iran, for its part, took a more forceful approach, sending in four thousand Revolutionary Guards to join the Russian assault.

The more Russia and Iran stepped up their military presence in Syria, the less "doctrinaire" the position of the United States. By October 26, headlines were announcing that the United States saw "new need to engage Russian and Iran on the Mideast." At Indiana University on October 16, Kerry naïvely appealed to Russia's supposed reason as a way to encourage moderation of Russia's policies and at the same time, in defiance of reason, allowed room for a positive interpretation of Russian policies:

> He [Putin] is not going to be able to stop the war by being there. It could be ISIL that actually winds up gaining in that process, and that would be absurd, it would be a farce, and I think President Putin understands that....
>
> It remains to be seen what their full strategy is in Syria.... If Russia is there to go after ISIL, and to in fact help prevent the takeover of the country and to secure a political track that could result in the end of the war, that could be positive.

If Russia is there to uphold Assad, and fake it with respect to the extremists and terrorists, that's a serious problem.[56]

Thus, the Obama administration succumbed to the course that—with its acquiescence to Russian plans for Syria, its granting to Iran the leadership role in the battle against ISIS, and its heedlessness regarding the dire geopolitical and humanitarian consequences of the Syrian war—it had been heading toward all along. As 2015 came to a close, the White House endorsed yet another plan for a peace conference on Syria, with Kerry, yet again, heading to Russia in advance of the planned talks, and announcing afterward that in spite of differences on Assad, he and Putin had found "common ground." For the first time, the United States invited Iran to participate in the talks. Not for the first time, it indicated willingness to accept Assad staying on during a transition period.

Such cooperation with Russia and Iran, and such willingness to abide Assad, guarantees the United States a disadvantage in the battle for hearts and minds; it neglects the facts that ISIS propaganda appeals to those *against* Shiia/Arab tyrannical rule, and that Iran's own Islamic fundamentalism constitutes a global threat. As President-elect of the National Council of Resistance of Iran Maryam Rajavi testified to the House Foreign Affairs Committee, "Islamic fundamentalism and extremism emerged as a threat to regional and global peace and tranquility after a religious dictatorship . . . came to power in Iran in 1979. Since then, the regime in Tehran has acted as the driving force for, and the epicenter of, this ominous phenomenon regionally and worldwide." [57] As retired Ambassador Robert Ford emphasized in the same hearing, it is "extremely important to remember" that ISIS draws from "aggrieved Sunni Muslim communities in places like Lebanon, Syria and Iraq who are angry at and afraid of Iran and the Arab Shia." Therefore, "if we ally with Iran against the Islamic State, directly or indirectly, we play into the Islamic State's narrative and help its recruitment." We must also remember moderate Shiites who are being forced into Iran's orbit, and Middle Eastern Christians whose plight is now so dire that some observers are calling it genocide.

In a telling inversion, in late 2015 and early 2016, the Pentagon sent a small number of special operations forces to Syria to advise Arab and Kurdish forces fighting against ISIS, marking the first full-time deployment of US troops there, and sent an elite special operations "targeting force" to Iraq. And, it said it was considering deploying a squadron of Apache attack helicopters to Iraq as part of new assistance programs to counter ISIS, a move that could ultimately require further deployment of American troops. Hadn't aversion to military as opposed to "smart power" solutions been a main excuse for US inaction and refusal to give pro-democracy forces aid?

Again, we learn that burying our heads in the sand in the face of escalating atrocities and hostilities and apocalyptic ideologies only increases the chance that we'll be *forced* into action by events spiraling out of control. The Syrian regime has, again, bought time to crush the resistance. Iran has found yet another opening for its regional designs. Islamic State holds strongholds on Europe's doorstep. Russia has become a major power player in the Middle East for the first time in decades. Then there is the human toll, the catastrophic loss of life and property, the explosive violence, the systematized torture and terror, and the sea of humanity trying to flee. Desperately needed in this complicated and inflammatory environment: the formation of American foreign policy that is principled and wise.

CHAPTER 7

TRAGEDY INTENSIFIES
North Korea Tightens Its Grip while America Looks the Other Way

The real cruelties of this world are caused by governments that are too big and governmental leaders that are too powerful—not by ordinary people going about their lives trying to earn a living. It is not even "the rich" who have earned a big living or the "privileged" who have familial advantages that are the main problem. Nor is it even the "wealthy nations" for which President Obama blames many of the world's problems. It is humans in power who see other humans as means to their grandiose and socialistic but, in the end, cold and impersonal political ends that cause the worst pain.

Although North Korea is an extreme example of the cruelties of governments that are too powerful, it is nevertheless the most important example. The very existence of this brutal totalitarian regime is a crime, and we are all culpable in our indifference. It is not just that the North Korean gulags and prisons are as bad as the concentration camps that we vowed would "never again" mar this earth and degrade the human being. It is that the country itself is a concentration camp, wherein the people endure ubiquitous, omnipresent repression and routinely suffer unimaginable horrors.

In North Korea, the state and state leaders are everything; the individual is nothing. Central plans—"toward the state," that is glorified, and toward the leaders, who are deified—are everything; individual initiative and human longing are nothing. Every North Korean is taught from infancy that individual goals are capitalist sins and that communal-state

234

goals constitute the duty, the pride, and the purpose of every communist. The state controls every aspect of life—where one lives, what one says, whom one associates with, what one does for a career, what one eats, what one wears, what songs one listens to, what art one sees, what books one reads, how one spends time after work, whom one associates with, what rank one has in society, and what regions, if any, one can travel to.

The state restricts just about everything that makes life worth living. Love is discouraged because families are encouraged to spy upon each other; because most mothers spend all day working in factories, after which they must attend several hours of indoctrination sessions; because totalitarian communist ideology demands that the greatest love be directed toward communist leaders and that the "struggle" for communal material goals subsume human affection; because one's "rank," having to do with military status and family origin, dictates whom one can date and marry. Creativity is outlawed, as all forms of independent art and all forms of independent enterprise are prohibited. Photographs and paintings other than communist propaganda are illegal; the only pictures permitted on the walls of homes are portraits of "Eternal President" and "Dear Leader" Kim Il-sung, "Supreme Leader" Kim Jong-il, and "Supreme Leader," Kim Jong-un. By law, these must be dusted and cared for every day. About once a month, inspectors from the Public Standards Police check the cleanliness of the portraits.

Wearing non-state-sanctioned clothing or "decadent capitalist" jewelry is likely to lead to arrest. Listening to, singing, or composing non-state music are punishable offenses. Prominent human rights investigator and advocate David Hawk describes the case of a woman imprisoned in a penitentiary because she had disturbed the "socialist order" by singing a South Korean pop song in a private home.[1]

Learning itself, in any real sense of the term, is forbidden and punishable by hard labor and even death. Libraries have only books that prop up the regime; televisions receive only the propaganda channel of the government; and movie theaters show only propaganda films. Reading a novel or a work of history, religion, or philosophy; watching an unapproved movie or using a film camera; listening to non-Korean news or privately questioning the regime—all are "political crimes" that could send one to the gulag for life. Note Stephan Haggard and Marcus Noland of the East-West Center, "The definition of felony crimes in North Korea includes a range of activities which appear political rather than criminal: 'anti-state, anti-people crimes,' 'crimes injurious to socialist culture,' and so on." They add, "In fact, statistical analysis of detention experiences suggests that the regime disproportionately targets politically suspect groups, particularly those involved in economic activities beyond direct state control. The penal system subjects them to terror in an attempt to keep them atomized and quiescent."[2]

In spite of all the restrictions and regulations, it goes without saying that there is no impartial rule of law or fair trial system in North Korea. Thus, the tightness and rigidity of legal control is juxtaposed with the arbitrariness and capriciousness of the legal process. People in custody are generally subject to whatever level of torture and humiliation their captors decide to deliver. Moreover, interviews with former inmates indicate that most are never told the reason for their arrest.

In *Nothing to Envy: Ordinary Lives in North Korea* (so named because one of the verses Korean children are required to memorize contains the line "We have nothing to envy"), Barbara Demick compassionately and professionally catalogues the stories of Koreans who, defying all odds, managed to escape North Korea and lived to tell the story. Demick cared enough to ask, "What was it like to live in the world's most repressive regime?" I suggest reading this important book, but here I will provide a few snapshots of the living and housing conditions Demick portrays. "In the cities there are 'pigeon coops,' one-room units in low-rise apartment buildings, while in the countryside, people typically live in single-story buildings called 'harmonicas,' rows of one-room homes, stuck together like the little boxes that make up the chambers of a harmonica."[3] Outhouses are shared with other families, while running water and plumbing are extremely rare. Families sleep side by side on mats that they roll up during the day. "Occasionally, door frames and window sashes are painted a startling turquoise, but mostly everything is whitewashed or gray. . . . In the future dystopia imagined in *1984*, George Orwell wrote of a world where the only color to be found was in the propaganda posters. Such is the case in North Korea."[4]

In monochrome, uniform dwellings such as these, everyone in North Korea lives on edge and in fear as neighbors denounce neighbors, friends denounce friends, and lovers denounce lovers. One has to be on guard at all times, even around relatives. North Koreans are organized into *inminban*, which means "people's group"—cooperatives of twenty or so families "whose job it is to keep tabs on one another and run the neighborhood." The *inminban* has an elected leader who must report anything suspicious to higher authorities. The rewards for denouncing enemies of the state are great by North Korean standards. They might include a bit of rice, or exemption from attending all the evening hours of ideological training.

Teenagers' lives are strictly state-controlled and guided. They are expected to join the Socialist Youth League and other state-sponsored organizations and to spend countless hours performing their "socialist duty" in countless ways, from attending ideological "self-criticism sessions" to doing hard labor on farms to fulfilling required years of military service. Their careers are chosen by the state, and the desires, passions, and yearnings of young hearts and minds have nothing to do with state decisions. To its already severe restrictions on dating itself, the state adds the proscription of intermingling between the "classes"—the core class, the wavering class, and the hostile class. Hostile class members include any whose parents or grandparents were born in foreign countries or who had once done or said something that appeared to indicate a questioning of the regime. Once in the hostile class, North Koreans remain there for life.[5]

Teenagers are encouraged to spy on their parents, whether within civilian life or within the infamous camps, and are rewarded for doing do. They are assigned uniforms—even in college—and must adhere to strict dress codes. Hair too long, dresses too short, and blouses that bare the arms are forbidden, as are blue jeans and other signs of "capitalist" inclinations. Offenders can be arrested by the Public Standards Police. Teenagers typically have to collect "night soil" from the outhouses or toilets in and around the buildings in which their families live—since North Korea lacks chemical fertilizer and has few farm animals, human excrement is used.

This is not to say that North Koreans are automatons. If the twentieth century revealed new depths of human cruelty and depravity, it also revealed new levels of human resilience and moral fortitude. The human spirit is a very hard thing to crush.

The standard of life in North Korea is so low that the highest class, except for the ruling leaders themselves, lives in worse conditions than the poorest of the poor in Western countries. Running water, enough food that one isn't constantly hungry, apartments with more than one room, appliances that work, bicycles or any other form of transportation, fabrics made of cotton and other natural fibers, more than one pair of shoes, even rice and grains—all are rare privileges, even within the top ranks of North Korean society. The norm is to have too little to eat, shoes that are falling apart, and clothing made from cheap, brittle, state-made synthetics. Those with transportation do not own it; every "possession" is owned by the state and can be taken away when the state pleases. Traveling within North Korea requires governmental permission and documents, called traveler's certificates. Most people are forbidden from travelling to Pyongyang so that North Korea can show its better side to the rare visitors, who are always accompanied by at least two "minders."

If all of this is not enough to make relatively wildly free American citizens and American leaders stand up for human rights in North Korea and lend their support to such groups as LINK (Liberty In North Korea) and the Democracy Network Against the North Korea Gulag, let's look at the North Korean system of gulags and prisons. Perhaps then we will hear the outcry of dissidents who implore us to act and to care. The 2009 *White Paper on North Korean Human Rights Statistics* had this to say: "The horrendous human rights situation in North Korea, as disclosed by the statistics in this and previous NKDB White Papers, remind us once again that we dare not avert our gaze from the painful reality of the human tragedy that continues to take place in North Korea to this day. In fact, every new defector testimony causes us to be shocked by the gravity, ruthlessness, and particularly the routine nature of human right violations perpetuated in North Korea. That these conditions have persisted for nearly six decades is difficult for most to comprehend."[6] Note how much longer the North Korean system of camps and oppression has existed than did the Nazi and Soviet systems.

Stephan Haggard and Marcus Noland observe in their survey of North Korean prison camp experiences that technology, including satellite images, have played a "surprising role" in revealing the truth about North Korea's camps and detention centers. Yet, they say, "the core of our understanding" is information provided by refugees, including both prisoners and guards, who have managed to flee North Korea. This information has appeared in the form of memoirs, interviews, and databases of individual cases of human rights violations. "The portrait that emerges is of a Soviet-style gulag characterized by an arbitrary judicial system, an expansive conception of crime, and horrific abuses. These abuses include extreme deprivation, particularly with respect to food and medical treatment, torture and public executions."[7]

In *The Aquariums of Pyongyang: Ten Years in the North Korean Gulag*, Kang Chol-hwan portrays the barbarity of life inside the camps. When he was nine, security agents arrived at his relatively luxurious family home, "turned the place inside out," took almost everything, and ordered the family to prepare for "Yodok," a name that filled his parents with dread. The family was deposited to one of ten huts that formed one of the "villages" in the infamous labor camp, and soon learned how to make do with inadequate water and without subsistence levels of food and heating fuel. Adult laborers toiled under backbreaking, slave-labor conditions and hours, berated and whipped by guards. Kang attended classes where most of the "instructors" used their position to terrorize as much as to teach. Beatings and verbal degradation were the method of one. Another "sometimes punished his students by making them stand naked in the courtyard all day with their hands behind their backs."[8] Once a year, prisoners were allotted uniforms that quickly turned to rags and provided no protection from the elements. Corn, sometimes supplemented with acorn paste or collected herbs, was the only diet, so that Kang "was always hungry and had problems digesting the little food." Diarrhea, all the maladies that come with malnourishment, and death by starvation were common.

The fear of punishment was omnipresent, as everyone was ordered to inform on everyone else, and punishment was extreme. Kang writes, "In North Korea—as I later learned was the case in the Soviet Union and Nazi Germany—camp guards aren't satisfied to do all the surveillance themselves: they designate prisoners, unwilling ones sometimes, to become local chiefs and carry out responsibilities the police can't execute on their own. They collect information and have the power to punish recalcitrants, most notably by denouncing them to their superiors. . . . The slightest wrong move, it seemed, could mean extra work or a stint of solitary confinement in a sweatbox. . . . The informants were at every turn."[9] Although prisoners were sent to the "sweatbox" for trivial offenses such as stealing corn or responding to a guard's command with insufficient zeal, the ordeal of the sweatbox was so great that the pour soul subjected to it either died or emerged damaged for life.

Kang Chol-hwan's description of the sweatbox should be enough to stir the hearts of even the most hardened "realists" and the most dogmatic "progressive pragmatists":

> The sweatbox breaks even the sturdiest of constitutions. It is possible to survive it, but the cost is often crippling and the aftereffects are almost always permanent. It is simply grisly: the privation of food, close confinement, crouching on one's knees, hands on thighs, unable to move. The prisoner's rear end presses into his heels so unrelentingly that the buttocks turns solid black with bruising. Hardly anyone exited the sweatbox on his own two feet. If the prisoner needed to relieve himself, he raised his left hand; if he was sick, he raised his right. No other gestures were allowed. No other movements. No words. If the watchman pacing back and forth in front of the sweatbox failed to notice the raised hand, well, that was too bad. The prisoner continued to wait in silence. If he talked, he was beaten, if he moved, he was beaten. And if it was not a beating he got it was a special punishment; he was made to crouch over the septic pit for half an hour, with his hands behind his back and his nose bowed downward.[10]

Kang describes the sweatbox as one of two extraordinarily horrific forms of punishment within the camps, forced labor being the other: "In the realm of horror, only punitive forced labor withstands comparison with the sweatbox. In a way, the two are equal and opposite. With forced labor, one has to move without stopping, excavate mountains of earth, lift massive logs into the back of trucks—all at an infernal pace. ... According to the Yodok veterans, the one appreciable difference between punitive forced labor and the sweatbox was that the latter automatically added five years to one's detention."[11] Unbelievable as it is, Yodok and camps like it are better than the ones reserved for "irredeemables," where conditions are even worse. As an example, in Yongpyong, a camp for irredeemables within the Yodok complex, "inmates are worked harder, locked up at night and allotted less food."

Another revealing book, *Escape from Camp 14: One Man's Remarkable Odyssey from North Korea to the West,* tells a similar story. Although portions of escapee Shin Dong-hyuk's personal account have recently been called into question, the grim portrait of the North Korean camp system painted by author Blaine Harden is still accurate and worthy of our attention. Harden reports that there are six sprawling camps (in addition to the many political prisons) in North Korea. "The biggest is thirty-one miles long and twenty-five miles wide, an area larger than the city of Los Angeles. Electrified barbed-wire fences—punctuated by guard towers and patrolled by armed men—encircle most of the camps." [12] In two of the camps, "some fortunate detainees" are given the possibility of release through "reeducation," but most camps "are 'complete control districts' where prisoners, who are called 'irredeemables,' are worked to death."

Harden points to a distillation of escapee testimony by the Korean Bar Association in Seoul that paints a detailed picture of daily life in the camps. "A few prisoners are executed every year. Others are beaten to death or secretly murdered by the guards, who have almost complete license to abuse and rape prisoners. Most prisoners tend crops, mine coal, sew military uniforms, or make cement while subsisting on a near starvation diet of corn, cabbage, and salt. They lose their teeth, their gums turn black, their bones weaken, and, as they enter their forties, they hunch over at the waist. Issued a set of clothes once or twice a year, they commonly work and sleep in filthy rags, living without soap, socks, gloves, underclothes, or toilet paper. Twelve to fifteen hour workdays are mandatory until prisoners die, usually of malnutrition-related illnesses, before they turn fifty." [13]

These horror stories are confirmed by the meticulous and scholarly but heartfelt work of David Hawk, who, in association with the US Committee for Human Rights in North Korea, produced *The Hidden Gulag: Exposing North Korea's Prison Camps.* The report exposes the forced labor colonies and camps, as well as the smaller shorter-term detention facilities along the North Korea–China border that are used to brutally punish North Koreans who flee to China but are arrested by Chinese police and forcibly repatriated.

The *kwan-li-so* are political penal labor colonies, where the sentences entail slave labor in mining, logging, and farming in the valleys of mountainous areas in north and north central North Korea. The combination of slave labor, below-subsistence-level food rations, and brutal mistreatment leads to early death. The bodies of prisoners are dumped into mass graves or thrown into the mountains. Forced abortions and baby killings are common, since prisoners are not permitted to have children. The *kyo-hwa-so* are prison labor facilities for those who have committed nonpolitical crimes such as stealing, but some of the prisoners in this system are also political. In these, prisoners perform "virtually slave labor" under dreadfully harsh conditions. There is "virtually constant semi-starvation among prisoners and high levels of deaths in detention." Hawk says that both the gulags and the detention facilities "involve extreme phenomena of repression" and that "the practice of torture permeates the North Korean prison and detention system."[14]

A particularly appalling finding of the East-West Center is that the treatment of inmates in lower-level prisons is not much different from the treatment of inmates in the camps. These findings, Haggard and Noland note, "provide insight into how to think about North Korean politics, and the centrality of discretion and terror to the maintenance of the regime's power."[15]

In late January 2011, the UN Special Rapporteur on Human Rights in the Democratic People's Republic of [North] Korea reported, "The information gathered during the meeting with defectors from the DPRK who are currently living in Japan reinforces [a] number of reports that emphasizes dire humanitarian situation and absence of civil, cultural, economic, political and social rights for the people of the DPRK."[16] The rapporteur also reported that the abduction of Japanese nationals by agents of the DPRK remained a problem and revealed that citizens from Thailand, Lebanon, and other countries had been victims of abductions as well. Adding that progress on the release of abductees had seemed possible in 2002 and 2008, he said hope for their release had recently diminished. Refreshingly, he asserted, "the question of abduction is not only a bi-lateral issue between Japan and the DPRK, but one that concerns the international community at large and one that has strong links to the human rights situation."[17]

In its 2012 *World Report*, Human Rights Watch urged, "The United Nations should immediately establish an independent commission of inquiry to investigate crimes against humanity in North Korea." It noted that the change in leadership had not translated into improvements in human rights. "Human rights abuses are systematic and pervasive in North Korea, with no sign of change despite the ascension of Supreme Commander Kim Jong-un, the new paramount leader of the Democratic People's Republic of Korea (DPRK), following the death of his father, Kim Jong-Il, on December 17, 2011."[18] David Hawk also came out with an updated report in 2012. Unbelievably, he found that the human rights situation was either the same or worse.

Robert Park, a Korean-American missionary from Arizona, illegally entered North Korea on Christmas Day 2009 with the purpose of drawing attention to North Korea's human rights abuses. Caught and imprisoned, he was released on February 6, 2010. Park has remained publicly silent about his time in captivity, but it has been reported that he was severely tortured. Park's silence is painfully understandable; US government and "international community" silence is not. The Obama-Clinton approach to foreign affairs emphasized *speech* in its call for negotiation and dialogue between adversaries, but it rejected speech in its refusal to *speak up* for the oppressed and for human and individual rights, in North Korea and other places of extreme repression. The same administration that placed so little faith in the power of words, ideas, and language nevertheless placed naïve hope in verbal interaction with and verbal assurances from dictators.

The real heart of American exceptionalism is the idea that rights are not exceptional; they are universal. The very thing that makes America exceptional is that we, in our very institutions and laws and documents, recognize the universality of rights. We reject the idea that rights are bestowed by government, and that government can create rights or take them away. We take this position because we believe in the permanence and spiritual foundation of human nature and reject communist/utopian attempts to re-create human nature or to re-create man. Harry Truman articulated the idea beautifully: "Democracy has a spiritual foundation because it is based upon the brotherhood of man. We believe in the dignity of the individual. We believe that the function of the state is to preserve and promote human rights and fundamental freedoms. We believe that the state exists for the benefit of man, not man for the benefit of the state. Everything else that we mean by democracy arises from this fundamental conviction. We believe that each individual must have as much liberty for the conduct of his life as is compatible with the rights of others."[19] The human being—the individual—is thus prior to the state, and this concept is the very source of our liberty.

John W. Danford articulated the same concept in *Roots of Freedom*: "Liberty, at least individual liberty, cannot develop so long as the political community is regarded as higher in rank than the individual. The modern project challenged this ancient principle by suggesting that human beings are first and foremost individuals, and that political communities are not natural but artificial."[20] Danford saw that what British historian Paul Johnson called the "century of the state" threatened this advance in human understanding and dignity, and that many still exhibit that "enthusiasm for government" that seems to be the "product of faith in the social sciences, or the ability of human analysis and planners to identify problems and fix them."[21]

In spite of the enormously meaningful and consequential differences between our regime type and that of North Korea, the response of the United States to North Korean totalitarianism has, for the most part and throughout the years, been detached and apathetic. We were understandably demoralized and resigned after the Korean War, which, after so much bloodshed, returned the peninsula to the same demarcated line between north and south that existed before the war. Since then, we have taken sporadic stands for human rights in North Korea, but we have never done so consistently or for a sustained period of time. In recent decades, we have often even *retracted* human rights concerns in order to focus on negotiations regarding North Korea's nuclear program. The leveling one-world vision that comes at the expense of the American tradition, and that influenced the Obama administration, allows some to claim that overlooking the internal practices of other regimes is the progressive (i.e., "tolerant") stance anyway.

In chapter 2, I referred to academic panelists who agreed that a focus on human rights was an arrogant attempt to "impose" one civilization upon another. They claimed North Korea was a "fear regime" and that fear of the United States explained (i.e., justified) North Korea's behavior. One panelist blamed the tension in relations between the United States and North Korea entirely on US "insults." In order to feign moral neutrality, some professors resort to such sophistry. They insist that toning down American ideals is the path to a "unified" world;

that democratic ideas are "culturally specific" and invalid for others; that, for the sake of peaceful compromise, the United States must with-hold its principles and its "judgment." But, *the truth of the matter is that you can't honestly say you're for world harmony without also saying you're for individual and human rights, for it is only respect for human and individual rights that enables people within regimes and between regimes to get along.* The actual effect of one-world socialism is that tyrants may act with impunity and may spread hate-filled propaganda, while democracies are expected to act timidly and to keep their democratic ideals to themselves.

Whether we have interjected human rights into the discussion or have left them out, North Korea has played to our weaknesses—which include our own academicians who apologize for the regime and blame its behavior on our "insults"; which include our tendency to believe that even totalitarians are "rational actors" who will abide by hard-fought negotiated agreements; and which include our susceptibility to lies, prevarications, and verbal games. We must see that North Korea has used the negotiating process to play for time, has violated every nego-tiated agreement, and has methodically continued on with its nuclear program and bellicose posture toward its neighbors and the West.

A survey of decades of negotiations with the North Koreans reveals that our circumspection and politeness regarding their regime type has done absolutely no good. Sure, they might be more willing to come to the table if we remain silent regarding that country's internal condition, but that does not and has not meant that they will keep their agree-ments or change their course. As did Hitler and as do today's Iranian leaders, the Kim dynasty uses negotiations as mere cover for real plans. And, as with Nazi Germany and fascist-Islamist Iran, the only thing that will really change North Korea's foreign policy course is a change in the regime itself.

We must face the fact that negotiation with fanatical regimes is most likely negotiation for its own sake. Totalitarians use negotiations to buy time, build weapons programs, deceive the naïve West, refine war plans, and deflect attention away from their atrocities. Thus, even the most hard-hearted "realists" should not object to the inclusion of human rights concerns in our Korean policy. If the regime collapses due to being unable to extract more concessions from the West and due to strategic and moral pressure from the "international community," this will surely benefit realist geopolitical goals.

■ ■ ■

In the 1980s, when the Soviet Union underwent glasnost and in the process removed much of its financial and military support of the North Korean regime, the truth about the communist-Orwellian experiment began to emerge. Without the propping up of Russia, the North Korean economy, infrastructure, architecture, and food supply rapidly deteriorated. The emperor had no clothes. Soon, the country and the people were impoverished, kept alive only by the Kim dynasty's reign of terror and by the intermittent infusion of food and energy aid from the UN and Western countries, particularly the United States.

The famine and floods of the 1990s nearly destroyed the state-run economy and threatened the regime itself. Starvation killed between six hundred thousand to one million people and scarred millions of others with stunted growth and mental and physical deterioration. The search for food became everything, while people dropping dead in the middle of the street became unsurprising. Rice became a rare, coveted, and fought-after grain. Corn husks were the common dietary staple around which meals were built.

Prior to the 1990s, the crowning achievement of the regime had been subsidized food. When the food supply and distribution system collapsed, the regime itself, by any reasonable reckoning, was therefore implicated and vulnerable. As Haggard and Noland assert, "While authorities blamed the collapse of the food economy on weather, the famine was a classic case of state failure."[22] In the face of possible collapse under the weight of its own failed statism, the North Korean regime stepped up repression, expanded its system of camps, and resorted to ever more gruesome methods of terror and intimidation. It also accelerated its pursuit of nuclear weapons and claimed the program was a necessary defense against the aggressive West, particularly the United States. Anti-Americanism was at the core of every school curriculum.

All of this provides the backdrop to President Bill Clinton's policies. As would most of the Obama foreign policy team, the Clinton foreign policy team believed that the strategic and ideological rivalries of the Cold War no longer applied, and that we were entering a world that would be defined by economic rather than strategic and ideological priorities. As George Friedman of Stratfor Global Intelligence writes, the "consensus" was that war and geopolitics no longer governed the world. "Except for a few rogue states, everyone was in fundamental agreement about what was important: economic growth and prosperity. Modern prosperity was global in nature, and all reasonable people and nations would want to participate in the global adventure."[23]

Beneath the globalist surface, however, there were troubling signs. Although the Soviet empire had fallen, much of the Middle East still operated according to Stalinist rules, while many Middle Eastern countries were procuring components of the (old) Soviet Union's military arsenal. Communists in Asia were asserting regional influence and engaging in weapons proliferation. Oppressive states and terrorist organizations were pursuing weapons of mass destruction with unprecedented intensity. Islamist ideology was becoming more incendiary. Terror attacks were on the rise.

The Chinese and North Korean realities belied the globalist illusion. Asserting that President Clinton had "delusions of supra-national security," *FrontPage Magazine* editor Ben Johnson reminds us that Clinton "famously misled the public that 'there's not a single, solitary nuclear missile pointed at an American child tonight' before asking China to reorient its missiles away from U.S. population centers."[24] "Evidence that North Korea was violating the nuclear Non-Proliferation Treaty surfaced within weeks of Clinton's first inauguration. After a year of inaction allowed Pyongyang to create at least one nuclear weapon, the emboldened Stalinists announced their formal withdrawal from the treaty. It seemed North Korean officials were angling for a payoff. They must have realized they struck the jackpot when Clinton named tough-as-nails Jimmy Carter as his principle negotiator."[25] (In 2010, Carter would write an op-ed for the *Washington Post* that characterized Pyongyang's shelling of a South Korean island and clandestine construction of a uranium facility as merely "designed to remind the world that they deserve respect in negotiations that will shape their future.")

Although the resultant nuclear treaty is cited as evidence of concern for proliferation, and although the treaty process itself came about because Clinton rightly saw that North Korea would be crossing a line if it reprocessed fuel rods into plutonium, the terms provided the North

Koreans with more loopholes and economic benefits than restrictions. The Agreed Framework approved in October 1994 provided North Korea with two light water nuclear reactors and a massive allotment of oil, thus helping the regime with its energy crisis and giving it the very materials that could potentially bolster its non-peaceful nuclear program. It also provided technology and materials that would supposedly go toward a "peaceful" nuclear program in exchange for North Korea agreeing that the IAEA could conduct a one-time inspection of seven declared nuclear sites. In addition, it offered an end to our joint military exercises with South Korea. This in spite of the fact that North Korea was violating the Non-Proliferation Treaty it had *already* signed and that that treaty *already* required regular inspections not only of "self-declared" sites but also of "undeclared" sites.

As events unfolded, we appeared to be the unwitting fools of North Korea's deception. It soon became clear that North Korea had no intention of living up to its side of the bargain.

In forming policy toward North Korea, the Bush administration was torn between the Colin Powell and Richard Armitage camp in the State Department that wanted some continuation of the Clinton approach of engagement and negotiations, and the Dick Cheney and Donald Rumsfeld camp that wanted a harder line on nuclear proliferation and more focus on human rights. In the end, President Bush and his (next) secretary of state, Condoleezza Rice, tried all of the above, but none of it worked insofar as North Korea's nuclear program was concerned.

In 2002, North Korea conducted nuclear weapons tests and flight tests of missiles and admitted to a clandestine uranium enrichment program. It built a uranium enrichment plant and started constructing a new nuclear reactor. As if to confirm fears that this was a regime that would actually consider *using* nuclear weapons once it possessed them, North Korea also repudiated the 1953 Armistice Agreement, sank a South Korean warship, and bombarded a South Korean island, killing four people. Its rhetoric was ceaselessly hostile and bellicose. President Bush and Secretary Rice responded to all of this by demanding a dismantling of North Korea's nuclear program as a precondition to further negotiations.

In the same year, Bush famously delivered the "axis of evil" line in his State of the Union address. He proclaimed the goal of preventing regimes that sponsor terror "from threatening America or our friends and allies with weapons of mass destruction," and elaborated:

> Some of these regimes have been pretty quiet since September 11, but we know their true nature. North Korea is a regime arming with missiles and weapons of mass destruction, while starving its citizens. Iran aggressively pursues these weapons and exports terror, while an unelected few repress the Iranian people's hope for freedom. Iraq continues to flaunt its hostility toward America and to support terror. The Iraqi regime has plotted to develop anthrax and nerve gas and nuclear weapons for over a decade. This is a regime that has already used poison gas to murder thousands of its own citizens, leaving the bodies of mothers huddled over their dead children. This is a regime that agreed to international inspections, then kicked out the inspectors. This is a regime that has something to hide from the civilized world. States like these, and their terrorist allies, constitute an axis of evil, arming to threaten the peace of the world. By seeking weapons of mass destruction, these regimes pose a grave and growing danger. They could provide these arms to terrorists, giving them the means to match their hatred. They could attack our allies or attempt to blackmail the United States. In any of these cases, the price of indifference would be catastrophic. We will work closely with our coalition to deny terrorists and their state sponsors the materials, technology and expertise to make and deliver weapons of mass destruction. We will develop and deploy effective missile defenses to protect America and our allies from sudden attack.[26]

This speech appalled and apparently outraged most pundits, political scientists, and Democratic Party leaders. It was widely and emotionally ridiculed and was seen as one more example of Bush's "cowboy" approach to foreign policy. In response to all the supposed furor, Ben Johnson pointed out that all the attempts to appease North Korea during the Clinton years "failed to quell the North's atom-lust" and, instead, played right into North Korea's hands:

> In August 1998, North Korea lobbed a Taepo Dong 1 missile over Japan. Four months later, officials refused U.S. inspectors access to a suspected underground nuclear reactor at Kumchang-ni. President

Clinton then sweetened the deal by rewarding Kim Jong Il's half-year-long stall tactics with 11 million tons of food worth nearly $200 million. Not surprisingly, American inspectors found no signs of wrongdoing at the long-sanitized facility. Even this seemingly humanitarian food aid turned into a weapon in North Korea's hands. Reports abound that rations have been re-directed to the DPRK's military, the fifth largest in the world. This is nothing new. Using food as a weapon dates back at least to Stalin. Communist Ethiopia similarly misused international aid in the 1980s. With this in mind, Rep. Benjamin Gilman, R-NY, warned in 1999, "Any food aid we provide to North Korea . . . must be monitored to prevent diversion to the military and the party cadre. Unscheduled, unsupervised visits by American Korean-speaking monitors would assist us in this regard." It didn't happen. . . . Even as floods and famine emaciated its nearly 22 million citizens, regime leaders in this "worker's paradise" earmarked every available dollar for guns, not butter, in the hope that Uncle Sam would pay their price without demanding accountable disarmament. Their gamble paid off.[27]

Indeed, the gamble did pay off, as North Korea became the leading recipient of foreign aid in the Asia-Pacific region. According to the testimony of defectors, the North Korean government funneled aid directly to the military rather than to starving citizens. Savvy military members became part of a growing black market, selling just enough of the food aid to starving citizens to keep the economy from utter and total collapse.

In January of 2003, North Korea expelled the IAEA, reopened the Yongbyon nuclear facilities, and withdrew from the Non-Proliferation Treaty. By then, North Korea was announcing, not denying, that it possessed nuclear weapons, and was threatening to export them unless the United States signed a nonaggression pact. Bush considered this blackmail and refused. In May 2003, North Korea abandoned the 1992 Joint Declaration on the Denuclearization of the Korea Peninsula.

Facing lack of success in convincing North Korea to give up its nuclear ambitions, and still facing heated criticism for the Axis of Evil speech, President Bush and Secretary Rice decided to give outreach and negotiations a try. This led to the Six-Party Talks between North Korea, South Korea, China, Russia, Japan, and the United States. North Korea agreed to abandon its nuclear program, to rejoin the Non-Proliferation Treaty, and to allow IAEA inspectors back in, in exchange for more energy assistance, normalization of relations with the United States and Japan, and a peace agreement with South Korea. But, in July 2006, North Korea test-fired a Taepodong-2 missile, giving the lie to its supposed abandonment of its nuclear program. The UN responded with a resolution demanding North Korea halt its ballistic missile activity and requiring all UN members to refrain from exporting materials to North Korea that could contribute to the program. Nevertheless, North Korea conducted its first nuclear test in October 2006. The UN responded with another resolution with more stringent sanctions. In December 2006, the Six-Party Talks resumed, resulting in agreement to implement the steps of the September 2005 statement of principles. In July 2007, the IAEA verified the shutdown of the Yongbyon nuclear facility.

Partly in response to apparent progress on the nuclear issue, in a move hurtful and shocking to human rights activists, the Bush administration removed North Korea from the Trading with the Enemy Act and from the State Sponsors of Terrorism list. North Korea did not return the favor. At the end of the second Bush term—the one in which the Bush team had tried engagement—North Korea refused further discussions until Obama took office; scrapped all military and political deals with South Korea; informed the United States it had enough weaponized plutonium for four to five nuclear bombs; and refused to allow verification of the shutdown of its nuclear programs. In addition, North Korean leaders brandished the word "war," proclaiming that a routine South Korean military exercise had so inflamed tensions that "war might break out at any time."

The lesson was clear: *North Korea had used negotiations as cover for its nuclear program, and had not let negotiated agreements get in the way of its program.* Neither intensifying sanctions nor engaging in negotiations with this hostile regime bore much fruit regarding North Korea's bellicose posturing and nuclear ambitions. Such behavior is characteristic of totalitarian regimes. As Robert Kaufman of the Pepperdine University School of Public Policy puts it, "All regimes do not behave alike. Some are more aggressive; others are more peaceful. There is a vital moral and practical distinction between totalitarian regimes animated by messianic ideologies on the one hand, and stable liberal democracies, on the other. The difference between Nazi Germany and a stable, liberal, democratic West Germany puts this vital distinction in high relief."[28]

What is not clear is whether differently constructed sanctions might have helped move North Korea or might help in the future. Moreover, China's persistent support of North Korea means that costs and pressure must be applied in that direction as well. Because the West's imposition of sanctions has been inconsistent, and often interrupted by food and technical aid, it is impossible to say what effect the long-term imposition of serious sanctions might have. In a 2011 article entitled "Old News from North Korea," Mark Guzylak-Shergold confirmed that, then and now, North Korea uses energy and food aid not to help citizens but to support its military operations.

■ ■ ■

A November 2010 report by former director of the US Los Alamos National Laboratory Siegfried Hecker, in association with the Center for International Security and Cooperation, warrants attention. It was based upon Hecker's fourth trip (since his first in 2004) to the Yongbyon nuclear complex. He found the uranium enrichment facility advanced by leaps and bounds: "Instead of seeing a few small cascades of centrifuges, which I believed to exist in North Korea, we saw a modern, clean centrifuge plant of more than a thousand centrifuges all neatly aligned and plumbed below us. . . . The chief processing engineer told us (in response to persistent questioning) that the facility contained 2,000 centrifuges in six cascades (one thousand centrifuges and three cascades on each side.) . . . The control room was astonishingly modern." Hecker stated that "the 2,000 centrifuge capability significantly exceeds my estimates and that of most other analysts."[29] His "greatest concern" was that "a facility of equal or greater capacity, configured to produce HEU [highly enriched uranium], exists somewhere else." Such a facility, he explained, would be difficult to detect.[30] In an understatement, Hecker went on, "The issue is complicated by the inherently dual-use nature of nuclear technology."[31] He concluded that sanctions were useless, but did recommend continuing attempts to engage with North Korea in order to urge them to use their substantial nuclear capability "for nuclear electricity in lieu of the bomb."

We will see, however, that Obama's engagement policy provided North Korea with *more* opportunities for deception. North Korea's supposed willingness to negotiate with the Obama administration over the dismantling of its nuclear program, which was widely attributed to a toning down of criticism of the regime, turned out to be yet another cover for the program. The initial appearance of cooperation provided camouflage and bought time.

Before turning to Obama's policy, one more thing about the Bush policy needs to be said. In spite of his eventual willingness to give engagement and negotiations a try, Bush could not bring himself to simply ignore the atrocities in North Korea. Perhaps hearing the call of dissidents and activists who expressed dismay at his second-term outreach policies, President Bush made the exposure of North Korean human rights abuses one of his last missions before he left office. He signed a law promoting the US special envoy on North Korean human rights to ambassador and making it easier for North Korean refugees to settle in the United States. Senior US envoy Christian Whiton publicly called on world leaders to meet with North Korean human rights activists "just as President Bush met with the Dalai Lama," saying such meetings would send "powerful signals" to the Pyongyang regime. "When government leaders speak clearly about human rights, it can help those in repressive countries immensely," he said.[32] That is the way defectors saw it. Wouldn't you see it that way if it were your family in the camps, or your son or daughter or parents being routinely tortured by the regime, or if you yourself were languishing in solitary confinement?

In the preface to the revised edition of *The Aquariums of Pyongyang*, defector Kang Chol-hwan emphasizes how much it meant to him and others that President Bush decided at the end of his term to meet with him. Appalled by the way South Koreans and the South Korean government were downplaying North Korean atrocities under the "Sunshine Policy"—to the point that many claimed the "progressive" position was simply to seek peaceful coexistence—Kang was losing hope. "I found God in South Korea, but He seemed determined to not respond to my prayers. I asked the Lord: 'Why do they have to go through all the pain they suffer?' ... My heart broke anew each night as I contemplated their misery." Then, everything changed when Kang Chol-hwan "heard that the president of the world's most powerful nation wanted to meet the author of a gulag memoir he had just finished reading. That was me!"[33] Kang portrays the compounded significance of that singular gesture:

> I now realize that the Lord wanted to use President Bush to let the blind world see what is happening to His people in North Korea. With one simple stroke of God's finger, the bleak reality, in which nearly no one cared about the ghosts of three million famished souls and hundreds of thousands more in concentration camps in my home country was instantly changed. . . . Some inside North Korea said that this single event could wipe out years of anti-American propaganda. And in South Korea, the effects have been most visible on the youth who have been uninformed and, therefore, indifferent to the plight of their fellow Koreans in the North. As for me personally, meeting with President Bush gave me such a visibility that I have been bombarded with requests for one public speech after another. I have been speaking out about human rights violations ever since.[34]

What better testimony to the *power* of moral decency and democratic principles? That power is something understood since our country's founding: Our power does not come primarily from our material strength; it comes primarily from the revolutionary potential of our ideals and from the unleashing of human potential that our political system begets. Our early leaders realized that as the American people reached the heights of accomplishment and creativity that their political freedom inspired—and as the world came to admire and emulate their example—this would be a victory not only for our democracy, but also for our power. In addition, the founders counted on Americans, so many of whom had come to America looking not only for freedom but for freedom of religion and conscience, to be a particularly moral people—who would use their freedom for good purpose. They were thus determined that our relations with the world occur on our own democratic terms and not solely in terms of power politics and the balance of power.

Of course, the founders also recognized that we could not protect the rights of free citizens if we did not protect their very existence. We could not stand for liberty if we did not first stand; if our geopolitical position were not secure. Thus began the hard and complicated task of forging a foreign policy that considered liberty and individual rights, but also *protected* liberty and individual rights. The complexity of that task still confounds us today, but that does not lessen its worthiness. *The defense and the invigoration of the civilization in which the American way of life is rooted remains our consummate foreign policy challenge.* We must see that if we lose the clarity of our democratic principles for the sake of negotiations, then we have lost the reason we're negotiating in the first place. But we must also see that it is essential to keep our national security strategy energized and our military defense posture robust. Until the day when hostile, immoral ideologies and hostile, immoral regimes no longer threaten our way of life, surrendering ourselves to complacency regarding the post–Cold War world is dangerous and unwise.

■ ■ ■

With the Bill Clinton foreign policy team setting the stage for such an approach, the Obama-Clinton foreign policy team chose to see the world in post–Cold War, post-moral, post-ideological, post-strategic terms. In place of the assertion of democratic principles and the construction of grand strategy were attempts to reach out and "talk" with dictators and extremists alike—and to limit the terms of that dialogue to "practical" matters such as proliferation and economic relations (as opposed to "subjective" matters such as political freedom). In forming policy toward North Korea and other extremist regimes, the Obama-Clinton foreign policy team took ideas and principles out of the equation for the sake of a "smarter" approach. The end goal was some sort of workable compromise that enabled us all to get along.

Noting that "Obama depreciates the importance of regime type and ideology in discerning America's friends and foes," Robert Kauffman calls this "unrealistic realism." Why is the "realistic" willingness to overlook regime type and ideology actually unrealistic? Take the case of Russia: "Historically, stable liberal democracies do not fight each other; they also have less serious disagreements with one another and are more likely to cooperate with one another. Conversely, the more tyrannical a powerful regime becomes, the more aggressive and expansionist it tends to be. This holds true with Russia. When Vladimir Putin called the collapse of the evil empire a great tragedy, this statement encapsulated the problem bound to intensify as Putin consolidated his power."[35] True to his expressed ideas, Putin has assailed democratic currents in Russia and reinstated imperial strategies in Eastern Europe and former Soviet territories. In addition, at every turn, he has thwarted the efforts of democracies to contain and restrain hostile and extreme regimes, such as North Korea, Iran, and Syria. Degrading our democratic tradition by ignoring regime type and ideology has emboldened men like Putin.

Given that North Korea scrapped all military and political deals with South Korea, informed the United States it had enough weaponized plutonium for four to five nuclear bombs, and refused to agree to a system for verifying the shutdown of its nuclear programs, it is no surprise that the Obama team's relations with North Korea got off to a strained start—in spite of President Obama's outstretched hand. One month after Obama's first inauguration, North Korea announced that it was preparing to shoot a communication satellite into orbit and threatened to "destroy meddlers." The "communication satellite" was a Taepodong-2 missile believed capable of reaching Alaska. The country's official Korean Central News Agency declared, "If the puppet warmongers infringe upon our inviolable dignity even a bit, we will not only punish the provokers but reduce their stronghold to debris." Still, Obama and Clinton enunciated a diplomatic solution and the improvement of relations with North Korea as their goals.

Regarding Secretary Clinton's high-publicity tour to the Far East in February 2009, Indira A. R. Lakshmanan of *Bloomberg* reported: "'Not everyone will unclench their fist,' Clinton said, echoing words Obama used in his inaugural address last month. 'But the message of our extended hand has impact.' All week, Clinton has repeated that the U.S. will normalize ties with North Korea and sign a peace treaty if the North agrees to verifiable and complete nuclear disarmament."[36] Clinton did garner attention when she once went off-script and referred to the North Korean regime as a "tyranny" while on the Asian tour, but during the same time she was volunteering that the United States would not focus on human rights as it negotiated with tyrannical regimes.

Of particular concern to human rights groups was Secretary Clinton's indication, in a question-and-answer session with the press in Seoul, that economic issues, climate change, and security threats would be the focus of talks with China and that human rights violations, while of concern, would not be permitted to block progress on these other issues. (Amnesty International and North Korean Refugees had written Secretary Clinton urging her to make human rights a priority.) She said:

We have an opportunity, we hope to engage with the Chinese on a range of issues. Let me just mention three of them. One is the economic crisis. China and the United States are intertwined when it comes to our recovery. . . . Secondly, global climate change. It's one of the reasons why I asked Todd Stern, another envoy that we have appointed, to come on this trip, because so many of the opportunities for clean energy, technology and the like are going to come out of this region of the world. . . . And, finally, a range of security issues. What will China be willing to do with respect to the Six-Party Talks and their bilateral relationship with North Korea? . . . Now that doesn't mean that questions of Taiwan and Tibet and human rights, the whole range of challenges that we often engage on with the Chinese, are not part of the agenda either. But we pretty much know what they're going to say.

Clinton elaborated, "I don't mean to in any way say that we know everything that's going to happen. But successive administrations and Chinese governments have been poised back and forth on these issues, and we have to continue to press on them. But our pressing on these issues can't interfere with the global economic crisis, the global climate change crisis, and the security crisis."[37] In response to her remarks, Amnesty International said in a statement, "The United States is one of the only countries that can stand up to China on human rights issues. . . . The Chinese people face a dire situation. . . . Half a million people are currently in labor camps. Women face forced abortion and sterilization as part of China's enforcement of its one-child policy."[38]

While human rights groups unanimously urged the administration to confront human rights violations in China and North Korea, the media was divided on whether this downplaying of human rights was a positive or negative development. John C. Bersia of McClatchy-Tribune Information Services applauded Clinton's "creative engagement" with China, which included not letting human rights "interfere" with economic, climate, and security issues; instead putting human rights on a "separate track." Merle Goldman, in the *Boston Globe*, deemed her approach a "missed opportunity" given that the popularity of the Charter 08 movement for human rights in China, which was modeled after Czechoslovakia's Charter 77 movement, revealed "widespread dissatisfaction with China's authoritarian market economy." (China was in the midst of a crackdown on the movement at the time of Clinton's visit.) "Such a movement needs the support of the international community. The worldwide outcry over the crackdown of the Charter 77 movement in Czechoslovakia marked the beginning of the unraveling of the Communist system in Eastern Europe. Clinton's recent visit to China would have been the appropriate venue for criticism of China's suppression of Charter 08."[39]

Perhaps most interesting was the take of the *China Daily*: "If the point of Hillary Rodham Clinton's maiden voyage overseas in her new role as United States secretary of state was to assure and reassure, she made it. If her four-country Asia trip was to present a fresh American approach to world affairs, she did so," the official government paper said.[40]

As in the case of negotiations with Russia, Iran, and the Palestinians, the Obama administration had surrendered leverage before talks even began. Even if we accept an approach that demotes democratic principles and humanitarian concerns, we would be justified in asking: Why didn't the administration hold onto human rights points as a way to get China to compromise on the issues the administration *was* interested in, such as instituting stricter emissions standards and stopping weapons proliferation? And why wouldn't the administration take a similar tack with North Korea, which required periodic injections of much-needed aid to stave off societal collapse?

Another remark by Clinton on the Far East trip that received attention because of its "bluntness" should also have received attention because of the significant signal it sent regarding her position on human rights. In what was, according to ABC's Martha Raddatz, "refreshingly undiplomatic language," Secretary Clinton broke "an informal taboo" and talked about North Korea's possible succession after Kim Jong-il. Saying she would press to restart the stalled six-nation talks on North Korea's nuclear programs, she added, "Our goal is to try to come up with a strategy that is effective at influencing the behavior of the North Koreans at a time when the whole leadership situation is unclear. . . . If there is a succession, even if it's a peaceful succession, that creates more uncertainty, and it may also encourage behaviors that are even more provocative, as a way to consolidate power within the society."[41]

Some journalists saw this statement as unnecessarily provocative, pointing as it did to the possibility of the Supreme Leader's demise. But the statement can be seen another way. Notice that Clinton expressed concern about the succession insofar as it might affect progress on nuclear proliferation. Given the severity of the suffering and repression in North Korea, bringing up the succession in terms of concern about nuclear weapons, but explicitly *not* in terms of hope that succession might lead to an improvement in conditions for the people there, constitutes an unbelievable omission. In addition, pointing to negative rather than positive ramifications of succession—i.e., government change—could only serve to bolster the horrible status quo.

Notice also that Clinton used the word "crisis" for climate change and the economic meltdown, but that she made no mention of the crisis of humanity in North Korea. In one of her *strongest* statements regarding that awful regime, Clinton would say, "North Korea is not going to get a different relationship with the United States while insulting and refusing dialogue with South Korea."[42] Even in this statement, she objected to how North Korea treated the United States and South Korea but specifically did not object to how North Korea treated its own citizens.

In addition to sending no signals regarding North Korean human rights, the Obama administration did not initially send signals that stopping North Korea's nuclear program and weapons proliferation was the highest priority. The higher priority appeared to be engagement itself. In her confirmation hearing, Clinton had downplayed North Korea's uranium enrichment efforts, saying they "were never quite verified." Pressed on the point at a State Department briefing, she said "we don't know" whether such a program exists.

In an editorial entitled "Now Is No Time to Downplay North Korea," former UN ambassador John Bolton expressed concern that the administration believed North Korea was not a "truly pressing problem. . . . After all, the argument goes, the North already has nuclear weapons, so unlike Iran there is no line to prevent it from crossing."[43] In reality, Bolton argued, the danger was very real: "The belief that North Korea is not an imminent danger is closely related to the fallacy that it is 'merely' a threat to peace and security in Northeast Asia, a longstanding State Department fixation. In fact, North Korea is an urgent threat in the Middle East, both because of its nuclear program and its strenuous efforts to proliferate ballistic weapons there. The clone of North Korea's Yongbyon reactor, under construction in Syria until it was destroyed by

Israel in September 2007, demonstrates beyond debate how the North's nuclear program contributes directly and palpably to Middle East tensions. Trying to ignore or downplay the relationship guarantees that we will resolve neither Pyongyang's, nor Tehran's nuclear ambitions."[44]

Whether the North Korean nuclear program was an early priority for the administration or not, there is no question that the administration downplayed North Korea's hostility. In a September 18 interview with *Bloomberg*, Leon Panetta famously said that the US and North Korea were in a "honeymoon situation right now." *Bloomberg* reported: "Panetta [also] said the U.S. may get the opportunity to negotiate with North Korea to scale back its nuclear and missile programs. The U.S. is ready to engage directly with North Korea in an effort to bring the nuclear-armed regime back to multinational talks on disarmament, Philip J. Crowley, the top State Department spokesman, said in an interview Sept. 11. The U.S. and North Korea 'are discussing the ability to try to talk with one another.'"[45]

As we look into the further development of relations between the North Korean regime and the Obama administration, we see that this pattern of priorities continued. *No matter what obstacle or provocation North Korea put in our way, the administration was very quick to indicate that negotiations and the normalization of relations were still possible.* As we turn to the further sequence of events, we will see that, even when issuing sanctions or condemning the latest hostile act, the administration opened the door to more negotiations, more assistance if cooperation ensued, and more understanding between North Korea and the United States.

Relations were again strained in March 2009, when American journalists Euna Lee and Laura Ling were imprisoned and sentenced to twelve years of hard labor for their alleged illegal entry into North Korean territory. After their arrest, Clinton disassociated the incident from proliferation issues, stating that there was still an "open door" to the Six-Party Talks. When North Korea refused to return to the talks, presidential envoy Stephen Bosworth said the United States was "still committed to dialogue."

In April, North Korea fired a long-range missile over Japan. At a Senate hearing, Clinton condemned the launch, but also held out the carrot of economic assistance in return for a change in behavior. She said, "We have absolutely no interest and no willingness to give them any economic aid at all." But she also said, "That money is there in the event, which at this point seems implausible if not impossible, the North Koreans return to the Six-Party Talks and begin to disable their nuclear capacity again."[46]

In May, North Korea conducted more nuclear tests, further testing the administration's engagement policy. Along with an underground detonation that registered on seismic stations as far away as Texas, North Korea tested three short-range missiles, including one from the same site from which it had fired the missile over Japan the month before. The US and other countries condemned the action, with President Obama stating, "North Korea's nuclear and ballistic-missile programs pose a great threat to the peace and security of the world, and I strongly condemn their reckless action."[47]

Noting that the Bush administration's overtures had failed as well, the *Wall Street Journal* observed, "Recent diplomatic overtures by the Obama administration to Pyongyang have failed to entice or subdue the regime." The *WSJ* sensibly added, "If history is any guide, Kim's strategy is to keep escalating until he extorts more money, aid and global recognition. This time in particular he's testing President Obama and his vow to 'engage' the world's worst rogues."[48] Confirmation of this theory, if any is needed, is found in the *Foreign Policy* article "The Secret History of Kim-Jong Il," written by Kim's former schoolteacher Kim Hyun Sik in 2008. Kim Hyun Sik revealed that Western overtures serve to prop up the very military aspect of the regime they supposedly target. (Remember that the end-goal and reason for overtures that overlook North Korea's regime type is progress on *military* issues.) Hyun Sik elaborated:

> In the 1990s, after the fall of the Soviet Union, and with a tide of democratization and reform spreading across the world, Kim Jong Il chose to buck the trend and implement a "military first policy." True to his familiar slogan, "The military is the core force of the revolution and the pillar of the state," Kim called for the militarization of the entire society. He believed that even though North Korea was a small state, he could stabilize the nation and make the country powerful and prosperous by growing the military. Today, just as he hoped, Kim Jong Il's vision has been realized—albeit through a continuing policy of military extortion. Whereas international trade and finance have only

played a marginal role in North Korea's economy and security, Kim has managed to extract resources from wealthier and stronger states by manufacturing crisis and generating international instability. His brand of nuclear blackmail is a virtual guarantor of bottomless international aid for the world's most militarized society.[49]

In its next move, the Obama administration sent Bill Clinton to North Korea to seek the release of the captive American journalists. He succeeded on that front and also succeeded in getting North Korea back to the negotiating table, this time for bilateral talks. Testimony to Kim Hyun Sik's assertions regarding North Korea's successful tactics, as the administration prepared for the talks, the *Asia Times* observed a very significant change in the goals of the administration: While it had previously insisted that North Korea end its nuclear program if it wanted improved relations with the United States, "in a major shift" Clinton said in a November 20 interview in Kabul that the United States was ready to explore the issues of *"normalization of relations, a peace treaty instead of an armistice, and economic development assistance"* as long as North Korea agreed to *"commit"* to *"denuclearization."*[50] (italics mine)

The word *commit* indicates future action rather than prerequisite action and heralded what the *Asia Times* called an "unmistakable change" in America's stance. Clinton backed away from demands for the elimination of North Korea's nuclear program and insisted instead on its recommitment to denuclearization. Indeed, envoy Bosworth was sent to North Korea with the primary goal of containing the nuclear program. Just as in the case of Iran, the administration collapsed its own original plan for the sake of achieving something—anything—with one of the world's worst regimes. Echoing his letter to the Iranian "Supreme Leader," Obama wrote a personal letter to Kim Jong-il for Bosworth to personally deliver. Bosworth reported that the two sides had reached "common understanding" on the need to restart nuclear negotiations.

In spite of new US overtures, in March 2010, North Korea torpedoed and sank a South Korean warship, killing forty-six South Koreans. North Korea denied it was responsible, but investigators from Australia, Britain, Sweden, and the United States confirmed that it was. In response, the United States and South Korea turned to the UN Security Council and worked on the construction of new sanctions. As is usually the case in the Security Council, Chinese and Russian resistance prevented a binding resolution, instead producing what the Heritage Foundation termed a "timorous" presidential statement. "As for the U.S. Administration, the problem was in not confronting the obstructionism more forcefully and not putting Moscow and Beijing on the diplomatic spot."[51]

In a visit to Seoul in July 2010, Secretary Clinton announced the imposition of sanctions on the individuals in the North Korean government and the banks that aid in the trade of arms to North Korea. But these sanctions were really nothing new, since UN sanctions already banned North Korea from importing or exporting weapons. As if to emphasize the futility of the sanctions, in November, North Korea ratcheted up its aggression, launching an artillery attack on Yeonpyeong Island in South Korea. Although the Western press was quick to rationalize this provocation as a "reaction" to President Lee's recent retraction of South Korea's Sunshine Policy, another way to look at this is that sunshine policies had failed.

This was the thanks South Korea got for seeking a normalization of relations and for trying to "live and let live" with its brutal northern neighbor by looking the other way when it came to North Korean repression and atrocities. For the sake of peace and harmony on the peninsula, the people within North Korea had been forsaken. But, oh how little peace and harmony that policy of indifference had produced. In announcing an end to the Sunshine Policy, the South Korean Unification Ministry's annual report called "the Sunshine Policy of peaceful engagement with North Korea . . . a failure." The ministry issued a paper showing that "a decade of cooperation, cross-border exchanges and billions of dollars in aid did not change Pyongyang's behavior or improve the lives of North Korean citizens." Indeed, in an April 2010 speech in Louisville, Kentucky, Secretary Clinton confirmed that North Korea had as many as six nuclear weapons. She nevertheless expressed confidence that the Six-Party Talks would resume.

The United States reaffirmed its commitment to South Korea, called on North Korea to cease its hostile acts, and, once again, turned to the Six-Party Talks, with China trying to pave the way. In the meantime, "Supreme Leader" Kim Jong-il was ill, and there was speculation that he would die soon. If other such moments in history are any indication, the passing of this dictator, who held total power and whose very name evoked terror, provided an opening, even if a small one, for the promotion of democratic ideals or at least reform. Bruce Klingner stressed the need for a contingency plan for securing North Korea's weapons in the event of an unstable succession, but also stressed that a "successful" succession meant "the continuation of a vicious dictatorship that subjugates its population, threatens its neighbors, and pursues nuclear weapons for coercive diplomacy." A "successful" succession also meant "the North Korean tiger would continue to have fangs of nuclear, biological, chemical, and conventional weapons." The regional security balance would become an "increasingly dangerous status quo" as North Korea refined its nuclear and missile delivery capabilities.[52]

Klingner thought the regime was at a "tipping point," noting the "combination of stresses" it was dealing with. But, Obama and Clinton did not seize the occasion. They neglected to use their positions as president and secretary of state to give the liberalization of North Korea moral support or to speak for the miserable and the oppressed. Recall the concrete effect Winston Churchill's soaring oratory had upon freedom's fate; he so inspired the British that they were able to "carry on" in the face of imminent ruin and close to impossible odds. Recall the passionate speeches President Reagan made for those behind the Iron Curtain and behind the Berlin Wall. He saw opportunity in the failure of the Stalinist economy and in signs that there were chinks in the armor of Soviet rule. But, neither before Kim Jong-Il's death, nor afterward, as his son Kim Jong-un succeeded him, did the United States take advantage of the fact that when leaders of the United States speak, the world listens.

In any foreign policy speech, any American president has the bully pulpit, since he is widely considered the most powerful person in the most powerful country in the world. But President Obama doesn't make foreign policy speeches, preferring to have his policies simply announced by his subordinates or through internal memos. This is another indication of the low priority he gives to American-democratic ideas, for how, without speech, can he articulate and defend them? It is also another indication of his administration's amoral approach to North Korea.

American journalists Euna Lee and Laura Ling were apparently more willing to use their position to promote democratic reform than

American leaders. While expressing relief and gratitude at their release, they stated, "We know that people would like to hear more about our experience in captivity. But what we have shared here is all we are prepared to talk about—the psychological wounds of imprisonment are slow to heal. Instead, we would rather redirect this interest to the story we went to report on, a story about despairing North Korean defectors who flee to China, only to find themselves living a different kind of horror. We hope that now, more than ever, the plight of these people and of the aid groups helping them are not forgotten."[53] The "different kind of horror" Lee and Ling referred to was the Chinese mistreatment and forced repatriation of North Korean defectors (which I discuss in the next chapter).

In October 2011, President Obama hosted South Korean president Lee Myung-bak at the White House, and, in announcing a new trade agreement with "one of our strongest allies," came as close as he ever comes—which is not very close—to taking a stand for liberty. Obama had firm words for North Korea, stating that "if Pyongyang continues to ignore its international obligations it will invite even more pressure and isolation."[54] Asked by a reporter whether North Korea might one day undergo the kind of popular uprising that toppled governments in the Arab Spring, Obama suggested that someday it might, answering, "I think that obviously the people of North Korea have been suffering under repressive policies for a very long time, and none of us can look at a crystal ball and know when suddenly that type of government collapses on its own. What we know though is that what people every-where . . . are looking for is the ability to determine their own destiny."[55] President Lee added that South Korea and the US "speak with one voice" on North Korea. He told lawmakers he would never accept the division of the Korean peninsula as a "permanent condition" and that in order for peaceful reunification to occur, the North must give up its nuclear ambitions.

For all its politeness regarding North Korea's regime type, all its overtures to North Korean leaders, all its willingness to hold out the possibility of a generous negotiated agreement no matter what prov-ocation North Korea threw our way, the United States got nothing in return. Incredibly—given all the verbal references to the Six-Party Talks by the Obama foreign policy team and all the respectful references to the concept in the American press (so many that a well-read person could be excused for thinking Six-Party Talks were a successful reality)—the talks didn't exist during the Obama first term except as a future goal!

By December 2011, the Brookings Institution had produced a paper entitled "Strategic Patience has Become Strategic Passivity." James E. Goodby and Donald Gross summed up the failure of accommodation with North Korea as follows:

> In this period and during the last years of the Bush administration as well, North Korea conducted nuclear weapons tests and flights of missiles. It built a uranium enrichment plant and is constructing a new nuclear reactor. It repudiated the 1953 Armistice Agreement that suspended hostilities, but did not legally end the Korean War. It recently sank a South Korean warship and bombarded a South Korean island, killing four people, wounding several and severely damaging civilian property. The Obama administration says that is will not return to a process which rewards North Korea for bad behavior. But the bad behavior goes on. Sanctions have not yielded results. Toughening the already strict sanctions against North Korea requires a level of cooperation from China that is not likely to occur. Tough action just by the United States, South Korea and Japan will not suffice. . . . A policy of so-called 'strategic patience' will not fix that problem."[56]

The new North Korean leader Kim Jong-un, who succeeded to power as planned, at first appeared willing to take part in Obama's engagement policies, sending signals that he was particularly interested in seeking more food aid in exchange for concessions on North Korea's uranium enrichment program. (The food situation in North Korea, although perhaps not as bad as the 1990s, is still dire and only appears to be getting worse. The *Guardian* reported in April 2014 that regular food rations were no longer being distributed beyond Pyongyang.[57]) The Obama administration hardly acknowledged the historic transition, which was also a historic opportunity. Moreover, President Obama didn't mention North Korea in his 2012 State of the Union speech even though North Korea has been cited in nearly every State of the Union address since 1995.

Behind the scenes, more was happening—on food aid in exchange for a weapons freeze, that is. In late February 2012, the United States and North Korea announced a "Leap Day" agreement in which the United States once again pledged food aid—*240,000 metric tons of food over the following year*—in exchange for a freeze on nuclear and missile tests and a return of UN weapons inspectors. Note that the condition for food aid was no longer an *end* to the nuclear program but simply a *freeze* on nuclear tests. On human rights, the behind-the-scenes story was as lacking in moral conviction as the surface story. As usual, President Obama and his foreign policy team ignored the potential power of American principles and words (for human rights, individual rights, and democracy) while falling for the words of Korean leaders who, when they want and need something from us, tell us what we want to hear.

The agreement led to a fleeting "resumption" of the Six-Party Talks. But, like the previous ones, the talks were over before they started. On March 16, 2012, North Korea announced it was planning to launch a satellite to commemorate Kim Il-sung's one-hundredth birthday, drawing condemnation by the other five participants in the talks and casting doubt on the Leap Day agreement. What a cogent reminder of the futility of appeasement, and how sad that we had to learn the lesson again. Six-Party Talks had occurred in 2003, 2004, 2005, 2006, and 2007, with multiple talks held each year. The very administration that was willing to pay a high price for talks, that offered to keep quiet about North Korea's regime-type and atrocities, that promised recognition of the "legitimacy" of the regime if only "progress" were made on the nuclear issue, that was willing to change US goals from eliminating the nuclear program to limiting it, that saw "talking" (engagement and diplomacy) as the key to resolving international issues, could not get the talks going!

The North Korean people paid a price for the Obama administration's repeated attempts to jump-start discussions with North Korean leaders. Lamented human rights blog *FreeKorea* regarding special envoy for human rights Robert King's State Department website, "Jesus wept. Where are the plans to mobilize global opinion, bring Twitter to North Korea, sanction the leaders of North Korea's internal security forces, or bring Chapter VII sanctions at the Security Council over the matter of North Korea's concentration camps? There isn't even a schedule of the conferences King attends to strike a sagacious pose and avoid saying anything controversial or noteworthy."[58]

Very shortly after what many called the "food for nukes transaction," evidence arose that North Korea was nevertheless planning a third nuclear test. This time the White House verbally warned North Korea, with White House press secretary Jay Carney linking such an act with the retraction of desperately needed aid. North Korea should "refrain from engaging in any more hostile or provocative actions," he said. Such acts would "do nothing to help the North Korean people, many of whom are starving because of the predilection of the regime to spend money on weapons systems rather than on economic development."[59] At least that point was finally made.

Obama, too, gently stepped up his rhetoric, saying North Korea risked "deepening its isolation in the international community" if it proceeded with the planned rocket launch. In his first visit to the demilitarized zone he finally noted the stark contrast between the two sides: "It's like you're in a time warp. It's like you're looking across fifty years into a country that has missed forty or fifty years of progress." He added, "Bad behavior will not be rewarded."[60]

It goes without saying that this statement, although an improvement over previous statements, stands in weak contrast to the statements of Kennedy and Reagan when they stood at the Berlin Wall. *"Bad behavior" had been rewarded—again and again.* Thanks to our renewed promise of food aid, Kim would be able to point to concessions he'd wrested from the "imperialist pigs." He would be able to promise the starving people greater prosperity. And, he would be guaranteed even more cover for his loathsome regime. In an editorial entitled "The U.S. Falls Again for North Korea's Tricks," the *Washington Post* intoned, "As part of the bargain, the Obama administration effectively ratified the next generation of one of the world's worst tyrannies, declaring that it has 'no hostile intention' toward North Korea."[61]

In April 2012, North Korea went ahead with the rocket launch, which was widely assumed to be a cover for testing long-range missile technology. The rocket disintegrated over the Yellow Sea, indicating failure, but not total failure; although revealing flaws in North Korea's nuclear technology, it constituted another step toward testing and refining that technology and another successful slap in the face of the United States. While displaying North Korea's own challenges, the launch also displayed for all the world to see the failure of United States policy. Presidential candidate Mitt Romney said that appeasement had led to "a food aid deal that was as naïve as it was short-lived." Soon after the failed rocket launch, the administration suspended the Leap Day food aid package.

Our country, which should stand for freedom, and which is still the most powerful in the world, had again been humiliated on the world stage—this time by the least free country in the world, and one whose power is nothing compared to ours, but which keeps expanding its nuclear program, and which sends its military technology around the world to other oppressors and terrorists. American policy during the Obama/Clinton years was centered around trying to engage with the world's worst tyrants, being careful not to offend them, and *offering them concessions in exchange for keeping their ruthlessness confined within their own borders*. Even aside from the absence of principle in this approach, it didn't work. In the Associated Press, Anne Gearan observed, "Obama had insisted that 'bad behavior' would not be rewarded and now has few options to restart negotiations without appearing to let North Korea off the hook."[62] North Korea already *was* off the hook, with the "diplomatic" approach of the Western world, combined with the sponsorship of China, working to its advantage at every turn.

As if more evidence of this were needed, the UN Security Council refused to impose additional sanctions in response to the launch even though the launch violated two of its previous restrictions. US Ambassador Susan Rice announced, "Members of the Security Council agree to continue consultations on the appropriate response." In an editorial entitled "A Pyongyang Joke," the *Wall Street Journal* pointed to their own warning in a previous editorial that "the North was certain to break the deal," adding: "The larger Administration error is that it continues to bounce between the equally futile alternatives of engagement with the regime and condemnation at the U.N. That may suit Barack Obama's re-election interest in being seen as the President who ended all wars and other global unpleasantness. But it all but guarantees that the North will continue to provoke an 'international community' that it reasonably has concluded will impose no serious penalties."[63]

In addition to concluding that the "international community" would do little to stop its nuclear program, the North Korean regime concluded that it could inflict terror and misery on its entire populace

with impunity since the United States and the "international community" were impassive and ineffective on this issue as well. Impassioned
pleas for the North Korean people have been and remain exceedingly
rare. After all the provocation and all the new information regarding
North Korean repression, we are still terribly far from having any nerve
when it comes to confronting evil. With our cultural relativism and
our stated belief that the economy matters more than ideology, we are
embarrassed to admit we believe in such a thing as right and wrong.

How distant Reagan's words at his first inaugural address sound
today: "No arsenal or no weapon in the arsenals of the world is so formidable as the will and the moral courage of free men and women." How
strangely moral seem these words of Harry Truman: "Nowadays in politics and just about everywhere else, all anybody seems to be interested
in is not how much he can do but how much he can get away with. And
I don't like to see it. I don't know what's going to become of us if everybody starts thinking and acting that way."[64]

Once the administration's and previous administrations' engagement policies were more widely acknowledged to have failed, an
interesting twist emerged. Some of those who previously argued that
we shouldn't mention North Korea's internal horrors because it might
"insult" the regime and thereby "provoke" it, began, after the failed
rocket launch, to say that we shouldn't insult the regime because it was
no threat to the powerful United States anyway! We must ask, *Which is
it?* The first reason for ignoring human rights and forsaking the Korean
people is that it might inspire a threatening response. The second reason
for ignoring human rights and forsaking the Korean people is that the
regime isn't really a threat.

The truth about people who make these contradictory arguments
is that they just don't care; their policy recommendations are based less
upon progressive pragmatism than upon moral indifference. These
supposed intellectuals get caught up in their own illogic. Their combined
words require that the United States be *afraid* of a regime exponentially
weaker (both militarily and in terms of international influence) than we
are. At the same time, they require that the United States *not be afraid* of
the intent behind the rants of Korean leaders who state the destruction
of "disgusting imperialists" and "capitalist pigs" (us) as their goal.

In the end, this is all part of the hyper-paranoia of political correctness, which cowers and complains if democracies call oppression *oppression*, but looks the other way when totalitarian thugs murder and torture their own people, launch missiles at democratic neighbors, and call *us* "puppet warmongers." Let's be grown-ups and get back to the actual formation of foreign policy and grand strategy. If the rare instances when, with generous understatement, we call North Korea a "tyranny" were really the cause, as some academicians argue it is, for the North Korean "fear regime," then why, during years when we flatter and mollify the regime, does it pursue nuclear weapons, sink ships, lob missiles, and step up repression?

Just look at all the belligerence and atrocities that occurred right in the middle of our accommodative policies. In March of 2010, Vitit Muntarbhorn, UN special envoy on human rights, announced that the human rights situation in North Korea had gotten worse, not better. He reported to the Human Rights Council on "harrowing and horrific" human rights violations, stating in a news conference afterward that "sadly on many fronts the situation has actually gotten worse." Then, in 2012, David Hawk issued an updated report in association with the US Committee for Human Rights in North Korea. His findings detailed an unimproved and perhaps deteriorating human rights situation and presented yet another picture of a country beset by repression, terror, prison camps, torture, and executions.

So too, Kim Jong-un stepped up intimidation and persecution of would-be escapees. In recent years, the North Korean government had mostly ignored the refugee problem, partly due to not wanting to draw attention to the fact that people in North Korea's "paradise" were desperate and unhappy, partly due to the fact that there were too many mouths for the economically decrepit regime to feed. But, the new leader soon chose to step up border security and to launch a propaganda campaign against refugees, which includes forced public confessions of regret and remorse by North Koreans captured as they tried to escape.[65] (On the subject of escapees and trafficking, it is worth looking at the testimony to Congress of Suzanne Scholte, chairwoman of the North Korea Freedom Coalition.[66])

The regime remained fanatical as well as cruel: Just when it was about to receive massive quantities of desperately needed food aid, it sabotaged the aid program by launching a missile (discussed above). When, in spite of this, the Obama administration indicated it still wanted negotiations and hinted it would still consider food aid if North Korea came back to the negotiating table, North Korea stridently announced in October 2012 that the US mainland and South Korea were "within range" of its missiles. Also in October, the regime defiantly launched a satellite carrier rocket into orbit that uses the same technology as a missile with a warhead. Unlike the one in March, this missile launch was a success. David Chance of Reuters logically asserted, "North Korea's next step after rattling the world by putting a satellite into orbit for the first time will likely be a nuclear test, the third conducted by the reclusive and unpredictable state."[67]

Chance was correct. In February 2013, North Korea announced it had successfully conducted its third nuclear test, detonating a miniaturized nuclear device in defiance of threatened further sanctions by the UN Security Council. Coming so close on the heels of the previous year's missile launch, the test was seen by observers as putting North Korea one step closer to developing a nuclear warhead. President Obama released a statement in response to this latest, serious provocation: "Far from achieving its stated goal of becoming a strong and prosperous nation, North Korea has instead increasingly isolated and impoverished its people through its ill-advised pursuit of weapons of mass destruction and their means of delivery."

Feeding the people has always been a problem for the communist regime, but, in the end, it would rather put money toward weapons than food, and would rather be complicit in the starvation of the people than allow them a glimpse of freedom. Interestingly, it was starvation that for a very brief period generated an opening toward liberalization. As the 1990s famine took its incredible toll, a positive movement arose amidst the desperation and chaos. Barbara Demick explains, "Just when things were hitting bottom, with deaths reaching hundreds of thousands, a new spirit of enterprise was born. The collapse of the socialist food distribution system presented an opportunity for private businesses. It wasn't as though everyone could trek out to the mountains to pick leaves and berries and scrape pine bark; people had to buy their food somewhere and somebody had to supply it to them. North Korea needed vendors: fishmongers, butchers, and bakers to fill the collapse left by the public system. . . . [But] out of hunger and desperation, they were reinventing the concept of the free-market economy, which required the unlearning of a lifetime of propaganda."[68]

The people's own black market indeed began to improve conditions, and for a while the regime looked the other way, especially since government and military officials extracted kickbacks for doing so. But, in 2004, the regime rescinded its minimal economic liberalization and cracked down, both physically and economically, by stepping up repression and imposing crippling limits on the amount of *won* that could be exchanged for foreign currency. Of course, the centralized regime realized it couldn't survive if the people kept improving their own lives.

By 2008, the food situation was again dire, with a survey showing that two-thirds of North Korean households were still supplementing their diets by picking grass and weeds in the countryside. Incredibly, public protests resulted in a rare policy retreat, with the government rescinding its ban on foreign currency. Did this present a small opening, which we failed to notice?

A similar dynamic might be developing today. A February 2013 cover story in the *Economist* detailed a burgeoning black market in North Korea, what the magazine quotes Stephan Haggard and Marcus Noland as being natural "entrepreneurial coping behavior."[69] Suzanne Scholte confirms that the food distribution system, which created total dependency on the state, has fallen apart. Are these signs that the people of North Korea are ripe for change and ready to grasp President Obama's "outstretched hand"—if he would only extend it to them instead of to their nominal leaders?

■ ■ ■

All too often, we extend particularly lopsided globalist gestures to the regimes most dead set against globalism. As Sung-Yoon Lee of the Fletcher School of Law and Diplomacy at Tufts University points out, North Korea operates precisely on blocking out cultural infiltration and forces of globalization, describing them as tools of capitalist imperialism. We provide carrots and sticks (mostly carrots) in the attempt to bring North Korea into some kind of relationship with the "international community" and to convince North Korea to relinquish its nuclear program.[70] But, North Korea cooperates only long enough to extract desperately needed aid, and technical assistance. It backs out of and violates agreements as soon as it has gotten what it wants, and accelerates its nuclear program at the very time it hints at willingness to disband it.

As the Obama administration entered its second term, it appeared that North Korea's nuclear program had advanced so far that DPRK leaders no longer saw the need to downplay it. North Korea declared its nuclear weapons were not a "bargaining chip" and formally rejected a UN Security Council resolution that called for an end to its nuclear program. Making a bad situation worse, it threatened the United States and its Asian allies with destruction, conducted missile and rocket launches, announced the nullification of the 1953 armistice, intentionally provoked South Korea with cyber-attacks and military provocations, and stepped up already horrific human rights violations against its citizens.

Still, North Korean leaders suggested they might be willing to negotiate in the future on matters *other than* nuclear weapons and human rights. In other words, they demanded that we go even further toward divesting our globalist policies of strategic and humane concerns. Some in the West and in Asia apparently agreed that we should do just that in the attempt to prevent war and foster dialogue. Others, notably the new South Korea president, Park Geun-hye, appeared less willing to surrender our democratic principles and squander our military and geopolitical leverage.

John Kerry began his term as secretary of state with the globalist approach of his predecessor. He reached out on the nuclear front and avoided strong statements on North Korean human rights. But as the term went on, in tandem with the UN's newfound voice on the matter, Kerry began to speak out against North Korea's crimes against humanity—and he did so with conviction. At least on North Korea, Kerry became willing to interrupt globalism's trajectory—to move away from relativistic hopes of a unified if morally mute one world order, in which we could all, somehow, coexist. He *took a stand* for human dignity and against North Korean atrocities and, in so doing, showed that some of the free world's differences and disagreements with others are worth emphasizing and arguing about.

At first, however, outreach was again tried. Although the United States did initiate a 2013 Security Council resolution to censure and sanction North Korea for its December rocket launch, Kerry showed that he was nevertheless willing to reach out. In April 2013, in tandem with his trip to Asia, he said talks with North Korea were possible and that the United States was "prepared to reach out" to Kim Jong-un at the "appropriate moment" and under "appropriate circumstances." Continuing its song and dance, North Korea said it would be willing to hold "disarmament talks," but not over its nuclear program! Human rights groups that had urged Kerry to take a stand on the trip were disappointed, as they had been when Hillary Clinton took her Far East tour. In a news conference with South Korean foreign minister Yun Byung-se, Kerry stated, "North Korea will not be accepted as a nuclear power. . . . The rhetoric that we are hearing is simply unacceptable." As per usual, the administration chose not to focus on the unacceptability of the North Korean regime. This, in spite of the fact that David Hawk published a devastating second edition of *The Hidden Gulag* in 2012, and that the Human Rights Watch North Korea report for events of 2012 showed that conditions were abysmal and dire.

In the meantime, a US institute tracking North Korea's nuclear weapons said its satellite photos showed it was *doubling* the size of its uranium enrichment plant.[71] In September, North Korea moved two more launchers to its east coast for a possible test-firing of Scud missiles, and was believed to have two mid-range missiles positioned there as well. In December, signs of new activity at North Korea's main nuclear complex followed the regime's repeated assertions that it was strengthening capabilities to produce nuclear arms.

Then, in February 2014, North Korea fired four short-range Scud missiles in what was the first confirmed launch in more than nine months. Interestingly, the provocation occurred just after the North and South had held their first high-level talks in more than six years (agreeing to have more discussions) and just after North and South Korean families divided by the Korean War had had their first reunions in more than three years—in other words, just at a time of engagement. In March, North Korea reinforced its attitude toward the "international community" by test-firing two medium-range ballistic missiles for the first time since 2009, and in violation of UN resolutions—just hours after the United States, South Korea, and Japan met for talks.

In other words, nothing in North Korea had changed. But something, in the UN and the US, had. Both the international body and the American secretary of state started to overtly condemn North Korean atrocities. In February 2014, the UN Human Rights Council released a report on North Korean crimes against humanity, which was presented as the most detailed and authoritative body of data on the subject to date, and a milestone in "international debate." It spoke of "unspeakable atrocities," cited "systematic, widespread and gross human rights violations," and pointed to extermination, murder, enslavement, torture, rape, starvation, forced disappearances of foreign citizens, and persecution on the grounds of race, religion, and gender. In the *New York Times*, Nick Cumming-Bruce recognized the significance of this report, not just because of its exposure of North Korean atrocities, but also because it represented the international community finally speaking out:

> Human rights activists had pushed for the creation of the panel in a bid to broaden what had been the international community's focus on the North's nuclear program and bellicose security policies to the near exclusion of its human rights record.
>
> North Korea's practice of what the report called "crimes that shock the conscience of humanity" for decades "raises questions about the inadequacy of the international community."
>
> "It really opens up a whole new chapter in the international reaction to North Korea," Lee Jung-hoon, South Korea's ambassador for human rights, said by telephone. "It's not just an investigation and a report and that's the end of it. It's giving a road map and blueprint to end this thing. There's a very strong sense of urgency."
>
> There appears to be little immediate prospect of winning approval for International Criminal Court prosecution, however. Approval is necessary from the Security Council's permanent members, which include North Korea's long-term protector, China.
>
> Still, Mr. Lee said, "just the fact that they are getting the vocabulary of crimes against humanity, the International Criminal Court and Kim Jong-un on the same page is a huge step forward in the debate on North Korean human rights."[72]

At a minister's meeting at the United Nations, Secretary Kerry stressed that the international community could no longer ignore the situation in North Korea, given the findings in the UN report: "So we say to the North Korean government, all of us here today, you should close those camps. You should shut this evil system down. As the Commission of Inquiry report concludes, the gravity, scale and nature of these violations reveal a state that does not have a parallel in the contemporary world." Yes, he did it: our secretary of state called an evil system an evil system.

On Human Rights Day 2014, the State Department backed up Kerry's words with action by releasing profiles on six of the most notorious North Korean prison camps on HumanRights.gov. Asserted Secretary Kerry, "You may be hidden, but we can see you. We know you're there. Your captors can silence your voice and assault your dignity, but they cannot deny your basic humanity."[73] In May of 2015, Kerry's later willingness to take a stand on human rights in North Korea was still in evidence as he condemned the country's "grotesque, grisly, horrendous public displays of executions" after Kim Jong-un ordered the death of his defense minister.

When it came to North Korea's ongoing military provocations, the messages Kerry sent were still more mixed. In Seoul in May 2015, Kerry stated, "We are not seeking conflict, we are seeking a peaceful resolution of the differences that still exist after so many years on the peninsula. . . . Never has the international community been as united as we are now that No. 1, North Korea needs to denuclearize and No. 2, that they have not only not taken steps in that direction but have grown their program and have acted with a kind of reckless abandon."[74] While the United States was certainly right not to seek conflict, it was not necessarily right to tout "peaceful resolution of the differences" on the peninsula, since those words implied that the North Korean regime might somehow decide to negotiate in good faith on weapons issues, and indirectly consigned the North Korean people to living under that regime. As Evan Moore of the Foreign Policy Initiative observed, the core of the nuclear and ballistic crisis (just as the core of the human rights crisis) is the nature of the North Korean regime.[75]

It is time to apply more pressure to the regime itself. An early 2015 report from the US-Korea Institute at Johns Hopkins University and the Institute for Science and International Security analyzed how the recent growth of North Korea's nuclear program could impact its future stockpiles, and reached a grim conclusion. The report determined that North Korea will have a minimum of twenty-nine bomb's worth of weapons-grade materials (with a medium projection of sixty-nine weapons' worth of materials and fifty actual weapons) by 2020. The study noted a "dramatic build-up in North Korea's nuclear weapons capability" in the last several years: North Korea has restarted and renovated a five-megawatt nuclear reactor, built an additional experimental light-water reactor for plutonium production, doubled the size of a known uranium enrichment centrifuge plant, and possibly constructed a second enrichment plant. It has also definitely constructed several additional buildings at the Yongbyon nuclear facility.

We must, again, learn that weak engagement policies don't work, that peace is at stake, and that the North Korean people who are denied their God-given rights by the despicable regime are left behind by those policies. As Bruce Klingner warned in a policy paper, "Respond Cautiously to North Korean Engagement Offers,"

> In what is now something of an annual rite on the Korean Peninsula, 2015 dawned with perceived signals of North Korea's supposed desire to resurrect diplomatic ties with the United States and South Korea. Although these signals were met with predictions of another inter-Korean summit, Pyongyang's offer to refrain from nuclear tests in return for a freeze on allied military exercises was quickly— and correctly—rejected. The regime subsequently added ever more preconditions, ultimately rejecting even the possibility of talks with either Washington or Seoul.
>
> By late February, hopes of improved inter-Korean relations and a diplomatic resolution to the North Korean nuclear problem had, once again, dissolved. On the eve of the latest annual U.S.–South Korean military exercises in March, Pyongyang abandoned its charm offensive and threatened to wage a "merciless, sacred war" against the United States.[76]

Indeed, in January 2016, North Korea rattled the world by launching its fourth nuclear test (its third in seven years) and claiming it had detonated a hydrogen bomb. While experts determined that the claim was exaggerated, North Korea had nevertheless conducted a test that moved its nuclear program further along. The US House swiftly passed legislation to broaden sanctions, while South Korea pledged to work on strong international sanctions. Sanctions should be severe, continual, and consistent. The US and UN must designate enablers, especially China, which abets North Korea's WMD program, and has long failed to enforce sanctions.[77] In order to pressure both North Korea and China, the defense posture of the United States should be enhanced instead of degraded, and joint military exercises and military cooperation with Asian allies should be a priority.

Ultimately, only regime change will stop that country's bellicosity and atrocities. Given the way North Korea's leaders use deception and manipulation to string the United States and its allies along; given the dramatic advances in North Korea's nuclear program and its hostility, threats, and brinkmanship; and given the regime's cruelty and totalitarian extremes, engagement and diplomacy in lieu of other actions is unprincipled and unwise. Radio Free Asia and the Voice of America should be modernized and used in conjunction with the spread of radios and cell phones to counter the regime's relentless propaganda. Leaders of the "free world" should make Truman-esque and Reagan-esque speeches for human freedom and dignity. As Suzanne Scholte insists, it is important "to name names"—to expose those authorizing and committing the atrocities, and to emphasize and support HR 1771 and HR 757, the North Korea Sanctions Enforcement Acts. Unwavering efforts to save and assist North Korean escapees should be made. We must be on the alert for opportunities to promote freedom.

The United States should refuse more food aid without unconditional and total access to distribution sites, thus ensuring food aid gets to the people. The same goes for nuclear negotiations. Until and unless we are granted access to all production sites, we should refuse further technical aid or "food for nukes" concessions. We should not trust until we can verify. *Verifiable* should be our new diplomatic word, and we should use it again and again. We should never again give North Korea the very technology it needs to proceed with its nuclear program in exchange for "promises" it will halt the program. We should press and press again for openness and transparency. Using words as weapons, we should cast light onto that dark, otherworldly place on the map called the Democratic People's Republic of Korea.

When we downplay the truth about the regime, we provide cover for the regime. That is a fact that "smart power" and "one world" advocates must finally acknowledge. As Kim Hyun Sik asserts, "Living under a totalitarian regime requires a daily suspension of disbelief. Nowhere is that more true today than in North Korea, where otherwise ethical people contort themselves into untenable moral positions because they've bought into the oft-repeated notion that their country is 'Paradise on Earth.'"[78] Hyun Sik reveals, however, that even when members of the North Korean elite tried to convince themselves that "purifying" North Korea of "subhuman" disabled and short people was for the good, they struggled with their consciences. Would it be "unrealistic," then, to return to an American foreign policy tradition that includes appeals to conscience?

CHAPTER 8

A PAPER TIGER
The Moral and Strategic Inadequacy of US China Policy

In its dealings with China, even more so than with North Korea, the United States has *consistently* downplayed human rights, emphasizing economic relations and balance of power concerns instead. During the period of détente, the precedent was set. Communist revolutionaries seized power all over Asia with brutal programs of social engineering and the mass murder of civilians. As the Khmer Rouge in Cambodia inflicted unimaginable atrocities, American leaders usually said little. When it came to Mao's brutal reign in China, many in the West not only overlooked the atrocities; they excused them. Here was the beginning of that cultural relativism combined with fondness for socialism (with which we are faced today) that consciously excuses communist repression.

As James Mann recalls, "At first it was suggested that Mao Zedong's regime really did reflect the overall wishes of the Chinese people, even if there were no elections to substantiate this claim. China was said to be different, in cultural terms from the West; there was no need for the formalities of voting or ballots or polling stations."[1] That idea became an obvious delusion when Mao's Cultural Revolution took its horrific toll, reaping terror and misery, but most in the West continued to look the other way. The whitewashing of China's human rights abuses continued after Mao was gone, and it continues to this day.

As in every place and time when the people succumb to what Jean-François Revel called the totalitarian temptation (until its horrors come back to haunt them), Mao's Cultural Revolution had to do with the successful dissemination of propaganda, with pitting supposed "classes" of people against each other, and with concepts of historical inevitability and moral relativism. In her intelligent and moving memoir, *Wild Swans*, Jung Chang recalls, "In the days after Mao's death, I did a lot of thinking. I knew he was considered a philosopher, and I tried to think about what his 'philosophy' really was. It seemed to me that its central principle was the need—or the desire?—for perpetual conflict. The core of his thinking seemed to be that human struggles were the motivating force of history, and that in order to make history, 'class enemies' had to be continuously created en masse. . . . He understood ugly human instincts such as envy and resentment, and knew how to mobilize them for his ends. He ruled by getting people to hate each other. . . . In bringing out and nourishing the worst in people, Mao had created a moral wasteland and a land of hatred."[2]

China emerged from the horrors of Mao's reign with an attempt to combine authoritarian government with aspects of a capitalist economy. There was good reason for the West to engage with China once this occurred; China genuinely "opened up" after the Mao days, and its human rights situation improved significantly. We could benefit from trade between our countries while holding onto the hope that, in facilitating interaction between the Chinese and American people, trade might increase chances for democratic reform.

This need not have meant, however, that we remained simply silent regarding China's history and its treatment of dissidents and reformers. In *Out of Mao's Shadow*, documentary journalist Philip Pan shows that at the very time that the West was praising China for capitalist advances, China was issuing new laws to wipe out accurate history of the terror, mass murder, and atrocities Mao inflicted upon the Chinese people, and was continuing on with lesser, though still grave human rights abuses. China's "capitalist advances" benefited the American pocketbook. As profits soared for those doing business with China, the economic incentive for ignoring those abuses increased.

Today, the press, the courts, and the labor unions in China are still strictly controlled by the Communist Party. Although economic and commercial law are relatively more liberalized, criminal law is a political tool of the government. The Party *is* the law and there is no alternative to it. The lack of legal rights, an independent judiciary and due process allows the Party to do whatever it wants with the accused, and translates into punishing restrictions on those who interfere with the Party's goals. China still maintains stringent restrictions on speech and assembly and is cracking down on reformers and on Christians with renewed intensity. Still, we generally ignore the fate of those who dare to speak out against the Chinese government. We also ignore the fate of ordinary Chinese citizens who don't conform to China's grand economic plan—such as the peasantry, who are treated like second-class citizens and are subject to special laws and mandates designed to control them. We don't talk much about China's one-child policy (now a two-child policy) and its human rights implications, nor do we pause to picture the forced abortions of women or the punishment of parents "caught" with more than one child. We stifle our disagreement with China over its repression of Christian, Tibetan Buddhist, and Falun Gong groups.

We overlook the fact that China is North Korea's best ally, providing the regime with military technology and economic assistance and doing everything it can to prevent North Korea's collapse. The American press generally doesn't report on China's detestable policy—in violation of the Status of Refugees Convention, to which China is a party—of forcibly repatriating North Korean escapees. (Nor is much said about China's support in the UN for the brutal Assad regime.) In addition to sending escapees to horrible fates, a report by Human Rights Watch entitled "Denied Status, Denied Education" documents the devastating effects of the policy on Korean and Chinese-Korean children. These children are treated as outcasts and risk being deported along with their parents. Children with Chinese fathers have access to the *hukuo* citizenship status of Chinese children only by way of a police document verifying their mother's arrest. Human Rights Watch observes: "The tragic reality for such children is that they obtain nationality—and the chance to go to school—only by losing their mothers."[3] In her moving book, *Escape from North Korea: The Untold Story of Asia's Underground Railroad*, Melanie Kirkpatrick exposes the tragic human toll of China's repatriation policies as she relates the harrowing tale of North Koreans who go to extreme lengths to escape.

We forget that—if the Marshall Plan, Radio Free Europe, and our salutary postwar occupation of Germany and Japan are any indication—an intelligent and moral political position can help improve the geopolitical position. The revolutionary potential of a strong moral position is especially potent now, when Christianity is spreading like wildfire throughout China. Christianity's combined emphasis on the individual and on universal values constitutes a countermovement to atheist, statist communism. The number of Christians in China is strikingly high and growing exponentially. Exact figures are hard to come by, but it is estimated that there are at least sixty-seventy million Christians in China (the government acknowledges far fewer).

By the time of the Obama presidency, China had come a long way from the Mao days when citizens could be tortured and murdered for thinking Christian thoughts. But, as Pastor Bob Fu's memoir *God's Double Agent* shows, the government still harassed Christians, and still periodically detained and tortured them, in order to contain the movement. Another way it sought to contain Christianity was to permit meetings only within the confines of sanctioned Christian organizations. Nevertheless, Christians continued to meet in "unregistered" house-churches, and Christianity continued to grow. After Xi Xingping assumed power in 2012, the Chinese government resorted to more pervasive and excessive methods of persecution.

Philip Pan seeks to understand why so many in China went along with the murderous Cultural Revolution and why, decades later, so many succumbed to repressive post-Tiananmen policies with resignation and/or complicity. As in the case of Nazi Germany, a philosophy of life that devalues individual human life and glorifies the state, and propaganda that successfully spreads that philosophy, has a lot to do with it. Lin Zhao, who was arrested in 1960 during the "anti-rightest" campaign of terror, bravely stated: "If this so-called 'socialism' means tyrannizing, persecuting, and humiliating people, then there is absolutely no shame in opposing socialism or attacking socialism! . . . According to the principles of Marxism-Leninism, the 'law' is merely the 'will of the ruler!' Resistance is a crime, struggling for freedom is a crime, demanding human rights is even more of a crime, so what need is there for 'evidence and witnesses?'"[4] Xi Qisheng, who joined Mao's Red Guards, described his generation's upbringing in a "culture of violent propaganda," telling Pan, "The children were fed a steady diet of stories that extolled Communist heroes who sacrificed their lives in 'class struggle' and had demonized 'class enemies' who were hiding and scheming to undo the Communist Revolution. . . . We had no humanity. . . . We were told that we needed to use violence to destroy a class spiritually and physically. That was justification enough for torturing someone."[5]

In seeking to understand why, after Tiananmen, the human rights movement died out, Pan concludes, "Prosperity allowed the government to reinvent itself, to win friends and buy allies, and to forestall demands for democratic change. It was a remarkable feat, all the more so because the regime had inflicted so much misery on the nation over the past half century. . . . Prosperity for some and 'stability' and repression had allowed/forced many to suppress hopes for political freedom. The party used fear to keep people from concerning themselves with politics or public affairs."[6] Fear and steadily improving economic conditions kept the Chinese human rights movement mostly quiet for a while.

We must remember that, in communism, matter is what "matters." Spirituality and individuality are cast aside for the sake of economic equality. Because of this, a communist government is in a better position to convince people to be satisfied with material comfort, and not to want more out of life, than a capitalist one! Of course, as Loung Ung shows in her beautiful memoir about her life as a little girl in Khmer Rouge Cambodia, the communist attempt to impose equality on society there relied on slavery and never resulted in economic equality, let alone material comfort. The more total or totalitarian the programs for equality, the more certain groups are elevated above others due to their conformance to state plans, and the more other groups and individuals are targeted and persecuted. *Equality is a cruel sham.* "Though the Angkar says we are all equal in Democratic Kamphuchea," recalled Loung Ung, "we are not. We live and are treated as slaves."[7] Indeed, the Cambodian people were slaves, living in camps where they were forced into backbreaking labor; where they were separated from their families and made to avoid words like mother and father; where they were incessantly indoctrinated, monitored, and spied upon and lived in constant fear of arrest, torture, and execution; where they had almost nothing to eat unless they were of the preferred "class," and died one after another of starvation.

By the time President Obama took office, the human rights movement in China had come out of its slumber. With the Chinese government engulfed in scandals over corruption, and with the Chinese people starting to see rampant corruption as inevitable in a society that did not uphold the rule of law, communists in power were vulnerable. With the heightened expectations that came with relative prosperity came unwillingness to settle for a standard of living previously considered acceptable. With Christianity expanding exponentially, the Charter 08 movement burning intensely beneath the shroud of repression, and the Chinese citizenry frustrated with the lack of free access to information, this was not the time to downplay human rights. This was not the time to embrace a "realist" foreign policy that sees nations as hard shells to be balanced against each other without concern for the people within, or to emphasize the economy to the *exclusion* of broader concerns.

Pan documents the resurgence of the human rights movement, seeing the death of Zhao Ziyang as a turning point. Zhao Ziyang was a general secretary of the Communist Party who refused to move against the Tiananmen protestors, and even emerged among them, warning them of coming reprisals and urging them to go home. He was placed under strict house arrest, and his very existence was erased from public record. When he died on January 17, 2005, state television and radio were ordered not to announce his death. Zhao's death, according to Pan, "revealed a scar on the nation's conscience." . . . "For years, people had tried to put Tiananmen behind them. Friends avoided the subject, and parents told their children not to ask about it. Many of those who had been part of the democracy movement threw themselves into making money, claiming they no longer cared about their country's political fate. The pain of remembering, the guilt of giving up and moving on—for many, it was too much to bear, and looking away seemed the only way to live. But when Zhao died, people allowed themselves a moment to reflect again on those young men and women killed in 1989, and to ask whether their sacrifice had meant anything."[8] Asserts Pan, "What progress has been made in recent years—what freedom the Chinese people now enjoy—has come only because individuals have demanded and fought for it, and because the party has retreated in the face of such pressure."[9]

We have seen that, as China allowed the capitalist model to coexist with authoritarian politics, and in so doing became an economic powerhouse (mostly through imitation and production of products made in democratic countries), and as China's military power ascended, the

United States usually overlooked human rights for the sake of lucrative economic relations and geopolitical strategy. The first Obama administration was unique only in the *extent* to which it emphasized the economic side of relations and ignored human rights. This administration's particular emphasis on economic goals rather than political or even strategic ones was substantiated by its one-world vision: a truly global citizen has no strong attachment to family, community, or country. *Such a citizen is tailor-made for the global economy and for the emphasis upon the prosperity we can all supposedly share, as opposed to the political principles or national interests that might divide us.* That is why those who believe in "globalism" say such things as "it's the economy, stupid." The emphasis on the economy instead of liberty goes hand in hand with the attempt to create a unified, if morally muted, world.

This helps to explain why President Obama spoke the words *prosperity* and *international order* so often, but almost never the words *liberty, democracy, freedom, human rights,* or *individual rights*. It helps to explain why Obama and Clinton began their China policy by focusing almost exclusively on the economic relationship. It also explains why, once faced with China's unwillingness to nurture that relationship, they sometimes criticized China for its unfair economic practices, while almost never mentioning its political or military practices.

Secretary Clinton declared in advance of her 2009 Asia trip that the US-China relationship was "the world's most important in the twenty-first century." She emphasized the "interests" China and the United States had in common, saying, "Some believe that China on the rise is, by definition, an adversary . . . To the contrary, we believe that the United States and China can benefit from each other's successes."[10] During the trip, she indicated that human rights would not be permitted to block progress on economic issues. President Obama called China a "strategic partner" with "common economic interests," then treated it like one, offering military-to-military exchanges, downgrading the National Security Council's intelligence gathering from China, and carefully avoiding the subject of human rights. In departures from presidential tradition, he initially refused to meet with the Dalai Lama and stonewalled Taiwan's request for F-16 fighter jets.

In the president's May 2010 speech at West Point, the de-emphasis on political and military power, and the emphasis on economic power, was clear. Obama stated that "our strength and influence abroad begins with steps we take at home." He explained, "We must educate our children to compete in an age where knowledge is capital, and the marketplace is global. We must develop clean energy that can power new industry and unbound us from foreign oil and preserve our planet. We have to pursue science that unlocks wonders as unforeseen to us today as the microchip and the surface of the moon were a century ago. Simply put, American innovation must be the foundation of American power—because at no time in human history has a nation of diminished economic vitality maintained its military and political primacy."[11] The speech foreshadowed a national security document that advocated increasing cooperation with international institutions, engaging with governments around the globe, and redefining American power in terms of our economic, scientific, and environmental achievements.

The academic idea that all the capitalist United States cares about is the "financial motive"—which began as a critique of the United States by such leftist critics as William A. Williams and Michael H. Hunt—can become a self-fulfilling prophesy. Some of the very intellectuals who made that claim now urge the United States to forget its ideas and ideals, to retract its power and influence, and to realize the advantage that can come to the entire world if America emphasizes the economic side of relations with other countries. In the end, this emphasis on the economy suits their socialist worldview, which values economic equality over individual rights, political freedom, and spiritual well-being. The very reason they see America in terms of economic greed, and fail to acknowledge America's attributes, is that they themselves see the world in terms of impersonal economic forces.

The rewriting of history makes it easy to do so. *It is one thing for China to remove Mao's reign of terror from its history books, but it is another thing for the United States to do so.* Propaganda and censorship aren't supposed to happen here. And yet, in the majority of American high schools and universities, the truth about communist countries is eluded. Emblematic of today's approach, my childrens' middle school textbook on China focused on China's geography and "unique traditions" and celebrated China's clothing, food, and architecture. The text supported a "culture studies" curriculum that whitewashed uncomfortable facts about other cultures and focused obsessively on American misdeeds and prejudices.

In announcing the end of our mission in Iraq in August 2010, Obama again defined American significance and American priorities in economic terms. The president asserted:

> Throughout our history, America has been willing to bear the burden of promoting liberty and human dignity overseas, understanding its links to our own liberty and security. But we have also understood that our nation's strength and influence abroad must be firmly anchored in our prosperity at home. And the bedrock of that prosperity is a growing middle class. Unfortunately, over the last decade, we've not done what's necessary to shore up the foundations of our own prosperity. We spent a trillion dollars at war, often financed by borrowing from overseas. This, in turn, has shortchanged investments in our own people and contributed to record deficits. . . . Our most urgent task is to restore our economy, and put the millions of Americans who have lost their jobs back to work. . . . This will be difficult. But in the days to come, it must be our central mission as a people, and my central responsibility as president.[12]

Note that the economy is our "foundation of power," our "central mission," the "anchor" of our influence, and our "most urgent task." Would that the president used such words for freedom itself.

In October 2011, Secretary Clinton gave a similarly revealing speech, widely seen as an important foreign policy statement, at the Economic Club of New York. Clinton touted "economic statecraft" and said we were "updating our foreign policy priorities to include economics every step of the way." She depicted our own strong economy as the key to our influence and strong economic relations as the key to international relations. We were committed, she said, "to strengthening the economic dimensions of our closest relationships." To do so, she advocated a shift in American foreign policy priorities and methods: "As we embrace economic statecraft, it's not just our priorities that are changing. The way we pursue them is evolving as well. . . . We are honing our ability to develop and execute economic solutions to strategic challenges."

Clinton asserted that, essentially, economic power mattered more than military power, and she placed her focus on economic relations in the tradition of Truman's Marshall Plan: "It was, after all, Harry Truman who said, 'Our relations, foreign and economic, are indivisible.'

Because President Truman understood that if America wanted to shape the postwar world, America had to lead—not just diplomatically or militarily, but critically, and maybe most importantly, economically. And so we marshaled our forces to rebuild friends or even former enemies, we led the charge to create a new international economic order, and we made the investments we needed here at home to advance our ideals and promote shared prosperity."[13] But, as my discussion of Truman shows, this is a misrepresentation of the man. Truman was not seeking a "new international economic order." He was seeking the protection and extension of the realm of liberty. Truman valued the Marshall Plan primarily for the assistance it provided to war-ravaged Europe, and for the sympathy it inspired in Europeans for our way of life (with our way of life including the practice of free enterprise). The building up of strategic alliances had the same purpose—defending and promoting freedom's realm. To Truman, individual rights and human worth were primary, not secondary.

In the very speech in which she claimed Truman's legacy, Clinton downgraded foreign policy based upon military strategy and American principles. Yet, it is hard to find a president that upgraded America's military strategy and asserted American principles more than Truman. In the long speech, she mentioned principles only once—in the context of stating that they were outdated as markers of American foreign policy: "Now, there will always be times when we put cost aside to keep Americans safe or to honor our principles. And for the last decade, our foreign policy has, by necessity, focused on the places where we faced the greatest dangers. . . . But it cannot be our foreign policy. In the decades ahead, our foreign policy must focus just as intensely on the places where we have the greatest opportunities. And often, they will be economic in nature."[14]

To move toward the "new international economic order," Clinton proposed helping reform economies "designed to keep autocrats and elites in power" in the Middle East, supporting Russia in its bid to join the World Trade Organization, passing trade deals in South America, and pressuring China regarding its unfair valuation of currency. She spoke for the importance of women's participation in the "global economy." She stated, "It's also not enough for our commercial diplomacy to promote the flow of goods and services. We also need to promote the free flow of capital."[15] She noted that states are often the ones deploying cash, companies, and natural resources and called for "international norms" to regulate state behavior.

Leslie Gelb of the Council on Foreign Relations praised the speech in the *Daily Beast*, saying, "The secretary tries to help the Washington uncaring comprehend the vast array of economic connections between America and the world—on which rise or fall America's prospects, standard of living and international power—trade, investment, currency exchange rates, the role of the dollar as the world's reserve currency, aid, technology transfers, the roles of the World Bank, International Monetary Fund, World Trade Organization, the sale or withholding of natural resources, the debt and banking crises in American and Europe, and on and on."[16] In an article entitled "Clinton Adopts Jobs's 'Think Different' Motto for Diplomacy," Flavia Krause-Jackson and Nicole Gaouette noted Clinton's positioning of the economy as "the basis for our security, power and influence" and quoted Stephen S. Cohen of the Berkeley Roundtable on the International Economy, who thought the emphasis on the economy should go even further. The State Department, Cohen said, should "get serious about opening markets and leveraging the advantage to the U.S. side now," while the administration should "forget ideas and just look very concretely at the economy."[17]

Cohen captured the spirit of Hillary Clinton's foreign policy agenda: Her "idea," which recurred in various forms (including her early declaration that "ideology is so yesterday"), was to downplay ideas and ideals for the sake of pragmatism and prosperity. The problem with this is that individuals, groups, and countries always live according to ideas—sometimes very low ones, sometimes very high ones, sometimes silly ones, sometimes practical ones. But one cannot live or act without ideas.

The question then becomes, what *are* Clinton's ideas and what does her de-emphasis on ideas tell us about *her* ideas? As we have seen, she has clear ideas about the arrogance of American power, about the need to tone down American principles for the sake of a new world order, about the priority that should be given to international institutions and shared economic interests, and about the leveling of the playing field that needs to occur if we are all to get along. As we have seen, the globalism of today is wrapped up in the "toleration" of differences—even if the differences include the imposition of Sharia law, the repression of citizens with communist mandates and methods, and the organization of society according to militaristic goals. We've also seen that the globalism of today is often tied up with what some call the "blame America first" mentality, which calls upon America to voluntarily relinquish some of its power and influence, while confessing its faults. Taken together, these tendencies lend a provincialism to our globalism: We "remember" Selma (as we should), but we overlook Iranian atrocities. We concern ourselves with the inequalities of our own capitalist system, but we refrain from criticizing the treatment of factory workers, religious minorities, or the peasantry in China.

It is this leveling compulsion—that defers to international "norms," elevates our enemies and depreciates our friends, and lessens the distinction between democratic nations and undemocratic nations—that explains Clinton's de-emphasis on ideas. For, *claiming to disregard ideas not only provides an excuse for shoving American ideas aside; it also provides an opening for internationalist ideas that Clinton would like Americans to consider. Perhaps most importantly, it provides cover for proceeding on with what is actually a strong cultural, political, and ideological agenda.* Clinton could insert her agenda into American policy more easily if she claimed not to have an agenda. Many in the press fell for her line and portrayed Secretary Clinton as she described herself: a "smart power" pragmatist.

Obama, Clinton, and the rest of the foreign policy team *were* plenty smart enough to realize globalism's conundrum. They knew that the thuggish dictators we were reaching out to did not themselves want one-world harmony and global prosperity. Extremist leaders prefer that their "will to power" be successfully imposed upon others—both within and without—than that the world reach a compromise based upon toleration and mutual respect.

In the face of America's policy of indifference, the Dalai Lama declared in 2009 that Tibet had become "hell on earth" and that Chinese oppression was driving Tibet to the "verge of extinction." Also in 2009, China began to take a harder line on the Charter 08 democracy movement and began to draw sharper distinctions between Chinese government and Western-style democracy. In a March 2009 speech, National People's Congress chairman Wu Bangguo said China would "never" be a multiparty state with separation of powers and/or an independent judiciary. He announced that elections would continue to have government-approved candidates on the ballot. In December 2009, China sentenced pro-reform author Liu Xiaobo to eleven years in prison in what human rights groups said was a warning that punishments for human rights activists would be increasingly harsh. Indeed, the years 2010 and 2011 were worse. A researcher with Hong Kong–based Chinese Human Rights Defenders, Wang Songlian, said, "This is the harshest crackdown we have seen in the past fifteen years. Every day, someone is disappeared, taken away, detained or charged."[18] Among the victims of the crackdown was prominent artist and critic of the regime, Ai Weiwei.

Too few take seriously the warning issued by Lincoln in his 1838 Lyceum address. Lincoln feared that the "the silent artillery of time" would lull complacent Americans into forgetting their founding ideas and predicted that, if they did forget them, it would be their undoing. Given the incredible bounty of our territory and the inherently strong position of a free people, Lincoln stated that he did not fear America's undoing by a foreign threat—unless Americans would forget their indebtedness to the Revolution and the Constitution and so undo the sources of their strength. "At what point then is the approach of danger to be expected?" he asked. "I answer, if it ever reach us, it must spring up amongst us. . . . If destruction be our lot, we must ourselves be its author and finisher."[19] Since Americans no longer had access to the "living history" of the Revolution, Lincoln urged us to preserve our history in our teachings and books: "They were a fortress of strength; but, what invading foeman could never do, the silent artillery of time has done; the leveling of its walls. They are gone. . . . They were the pillars of the temple of liberty; and now, that they have crumbled away, that temple must fall, unless we, their descendants, supply their places with other pillars, hewn from the solid quarry of sober reason."[20]

The intentional and unintentional forgetting of American ideas and American history has everything to do with the current lack of emphasis upon individual rights and human rights. It explains why, unlike previous administrations that at least began their tenures with an attempt to promote human rights in China, the Obama-Clinton administration never made the attempt in the first place. In a paper presented to the Fulbright Symposium on Australia-US Relations and the Rise of China, Suisheng Zhao noted the difference. Seeing the ultimate move toward a more "centralist" approach by previous presidents as a good thing, Zhao observed that Reagan at first restored official relations with Taiwan and put restrictions on Chinese textile exports to the US and American technology transfers to China; President Clinton at first issued an executive order establishing human rights conditions for China's most favored nation status; and George W. Bush at first emphasized US obligations to Taiwan and sought a reversal of Clinton's policy which had ultimately accommodated China.

The reality of China's economic and military power, according to Zhao, convinced these presidents to back away from their initial stands. President Obama, however, *immediately* proposed a "positive, cooperative, and comprehensive" relationship with China to replace Bush's "cooperative, constructive, and candid" relationship. Observed Zhao: "Using 'positive' to replace 'candid' reflected the Obama administration's reluctance to challenge China on issues of fundamental disagreements and its intention to make sure that disagreements on these issues would not interfere with the engagement to pursue shared interests."[21]

To confirm that US policy would be based upon respect for China's "interests" and not upon concerns of human rights, the US-China joint statement after President Obama's first state visit to Beijing stated that for the first time "the two sides agreed that respecting each other's core interests is extremely important to ensure steady progress in U.S.-China relations."[22] As Zhao observed, "President Obama also had no hesitation to elevate his high level dialogue with China as 'strategic' and describe China as a 'strategic partner.'" The latter was "a label much desired by Beijing," whereas Bush characterized US security dialogue with China as "senior" to preserve "strategic" for US allies. "Because the focus on shared interests was more or less in line with China's call for building a harmonious world to avoid the clash of civilizations," Zhao wrote, the Obama administration enjoyed a brief "honeymoon relationship" with China.[23]

Our close ally Japan viewed this policy with alarm. "Japan is very concerned about the attitude of the United States toward China," said defense analyst Hisao Yuwashima. "It is important that the two countries have a friendly relationship, but a military alliance would be dangerous, I fear, because it is not clear how much control the Chinese government has over its military."[24] The fact that Japanese analysts feared US-Chinese military (not just economic) cooperation shows that the level and kind of partnership the United States was offering China was a watershed in US policy.

The "honeymoon period" for US-Chinese relations was short, however. Rather than responding in kind to America's generous offer, China saw it as a sign of weakness. While the Obama administration worked assiduously in its first year to improve the US-China relationship and lay the groundwork for cooperation on major global challenges, it soon found itself responding to a series of increasingly uncooperative Chinese moves. China ratcheted up its rhetoric about the consequences of routine US arms sales to Taiwan and about regular US naval operations in international waters off its coast; refused to cooperate with efforts to contain Syria and Iran; obstructed US initiatives in the UN Security Council; expanded its designs on the South China Sea and attempted to create a sphere of influence in the Sea and around India; fielded an array of new weapons systems and anti-satellite missiles, the stated purpose of which was to defeat the United States; and clamped down further on dissidents, freedom of speech, and the free flow of information. China continued to prop up the loathsome North Korean regime by failing to pressure it on its weapons programs and continuing the horrible practice of forcibly repatriating North Korean escapees. In addition, evidence increased that China was complicit in Iran's acquisition of weapons.

The Obama administration was thus forced to rethink its China policy. The administration turned to a "rebalancing" that, to the relief of Japan and other Asian countries, stepped up engagement with America's traditional allies and partners in Asia. By 2010, the US was seeking to remind China of US strategic power and influence in Asia and was reestablishing strategic and security ties with Japan, India, and even Vietnam in order to offset a resurgent China. By 2011, Obama was declaring a "pivot" to Asia that increased deployment of US troops around the region and sent new US warships to Singapore. In early 2012, a Department of Defense document entitled "Sustaining US Global Leadership Priorities for 21st Century Defense" stated that the US "will of necessity rebalance toward the Asia Pacific Region" and said the reason for this change was "economic and security interests inextricably linked to developments in the arc extending from the Western Pacific and East Asia into the Indian Ocean region and South Asia."[25]

Clinton had explained the shift in American policy in an October 2011 article in *Foreign Policy* entitled "America's Pacific Century."

Zhao saw President Obama's pivot as "the return to the centralist engagement policy successfully held by his predecessors that sought to engage and interact economically with China, but also sought to provide military and strategic counterweights to Chinese influence."[26] He concluded, "In contrast to his predecessors who started with tough positions toward China and adjusted their positions toward more cooperative direction, President Obama has gone the other way around. Starting with a reconciliatory tone, he has scaled back and took a tougher position."[27] In other words, according to Zhao, although Obama and Clinton took a different route, they ended up where American policy usually ends up.

Although I find Zhao's thesis helpful, on this point I disagree with his argument. It is true that on the surface the administration's "tougher position" resembled the tougher position ultimately adopted by Obama's and Clinton's predecessors, but it differed in fundamental ways. First, a policy that never did emphasize concern for human rights is fundamentally different from policies that initially or occasionally made human rights a priority. Second, a policy that represents "interests" instead of American ideals, and that only changed its definition of interests because Chinese actions forced it to change, is a policy beholden to the international turn of events, that has no steady compass to guide it. Third, the Obama administration and the Chinese government still shared a stated desire for a new world order based on economic interests and a downplaying of ideological differences. Fourth, while China steadily increased its defense spending and decreased the transparency of its military modernization program, the Obama administration decreased support for the US military, both in word and in deed.

At the February 2012 Munich Security Conference, Defense Secretary Leon Panetta stated, "Let me summarize the key elements of the new U.S. defense strategy. First, the United States military will be smaller and will be leaner. That was something, frankly, that was going to happen under any circumstances by virtue of the drawdown we were involved in."[28] Accordingly, the Obama administration announced plans to cut up to $1 trillion from defense spending over the next ten years. *Washington Times* editor Bill Gertz warned regarding this plan, "There the story of America's education on China's military should serve as a lesson for those who still seek to shrink U.S. fighting capabilities in the face of growing threats. Barack Obama, in looking to cut defense spending across the board, is repeating the mistakes of the benign-China school on a much larger scale. Motivated by faith in a benign global order, against all evidence, this would undercut America's ability to lead the free world. . . . The Obama administration deserves credit for shifting American strategy to respond to the genuine Chinese threat. . . . But Cold War strategy wasn't implemented along with a simultaneous effort to defund it."[29]

My final disagreement with Zhao's thesis has to do with its argument that the "pivot" toward Bill Clinton-style pragmatism is an effective strategy for dealing with China. In a January 1999 article entitled "Clinton's China Policy Invites Disaster," University of Pennsylvania professor Arthur Waldron made a convincing case that President Clinton's supposedly pragmatic policy had not worked. The Cox Report—a 1999 congressional investigation of China's covert efforts to steal advanced weapons technological information from the US—found, among other things, that the People's Liberation Army was pushing for a very hard line, with PLA generals signing a strong protest against President Jiang Zemin's "weak" policies toward the US, Japan, and Taiwan and with Premier Zhu Rongji taking the same stance. Waldron argued, "The U.S. could have strengthened the hand of reformers in China by making clear that the revival of authoritarianism would lead to trouble in the China-U.S. relationship. Instead the administration did just the opposite—it shunned the reformers and embraced the oppressors. That solicitude convinced China's military leaders that Washington is afraid and hence malleable, and that has emboldened them to take a harder line. U.S. policy, in other words, has smoothed the road for an ultra-nationalist dictatorship in China—even as U.S. security failures have ensured that the dictatorship will have state of the art weapons."[30]

In an unpublished article at the time, I chimed in:

> Recent policy tells China that our national resolve and our democratic convictions are faltering. The decline in defense spending and in anti-proliferation measures, and the security lapses, technology transfers and military "exchanges" which benefit the Chinese military, suggest that we do not take deterrence seriously. The collusion

between the US government and American companies which profit from modernizing China's missile technologies suggest that the desire for short term gain (financial and political) blindsides us to our principles. The administration's deafening silence regarding China's increased bellicosity toward Taiwan and its apparent indifference to China's inroads into our own hemisphere support these claims. As but one example, at a November 1998 press conference, President Clinton admitted that, once the United States relinquished control of the Panama Canal, communist China would be running ports at both ends of the canal through a Hong Kong company, Hutchison Whampoa, Ltd. (a firm widely said to have close links to the Chinese military). He seemed recklessly unconcerned, speculating that the Chinese would "in fact be bending over to make sure that they run it in a competent and able and fair manner" and stating that he'd be "very surprised if any adverse consequences flowed from the Chinese running the canal." Clinton's indifference to China's strategic gains is tied in with a whole lot of wishful thinking.[31]

As all astute observers of China know, China does see solicitude as weakness, and does seize opportunities provided by American solicitude to bolster the authoritarian state and test expansionist goals. Given this, there is an un-pragmatic result of our pragmatic offer to keep human rights off the table. In doing so, we are relinquishing our ace in the hole. Dave Lindorff, who lived in and reported on China for several years, described the conundrum well: China, he said, views the United States as a "paper tiger," with its military might spread thin around the globe and its serious financial troubles. "Given this situation, with China holding most of the cards, the last thing Clinton and the Obama administration should have ever done, from a purely practical point of view, was to telegraph that it would not seriously press the one issue that does cause the Chinese ruling elite to lose sleep at night, and that is the powder keg that is the long-repressed Chinese people."[32]

As if to showcase its response to American weakness, in April 2012, China deployed a third ship into a disputed area of the South China Sea, where a tense standoff developed with Philippine vessels. One of the Chinese ships blocked entrance to a lagoon, while others ordered a Philippine warship to leave the area.

The fact is that when it came to perpetuating the traditional American stance for liberty or to traditional strategies of containment and deterrence, President Obama's heart just wasn't in it. His attitude toward national security was that we no longer needed grand strategy for the sake of it; we were supposedly reaping the "peace dividend" of a post-Cold War world. As we have seen, he showed only lukewarm support for the US military and pushed plans for major decreases in defense spending. Countless opportunities for strategic alliances and strong relationships with democratic allies in Asia and elsewhere were lost. When it came to human rights, the best his administration mustered was an unenthused and detached nod. President Obama's response to the problems of those stuck in repressive regimes was notably lethargic and indifferent. Their cries for American support and attention to their plight did not move him.

Human Rights First reported that 2011 and 2012 were sad and deteriorating years for human rights in China. North Korean children were still forcibly separated from their mothers and denied status. The country sentenced several prominent human rights activists to lengthy prison terms. Many other activists were harassed, detained, and tortured by the government.

Determined to prevent the wave of democracy movements that swept Arab countries from spreading across its borders, the Chinese government stepped up the pressure. Chinese human rights defenders in the legal profession were increasingly vulnerable. In 2011, at least two hundred people, including many lawyers, "disappeared," and in 2012, the government increased its use of unofficial detention centers—so-called "black jails"—to hold dissidents.[33] Human Rights First urged the United States to go beyond occasional shows of support and to establish a consistent policy of engagement with defenders of civil society in China and other countries: "Reliable U.S. support—through embassies or other means—is critical in bolstering the work of human rights defenders around the world and increases protection to those at risk."[34]

The crackdown intensified not just on activists but on their modes of communication and expression. Beijing-based analyst and professor Russell Leigh Moses reported in August 2011 that politburo member Liu Qi visited the offices of Sina.com's popular microblogging service

Weibo and "impressed upon the staff there the need for 'the Internet's healthy development'—code words for staying away from topics which attack the Communist Party or hold officials up for public ridicule." Moses added, "Liu's strong-arm visit follows a series of admonitions in the Party media, warning journalists to get back into the government fold and to play the role of conveying to a skeptical society that cadres care. The hardline view, expressed in a recent article posted in the 'People's Forum' run by the official *People's Daily*, is that microblogging is best confronted, not by embracing it as a way for the public to supervise the Party, but by the Party's use [of] the mass media to tell the truth."[35]

An April 2011 *Bloomberg* headline read, "China's Crackdown on Human Rights Sparks Little Outcry in Washington." The article noted that "neither President Barack Obama nor Secretary Clinton has singled out China for public criticism over the latest wave of arrests, though both have said they always raise human rights in their private conversations with Chinese officials."[36]

Perhaps starting to realize deficiencies in the administration's China policies, perhaps feeling more sympathy for Chinese dissidents, perhaps wanting to shore up her recorded statements on human rights for the sake of a future presidential run, Clinton did begin to speak up occasionally for Chinese dissidents in mid-2011, although such other statements as those made at the Economic Club of New York (discussed above) served to reassure realists that the administration's foremost concern would continue to be economic relations. In an interview with the *Atlantic* in May, she called China's human rights record "deplorable" and added, "They're worried, and they are trying to stop history, which is a fool's errand. They cannot do it. But they're going to hold off as long as possible."[37] In her October 2011 "America's Pacific Century" address, Clinton criticized China's record on human rights and mentioned "reports of lawyers, artists, and others who are detained or disappeared."[38]

If it weren't for the high-profile escape of Chinese activist and dissident Chen Guangcheng, the administration would have been able to leave it at that. A blind campaigner for disabled rights and against forced abortions and sterilizations, Chen's dramatic appearance at the US embassy and his corresponding plea for political asylum for himself and his family couldn't help but grab international attention. As Chinese filmmaker Ai Xiaoming put it, "If a blind person can break out of the darkness to freedom, then everyone can."[39]

The administration hoped the world's attention span would be short-lived as it is so often is in today's media age. Chen passionately appealed to Secretary Clinton for help. He said he was "really afraid" for the lives of his other family members. This appeal, combined with statements in support of asylum by Republican lawmakers and sympathy for Chen in the American press, pressured the administration. But the State Department forged an agreement with the Chinese government that would ultimately require Chen to leave the US embassy in exchange for Chinese pledges to allow him to "reunite" with his family and pursue his education. In an attempt to deflect attention away from the human rights issues, American diplomats said they had "determined Mr. Wang's case did not involve national security." In another attempt to shift attention back to issues such as the economy, White House spokesman Jay Carney responded to questions on the human rights implications of Chen's case by saying of President Obama: "He is focused on the need to advance US interests in our broad-based relationship with China— very important economic, diplomatic relationship with China. He has and will continue to make a priority in that relationship or a part of that relationship an open and frank discussion of our concerns about human rights."[40]

This time, however, the administration failed in its attempt to lead the American people where it wanted them to go. Said Representative Frank Wolf of Virginia, "The Obama administration has a moral, and a high moral, obligation to protect Chen and his family. . . . To do anything less would be scandalous."[41] Realizing that it was indeed creating a scandal, the administration reconsidered. Negotiations with the Chinese government ensued, and Chen and his family were ultimately allowed to come to the United States so that Chen could "study" in an American university. The agreement fell short of asylum, but was enough to stem the rising tide of condemnation of the US position. Otherwise, US policy remained unchanged.

Dissident and expatriate Bob Fu, who founded the influential Christian human rights group ChinaAid, begged Obama administration officials to publicly take up the cause of Chinese dissidents as soon as they entered office. President George W. Bush met Fu's delegation of top Chinese human rights lawyers three times, but President Obama was unwilling to meet with them. According to a *Wall Street Journal* interview with Fu, in 2011, ChinaAid's request for a meeting was "totally ignored." The *WSJ* further reported that Fu had supplied the State Department with information that Chen's family was mistreated and threatened when Chen took his stand at the US embassy.[42] But it was only after a great deal of international pressure, and two congressional hearings, that the United States granted Chen a student visa to study at New York University and permitted his family to accompany him. Fu's take on this was that the United States had sent "a very chilling message to the Chinese freedom fighters." The extreme reluctance to aid Chen Guangcheng suggested to him that if others "in the future seek this kind of U.S. help, we'll shut the door."[43]

■ ■ ■

As the Obama/Clinton period came to a close, and as the Obama/Kerry period began, it was clear that, even apart from the deterioration in human rights, China was not responding favorably to America's globalist gestures. While the United States had emphasized "international rules" and a world economy, and had stressed "common interests" with China, China had become more, not less, assertive in pursuing *its own* interests. A report entitled "Asia in the Balance: Transforming US Military Strategy in Asia" demonstrated that China was not the "strategic partner" the Obama administration had hoped for. Noting "the scope and pace of Chinese military developments," the authors said: "China has been working systematically to undermine the American approach to assurance, deterrence, and warfighting. Specifically, China's military modernization lends it the ability to decouple America's allies from the US extended nuclear deterrent, to destroy US and allied fixed bases in the Asia-Pacific region, and to threaten US power projection forces. This, in turn, could allow China to coerce US allies and friends in the region (regarding territorial disputes for example), hold US forces at arm's length, and control the rear along the Asian periphery."[44]

China's geopolitical and military positions were advancing steadily, while US leverage in Asia, in spite of the US "pivot" to that region, was declining. China was seeking control over waters extending two hundred nautical miles from Chinese shores. China was undergoing aggressive land reclamation and island-building projects in the South China Sea. China was adopting a "String of Pearls" strategy of developing relations and bases in the Indian Ocean in order to have greater control over passageways into East Asia. In addition, China was pursuing the goal of unifying Taiwan with the mainland and preventing the US and Japan from coming to Taiwan's defense.

All of this, of course, had ramifications for America's Asian friends. Think, for example, of the kind of pressure this put on India, and on its decision (during the Bush years) to cooperate as never before with the United States. Think of the difference China's arsenal of ballistic and cruise missiles, submarines and mines, and integrated defense system makes to the balance of power in the region, particularly as it affects Japan and South Korea. China's increasing "command of the Commons" upended America's post–World War II role as the guarantor of regional stability in Asia (a role which allowed our allies to focus on political and economic goals as opposed to military ones).

As the US Defense Department's 2012 "Joint Operational Access Concept" indicates, such concerns were primary as the United States "rebalanced" toward Asia. The rebalance was underlain by the idea that backing away from commitments in Afghanistan and Iraq freed the United States to focus on Asia and China. (Recall that Secretary Clinton termed the US-China relationship the "world's most important in the twenty-first century.") Noboru Yamaguchi of the National Defense Academy of Japan speculated that the shift "may represent demobilization from a wartime posture rather than a [mere] change in US policy priorities." He noted, "Secretary Clinton has said that 'as the war in Iraq winds down and America begins to withdraw its forces from Afghanistan, the United States stands at a pivot point.'"[45]

Questions about our credibility and reliability were created when we announced that China was our most important partner, thereby demoting our relationships with Japan, South Korea, Taiwan, India, and Australia. When we then announced a pivot to Asia, we effectively downgraded our alliances in Europe and the Middle East, sending a message to our allies (then and now) that our allegiance and commitment might not last. Even apart from this, the rebalance damaged American credibility for the following reasons: First, the rebalance in some ways resembled the very balance of power tactics the administration decried for the sake of "soft power." It is true that it had economic and diplomatic dimensions, but the military emphasis drew into question the administration's early assumptions. Second, America's rebalancing activities were limited to some alliance building, sending some combat ships to Singapore and some marines to Australia, and conducting joint exercises with Japan and South Korea. Budget cuts negatively affected the numbers and the readiness of our ships, missile defenses, and bombers. As the authors of "Asia in the Balance" argued, "There is a danger that the vulnerability of US forces (and responses to this vulnerability) will undermine the credibility of America's security commitment to the Asia-Pacific region."[46]

US decreases in defense spending along with dramatically escalating violence and chaos in the Middle East made it difficult for the administration to make good on its commitment to pivot to Asia. The Middle East was, in the words of Chuck Hagel, secretary of defense from 2013 to 2015, "exploding all over," forcing the United States to think twice about focusing too many resources on Asia. Events were again overtaking the administration, exposing its lack of a steady moral or strategic compass. In April 2013 testimony before the House Foreign Relations Committee, Secretary Kerry fittingly stated:

> In the past few months, we've seen a number of developments that underscore the stakes for having a strong American presence in every part of the world. American engagement was essential to the rapprochement between two of our closest partners, Israel and Turkey, and that was a positive step toward stability in a volatile region of the world, where we need partnerships. This committee is more than immersed in Syria. We have contributed nearly $385 million to humanitarian relief to provide essential resources to the Syrian people, including sending flour to bakeries in Aleppo and providing food and sanitation in Atmeh in the refugee camp. . . . Having just returned from Seoul, Beijing, and Tokyo, where the North Korea issue took center stage, we are reminded once again that America is the guardian of global security. We should be proud of that and we should carry that mettle. We will not turn our back on the prospect of peace, but neither are we going to hesitate to do what we need to do to defend our allies and our interests.

And yet, Hagel announced 2014 Pentagon budget priorities that would shrink the Army to its smallest size since 1940 and cut the Navy to its smallest size since 1915, while Kerry presented a 2014 budget request for foreign operations that represented a 6 percent reduction. When asked to name the practical implications of the pivot policy, he mentioned the administration's commitment to passing the Trans-Pacific Partnership. Seeming to downplay the policy, he placed more emphasis on US engagement in the Middle East! Although he noted the grave situation in North Korea, when pressed on the administration's strategy for handling that country, he stated that diplomacy was the cornerstone of relations, and advocated the continuation of engagement policies. Tellingly, he stressed China's key role in bringing North Korea to the negotiating table. "The policy of Russia, the policy of China, the policy of South Korea, Japan and the United States is the policy of denuclearization. The single country that has the greatest ability to be able to impact that is China. . . . Absent China coming to the table, I believe [North Korean leader] Kim Jong-un calculates . . . that he can get away with anything if China is not going to hold [him] accountable."

A transparent summation of the Obama/Kerry approach to China and Southeast Asia can be found in John Kerry's August 13, 2014, speech entitled "US Vision for Asia-Pacific." While committing to "revitalizing" security partnerships with treaty allies Japan, Australia, South Korea, and the Philippines and claiming that "we are standing up for the human rights and the fundamental freedoms that people in Asia cherish," Kerry defined the "four specific opportunities" in Southeast Asia in this way and in this order: "creating sustainable economic growth, powering a clean energy revolution, promoting regional cooperation, and empowering people." Philosophically, Secretary Kerry's China position was similar to Secretary Clinton's. He emphasized all the good that should come from great power cooperation defined by adherence to international norms and pursuit of common interests:

> Now, one thing that I know will contribute to maintaining regional peace and stability is a constructive relationship between the United States and China. President Obama has made it clear that the United States welcomes the rise of a peaceful, prosperous, and stable China— one that plays a responsible role in Asia and the world and supports

rules and norms on economic and security issues. The president has been clear, as have I, that we are committed to avoiding the trap of strategic rivalry and intent on forging a relationship in which we can broaden our cooperation on common interests and constructively manage our differences and disagreements.

But make no mistake: This constructive relationship, this "new model" relationship of great powers, is not going to happen simply by talking about it. It's not going to happen by engaging in a slogan or pursuing a sphere of influence. It will be defined by more and better cooperation on shared challenges. And it will be defined by a mutual embrace of the rules, the norms, and institutions that have served both of our nations and the region so well. I am very pleased that China and the United States are cooperating effectively on the Iran nuclear talks and we've increased our dialogue on the DPRK. We're also cooperating significantly on climate change possibilities, counter-piracy operations, and South Sudan.

So we are busy trying to define a great power relationship by the places where we can find mutual agreement and cooperation.[47]

Occasions such as Chen Guangcheng's escape to our embassy could instead (or, at least, in addition) have prompted speech about the moral, political, and economic benefits of a free society. We can and should speak for human rights and individual rights in a measured way that distinguishes us from regimes that spew propaganda. We can and should reach out to both the Chinese government and the Chinese people. We can and should maintain a viable defense posture and heed the valuable lessons learned from our exceptionally successful Cold War containment policy. Post–World War II American foreign policy depended upon both American power and American ideals, and it still holds valuable lessons.

We should, furthermore, seize every opportunity we can to press the Chinese government regarding policies that affect North Korean escapees and citizens. Following Kim Jong-il's death in 2011, the Chinese government publicly expressed "confidence" in Kim Jong-un's ability to succeed his father. (Shortly thereafter, North Korea announced it would launch "special actions" to wipe out South Korean president Lee Myung-bak's administration.) When China expresses support for North

Korea, the United States should, in turn, publicly expose the internal practices of North Korean leaders and the human rights consequences of China's support for the North Korean regime. It should make clear that constructive dialogue and trade with China does not translate into our indifference to the plight of North Koreans.

Mutually profitable economic interaction and cooperation in areas of mutual interest *are* important, as long as we don't allow them to harden our hearts and blind us to humane responsibilities. They *are* important, as long as we don't allow them to lull us into complacency and blind us to strategic imperatives.

Events in China from late 2012 through Obama's second term illuminated the inadequacy of an approach to foreign relations that overemphasizes shared interests and the economy. In December 2012, a prominent group of Chinese academics, including well-known legal experts, warned in a courageous open letter that the country risked "violent revolution" if the government didn't respond to public pressure and allow long-stalled political reforms. They complained that political reform had not accompanied the economic reforms that had allowed China's tremendous economic expansion. "If reforms to the system urgently needed by Chinese society keep being frustrated and stagnate without progress, then official corruption and dissatisfaction in society will boil up to a crisis point and China will once again miss the opportunity for peaceful reform, and slip into the turbulence and chaos of violent revolution," they warned.[48]

> In the face of this longing for more freedom, president of China and general secretary of the Chinese Communist Party Xi Jingping, who took office in November 2012, has taken China in the opposite direction. Although he did modify the one-child policy, he has otherwise cracked down on civil society, religious and political expression, and dissent. Although he did target corrupt business managers, party officials, and generals, the anticorruption campaign provided cover for a correlated political purge. Seeking to strengthen the power and control of the Communist Party, in the words of Evan Osnos, whose exposé appeared in the *New Yorker*, Xi "unambiguously opposes American democratic notions." Xi's government has engaged in a series of coordinated detentions and interrogations of human rights lawyers,

Christians, and others, prompting rights defenders inside and outside of China to identify a serious deterioration in China's human rights situation. The government has stepped up censorship of the press, the Internet, print publications, and academic research. In 2013, the government launched an aggressive effort to rein in microblogging. As people who dare to oppose the Party's stranglehold have been intimidated, arrested, or "disappeared," more and more Chinese churches have been subject to demolition. Severe prosecution and harassment of anyone involved in the 1989 pro-democracy movement has continued, with China expanding a crackdown on dissent in the run-up to the 2014 anniversary of the Tiananmen massacre.

Detention and treatment of women's rights activists has been severe, prompting Secretary Kerry to issue an April 2015 statement urging China to "immediately and unconditionally release" the five Beijing+20 women who were detained after they organized a peaceful campaign to help end sexual harassment and promote equal rights for women.

An August 2015 Human Rights Watch report entitled "Dispatches: Gagging the Critics in China" states that China's human rights activists often face imprisonment, detention, torture, commitment to psychiatric facilities, house arrest, and intimidation. In Hong Kong, it notes the "slow erosion of the rule of law in recent years" and "increasingly strict police control." In Tibet, "arbitrary arrest and imprisonment remain common, and torture and ill-treatment in detention is endemic." In Xinjiang, there is "pervasive ethnic discrimination, severe religious repression, and increasing cultural suppression" of Uyghurs, Han, and other ethnicities. The report aptly observes, "Chinese government is once again demonstrating that under 'rule of law' in China today, the state always prevails."

On the geopolitical front, too, China under Xi ratcheted up the pressure. In December 2012, China's assertiveness in the South China Sea intensified, as China issued a declaration claiming exclusive jurisdiction over disputed islands and establishing new rules to allow for interception of ships passing through the sea's international shipping lanes. Defense analysts saw this as another step in China's bid to solidify its control over crucial navigation lanes over which more than a third of global trade passes, and to shift the balance of power in Southeast Asia even more to its favor. President Obama had sensibly joined other heads of state at the 2012 East Asia Summit in Cambodia in objecting to unilateral Chinese claims over the disputed waters. Interestingly, as China ignored these objections and hardened its position, Chinese state councilor Dai Bingguo defended the move by insisting to Indian security advisor Shiv Shanker Menon that both countries needed "to prevent noise from diverting friendly cooperation and common development."[49]

As the Obama administration continued nevertheless to hold out hope for a cooperative and constructive big-power relationship with China, China continued to pursue expansive strategic goals and to flex its military muscle. In 2013, China unilaterally declared an "air defense identification zone" in the East China Sea, including over islands administered by Japan. It made forceful assertions of claims to South China Sea waters potentially rich in oil and gas, alarming neighboring nations. In July 2014 talks designed to address rising tensions, Kerry made little progress convincing China to change course. Stated he, "I can tell you that we are determined to choose the path of peace and prosperity and cooperation and, yes, competition, but not conflict." In August 2014, an American P-8 Poseidon antisubmarine aircraft on routine patrol in international airspace off the east coast of China was intercepted and combatively harassed by a Chinese J-11 jet fighter. The Chinese government announced that it would raise its military budget by about 10 percent in 2015. In February 2015, the *Wall Street Journal* reported that satellite images showed "a dramatic expansion in China's construction of artificial islands on disputed South China Sea reefs, intensifying concerns about Beijing's territorial ambitions."

In a September 2014, article, Arthur Waldron posed this scenario:

Friendship is on track, with the long chain of incidents doing no more than to "slow" what is described as a "warming trend" in relations. . . . Thus we warmly welcomed her navy to participate in the annual Rim of the Pacific naval exercises this past July—while excluding, for "human rights" reasons, our long-time ally Thailand, which has processed quantities of American diplomatic and military dirty laundry over the decades. Thailand is currently administered by a relatively benign military government, as happens from time to time—but even so remains incomparably freer than China. What is going on? An objective observer might say that no amount of contrary evidence can dissuade Washington from its absolute conviction that, one way or another, China will ultimately emerge as a friend to the United States and her allies—"a responsible stakeholder" in regional security, as then-deputy secretary of state Robert Zoellick so optimistically put it in 2005. Suppose, however, that this belief in eventual friendship, the bedrock assumption of our perennial China policy, turns out to be completely wrong? Suppose China is in fact a "revisionist power" intent on changing the political configuration of Asia by a combination of military and diplomatic means?[50]

What better reminder that cooperation between powers is always for something and about something. In China, as elsewhere, the United States must define and clarify the terms of cooperation rather than seeing cooperation as an end in itself. Without the mitigating factors of American principles and national security strategy, cooperation makes us a paper tiger, all too easily overruled, outwitted, and deceived.

THE ONE-WORLD VISION
FALLS APART

A More Dangerous, More Oppressive World

The founders of the United States believed government "of the people, by the people, and for the people" would unleash human potential and attract others to our way of life. Our forefathers believed in the revolutionary potential of American ideals to improve the human condition. George Washington warned against premature entanglement in the world's problems, but he also saw the early American republic as a powerful example.

One need only look at a geopolitical map of the world today to know that the founders were right. Country after country has looked to the United States as a model, while person after person has come to the United States to find a better life. But the founders could not predict world wars, the rise of fascism and communism, or the power of totalitarian ideology. They could not possibly foresee a century so overwhelmed by policies of mass murder and terror that American responsibilities in the world would themselves become overwhelming. Building upon the founding idea of setting a democratic example, President Harry Truman believed that the fact that Europe and Asia had submitted to the disastrous consequences of *their* ideas (and that we too had paid the price) meant that we had to more actively promote our democratic alternative. Truman viewed the enhancement of defensive American power, the invigoration of American principles, and increased American involvement in the world as the best—and the necessary—responses to modern problems such as Bolshevism, fascism, and "total war."

Truman would be sad to know totalitarianism and twentieth century–style fanaticism still exist. He would be disheartened to know an entire school of American foreign policy now encourages the United States to turn a blind eye. It not only downgrades formidable defensive structures and alliances, and avoids the promotion of democratic ideals; it downplays the idea which has sustained us from the beginning: that individual rights are human rights, that they are particular in that they apply to each one, and at the same time universal in that they apply to everyone. Those rights are inalienable and prior to government. No government can grant them and no government can take them away.

Post–World War II presidents and their secretaries of state realized that, in this highly interconnected world, if we did not take the lead in influencing and helping others, others would take the lead in influencing and harming us. Here again, current policy forgets the postwar lesson. Although global threats, extremism, and atrocities are ever-present, President Obama and his secretaries of state have been reluctant to promote liberal-democratic values or to stand up for the oppressed. With rare exceptions, the administration was as mute as it was inactive in response to the atrocities and bellicosity of the regimes in Syria and North Korea, the aggression and human rights violations of Russia and Iran, and the persecution of Christians, women living under Sharia law, and religious minorities.

As America stays mostly quiet, enemies of freedom use propaganda with a sophistication and skill never seen before. Putin's Russia, Assad's Syria, Kim Jong-un's North Korea, Xi Jinping's China, Ali Khamenei's Iran, and the Islamic State pour resources into controlling information and spreading disinformation. From China's Confucius Institutes, which install teachers and funding in universities and secondary schools around the world, to ISIS's vast social media network, which propagates Islamist ideology and wins recruits, to Iran's Al-Alam News Network and PressTV, which broadcast the Iranian worldview to foreigners in both Arabic and English, these states use multifarious means to control the narrative.

Hostile regimes and transnational terrorist groups such as Islamic State use propaganda not only to spread division and hate, but also to justify their policies. ISIS appeals to devastated Sunnis by positioning itself as the best way to fight the brutal Assad regime. Assad, in turn, positions his regime as the only alternative to Islamist extremism. Iran defends its "right" to "peaceful" nuclear technology and spreads lies about "infidels" Israel and America. Putin appeals to Eastern Europeans with calls for justice for minorities, and with frightening tales about American/Western intentions.

In the time-tested approach of using the concepts of liberal democracies to deceive and disarm liberal democracies, Vladimir Putin told Russian ambassadors in a publicized 2012 speech, "We are seeing attempts by individual players in the international community to keep the influence they are used to by which our partners often use unilateral actions that contradict international law. . . . This can be seen from the so-called humanitarian operations . . . and intervention in internal conflicts. . . . The search for compromises in a peaceful way should become an imperative."[1] Putin knew that describing Russia's approach in internationalist terms would put pressure on the Obama administration to adhere to the internationalist approach *it* had doggedly promoted. He used claims of US unilateralism to obstruct US proposals in the UN and to avoid cooperating on urgent matters such as the Iranian nuclear program. Tellingly, in the same speech, Putin declared the Western world in decline, asserting, "Domestic socioeconomic problems that have become worse in industrialized countries as a result of the [economic] crisis are weakening the dominant role of the so-called historical West."[2]

Many around the world agree with Putin that the "so-called historical West" is debilitated and disrespected. A July 2012 article in the *Sydney Morning Herald* titled "Bald Fact Is US Power Is Waning" argued that "the loss of credibility and prestige, and consequently, the ability to lead and persuade" make American decline undeniable, and pointed to America's waning leverage and influence in various regions. In November 2013, Nikolas Gvosdev observed in *World Politics Review*, "Kerry's attempts to convince skeptical allies that the United States remains committed to their security and well-being, interrupted in part by the secretary's decision to travel to Geneva to attend the second round of talks over Iran's nuclear program, were confronted with concerns that the United States lacks both strategic focus and staying power. . . . In their search for a hedge against perceived American unreliability, U.S. partners have taken the first steps to diversify their relationships—starting with a reassessment of the desirability of expanded ties with Russia."

Indeed, Russia and Iran are moving into the void the United States left behind, while Egypt, Afghanistan, India, Pakistan, and other countries are strengthening strategic and defense ties with Russia and/or Iran. Iraq has joined Russia, Iran, and Syria in a new agreement to strengthen cooperation against Islamic State, further enhancing the Russian and Iranian lead in that battle. Jordan, which for four decades has had one of the most pro-American policies in the region, has quietly pursued ties with Iran. In light of US/Western abandonment of the pro-democracy movement in Lebanon, Saudi Arabia is stepping up involvement, thereby increasing the extent to which conflict in that beleaguered country will be defined in terms of the Sunni/Shiite divide. Four of the biggest and most strategically important democratic or moderate countries in the developing world—Brazil, South Africa, Turkey, and India—are increasingly at odds with American foreign policy. Eastern European allies, which so recently rejoiced at the chance to align with the United States, and looked to the United States Constitution for guidance, now view America with resentment and suspicion. Western European allies aren't cooperating any more than they did during the Bush years. Eastern Europeans, Asians, Middle Easterners, and Africans who are fighting for representative government and economic opportunity are more, not less, disillusioned with the United States.

Instead of increasing America's global stature as promised, President Obama, Secretary Clinton, and Secretary Kerry spurned the very passion for liberty that makes American stature important and gave up the very strategic advantage that undergirds it. The result of de-emphasizing American power and American ideals is a more hostile, more oppressive world. Both domestically in terms of its level of repression, and internationally in terms of its level of activism, China seized the day when America stopped speaking up for freedom, downgraded its alliances, and reduced its global presence. Iranian and North Korean nuclear programs advanced so far that the administration's goals evolved into containing the programs rather than eliminating them. The Israeli-Palestinian "peace process" is in shambles, while the Sinai region of Egypt is, increasingly, a harbor for terrorists. Iraq, Afghanistan, Lebanon, and Yemen are hostage to fanatical groups using them for cynical gain.

Ethnic strife and sectarian violence is rampant. Persecution of Christians by Islamists is on the rise, from Sudan and Nigeria, to Iraq and Iran. Christians are under such siege that a new study by a group called Aid to the Church in Need predicted that Christianity could face a Middle East purge within the decade. Cuban dissidents have been targeted more, not less, since the United States and Cuba formalized relations.

Russian incursions into Ukraine and Syria, the growing specter of hostile states with nuclear weapons, and Syria's, Iran's, and Russia's indifference to our globalist gestures must give us pause. So too must the way these countries have strengthened ties with each other, and exploited America's continual refusal to provide significant aid to moderate Syrian rebels. Iranian and Russian coordination and consultation on Syria have reached new heights. US complacency and acquiescence to Russian plans for Syria, and to Iranian leadership in the battle against ISIS in Syria and Iraq, have made the United States increasingly beholden to the two countries. China has expressed support for Russian actions in Ukraine, while Russia and China both declined signing the 2014 Nuclear Security Summit agreement. Since the Iran nuclear deal, Iranian hardliners have only pressured moderates in Iranian government and society more, and have pursued aggressive policies at home and abroad.

In short, what we have is the opposite of the peaceful one-world order that Obama's engagement and outreach policies promised. As we have pared down our military and toned down our democratic principles, aggressive anti-democratic powers have seen this as an opportunity. Policies designed to create peace, stability and unity end up having the opposite effect. Adversaries are less cooperative with us, and more aligned with each other. The world is more divided and more violent. Rather than a world free of nuclear weapons, there is proliferation of weapons of mass destruction on an alarming scale. Rather than benefiting from Obama's conciliatory gestures to the Muslim Brotherhood and the "Muslim world," the Middle East faces a stateless mass of terrorism spreading across and beyond Syria and Iraq.

The explosive Syrian War and refugee crisis threaten to bring suffering and bloodshed to an entire region. Human rights violations in Syria and North Korea are catastrophic. Areas controlled by Islamic State succumb to conditions of utter barbarism and terror. Atrocities in these dark places—which are so horrible it is difficult to comprehend that they are real—hurt our American conscience, whether we allow our feelings to the surface or not.

Crimes against humanity of the twentieth century now meet their match in the twenty-first century. In a nihilistic world, no one is off limits. Children in Syria are abducted and tortured. Children in North Korea are left to fend for themselves after their parents are taken away. If they, too, are taken to the gulags, they are subjected to the same forced labor, starvation diet, beatings, and abuse as the adults. Throngs of starving children in both countries have lost both their families and their homes due to state action and state violence. Non-Islamic women are captured and used as sex slaves by Islamic State. Women and teenagers in Iran languish in prisons from hell. Women and children in volatile parts of the world are at high risk for abuse and trafficking. Adopting a policy that consciously downplays their plight by focusing on good relations with the very regimes that allow such conditions is unconscionable.

We can re-strengthen our alliances with democracies young and old, and we can recapture our democratic influence, but we had better do so quickly because the strategic and ideological fault lines are increasingly lined up against us. We still have enough leverage to improve our standing in the world, and our stance toward the world. If we don't, we will not only have sold others short; we will have sold ourselves short as well. We can do better. We usually do. We can re-embrace the best of our traditions without leaving realism or the desire for global harmony and peace behind. It turns out that "smart" foreign policy is also strategically and morally strong policy.

Just look at all the twentieth century periods of mayhem and destruction and at their causes, and you will see that this is the case. Neither Europe's balance of power approach nor its negotiations with and concessions to extremist regimes prevented European wars. The devastating rise of fascism and communism in Europe and Asia was enabled by philosophies that dehumanize and stigmatize groups and classes of people—and by the initial indifference of the rest of the world to the horrible human implications of those philosophies. We should rethink our decision to make our foreign policy more like Europe's— for ethical reasons and because our "new" foreign policy, which in some ways resembles Europe's of old, is not working.

As the one world vision of President Obama and Secretary Clinton unravels, we should consider reconstructing our national security strategy and reasserting our principles. The world today is both crueler and more dangerous than when they took office. People suffering in the world's worst regimes still need America's voice. Struggling democracies still need our support. Totalitarian and extremist powers are still unwilling to respond in kind to our outreach. America at its best asserts moral authority. America has no choice but to maintain the geopolitical upper hand. Many would like to see us devolve into a wounded and demoralized Leviathan. Let's not show them the way.

ABOUT THE AUTHOR

Anne R. Pierce is an author, commentator, and scholar in the areas of American presidents, American foreign policy, and American society. With a Ph.D. from the University of Chicago, she is an appointed member of Princeton University's James Madison Society and a political science field editor for Transaction Publishers. Pierce has written three books and contributed to three others. Her articles have been published in *USA Today, Washington Times, Society, Washington Examiner*, USEmbassy.gov, Ricochet.com, *World and I,* and elsewhere.

BIBLIOGRAPHY

Aggarwal, Vinod K. and Kristi Govella, eds. *Responding to a Resurgent Russia: Russian Policy and Responses from the European Union and the United States*. New York: Springer, 2014.

Aswany, Alaa al. *On the State of Egypt: What Made the Revolution Inevitable*, trans. Jonathan Wright. New York: Vintage Books, 2011.

Bloom, Allan. *The Closing of the American Mind*. New York: Simon & Schuster, 2012.

Bracher, Karl Dietrich. *The German Dictatorship*. New York: Praeger Publishers, 1970.

Bush, George. *All the Best, George Bush: My Life in Letters and Other Writings*. New York: Scribner, 1999.

Bush, George and Brent Scowcroft. *A World Transformed*. New York: Vintage Books, 1999.

Chang, Jung. *Wild Swans: Three Daughters of China*. New York: Anchor Books, 1992.

Chol-hwan, Kang and Pierre Rigoulot. *The Aquariums of Pyongyang: Ten Years in the North Korean Gulag*. New York: Basic Books, 2002.

Cleveland, William L. and Martin Bunton. *A History of the Modern Middle East*. Boulder, CO: Westview Press, 2009.

Clinton, Bill. *My Life: The Presidential Years*. New York: Vintage, 2005.

Danford, John W. *Roots of Freedom: A Primer on Modern Liberty*. Wilmington, DE: ISI Books, 2000.

David-Fox, Michael, Peter Holquist, and Alexander M. Martin, eds. *The Holocaust in the East: Local Perpetrators and Soviet Responses*. Pittsburgh, PA: University of Pittsburgh Press, 2014.

Demick, Barbara. *Nothing to Envy: Ordinary Lives in North Korea*. New York: Spiegel & Grau, 2009.

Forest, James J. F. *Essentials of Counterterrorism*. Santa Barbara, CA: ABC-CLIO, 2015.

Freidman, George. *America's Secret War: Inside the Hidden Worldwide Struggle Between America and Its Enemies*. New York: Doubleday, 2004.

Fu, Bob and Nancy French. *God's Double Agent: The True Story of a Chinese Christian's Fight for Freedom*. Grand Rapids, MI: Baker Books, 2014.

Gaddis, John Lewis. *We Now Know: Rethinking Cold War History*. New York: Oxford University Press, 1997.

Gelvin, James L. *The Arab Uprisings: What Everyone Needs to Know*. New York: Oxford University Press, 2012.

Hamza, Khidir and Jeff Stein. *Saddam's Bombmaker: The Terrifying Inside Story of the Iraqi Nuclear and Biological Weapons Agenda*. New York: Simon & Schuster, 2001.

Harden, Blaine. *Escape from Camp 14: One Man's Remarkable Odyssey from North Korea to Freedom in the West*. New York: Viking/Penguin Group, 2012.

Holmes, Kim R. *Rebound: Getting America Back to Great*. Lanham, MD: Rowan & Littlefield, 2013.

Hook, Stephen W. and John Spanier. *American Foreign Policy Since World War II*. Washington, DC: CQ Press, 2007.

Iriye, Akira. *The Cambridge History of American Foreign Relations: Volume 3, The Globalizing of America, 1913–1945*. Cambridge: Cambridge University Press, 1995.

Jackson, Robert. *Classical and Modern Thought on International Relations*. New York: Palgrave Macmillan, 2005.

Johnson, Paul. *A History of the American People*. New York: Harper Perennial, 1999.

Johnson, Robert David, ed. *Asia Pacific in the Age of Globalization*. New York: Palgrave Macmillan, 2014.

Kagan, Robert. *The World America Made*. New York: Vintage Books, 2013.

Kahlili, Reza. *A Time To Betray: The Astonishing Double Life of a CIA Agent Inside the Revolutionary Guards of Iran*. New York: Threshold Editions, 2010.

Kane, John. *Between Virtue and Power: The Persistent Moral Dilemma of US Foreign Policy*. New Haven, CT: Yale University Press, 2008.

Kasparov, Garry. *Winter Is Coming: Why Vladimir Putin and the Enemies of the Free World Must Be Stopped*. New York: Public Affairs, 2015.

Keddie, Nikki R. *Modern Iran: Roots and Results of Revolution*. New Haven, CT: Yale University Press, 2003.

Kershaw, Ian. *Hitler: A Biography*. New York: W. W. Norton & Co., 1998.

Kirkpatrick, Melanie. *Escape from North Korea: The Untold Story of the Underground Railroad*. New York: Encounter Books, 2014.

Ledeen, Michael A. *Accomplice to Evil: Iran and the War Against the West*. New York: St. Martin's Press, 2009.

Lewis, Bernard. *The Crisis of Islam: Holy War and Unholy Terror*. New York: Random House, 2003.

Lieber, Robert J. *The American Era: Power and Strategy for the 21st Century*. New York: Cambridge University Press, 2005.

Lipson, Charles. *Reliable Partners: How Democracies Have Made a Separate Peace*. Princeton: Princeton University Press, 2005.

Mann, James. *The China Fantasy: How Our Leaders Explain Away Chinese Repression*. New York: Viking Penguin, 2007.

Marshall, Paul, Lela Gilbert, and Nina Shea. *Persecuted: The Global Assault on Christians*. Nashville, TN: Thomas Nelson, 2013.

Miller, Merle. *Plain Speaking: An Oral Biography of Harry S. Truman*. New York: Berkeley Books, 1974.

Mitchell, Lincoln A. *Uncertain Democracy: U.S. Foreign Policy and Georgia's Rose Revolution*. Philadelphia: University of Pennsylvania Press, 2009.

Nasr, Vali. *The Dispensable Nation: American Foreign Policy in Retreat*. New York: Anchor, 2014.

Oren, Michael B. *Power, Faith, and Fantasy: America in the Middle East—1776 to the Present*. New York: W. W. Norton & Co., 2007.

Pan, Philip. *Out of Mao's Shadow: The Struggle for the Soul of a New China*. New York: Simon & Schuster, 2009.

Pierce, Anne R. *Woodrow Wilson & Harry Truman: Mission and Power in American Foreign Policy*. New Brunswick: Transaction Publishers, 2007.

Pollack, Kenneth M. *The Threatening Storm: The Case for Invading Iraq*. New York: Random House, 2002.

Power, Samantha. *A Problem from Hell: American and the Age of Genocide*: New York: Basic Books reprint edition, 2013.

Ratnesar, Romesh. *Tear Down This Wall: A City, A President, and the Speech That Ended the Cold War*. New York: Simon & Schuster, 2009.

Redner, Harry. *Totalitarianism, Globalization, Colonialism: The Destruction of Civilization since 1914*. New Brunswick, NJ: Transaction Publishers, 2014.

Reid, Anna. *Borderland: A Journey through the History of Ukraine*. New York: Basic Books, 2015.

Remnick, David. *The Bridge: The Life and Rise of Barack Obama*. New York: Vintage Books, 2011.

Revel, Jean-François. *The Totalitarian Temptation*. New York: Penguin Books, 1978.

Rice, Condeleezza. *No Higher Honor: A Memoir of My Years in Washington*. New York: Crown Publishing Group, 2001.

Shambaugh, David, ed. *Tangled Titans: The United States and China*. New York: Rowman & Littlefield, 2012.

Shirer, William L. *Berlin Diary: The Journal of a Foreign Correspondent, 1934–1941*. New York: RosettaBooks, Kindle Edition, 2011.

Strauss, Leo. *Natural Right and History*. Chicago: University of Chicago Press, 1950.

Sussex, Matthew, ed. *Conflict in the Former USSR*. New York: Cambridge University Press, 2012.

Tabler, Andrew. *In the Lion's Den: An Eyewitness Account of Washington's Battle with Syria*. Chicago: Lawrence Hill Books, 2011.

Telhami, Shibley, Kenneth M. Pollack, Daniel L. Byman, Akram Al-Turk, Pavel K. Baev, Michael S. Doran, Khaled Elgindy, Stephen R. Grand, Shadi Hamid,

Bruce Jones, Suzanne Maloney, Jonathan D. Pollack, Bruce O. Riedel, Ruth Hanau Santini, Salman Shaikh, Ibrahim Sharqieh, Omer Taspinar, and Sarah E. Yerkes. *The Arab Awakening: America and the Transformation of the Middle East.* Washington, DC: Brookings Institution Press, 2011.

Tismăneanu, Vladimir, *The Devil in History: Communism, Fascism, and Some Lessons of the Twentieth Century.* Berkeley and Los Angeles: University of California Press, 2012.

Truman, Harry S. *Memoirs: Years of Trial and Hope.* Garden City: Doubleday & Co., 1956.

Truman, Harry S. "Speeches and Writings," *Public Papers of the President, 1946–1953.* Washington, DC: US Government Printing Office, 1966.

Ung, Loung. *First They Killed My Father: A Daughter of Cambodia Remembers.* New York: Harper Perennial, 2000.

Viereck, Peter. *Unadjusted Man in the Age of Overadjustment: Where History and Literature Intersect.* Piscataway, NJ: Transaction Publishers, 2004.

Wakin, Edward. *A Lonely Minority: The Story of Egypt's Copts.* New York: W. Morrow & Co., 1963.

Youssef, Michael, PhD. *Blindsided: The Radical Islamic Conquest.* United States: Kobri, 2012.

Zakaria, Fareed. *The Post-American World.* New York: W. W. Norton & Co., 2012.

Zimmerman, Katherine. *A New Model for Defeating al Qaeda in Yemen.* Washington D.C.: American Enterprise Institute: 2015.

ENDNOTES

CHAPTER 1

1 The most notable being Bill Clinton's successful 1992 campaign, which focused on James Carville's theme: "(It's) the economy stupid."

2 Ian Kershaw, *Hitler: A Biography* (New York: W.W. Norton & Company, 1998), 424.

3 Ibid., 480.

4 William L. Shirer, *Berlin Diary: The Journal of a Foreign Correspondent* (New York: RosettaBooks LLC, 2011), Kindle Edition, Loc. 2212.

5 Norrin M. Ripsman and Jack S. Levy, "The British Response to Rising Germany, 1933–1936," Social Science Research Network, APSA 2009 Annual Meeting Paper, 5.

6 Ibid.

7 Stacie E. Goddard, "Legitimacy in the Balance: Hitler's Rhetoric & British Foreign Policy, 1933-1938," Social Science Research Network, APSA 2010 Annual Meeting Paper.

8 Shirer, Loc. 457–458

9 Kershaw, *Hitler*, 431.

10 Karl Dietrich Bracher, *The German Dictatorship* (New York: Praeger Publishers, 1970).

11 Michael A. Ledeen, *Accomplice to Evil: Iran and The War against The West* (New York: St. Martin Press, 2009), 22–23.

12 Peter Viereck, *Unadjusted Man in the Age of Overadjustment: Where History and Literature Intersect* (New Jersey: Transaction Publishers, 2004), 275.

13 George Anastaplo, "Simply Unbelievable: Conversations with a Holocaust Survivor," (recorded conversations with Simcha Brudno, 2000-2001).

14 Ibid.

15 Ibid.

16 Harry S. Truman, *Memoirs: Years of Trial and Hope* (Garden City: Doubleday & Co., 1956), 111.

17 Anne R. Pierce, *Woodrow Wilson & Harry Truman: Mission and Power in American Foreign Policy* (New Brunswick: Transaction Publishers, 2003), chapters 6 & 7.

18 Harry S. Truman, "Speeches and Writings," in *Public Papers of the President 1946–1953,* hereinafter cited by specific year (Washington, DC: U.S. Government Printing Office, 1966), 1947: 174-175.

19 Pierce, *Woodrow Wilson & Harry Truman*, 171.

20 Truman, *Public Papers of the President—1953*, 1128.

21 Paul Johnson, *A History of the American People* (New York: Harper Perennial, 1999), 882.

22 Such a dynamic is discussed in Allan Bloom's *The Closing of the American Mind* and numerous other works.

23 James Mann, *The China Fantasy: How Our Leaders Explain Away Chinese Repression* (New York: Viking Penguin, 2007), 44.

24 Philip Pan, *Out of Mao's Shadow: The Struggle for the Soul of a New China* (New York: Simon & Schuster, 2009).

25 Jimmy Carter, "A Foreign Policy Based on America's Essential Character," Commencement Speech, University of Notre Dame, May 22, 1977.

26 Brett Stephens, "The Carter Ricochet Effect," *Wall Street Journal*, November 23, 2009.

27 Ibid.

28 Romesh Ratnesar, *Tear Down This Wall: A City, a President and the Speech that Ended the Cold War* (New York: Simon & Schuster, 2009), 188.

29 George H. W. Bush, "Address before the 45th Session of the United Nations General Assembly in New York, New York," October 1, 1990, http://www.presidency.ucsb .edu/.

30 George Bush and Brent Scowcroft, *A World Transformed* (New York: Vintage Books, 1999), xiii.

31 George Bush, *All The Best, George Bush: My Life in Letters and Other Writings* (New York: A Lisa Drew Book/Scribner, 1999), 233.

32 Charles Krauthammer, "Capitulation in Korea: Clinton's cave-in makes a joke of the NPT," *Washington Post*, January 7, 1994.

33 US State Department Office of International Information Programs, *The China Nonproliferation Act* by Fred Thompson (R-TN). Introduction at press conference, Washington, DC, May 25, 2000.

34 Mann, *The China Fantasy*, 6.

35 Donna Abu-Nasr, "Clinton Trip Disappoints Dissidents," Associated Press, July 3, 1998, http://apnewsarchive.com/.

36 Samantha Power, "Bystanders to Genocide," *Atlantic*, September 2001.

37 Leffler, Melvyn P., "The Foreign Policies of the George W. Bush Administration: Memoirs, History, Legacy," *Diplomatic History*, February 23, 2013.

38 Robert J. Lieber, *The American Era: Power and Strategy for the 21st Century* (Cambridge: New York: Cambridge University Press, 2005), 26.

39 Condeleezza Rice, *No Higher Honor: A Memoir of My Years in Washington* (New York: Crown Publishing Group, 2001), 169.

40 Ibid., 170.

41 Khidir Hamza and Jeff Stein, *Saddam's Bombmaker: The Terrifying Inside Story of the Iraqi Nuclear and Biological Weapons Agenda* (New York: Simon & Schuster, 2001).

42 Frank P. Harvey, *Explaining the Iraq War: Counterfactual Theory, Logic and Evidence* (Cambridge: Cambridge University Press, 2011).

43 George Friedman, *America's Secret War: Inside the Hidden Worldwide Struggle Between America and Its Enemies* (USA: Doubleday, 2004), 302.

44 Ibid., 175.

45 Andrew Tabler, *In The Lion's Den: An Eyewitness Account of Washington's Battle with Syria* (Chicago: Lawrence Hill Books, 2011), 174.

46 "Pratfall in Damascus," *Washington Post*, April 5, 2007.

47 Kenneth M. Pollack, *The Threatening Storm: The Case for Invading Iraq* (New York: Random House, 2002), book jacket.

48 See, for example, Jack Kelley, "Iraqis Pour Out Tales of Torture Chambers," *USA Today*, April 13, 2003.

49 Operation: Iraqi Freedom, "Depths of Saddam's Evil Plumbed," World Net Daily, April 14, 2003.

50 The National Security Strategy of the United States of America (2002), http://www .state.gov/documents/organization/63562.pdf.

51 Vladimir Tismăneanu, *The Devil in History: Communism, Fascism, and Some Lessons of the Twentieth Century* (Berkeley and Los Angeles: University of California Press, 2012), 1.

CHAPTER 2

 1 Barack H. Obama, "Final Primary Night: Nomination Speech," St. Paul, Minnesota, June 3, 2008.

 2 Barack H. Obama, "The American Promise," Democratic Convention Acceptance Speech, Denver, Colorado, August 28, 2008.

 3 Spencer Ackerman, "The Obama Doctrine," *American Prospect*, March 19, 2008.

 4 "Obama's Metapolitics," Daily Kos, February 5, 2008.

 5 Samantha Power, "Full Force," *New Republic*, March 3, 2003.

 6 Jeffrey Goldberg, "Did Samantha Power Just Rebuke Obama on Syria?," *Bloomberg View*, May 6, 2014.

 7 Samantha Power, "Rethinking Iran," *Time*, January 17, 2008.

 8 Sam Stein, "Samantha Power Unapologetic About Iraq Remarks, Hints at Return," *Huffington Post*, April 3, 2008.

 9 Molly Lanzarotta, "Samantha Power on U.S. Foreign Policy," Harvard Kennedy School, March 14, 2007.

10 David Remnick, *The Bridge: The Life and Rise of Barack Obama* (New York: Vintage Books, 2011), 273.

11 Ibid.

12 Valerie Jarrett comments at Netroots Nation Convention, August 12, 2009, https:// www.youtube.com/watch?v=Ud_yNFnfrSI.

13 Ryan Mauro, "Disturbing Facts About a Senior Homeland Security Adviser," *ClarionProject.org*, October 8, 2013. "Unreliable Advice from This Muslim Group," *Dallas Morning News*, November 11, 2009. See also: 9/11 Commission's findings on Qutb.

14 Ibid.

15 Frank Gaffney, "Charles Freeman Unfit, Beyond the Pale," *Newsmax*, March 10, 2009.

16 Bret Stephens, "Obama's National Intelligence Crackpot," *WSJ*, March 10, 2009.

17 Alan Dershowitz, "Defeating Freeman: A Patriotic Duty," *Huffington Post*, March 13, 2009.

18 David Rothkopf, "Hillary Clinton Redefining State Department and Her Own Role," *Washington Post*, August 23, 2009.

19 Pamela Meister, "A is for Arrogance, B is for Baloney," *American Thinker*, February 24, 2007.

20 Hillary Rodham Clinton, "Statement before the Senate Foreign Relations Committee," Washington, DC, January 13, 2009.

21 Daniel Halper, "Hillary: We Must Empathize with America's Enemies," *Weekly Standard*, December 4, 2014.

22 Barack H. Obama, "Barack Obama's Foreign Policy Speech," Council on Foreign Relations, DePaul University, Chicago, Illinois, October 2, 2007.

23 National Security Strategy of the United States of America (2002), http://www.state.gov /documents/organization/63562.pdf.
24 "Obama tells Al Arabiya peace talks should resume," *Al Arabiya*, January 27, 2009.
25 Barack H. Obama, "Remarks by President Obama at Strasbourg Town Hall," Strasbourg, France, (The White House: Office of the Press Secretary, April 3, 2009).
26 Barack H. Obama, "Remarks by President Obama to the Turkish Parliament," Ankara, Turkey (The White House: Office of the Press Secretary, April 6, 2009).
27 Barack H. Obama, "Remarks by the President at the Summit of the Americas Opening Ceremony," Port of Spain, Trinidad and Tobago (The White House: Office of the Press Secretary, April 17, 2009).
28 Ibid.
29 Barack H. Obama, "Remarks by the President on a New Beginning," Cairo, Egypt (The White House: Office of the Press Secretary, June 6, 2009).
30 Robert J. Lieber, "Obama's Can't-Do Style," *Los Angeles Times*, January 1, 2010.
31 Obama, "Remarks by the President on a New Beginning," Cairo, Egypt.
32 Ibid.
33 Barack H. Obama, "Remarks by President Obama," Prague, Czech Republic (The White House: Office of the Press Secretary, April 5, 2009).
34 Obama, "Remarks by the President on a New Beginning," Cairo, Egypt.
35 Ibid.
36 Jonah Goldberg, "Realism minus Reality, Idealism minus Ideals," *National Review*, November 2, 2009.
37 Doug Hagmann, "Obama Administration reports to the UN on human rights issues in US," Canada Free Press, August 25, 2012.
38 Barack H. Obama, "News Conference by President Obama," Strasbourg, France (The White House: Office of the Press Secretary, April 4, 2009).
39 Jonah Goldberg, "Realism minus Reality, Idealism minus Ideals," *National Review*, November 2, 2009.
40 Barack H. Obama, "News Conference by President Obama," Strasbourg, France (The White House: Office of the Press Secretary, April 4, 2009).
41 Ibid.
42 Ibid.
43 Barack H. Obama, "Remarks by the President to the United Nation Assembly," United Nation Headquarters: New York (The White House: Office of the Press Secretary, September 23, 2009).
44 Whittle Johnston, "Radical Revisionism and the Disintegration of the American Foreign Policy Consensus," *Orbis*, Spring 1976, 185.
45 Ibid., 199.
46 Nancy Spiller, "That Jammed VOA," *Chicago Tribune*, May 28, 1990.
47 John Noonan, "Lech Walesa Slams Obama's Foreign Policy," *Weekly Standard*, February 5, 2010.
48 *"Ich bin ein Berliner* Speech," Miller Center, University of Virginia, http://millercenter .org/president/speeches/speech-3376.
49 Barack H. Obama, speech at the Brandenburg Gate, June 19, 2013, http://blogs.wsj .com/washwire/2013/06/19/transcript-of-obamas-speech-in-berlin/.
50 Jennifer Rubin, "Havel Unplugged," *Commentary*, December 10, 2009.
51 "Obama's Defense Drawdown," *Wall Street Journal/Review & Outlook*, January 9, 2012.

52 Ibid.

53 Nile Gardiner, "Biden's Munich Speech: Obama Administration Foreign Policy Projects Weakness and Confusion," Heritage Foundation, February 9, 2009.

54 Ibid.

55 Robert J. Lieber, "A Contested Analysis of American Standing Abroad," *Chronicle Review*, October 1, 2009.

56 Daniel J. Goldhagen, "Ending Our Age of Suffering," *New Republic*, October 10. 2009.

57 Caroline Glick, "Column One: Obama's War on Israel," *Jerusalem Post* March 19, 2010.

58 Ambassador Howard Gutman/Speech, "Thinking about Anti-Semitism in Europe 'Conference on Fighting Anti-Semitism in Europe: What's Next?'" Brussels, Belgium, November 30, 2011.

59 Timothy J. Alberta, "Clinton Says Iran Process on 'Dual Tracks,'" *Wall Street Journal*, April 22, 2009.

60 Philip Sherwell, "Barak Obama and Hugo Chavez Shake Hands," *Telegraph*, April 18, 2009.

61 Shmuley Boteach, "Why Does Obama Smile at Dictators?" *Jerusalem Post*, April 20, 2009.

62 Aleks Tapinish, "Ahmadinejad joins China, Russia leaders at summit," Agence France-Presse, June 15, 2011.

CHAPTER 3

1 Garry Kasparov, *Winter Is Coming: Why Vladimir Putin and the Enemies of the Free World Must Be Stopped* (New York: Public Affairs, 2015), 5.

2 Vinod K. Aggarwal and Kristi Govella, eds., *Responding to a Resurgent Russia: Russian Policy and Responses from the European Union and the United States* (New York: Springer, 2014).

3 Matthew Sussex, editor, *Conflict in the Former USSR* (Cambridge: Cambridge University Press, 2012), 28.

4 Lincoln A. Mitchell, *Uncertain Democracy: U.S. Foreign Policy and Georgia's Rose Revolution* (Philadelphia: University of Pennsylvania Press, 2009), chapter 6.

5 "Georgia 'Overrun' by Russian Troops as Full-Scale Ground Invasion Begins," *Daily Mail*, http://www.dailymail.co.uk/news/article-1043236/Georgia-overrun-Russian-troops-scale-ground-invasion-begins.html#ixzz3qG9Xr9WY

6 Vinod K. Aggarwal and Kristi Govella, eds., *Responding to a Resurgent Russia: Russian Policy and Responses from the European Union and the United States* (New York: Springer, 2014), 97.

7 Robert Kagan, "Power Play," *Wall Street Journal*, August 30, 2008.

8 Ibid.

9 Robert Kagan, "Toward a Neo-Reaganite Foreign Policy," *Carnegie Endowment for International Peace*, July/August 1996.

10 Michele Kelemen, "Clinton Says She'll Hit 'Reset Button' with Russia," NPR, March 6, 2009.

11 Obama, "Remarks by President Obama," Prague, Czech Republic.

12 Theodore Kalionzes and Kaegan McGrath, "Obama's Nuclear Nonproliferation and Disarmament Agenda: Building Steam or Losing Traction?" Nuclear Threat Initiative, January 15, 2010.

13 Ibid.

14 Barack H. Obama, "Message from Obama on Peaceful Nuclear Agreement with Russia," Washington DC (The White House: Office of the Press Secretary, May 10, 2010).

15 Kim R. Holmes, "Crashing Obamas Nuclear Wedding," Heritage Foundation, April 1, 2010.

16 Editorial, "Apologies not accepted," *Investor's Business Daily*, October 11, 2011.

17 US Department of State, "Interview with Bob Schieffer of CBS's *Face the Nation*," (Washington DC: PRN, 2010), 422.

18 Charles Krauthammer, "Obama lowers the nuclear umbrella," *Washington Post*, April 8, 2010.

19 David E. Sanger and Peter Baker, "Obama Limits When U.S. Would Use Nuclear Arms," *New York Times*, April 5, 2010.

20 Frank Gaffney, "Obama's Missile Defense Capitulation Blow to Security," *Newsmax* September 17, 2009.

21 William J. Kole, "Eastern Europe Not Feeling the Love for Obama," Associated Press, September 14, 2009.

22 Marek Madej, "Obama's missile defense rethink: The Polish reaction," *Bulletin of the Atomic Scientists,* September 30, 2009.

23 Ibid.

24 Ariel Cohen, "Obama's Rookie Blunder on Missile Defense Concessions," *Foundry*, September 18, 2009.

25 Kole, "Eastern Europe Not Feeling the Love for Obama," Associated Press.

26 "Geopolitical Diary: Change in U.S. Foreign Policy," Stratfor Global Intelligence March 6, 2009.

27 Ibid.

28 Kole, "Eastern Europe Not Feeling the Love for Obama," Associated Press.

29 Alan Cullison, "Putin Reappoints Old Names as Kremlin Ally Starts Party," *Wall Street Journal/Europe*, May 21, 2012.

30 US Department of State press release, March 1, 2014, http://www.state.gov/secretary /remarks/2014/03/222720.htm.

31 John Kerry, remarks at US Embassy in Kyiv, Ukraine, March 4, 2014, http://www.state .gov/secretary/remarks/2014/03/222882.htm.

32 Niles Gardiner, "President Obama Goes AWOL on the Ukraine Front," *Daily Signal*, April 29, 2014.

33 Ellen Bork, et al, "Open Letter to President Obama: Secure Ukraine, Isolate Russia, and Strengthen NATO," Foreign Policy Initiative, March 21, 2014.

34 Gabriela Baczynska and Aleksandar Vasovic, "Pushing Locals Aside, Russians Take Top Rebel Posts in East Ukraine," Reuters, July 27, 2014.

35 Sabrina Tavernise, "Whisked Away for Tea with a Rebel in Ukraine," *New York Times*, July 15, 2014.

36 Steven Pifer, "Ukraine, Russia, and the U.S. Policy Response," Brookings, June 5, 2014.

37 "Obama Blames Russia for Violence in Ukraine; Calls Move 'Incursion,'" NPR, August 29, 2014.

38 Robert Kaplan, "The Long Game in Eastern Europe," Stratfor Global Intelligence, September 17, 2014.

39 "The West Can't Afford to Make Empty Threats on Russian Sanctions," *Washington Post*, July 1, 2014.

40 Peggy Noonan, "Warnings from the Ukraine," *Wall Street Journal*, March 14, 2014.

41 Keith Johnson, "New Russian Sanctions from Departing Congress," Foreign Policy, December 12, 2014.
42 Barack H. Obama, "Statement by the President on the Ukraine Freedom Support Act," (The White House: Office of the Press Secretary, December 18, 2014).
43 Michaela Dodge and David Poortinga, "Russia Broke the INF Treaty (Again). What the US Should Do," *Daily Signal*, October 1, 2015.
44 Michael Doran, "Ukraine Reveals to Us How Vladimir Putin Sees the Middle East," Brookings Institute, April 4, 2014.
45 Ibid.
46 Peter Pomerantsev, "Russia and the Menace of Unreality," *Atlantic*, September 9, 2014.
47 Ed Royce, "Countering Putin's Information Weapons of War," *Wall Street Journal*, April 14, 2015.
48 Anne R. Pierce, "Rediscovering America's Voice," *Washington Times*, May 17, 2015.
49 "US to Give Weapons and Troops to NATO Force Battling Europe's Security Threats," *Guardian*, June 22, 2015.
50 Matthew Lee and Bradley Klapper, "No Breakthrough as Kerry Meets Russia's Putin," Yahoo News, May 12, 2015.
51 Ibid.
52 Anne R. Pierce, "Beware ISIS Strategy that Fortifies Russia, Iran, and Syria," *Washington Times*, March 2, 2015.

CHAPTER 4
1 Thomas M. Franck, "Are Human Rights Universal," *Foreign Affairs*, vol. 80, no. 1 (January/February 2001), 195.
2 Tony Blair, "Tony Blair Speech to Chicago Council on Global Affairs," Office of Tony Blair, April 23, 2009.
3 Samuel R. Berger, "International Affairs and Obama's First 100 Days: Policies, Priorities and Politics," Council on Foreign Relations, May 7, 2009.
4 United Nations Development Fund for Economic and Social Development, "Arab Human Development Report 2002: Creating Opportunities for Future Generations," *United Nations Publication 2002*, Overview, 2.
5 Shibley Telhami et al., *The Arab Awakening: America and the Transformation of the Middle East* (Washington DC: Brookings Institution Press, 2011), 13.
6 Barack H. Obama, "Remarks by the President to the Turkish Parliament," Ankara, Turkey, February 2009.
7 Barack H. Obama, "Remarks of President Barack Obama—As Prepared for Delivery—A Moment of Opportunity," US Department of State, Washington, DC, (The White House: Office of the Press Secretary, May 19, 2011).
8 Secretary of State Hillary R. Clinton, "Remarks on the Human Rights Agenda for the 21st Century," Washington, DC, December 14, 2009.
9 Michael B. Oren, *Power, Faith, and Fantasy: America in the Middle East—1776 to the Present* (New York: W. W. Norton & Company, 2007), 285.
10 Ibid., 379.
11 Ibid., 346.
12 Ibid., 335.
13 Lieber, *The American Era*, 181.
14 Leeden, *Accomplice to Evil*, 118.

15 Human Rights Documentation Center, "Rights Disregarded: Prisons in the Islamic Republic of Iran," March 18, 2015.

16 Reza Kahlili, *A Time To Betray: The Astonishing Double Life of a CIA Agent inside the Revolutionary Guards of Iran* (New York: Threshold Editions, 2010), 93.

17 Ibid., 321.

18 William L. Cleveland and Martin Bunton, *A History of the Modern Middle East* (Boulder, CO: Westview Press, 2009), 538.

19 Ibid.

20 Barack H. Obama, "Videotaped Remarks by the President in Celebration of Norwuz," (The White House: Office of the Press Secretary, March 20, 2009).

21 Charles Krauthammer, "Obama Misses the Point with Iran Response," *Washington Post*, June 19, 2009.

22 Ken Timmerman, "Key Iranian Dissident Riled at Obama's Approach," Newsmax, June 23, 2009.

23 Christopher Layne, *American Empire: A Debate* (New York: Routledge, 2007), 83.

24 Amir Taheri, "A Student Rebellion," *New York Post*, December 10, 2008.

25 Doyle McManus, "Obama Doctrine Emerges in Oslo Speech," *Los Angeles Times*, December 13, 2009.

26 Michael Ledeen, "Accomplice to Evil," *National Review Online*, October 5, 2009.

27 Middle East Policy Council Journal, vol. xvi, number 2, Summer 2009.

28 Secretary Robert Gates, "Question and Answer Session with Secretary Gates following remarks at National Defense University's Distinguished Lecture Program at Ft. Leslie J. McNair," US Department of Defense News Transcript, Washington, DC, September 29, 2009.

29 Jay Solomon, "U.S. Allies Set October Target for Iran Progress," *Wall Street Journal*, May 15, 2009.

30 Blake Hounshell, "Obama's Iran Trap," *Foreign Policy*, September 28, 2009.

31 "Iranian Leader: Iran must stand firm against Western 'bullying' on nuclear program," Associated Press, March 7, 2012.

32 John Limbert, "Iran Primer: The Obama Administration," Tehran Bureau, November 3, 2010.

33 Josh Rogin, "Menendez livid at Obama team's push to shelve Iran sanctions amendment," *Foreign Policy*, December 1, 2011.

34 Mark Dubowitz and Toby Dershowitz, "Tearing Down Iran's Electronic Curtain," *Wall Street Journal*, April 13, 2012.

35 Alana Goodman, "Obama snubs Mark Kirk at AIPAC," *Commentary*, March 6, 2012.

36 Josh Rogin, "Hillary Clinton Celebrates the Iran Sanctions her State Department Tried to Stop," *Daily Beast*, May 15, 2015.

37 Tabassum Zakaria and Caren Bohan, "Obama's olive branch to Iran turned into sanctions hammer," Reuters, January 14, 2012.

38 Jay Solomon, "Iran Nuclear Fuel Hits Higher Grade, U.N. Says," *Wall Street Journal*, May 27, 2012.

39 Jay Carney, "Press Briefing by Press Secretary Jay Carney, 2/29/2012," (The White House: Office of the Press Secretary, Washington, DC, February 29, 2012).

40 Jay Solomon and Farnaz Fassihi, "Iran Balks at Nuclear Offer, Calls for End to Sanctions," *Wall Street Journal*, May 23, 2012.

41 "World Briefs: Nuclear Chief Rejects Limits on Enrichment," *Washington Times*, May 27, 2012.
42 Ali Akbar Dareini, "Iran: Uranium Enrichment to Be Expected," *Washington Times*, November 28, 2012.
43 Michael Scott Doran, "The Heirs of Nasser," *Foreign Affairs*, May/June 2011.
44 Ibid., 349–350.
45 Ibid., 357.
46 Barack H. Obama, "Remarks by the President in Address to the Nation on the End of Combat Operations in Iraq," Washington DC (The White House: Office of the Press Secretary, August 31, 2010).
47 "Officials Warn al-Qaida Making Comeback in Iraq," Associated Press, October 9, 2012.
48 Kenneth M. Pollack, et al., *The Arab Awakening*, 99.
49 Dexter Filkins, "What We Left Behind," *The New Yorker*, April 28, 2014.
50 Katherine Zimmerman, *A New Model for Defeating al Qaeda in Yemen*. (American Enterprise Institute, September, 2015).
51 "Iran Dispatches Warships to Sudan after Israeli Airstrike on Missile Base," *Telegraph*, October 30, 2012.
52 Anne R. Pierce, "Burying Our Heads in the Sand of Iran," Ricochet.com, November 18, 2012.
53 Michael Rubin, "Iran Justifies Israel's Annihilation in Islamic Law," *Commentary*, April 2, 2012.
54 Karim Sadjadpour, "The Supreme Leader," *Iran Primer*, ed. Robin B. Wright (Washington, DC: United States Institute of Peace, December 2010), 11.
55 Robert Marquand, "Iran Oil Embargo: How tough are the EU Sanctions?" *Christian Science Monitor*, January 24, 2012.
56 Michael Rubin, "Taking Tea with the Taliban," *Commentary*, February 2010.
57 Anne R. Pierce, "Burying Our Heads in the Sand of Iran," Ricochet.com.
58 Shahram Chubin, "A Grand Bargain with Iran," Carnegie Endowment for International Peace-Foreign Affairs, March/April 2011.
59 Robert J. Lieber and Amatzia Baram, "Containment Breach," *Foreign Policy*, December 22, 2009.
60 "U.N. Reports 'Striking Pattern' of Abuses," The Iran Primer, United States Institute of Peace, March 2012.
61 Sarah Morgan and Andrew Apostolou, "Why Obama Should Highlight Iran's Human Rights Abuses," *Foreign Affairs*, November 7, 2011.
62 Richard Spencer, "Iran May Hold Direct Talks with US," *Telegraph*, February 3, 2013.
63 Joby Warrick, "Iran's Bid to Buy Banned Magnets Stokes Fears about Major Expansion of Nuclear Capacity," *Washington Post*, February 13, 2013.
64 Omer Taspinar et al., *The Arab Awakening*, 274.
65 Daniel Byman, "Iran's Terrorism Problem," Brookings Institution, November 21, 2013.
66 Jeffrey Goldberg, "Obama to Iran and Israel: 'As President of the United States, I Don't Bluff,'" *Atlantic*, March 2, 2012.
67 "Iran: New President Must Deliver on Human Rights Campaign Promises," Amnesty International, August 2, 2013.

68 Mark Kirk and Marco Rubio, "Iran's Horrific Human-Rights Record," *Daily Beast*, November 7, 2014.

69 Michael Doran, "Obama's Secret Iran Strategy," Hudson Institute, February 2, 2015.

70 Mark Kirk and Eliot Engel, "Without Stronger Sanctions, Iran Will Go Nuclear," *Wall Street Journal*, August 12, 2013.

71 Daniel Pipes, "Saudis Bristle at Obama's Outreach to Iran," *Daniel Pipes Middle East Forum*, December 3, 2013.

72 Jay Solomon, "Iran Nuclear Deal Raises Fears of Proliferation Among Arab States," *Wall Street Journal*, November 29, 2013.

73 John Kerry, "Iran Nuclear Deal Still Is Possible, but Time Is Running Out," *Washington Post*, June 30, 2014.

74 Tzvi Kahn, "FPI Timeline: A Year of Iranian Defiance and Western Desperation in Nuclear Talks," Foreign Policy Initiative, December 8, 2014.

75 Anne R. Pierce, "Beware ISIS Strategy That Fortifies Russia, Iran, and Syria," *Washington Times*, March 2, 2015.

76 Mark Dubowitz, "Iranian Economy In Moderate Recovery Thanks to Sanctions Relief, New Report Finds," Foundation for Defense of Democracies, October 31, 2014.

77 Ibid.

78 "Ruinous Aftermath: Militias Abuses Following Iraq's Recapture of Tikrit," Human Rights Watch, September 20, 2015.

79 Anne R. Pierce, "Iran's Rising Star," *Washington Times*, March 7, 2015.

80 *Release of the 2014 Country Reports on Human Rights Practices*, US Department of State, June 25, 2015.

81 "Corker Highlights Concerns with Iran Nuclear Negotiations in Letter to the President," United States Senate Committee on Foreign Relations press release, June 15, 2015.

82 Jeffrey Goldberg, "John Kerry on the Risk of Congress 'Screwing' the Ayatollah," *Atlantic*, August 5, 2015.

83 Anne R. Pierce, "Iran Nuke Deal's Upside-Down Logic," *USA Today*, August 25, 2015.

CHAPTER 5
1 Elliott Abrams, "Egypt protests show George W. Bush was right about freedom in the Arab world," *Washington Post*, January 29, 2011.

2 James L. Gelvin, *The Arab Uprisings: What Everyone Needs To Know* (New York: Oxford University Press, 2012), 142.

3 Ali Akbar Dareini, "Ahmadinejad: Egypt Shows Middle East Breaking Free of 'American Interference,'" *World Post*, February 11, 2011.

4 Alaa Al-Aswany, *On the State of Egypt: What Made The Revolution Inevitable*, trans. Jonathan Wright (New York: Vintage Books, April 2011), 8.

5 Shadi Hamid et al., *The Arab Awakening*, 103.

6 Michael Youssef, PhD, *Blindsided: The Radical Islamic Conquest* (U.S.: Kobri), chapter 10.

7 Edward Wakin, *A Lonely Minority* (New York: W. Morrow & Company, 1963), 4, 30.

8 Gelvin, *The Arab Uprisings*, 148.

9 Daniel L. Byman et al., *The Arab Awakening*, 77.

10 Magdi Khalil, "The Muslim Brotherhood and the Copts." *ThreatsWatch*, April 20, 2006.

11 Ben Birnbaum, "Top Egyptian Presidential Candidate Doubts Al Qaeda Role in 9/11," *Washington Times*, May 31, 2012.

12 Sarah Lynch and Oren Dorell, "Egyptian President's Aims Unknown." *USA Today*, June 27, 2012.

13 "Cut Ties to Terror," *Investor's Business Daily*, November 26, 2010. Also of note: The Bush administration fostered ties with ISNA as well, but severed ties after the Holy Land trial. ISNA was again invited to Obama's inauguration in 2013, with Imam Mohamed Magid offering prayers at the National Prayer Service.

14 Liane Hansen, "Clinton Sticks to U.S. Principles on Egyptian Reform," *NPR News/ Weekend Edition*, February 6, 2011.

15 David D. Kirkpatrick and Steven Lee Myers, "Overtures to Egypt's Islamists Reverse Longtime U.S. Policy," *New York Times*, January 3, 2012

16 Michael Meunier, "Obama Gives Cold Shoulder to Egyptian Secular Democrats," *IPT News*, December 21, 2012.

17 http://arabnews.com/June 30, 2011 (source: Reuters).

18 Ryan Mauro, "Obama Administration Training Egyptian Islamists for Elections," *FrontPage Magazine*, November 18, 2011.

19 Caroline Glick, "America and the Arab Spring," *Real Clear Politics*, January 25, 2012.

20 Sarah El Deeb and Hamza Hendowi, "Egyptian Facing a Tough Choice In Picking a President," Associated Press, June 17, 2012.

21 Michael Wahid Hanna, "Clouded U.S. policy on Egypt." *Foreign Policy*, February 26, 2013.

22 Neil Hicks, "Egypt's Transition to Democracy One Year On: Recommendations for U.S. Policy," Human Rights First, January 26, 2012.

23 Josh Rogin, "Clinton Waives restrictions on U.S. aid to Egypt," *Foreign Policy*: "The Cable," March 22, 2012.

24 Ibid.

25 Ibid.

26 Frida Ghitis, "World Citizen: U.S., Arab Liberals Losing Ground in Middle East, "*World Politics Review*, August 4, 2011.

27 Arnaud de Borchgrave, "Commentary: Egypt's Tower of Babel," United Press International, October 11, 2011.

28 "Barack Obama and William Hague on the Maspero Massacre of the Copts by Egyptian Army 9-10-11—What their Pathetic Responses Tell Us? What Should We Do?" *Coptic Literature Wordpress*, October 16, 2011.

29 Jay Carney, "Statement by the Press Secretary on Violence in Egypt," Washington, DC, (The White House: Office of the Press Secretary, October 10, 2011).

30 Mary Abdelmassih, "100,000 Christians Have Left Egypt Since March: Report," *Assyrian International News Agency*, 27 September 2011.

31 Secretary of State Hillary R. Clinton, "Remarks at the Release of the 13th Annual Report on International Religious Freedom," Washington, DC, (US Department of State, September 13, 2001).

32 Youssef, *Blindsided*, 22–29.

33 Leo Strauss, *Natural Right and History* (Chicago: University of Chicago Press, 1950), 4 & 6.

34 "Clinton's Cause: Working for the Women of the World," *Newsweek*, September 18, 2011.

35 The documentary's subtitle is "culture is no excuse for abuse." For more information, see www.honordiaries.com.

36 Secretary of State Hillary R. Clinton, "Remarks at the Release of the 2011 International Religious Freedom Report," Carnegie Endowment for International Peace, US Department of State, July 30, 2012.

37 Michael Meunier, "Obama Gives Cold Shoulder to Egyptian Secular Democrats,", *IPT News*, December 21, 2012.

38 Dennis Ross and James F. Jeffrey, "Obama II and the Middle East: Strategic Objectives for U.S. Policy," Strategic Reports 12, Washington Institute for Near East Policy, Washington, DC, March 2013, 23.

39 David D. Kirkpatrick, "More Morsi Aides Resign as Egypt Deploys Tanks in Cairo," *New York Times*, December 6, 2012.

40 "Why We Shall Boycott the Referendum On the Islamist Constitution In Egypt," On Coptic Nationalism, *Coptic Literature Wordpress*, December 12, 2012.

41 Ahmed Eleiba, "F-16 Deal Redefines US relationship with Egypt's Morsi Administration." *Ahram Online*, January 14, 2013.

42 Shoshana Bryen, "Enshrining Ideologies: Egypt and the US," Gatestone Institute, January 22, 2013.

43 Brian Katulis, Ken Sofer, and Peter Juul, "Preparing U.S. Policy for the Next Phase of Egypt's Transition," Center for American Progress, March 1, 2013.

44 Michael Wahid Hanna, "The Seven Pillars of the Arab Future," *Democracy*, no. 28, Spring 2013.

45 Amir Taheri, "Will Egypt's Democrats Get Serious?" *New York Post*, February 27, 2013.

46 Paul Marshall, Lela Gilbert, and Nina Shea. *Persecuted: The Global Assault on Christians* (Nashville, TN: Thomas Nelson, 2013), 4.

47 Lela Gilbert, "Killed Because They Were Copts." Ricochet, April 7, 2013.

48 Ross and Jeffrey, "Obama II and the Middle East: Strategic Objectives for U.S. Policy," 21–22.

49 Glenn Kessler, "Obama's Claim that Aid to Egypt Was Based on Adherence to 'Democratic Procedures,'" *Washington Post*, July 20, 2013.

50 Bill Hoffmann, "Walid Phares: Egyptians Mad at US Embrace of Muslim Brotherhood," *Newsmax*, August 14, 2013.

51 James Jay Carafano and James Phillips, "Egypt: A Way Forward After a Step Back," Heritage Foundation, July 9, 2013.

52 "Egypt Protest Camps Cleared: International Reaction," BBC, August 16, 2013.

53 Josh Rogin and Eli Lake, "Obama Offers a Revisionist History of His Administration's Approach to Egypt," *Daily Beast*, July 2, 2013.

54 Eric Trager, "Sisi's Fearful Egypt," *Weekly Standard*, June 11, 2014.

55 "World Report 2015: Egypt," Human Rights Watch, https://www.hrw.org/world-report/2015/country-chapters/egypt.

56 Alan Krueger, "What Makes a Terrorist?" American Enterprise Institute, November 7, 2007.

57 Adam Kredo, "Muslim Brotherhood–Aligned Leaders Hosted at State Department," *Washington Free Beacon*, January 28, 2015.

58 "US 'Preferred' Compassionate Release of Lockerbie Bomber, says Alex Salmond," *Telegraph*, July 25, 2010.

59 Jason Allardyce and Tony Allen-Mills, "White House Backed Release of Lockerbie Bomber Abdel Basset al-Megrahi," *Australian*, July 26, 2010.

60 Josh Rogin, "How Obama Turned On a Dime Toward War," *Foreign Policy*, March 18, 2011, and Elise Labott, "How Clinton Got Behind the Military Coalition," CNN, March 20, 2011.
61 Patrick Goodenough, "Citing Libya, Clinton Extols Obama's 'Smart' Leadership in 'Complex, Dangerous World,'" *CNSNews*, October 24, 2011.
62 Joseph Lieberman and Susan Collins, *Flashing Red: A Special Report on the Terrorist Attack at Benghazi*, United States Senate Committee on Homeland Security and Governmental Affairs, December 30, 2012.
63 "Panetta: 'From the Beginning' I Knew Benghazi Was a Terrorist Attack," *Washington Free Beacon*, October 7, 2014.

CHAPTER 6
1 "After 29 years, Syria leaves Lebanon," *New York Times*, April 26, 2005.
2 General David H. Petraeus, "Report to Congress on the Situation in Iraq," Washington, DC, September 10–11, 2007.
3 Bernard Gwertzman, "Syria Looking for Improved Relations with the Obama Administration," Council on Foreign Relations, May 15, 2009.
4 Doran, "The Heirs of Nassar," 335.
5 Matthew R. J. Brodsky, "Syria and the Obama Administration," *National Security Policy Proceedings, Vol. 2—Center for Security Policy*, Jewish Policy Center, Summer 2010.
6 Tabler, *In the Lion's Den*, 120.
7 James H. Anderson, "Spoiler Alert: What Syria's President Really Wants," *World Affairs Journal*, January-February 2011.
8 Elias Bejjani, "Barbarism of the Syrian regime," *Global Politician*, July 18, 2011.
9 Ibid.
10 Patrick Goodenough, "Syrian President Assad Regarded as a 'Reformer', Clinton says," *CNS News*, March 28, 2001.
11 "Far From Justice: Syria's Supreme State Security Court," Human Rights Watch report, February 2009, 1.
12 "We've Never Seen Such Horror: Crimes Against Humanity by Syrian Security Forces," Human Rights Watch report, June 2011, 1 & 2.
13 Barack H. Obama, "Statement from the President on the Violence in Syria," Washington, DC, (The White House: Office of the Press Secretary, April 8, 2011).
14 Gelvin, *The Arab Uprisings*, 106.
15 Jake Tapper, "Clinton, No Longer a Believer that Assad is a 'Reformer,' Says He Can't Sustain the Armed Opposition in Syria," *ABC News*, November 18, 2011.
16 "In Syria, Protest and Disorder Grow," *Wall Street Journal/Middle East*, July 2, 2011.
17 Secretary of State Hillary R. Clinton, "Keynote at the National Democratic Institute's 2011 Democracy Awards Dinner," Washington, DC, (US Department of State, November 7, 2011).
18 Josh Gerstein, "Obama's Slow Burn on Assad," *Politico*, August 18, 2011.
19 Joby Warrick, "Clinton Defends U.S. Response to Crackdown in Syria," *Washington Post*, August 16, 2011.
20 Kori Schake, "Three Cheers for the Arab League," *Foreign Policy*, November 14, 2011.
21 US Department of State, "Remarks at a United Nations Security Council Session on the Situation in Syria," Remarks by Hillary Clinton, Secretary of State at United Nations (New York City, January 31, 2012).

22 Ibid.

23 "U.S. Should Cut Ties with Russian Arms Dealer Enabling Syrian Regime," Human Rights First, February 21, 2012.

24 Ilan Berman, "Obama Needs to Do More Than Pay Lip Service to Regime Change in Syria," *Daily Beast,* January 31, 2012.

25 Michael Young, "As Syria's Civil War Explodes, Preparing for the Aftermath," *National,* July 19, 2012.

26 "U.N. Suspends Syria Mission," Associated Press/*Politico,* June 16, 2012.

27 Elise Labott, "U.S. in Waiting Game on Syria," *CNN Blog,* May 16, 2012.

28 Victor Davis Hanson, "Syrian Ironies," *National Review Online,* March 6, 2012.

29 John Lavinger, "Kofi Annan on Syria: 'Things Fell Apart' at United Nations," *New York Daily News,* August 2, 2012.

30 Patrick Ventrell, U.S. Department of State Daily Press Briefing, Washington, DC, August 2, 2012.

31 Ibid.

32 Hillary Clinton, US House Of Representatives hearing, Foreign Operations and Related Programs Subcommittee of the Committee on Appropriations, February 29, 2012.

33 Michael R. Gordon and Mark Landler, "Backstage Glimpses of Clinton as Dogged Diplomat, Win or Lose," *New York Times,* February 3, 2013.

34 Mark Landler, "Attacking Obama Policy, Hillary Clinton Exposes Different World-views," *New York Times,* August 11, 2014.

35 Peter Nicholas, Adam Entous, and Carol E. Lee, "Hillary Clinton's Legacy at State Dept.: A Hawk with Clipped Wings," *Wall Street Journal,* May 30, 2014.

36 In a June 2012 forum at Brookings and on later occasions.

37 Frederic Hof Testimony, House of Representatives Committee on Foreign Affairs, December 14, 2011.

38 James L. Gelvin, *The Arab Uprisings: What Everyone Needs To Know* (New York: Oxford University Press, 2012), 112–114.

39 Anthony Cordesman, "U.S. Strategy in Syria: Having Lost Sight of the Objective," September 12, 2013.

40 Ernie Audino, "The Price of U.S. Timidity with the Kurds," *Washington Times,* October 15, 2015.

41 Ibid.

42 Scott Stewart, "The Jihadist CBRN Threat," Stratfor *Security Weekly,* February 10, 2010.

43 "Imagine If Hamas Was Backed by a Nuclear State," *Chicago Tribune,* November 12, 2012.

44 "Civil War Leaves Syrian Economy, Cities in Ruins," Associated Press, October 10, 2012.

45 "Secretary of State John Kerry Calls for Immediate Release of Syrian Human Rights Defender Razan Zaitouneh," PR Newswire, June 13, 2014.

46 John Kerry, remarks to the press, Washington, DC, January 26, 2014.

47 David Kenner Blogs, Foreign Policy, Fall 2013.

48 Michael Weiss, "How to Oust Assad," *Foreign Affairs,* August 28, 2013.

49 See "A Candid Discussion with Ayham Kamel," Foreign Policy, September 27, 2013.

50 "What a Strategy Would Look Like," transcript of Paul Gigot interview with General Keane, Fox News Channel, *Wall Street Journal,* September 1, 2014.

51 Whalid Phares testimony, House Foreign Affairs Committee Hearing, April 29, 2015. http://foreignaffairs.house.gov/hearing/subcommittee-hearing-isis-defining-enemy.

52 Anne R. Pierce, "Beware ISIS Strategy That Fortifies Russia, Syria, and Iran," *Washington Times*, March 2, 2015.

53 Eman El-Shenawi, "All Eyes on ISIS in 2014, but Was This Assad's Plan?" *Al Arabiya*, December 31, 2014.

54 Adam Garfinkle, "Putin, Obama, and the Middle East," Foreign Policy Research Institute, October 2015.

55 Felicia Schwartz, "Kerry to Meet with Putin in Russia on Tuesday," *Wall Street Journal*, May 12, 2015.

56 "John Kerry: Russia Has No 'Easy Track' in Syria," NPR, October 16, 2015.

57 House Foreign Affairs Committee Hearing, April 29, 2015. http://foreignaffairs.house.gov/hearing/subcommittee-hearing-isis-defining-enemy.

CHAPTER 7

1 David Hawk, *The Hidden Gulag: Exposing North Korea's Prison Camps* (Washington, DC: US Committee for Human Rights in North Korea, 2003), 11.

2 Stephan Haggard and Marcus Noland, "Repression and Punishment in North Korea: Survey Evidence of Prison Camp Experiences," *East-West Center Working Papers: Politics, Governance, and Security Series,* no. 20, October 2009, 9 & 27.

3 Barbara Demick, *Nothing to Envy: Ordinary Lives In North Korea* (New York: Spiegel & Grau, 2009), 8 & 11.

4 Ibid., 11 & 12.

5 Ibid., 27 & 28.

6 Kim Sang Hum, Board Director-Center for North Korean Human Rights, "Foreword—Human Rights: An Irreplaceable Component of a Strong Nation," *White Paper on North Korean Human Rights 2009.*

7 Haggard and Noland, "Repression and Punishment in North Korea," October 2009, 1.

8 Kang Chol-hwan and Pierre Rigoulot, *The Aquariums of Pyongyang: Ten Years in the North Korean Gulag* (New York: Basic Books, 2002), 67.

9 Ibid., 57, 58 & 77.

10 Ibid., 96.

11 Ibid.

12 Blaine Harden, *Escape from Camp 14: One Man's Remarkable Odyssey from North Korea to Freedom in the West* (New York: Viking/Penguin Group, 2012), 4 & 5.

13 Ibid., 5 & 6.

14 David Hawk, "The Hidden Gulag: Exposing North Korea's Prison Camps," US Committee for Human Rights in North Korea, 2003.

15 Ibid.

16 United Nations Human Rights, "Statement by the UN Special Rapporteur on the Situation of Human Rights in the Democratic People's Republic of Korea at the End of His Visit to Japan, 25 to 28 January 2011," Office of the High Commissioner of Human Rights, January 28, 2011.

17 Ibid.

18 "North Korea: UN Should Investigate Crimes Against Humanity," Human Rights Watch *World Report 2012*, January 24, 2012.

19 Truman, *Public Papers of the President—1947*, 165.

20 John W. Danford, *Roots of Freedom: A Primer on Modern Liberty* (Wilmington, Delaware: ISI Books, 2000), 184.

21 Ibid., 188.

22 Haggard and Nolan, "Repression and Punishment in North Korea," 1.

23 Friedman, *America's Secret War*, 46.

24 Ben Johnson, "Appeasing North Korea: The Clinton Legacy," *FrontPage Magazine*, January 3, 2003.

25 Ibid.

26 George W. Bush, "President Delivers State of the Union," The United States Capitol, Washington, DC (The White House: Office of the Press Secretary, January 29, 2002).

27 Johnson, "Appeasing North Korea," 2003.

28 Robert Kaufman, "The Perils of President Obama's National Security Policy," *Foreign Policy Initiative*, February 17, 2012.

29 Siegfried S. Hecker, "A Return Trip to North Korea's Yongbyon Nuclear Complex," Center for International Security and Cooperation, Stanford University November 2010, 4, 6 & 7.

30 Ibid., 7.

31 Ibid., 8.

32 Christian Whiton, US Department of State, "Promoting North Korean Human Rights: What the Free World Can Do," Brussels, Belgium, November 2007.

33 Chol-hwan and Rigoulot, *The Aquariums of Pyongyang*, x.

34 Ibid., x & xi.

35 Kaufman, "The Perils of President Obama's National Security Policy," February 2010.

36 Indira A. R. Lakshmanan, "Clinton Campaigns to Mend U.S. Image, Connect with Asian Public," Bloomberg, February 20, 2009.

37 Secretary of State Hillary Clinton, "Remarks: Roundtable with Traveling Press," Seoul, South Korea (US Department of State, February 29, 2009).

38 Glenn Kessler, "Clinton Criticized for Not Trying to Force China's Hand," *Washington Post*, February 21, 2009.

39 Merle Goldman, "Clinton's Missed Opportunity in China," *Boston Globe*, February 26, 2009.

40 "Clinton's Ears Wide Open," *China Daily*, February 23, 2009.

41 Mark Landler, "Clinton Warns of Risky Succession in North Korea," *New York Times*, February 19, 2009.

42 Jack Kim and Arshad Mohammed, "U.S. tells North Korea to End Insults, Return to Talks," Reuters, February 20, 2009.

43 John R. Bolton, "Now Is No Time to Downplay North Korea," *Wall Street Journal*, January 31, 2009.

44 Ibid.

45 Jeff Bliss, "CIA Adding Bases in Afghanistan as Taliban Gains, Panetta Says," Bloomberg, September 19, 2009.

46 P. J. Aroon, "Hillary Clinton Fed Up with North Korea," Foreign Policy, May 1, 2009.

47 Evan Ramstad, Jay Solomon, and Peter Spiegel, "Korean Blast Draws Outrage," *Wall Street Journal*, May 26, 2009.

48 "Korea's Obama Test: Pyongyang's Blast and White House' Engagement," *Wall Street Journal*, May 26, 2009.

49 Kim Hyun Sik, "The Secret History of Kim Jong II," *Foreign Policy*, September 1, 2008.

50 Kim Myong Chol, "Pyongyang Stage Set for Bosworth Talks," *Online Asia Times*, December 9, 2009.

51 Bruce Klinger, "Another Feeble Response to North Korean Aggression," Heritage Foundation, July 9, 2010.

52 Bruce Klingner, "New Leaders, Old Dangers: What North Korean Succession Means for the U.S.," Heritage Foundation, April 7, 2010.

53 Laura Ling and Euna Lee, "Hostages of The Hermit Kingdom," *Los Angeles Times*, September 1, 2009.

54 Barack H. Obama, "Remarks by President Obama and President Lee of the Republic of Korea in a Joint Press Conference," Washington, DC (The White House: Office of the Press Secretary, October 13, 2011).

55 Ibid.

56 James E. Goody, "Strategic Patience Has Become Strategic Passivity," Brookings Institution, March 1, 2012.

57 "North Korea: Fears of food shortages outside Pyongyang as distribution fails," *Guardian*, April 25, 2014.

58 "Nobel Prize Winning President Ignores World's Worst Human Rights Violations," Free Korea Blog, May 8, 2012.

59 Jay Carney, "Press Gaggle by Press Secretary Jay Carney Aboard Air Force One, 4/24/12," en route to North Carolina (The White House: Office of the Press Secretary, April 24, 2012).

60 "Obama Warns North Korea Against Rocket Test, Says It Would Isolate Regime," Associated Press, March 25, 2012.

61 Editorial Board, "The U.S. Falls for North Korea's Tricks," *Washington Post*, March 12, 2012.

62 Anne Gearan, "N. Korea's Rocket Attempt Scuttles Deal for US Food," Associated Press, April 14, 2012.

63 Editorial, "A Pyongyang Joke: The Missile May Have Fizzled, But So Did American Policy," *Wall Street Journal*, April 16, 2012.

64 Merle Miller, *Plain Speaking: An Oral Biography of Harry S. Truman* (New York: Berkeley Books, 1974), 135.

65 Andrei Lankov, "Kim Cracks Open Refugee Issue," *Asia Times Online*, January 16, 2013.

66 Suzanne Scholte testimony, House Committee on Foreign Affairs, April 18, 2013.

67 David Chance, "For North Korea, Next Step is a Nuclear Test," Reuters, December 13, 2012.

68 Demick, *Nothing to Envy*, 148, 149, & 151.

69 "Change in North Korea: Richer, Freer, Scarier," *Economist*, February 9–15, 2013, 11 & 24–26.

70 Sung-Yoon Lee, "Engaging North Korea: The Clouded Legacy of South Korea's Sunshine Policy," American Enterprise Institute, April 19, 2010.

71 George Jahn, "US Institute: N. Korea Expanding Nuclear Plant," *Pittsburgh Post-Gazette*, August 8, 2013.

72 Nick Cumming-Bruce, "U.N. Panel Says North Korean Leader Could Face Trial," *New York Times*, February 17, 2014.

73 "Prison Camps of North Korea," HumanRights.gov, http://www.humanrights.gov /dyn/news/features/prison-camps-of-north-korea/.

74 Elise Hu, "In Seoul, Kerry Calls N. Korea Provocations 'Egregious,' 'Reckless,'" NPR, May 18, 2015.

75 Evan Moore, "The Core of This Crisis Is the Nature of the North Korean Regime, Says FPI's Evan Moore," Foreign Policy Initiative, April 19, 2012.

76 Bruce Klinger, "Respond Cautiously to North Korean Engagement Offers," Heritage Foundation, April 20, 2015.

77 Joshua Stanton, "China Helps N. Korea Nuke Up and Break Sanctions, Then Says Sanctions Don't Work," One Free Korea, November 3, 2015.

78 Kim Hyun Sik, "The Secret History of Kim Jong II," *Foreign Policy*, September-October 2008.

CHAPTER 8

1 Mann, *The China Fantasy*, 44.

2 Jung Chang, *Wild Swans: Three Daughters of China* (New York: Anchor Books, November 1992), 495 & 496.

3 Human Rights Watch interview, Yanbian Prefecture, China, January 2, 2008. Quoted in "Denied Status, Denied Education: Children of North Korea Women in China," April 2008, 10.

4 Pan, *Out of Mao's Shadow*, 67.

5 Ibid., 106.

6 Ibid., xiv.

7 Loung Ung, *First They Killed My Father: A Daughter of Cambodia Remembers* (New York: Harper Perennial, 2000), 66.

8 Pan, *Out of Mao's Shadow*, 5.

9 Ibid., 325.

10 Glenn Kessler, "China Is at the Heart of Clinton's First Trip," *Washington Post*, February 15, 2009.

11 "Text of Obama's Speech to West Point 2010 Cadets," CBS News, May 22, 2010.

12 Barack H. Obama, "Remarks by the President in Address to the Nation on the End of Combat Operations in Iraq," Washington, DC, Oval Office (The White House: Office of the Press Secretary, August 31, 2010).

13 US Department of State, "Secretary Clinton's Speech at Economic Club of New York," New York, New York, October 14, 2011.

14 Ibid.

15 Ibid.

16 Leslie Gelb, "Hillary Hits The Mark," *Daily Beast*, October 14, 2011.

17 Flavia Krause-Jackson and Nicole Gaouette, "Clinton Adopts Job's 'Think Different' Motto for Diplomacy," Bloomberg, October 14, 2011.

18 Jim Meyers, "China Arrests Dissidents to Thwart Mideast-Like Uprising," *Newsmax*, April 4, 2011.

19 Abraham Lincoln, "Address Before the Young Men's Lyceum of Springfield, Illinois," *Constitution*, January 27, 1838, http://constitution.org/.

20 Ibid.

21 Suisheng Zhao, "Shoring Up US Leadership in the Asia-Pacific: The Obama Adminis-tration's Hedge Strategy against China," presented at the 2011 Fulbright Symposium, Melbourne, Australia (August 11–12, 2011), 5.

22 Zhao, "Shoring up US Leadership in the Asia-Pacific," 6.

23 Ibid.

24 Julian Ryall, "Hillary Clinton's Visit to China Sparks Alarm in Japan," *Telegraph* February 20, 2009.

25 US Department of Defense, "Sustaining US Global Leadership: Priorities for the 21st Century Defense," January 2012, 2.

26 Zhao, "Shoring up US Leadership in Asia-Pacific," 16.

27 Ibid., 24.

28 "Panetta and Clinton's Remarks at the Munich Security Conference, Germany," Council on Foreign Relations, February 4, 2012.

29 Bill Gertz, "China's High Tech Military Threat," *Commentary*, April 2012.

30 Arthur Waldron, "Clinton's China Policy Invites Disaster," American Enterprise Institute for Public Research, January 26, 1999.

31 Anne R. Pierce, unpublished article.

32 Dave Lindorff, "'Human Rights Won't Get In The Way': The Selling Out of a Chinese Dissident," This Can't Be Happening, May 4, 2012.

33 "US Ambassador Sees China Rights Worsening," *American Free Press*, January 16, 2012.

34 Marc Jayson Climaco, "Crackdown on Human Rights Defenders in China," Human Rights First, May 4, 2012.

35 Russell Leigh Moses, "China's Hardliners Take Aim at A New Target," CHINAREAL-TIME Blog/*Wall Street Journal*, August 26, 2011.

36 Indira A. R. Lakshmanan, "China's Crackdown on Human Rights Sparks Little Outcry in Washington," Bloomberg, April 5, 2011.

37 Secretary Hillary R. Clinton, interview by Jeffery Goldberg, "Hillary Clinton: Chinese System Is Doomed, Leaders on a 'Fool's Errand'," *Atlantic*, May 2011.

38 Secretary Hillary R. Clinton, "America's Pacific Century," *Foreign Policy*, October 11, 2011.

39 Alexa Olesen, "China Activist's Escape Raises Dissidents' Spirits, Official Ire," *Cincinnati Enquirer*, April 30, 2012.

40 Jay Carney, "Press Briefing by Press Secretary Jay Carney, 5/3/12," Washington, DC (The White House: Office of the Press Secretary, May 3, 2012).

41 Pete Kasperowicz, "Rep. Smith Says Obama Administration Failed to Connect Him In Phone Call with Chinese Activist Chen," *The Hill*, May 3, 2012.

42 Mary Kissel, "The Pastor of China's Underground Railroad," *Wall Street Journal*, June 2, 2012.

43 Ibid.

44 Thomas G. Mahnken with Dan Blumenthal, Thomas Donnelly, Michael Mazza, Gary J. Schmitt, and Andrew Shearer, "Asia in the Balance: Transforming US Mili-tary Strategy in Asia," American Enterprise Institute, May 31, 2012, 1.

45 Noboru Yamaguchi, "America's 'Return' to Asia Requires Japan's Strategic Response," *Association of Japanese Institute of Strategic Studies*, no. 147, April 25, 2012.

46 Mahnken, "Asia in the Balance," 8.

47 Secretary of State John Kerry, "U.S. Vision for Asia-Pacific Engagement," Honolulu, Hawaii (US Department of State, August 13, 2014).

48 Ben Blanchard, "China Academics Warn of 'Violent Revolution' If No Political Reform," Reuters, December 30, 2012.

49 Sudhanshu Tripathi, "Beijing's South China Sea Gambit: The View from India," *American Thinker*, December 5, 2012.

50 Arthur Waldron, "Put China On Notice," *National Review*, September 22, 2014.

CONCLUSION

1 "Meeting with Russian Ambassadors and Permanent Representatives In International Organizations," *Kremlin.ru* archives, July 9, 2012, http://eng.kremlin.ru/news /4145.

2 Ibid.